#2.8735

19093

My Life in Prison
Donald Lowrie

19093
C. Donald Lowrie
Los Angeles
Burglary
5 Years
Age 26
July 24th 1901
Mass.

HEATHEN EDITIONS
THEIR BOOKS. OUR WAY.

Published in the good ole United States of America
by Heathen Editions, an imprint of
Heathen Creative
P.O. Box 588
Point Pleasant, WV 25550-0588

Heathen Editions are available at quantity discounts.
For information and more tomfoolery, check us out online:

heatheneditions.com

@heatheneditions
#heathenedition

First published 1912
Heathen Edition published March 26, 2023

Book and cover design by Sheridan Cleland
Set in 11pt Plantin Std
Chapters set in Mom's Typewriter Redux

ISBN: 978-1-948316-22-4

FIRST HEATHEN EDITION

"To lighten your journey!" said Sam as he presented her with a book—"My Life in Prison," by Donald Lowrie.[1]

[1] Vanderbilt, C., Jr. (1929). *Reno* (p. 180). The Macaulay Company.

"Then in 1912 appeared a very influential work—Donald Lowrie's first book, *My Life in Prison*."
—H. Bruce Franklin, *Prison Literature in America*

"When Donald Lowrie finished the last chapter of *My Life in Prison* it seemed fairly certain that . . . a notable book had been accomplished, fully justifying the sensational success it achieved overnight." —*The New York Times Book Review*

"Written so simply yet with such power and such complete and evident sincerity."
—Thomas Mott Osborne, *Within Prison Walls*

"Some works boil down to, 'I'm here because of my social class,' a category tellingly defined by Donald Lowrie's 1912 classic, *My Life in Prison*, which presaged some of the writings of the black radicals of the 1960s and 70s."
—Ralph Blumenthal, *The New York Times*

"Donald Lowrie, whose writings did for American prisons what John Howard's did for those of England."
—Jack Black, *You Can't Win*

"His first contribution consisted of an installment of his studies, *My Life in Prison*. At once he attracted attention. As he went from day to day the interest grew. In two weeks he was the sensation of San Francisco. In the street cars, on the ferries, in trains, everywhere in public, people were eagerly reading Donald Lowrie, and discussing his revelations. The work revealed fine observation and dramatic power. As it went from week to week without a break, the marvel grew. Here was a new writer that could publish an interesting article each day for six days in the week. In a few weeks Donald Lowrie printed more than one hundred thousand words. The success of the articles made Donald Lowrie a notable figure not only in San Francisco but throughout California."
—John D. Barry, *The American Magazine*

"With swift, acid sincerity Lowrie describes his sensations in his one and only attempt at housebreaking. The psychologic analysis he makes of himself recalls in its power [Robert Louis] Stevenson's 'Markheim.' Donald Lowrie may not be a man of genius, but he is a cruelly keen observer of details. He has suffered, and his narrative quivers with compassionate indignation. He has lived in an atmosphere of overwhelming tragedy—tragedy which society is responsible for creating."   —Coningsby Dawson, *Everybody's Magazine*

"A book of such absorbing interest as this can do more than many volumes of penological discussion for the improvement of our penal system."   —*The Green Bag*

"Donald Lowrie's *My Life in Prison* is a narrative of real prison life by a real convict, and it extends, not over one week, but ten years. As giving an insight into the life of the convict in most of our prisons the book is unequaled. Lowrie was a keen observer and no phase of prison life has escaped his observation—the cells, the workshops, the treatment of women inmates, the man condemned to death and the manner of his execution, solitary confinement, the bullying of prisoners, their torture by the jacket, the light and dark sides of the inmate's character, all of these and may other things are set forth in a manner which throws the ordinary novel into the shade. There are men who are strong enough to pass through such an experience without being ruined morally, mentally, and physically, and who can use their experience for the benefit of their unfortunate fellows. Mr. Lowrie is one of these. It should be the duty of everyone who feels the least interest in humanity and who is not indifferent to his own responsibilities as a citizen, to read this book from beginning to end."   —*The O.E. Library Critic*

"Now comes another book, unpretentious, without the advertisement of any great literary name. But it is true and vital. Within its pages passes the myriorama of prison life. And within its pages may be found revelations of the divine and the undivine; of strange humility and stranger arrogance; of free men brutalized and caged men humanized; of big and little tragedies; of long sordidness and brief forgetfulness. There is humor, too, though sometimes the jest is made ironic by its sequel. And there is romance—the romance of the real; not the romance of Kipling's 9:15, but the romance of No. 19,093, and of all the other numbers that made up the arithmetical hell of San Quentin prison.

"The book is called *My Life in Prison*. It is written by Donald Lowrie. Why he went to prison does not matter. He tells the story himself. He has paid in full the debt due to society, and is now paying his share of the debt due from him, and from every free man and woman, to the outcasts of society, from the one-year convict to the man who is 'doing it all.' His story is not a lawyer's plea, for the defense or the prosecution. It is a statement of facts, set down simply and without exaggeration. Yet few novels could so absorb interest. It is human utterly. That is the reason. Not only is the very atmosphere of the prison preserved, from the colossal sense of encagement and defenselessness, to the smaller jealousies, exultations and disappointments; not only is there a succession of characters emerging into the clearest individuality and genuineness—each with its distinctive contribution and separate value: but beyond the details and through all the contrasted variety, there is the spell of complete drama—the drama of life. Here is the underworld in continuous moving pictures, with the overworld watching. True, the stage is a prison; but is not all the world a stage?"

—Charles Vale, *The Forum*

Heathenry:
Thoughts on the Text

This book is without a doubt one of the wildest I've ever read. Donald Lowrie's simple, matter-of-fact delivery of events as they transpired within the walls of San Quentin only amplifies their consistent absurdity and often brutality, and the narrative is full to the brim with mysterious and compelling characters, not least of which is Lowrie himself.

How we are the first publisher to both update and republish this book using a modern typeset—and why more people today haven't heard of this story—is beyond me. But I'm proud of the honor because panning the literary streams of yesteryear for gold nuggets such as these is why Heathen Editions exists. Hopefully, and maybe with a little luck, our edition will attract new eyes because this story and its host of characters are truly begging for a *much* wider audience.

With that notion in mind, we've striven to enhance the text that you're about to experience as much as possible, and we can only hope that this story may one day soon transcend its pages, whether that be a documentary or feature film, or a more aptly suited television series because these real-life characters deserve to be freed from the dusty bookshelves they've been relegated to for well over a century.

I say that not only because it's true, but for selfish reasons: I want to *see* Smoky Ryan in the flesh, with my own eyes, and barring the sudden appearance of a time machine, a television facsimile seems the quickest route. Smoky's hard-won, streetwise wisdom resonates every time he appears, and Lowrie renders his hillbilly dialect to such perfection that Smoky is practically narrating as you read. He's easily one of the greatest characters that I've ever read in literature. A bold statement, I know, but one that I firmly stand by. As a reader, [spoilers ahead!] when he is granted parole is such a bittersweet moment because you're happy to see him leave, yet sad to see him go. And as he walks away from Lowrie for the last time, I found myself wanting to follow Smoky, to know where his story went, to discover if a rascal's broken heart can ever be mended. Alas. . . .

Know what else I want to see? Ed Morrell's story. Because why that saga has *never* been mined for the screen, big or small, is also beyond me. It takes Lowrie three chapters to relay the telling of Morrell's five-year stint in solitary and the lie that put him there, and the entire time I was reading it all I could hear was David Holmes' *Ocean's Eleven* (or *Twelve* or *Thirteen*) soundtrack underscoring it. I could not read those three chapters (16–18) fast enough, editing it all together in my head with tracking shots, whip pans, and zip zooms. With the introduction of Harry Westwood Cooper, we meet a conniving doublecrosser who confoundingly decides to doublecross everyone around him in one of the most dou-blecrossiest doublecrossing stories that has surely ever been printed. That it is all true and the fact that Cooper's plan backfires spectacularly, landing him in solitary next to Mor-rell elevates it to something near legend. Seriously, *legend*.

Then, there's 14-year-old Claude, who you can imagine sitting on a bench, chewing gum nonchalantly—maybe even blowing bubbles, as he watches the Captain, the Warden, and a Sheriff argue back and forth over the whats of his age, the hows of his incarceration, and the whys of his delivery at San Quentin. Fourteen years old!

And never in my life did I think that I would suddenly learn the mechanics of how to hang someone, the ABCs of how to measure them to ascertain their "hanging height," or the 123s of the math involved to solve the problem of how long their hanging rope should be, or why it needs to be that length, *exactly*. Yet, I now unwillingly possess that information because Lowrie refused to shy away from the specifics. That chapter left me simultaneously appalled and mesmerized and unable to deny the mythological archetypes at play—the realization shooting cold chills up my spine.

And just when you think it can't get any worse, that's when Lowrie introduces the "Female" Department of San Quentin, which is to say he delivers us out of hell's frying pan and into its inferno, whose flames will surely elevate your body temperature as you learn of the many injustices delivered unto the women by their matron overlord. Tragically, the many wrongs those ladies endured makes Smoky Ryan's departing monologue all the more poignant. The bitter truth of it will claw at your heart, likely forever.

Through it all, there is Lowrie, his eye for detail ever-present. In review after review of the book at the time of its release (some on the praise pages at the beginning of this edition) you see his keen eye for detail noted more than once. It was a quality Lowrie expressed as essential to writing in the December 1912 issue of *The Editor*:

> ". . . learn to observe; be ready to tell the color of the eyes of the last person you spoke to, if asked to do so."[1]

At times, the details are simply too much. With my head swimming and reeling, I found myself audibly barking

---

[1] Lowrie, D. (1912, December). Letters From the Literati XII. *The Editor* 36(6). 245.

What?! at the insanities more than once—often, in fact. As the details cumulate, it's easy to see how this story became an overnight sensation in 1912. How can you not be moved? How can you not be stirred? How can you not be outraged at the atrocities these humans experienced, convicts or not? That this book instigated prison reforms still in effect today will come as no surprise, likely before you're even a quarter way through—because it's sheer wall-to-wall lunacy at every turn.

So strongly was I affected by what I read that after Chapter 3, in which Lowrie arrives at San Quentin and is processed, I wondered if the mugshots he describes were readily available. I wanted—no, I *needed* to put a face with the name. A quick search yielded zero results, but morbid curiosity prodded me forth, and after several days of fumbling through disparate sources—*suddenly*—there was the face of Convict #19093 staring at me, across time and space. His face seemingly as mysterious as he presents himself in his own narrative. Evelyn Wells, in her biography of Fremont Older (the newspaper editor who sponsored Lowrie's parole and put him to work at the *San Francisco Bulletin* upon release), even confirms his aura of mystery:

> "Lowrie was meek, shy, easily influenced, with eyes which did not show the pupils and never revealed his thoughts. Only his mouth revealed the suffering of a man sensitive beyond the normal."[2]

The Los Angeles Times, oddly, mentions his eyes too:

> "He is a tall young fellow, with brown eyes that shift and turn and are seldom still for an instant."[3]

[2] Wells, E. (1936). Prison Reform. *Fremont Older* (p.244). D. Appleton & Company.

[3] Lowrie Arraigned. (1901, February 27). *The Los Angeles Times*, A10.

What's more, I didn't discover one set of Lowrie mugshots, but two: he was also Convict #21873, a "two-time loser" at San Quentin—a fact that he doesn't reveal until the final chapter, almost as an afterthought.

Again, mystery.

However, I should note that biographers and writers adapting true stories will often condense timelines and create composite characters in order to streamline a narrative, so this mystery doesn't much bother me. Lowrie simply took his first 5-year term and his second 10-year term and combined them into a single 15-year term to simplify his story. Possibly at the behest of his editor who had word counts and column space in mind.

Still, though, who was Lowrie, really? Why such mystery? That he was educated is no question, the quality of his writing broadcasts it. Research into newspaper articles at the time of his first sentencing reveal that he was born in Boston and even briefly attended Harvard at some point.[4] His family was upper middle class, his mother a private physician in the home of a New Yorker on Fifth avenue, and his father was killed by Indians in Colorado while working as a surveyor on the Union Pacific railroad[5]—possibly the root cause of young Lowrie's troubles?

Or perhaps none of that was true as boldly stated in a *Los Angeles Times* headline: "Dude Lowrie a Liar as well as Burglar. Young Crook not a Harvard University Graduate."[6] The article goes on to quote a Cambridge, Massachusetts, police inspector who details Lowrie's record, which, if true, one can surely surmise why Lowrie hightailed it to the west coast soon after release, arriving in Los Angeles on Christmas Day 1900:

---

[4] College-Bred Man an Alleged Burglar. (1901, July 9). *The Los Angeles Times*, A1.

[5] Found Guilty of Lesser Burglary: Young Lowrie Convicted of Housebreaking. (1901, July 10). *Los Angeles Herald*, A9.

[6] Dude Lowrie a Liar as well as Burglar: Young Crook not a Harvard University Graduate. (1901, July 19). *The Los Angeles Times*, A1.

ends p. xx

My Life in Prison

"He was arrested in our city for several jobs, and was sent to the House of Correction (the same as a penitentiary) for two years. He has done time in Massachusetts, in Joliet, and at the Elmira prison, and has just completed a term at Washington, D.C., for house breaking . . . he is a good man to lock up. He is not a Harvard man, and never was."

Giving credence to the inspector's accusation is the 1900 census, which confirms Lowrie as an inmate at the Middlesex County House of Correction & Jail in Massachusetts. And moving backward in time, there appears this confirmation of allegations in a September 1898 Boston newspaper article claiming Lowrie was arrested while using an assumed name:

"At this time he gave the name of James H. Richards, and refused to tell anything about himself . . . it was found that the name had been torn from an inside pocket of the coat, but on the watch pocket of his trousers was found the name George Randall . . . Washington D.C. . . .

"For a time he said that his name was Randall, but later said that his real name was Lowrie . . . He admitted that he has been arrested once before for breaking and entering, and had been sent to the Elmira Reformatory for a term which was finished last June.

"Lowrie is a man of good appearance, being about six feet tall, and well proportioned. He is a stenographer by profession, and says he does not know how he happened to drift into dishonest ways."[7]

---

[7] Had Been Working in Suburbs: Man Brought Before Chief Watts Today Thought to Be Responsible for Breaks in Cambridge and Somerville. (1898, September 23). *Boston Evening Transcript.*

The second half of that final sentence would seem to become a recurring theme in his life; one that others would reflect on once they got to know Lowrie personally and the circumstances of his imprisonment(s), as noted again by Evelyn Wells:

> "What had happened to Lowrie that he had stumbled?"[8]

One vice that certainly contributed much to his recurring problems was alcohol—or maybe it was *a* problem greatly exacerbated by drinking, as observed by more than one of his peers:

> "Lowrie was a dipsomaniac,[9] given to long sprees, and had committed robbery while under the influence of liquor. He could fill long periods of time with intense constructive work. Then the reaction would set in. He drank. Drinking, anything could happen to Lowrie."[10]

> "Lowrie was invited to join [Thomas Mott] Osborne at Sing Sing as his private secretary, but Lowrie's heavy drinking was too much for Osborne, who let him go after six months . . . In a letter dated 28 March 1917, for instance, Osborne wrote to Lowrie and warned him . . . 'It is not the mere "lapses over the wine"— serious as these are . . . Your inability to keep sober is serious.'"[11]

---

[8] Wells, E. (1936). Prison Reform. *Fremont Older* (p.245). D. Appleton & Company.
[9] One who has an uncontrollable and recurring urge to drink alcohol.
[10] Ibid (p.244).
[11] Connelly, D. (2009, Spring/Summer). Research Notes. *The Courant*. 10, 4-5.

"Donald Lowrie, a gifted, sensitive, imaginative, troubled creature . . .

"Don's misdeeds must have arisen from a compulsion he couldn't control, not from a necessity of a more tangible sort. He had, perhaps without realizing it or understanding it, a quarrel with society.

"Yet he was gentle . . . much less at home in rough company."[12]

Even Fremont Older himself became troubled by Lowrie's many relapses:

"Older became certain that Donald Lowrie and his kind were doomed. Something in the man's nature and mind made him different from other men . . .

"How many times he had gone out to hunt Lowrie, traced him through detectives or reporters, found him at last struggling in the horrors of delirium! . . .

"'No power on earth could save Lowrie,' said Older sadly. 'Men like Donald Lowrie are different. In their making something went wrong. They are like cripples, stumbling along. Their minds are diseased.'"[13]

Much like the details in this book, as the observed traits of Lowrie cumulate—gentle, intense, meek, shy, troubled, different, sensitive beyond the normal—one may arrive at the conclusion that Lowrie's mind was more likely dis-eased rather than diseased. As you read this text, a question worth reflecting on may be: how could someone with such a keen eye for detail maintain even a shred of sanity in the world such as it was at the turn of the 20th century *and* in a place

[12] Duffus, R.L. (1960). Friends of Fremont Older. *The Tower of Jewels: Memories of San Francisco* (p.226). W.W. Norton & Company, Inc.

[13] Wells, E. (1936). Prison Reform. *Fremont Older* (pp.248-49). D. Appleton & Company.

such as San Quentin? How does one turn off a mind naturally geared for such astute and meticulous observation? I'm loathe to cite the oft-quoted cliché of "a riddle, wrapped in a mystery, inside an enigma," yet that's exactly what Lowrie seemed to be throughout the entirety of his life—and, I believe, why he so fascinates me. If he did stoop low enough to commit the burglaries that imprisoned him, then how did he also rise up enough to act as assistant counsel for his own defense in the trial that first sent him to San Quentin?[14] Who does that?

The more I learn about Lowrie and the deeper I dig, the more questions I have. History seems to have ultimately dismissed him as an alcoholic burglar who couldn't "make good," but, again, as the details cumulate, there's no single label you can hang on the man and make stick for long. Dipsomaniac? Okay, sure. Yet, after starting work at the *Bulletin* and serializing what would become this book, he wrote over one hundred thousand words in a few weeks[15] and single-handedly increased the *Bulletin*'s circulation by 41,000.[16] Anyone possessing even a modicum of knowledge concerning writing or newspaper subscriptions knows you can't balk at those numbers.

Frustratingly, I have joined what seems to be a long list of persons asking the same question so succinctly posed by Ms. Wells: What had happened to Lowrie that he had stumbled? Why did he vacillate between such extremes? Was it something in his youth? Rebellion against his upbringing? Was he far too sensitive for this world and had to self-medicate with alcohol? Was he undiagnosed bipolar, a condition worsened by liquor? Or was he simply a lying shyster who reveled in drink, conning everyone around him and putting

[14] Will Reside in San Quentin. (1901, July 11). *Daily Times Index*, A1.
[15] Barry, J.D. (1912, October). Donald Lowrie. *The American Magazine*, (74) 676.
[16] Wells, E. (1936). Prison Reform. *Fremont Older* (p.245). D. Appleton & Company.

on airs just long enough to make it to the rush of his next drunken criminal spree? Or was he some strange, complex amalgamation of all those things?

These are the questions that plague me because I don't think Lowrie should be so easily dismissed; there's just something about him, especially after reading this book, that seems worthy of further investigation—that's why we Heathens are already hard at work on the 1915 sequel *My Life Out of Prison*, which details his life after San Quentin, working at the *Bulletin*, and traveling the lecture circuit with Ed Morrell to educate the public on the need for prison reform, because maybe some of the answers I seek await within its pages.

And after much searching, we've finally located and are hard at work on his third and final book *Back in Prison—Why?*, which answers many questions as it was the serial Lowrie was working on in 1925 after once again being imprisoned for burglary in Arizona. Fremont Older sent Evelyn Wells to edit the story, and she sat with Lowrie every day for four months in a ward of the Arizona Penitentiary, but before Lowrie could finish he died of tuberculosis. Wells completed the book with notes she had taken at his bedside.[17]

A tragic end for a tragic man? That's the question I keep asking myself as I piece together more of the puzzle that was Donald Lowrie. . . .

As for the text of this book, the original surely could have used another pass by an editor, which is surprising considering this story was originally serialized in the *Bulletin*. We have corrected myriad spelling and punctuation errors, in addition to updating a few archaic and hyphenated words to reflect their modern usage. Additionally, we have added some 250 footnotes with further corrections and to supplement the text with context, clarification, and commentary

---

[17] Wells, E. (1936). Prison Reform. *Fremont Older* (p.248). D. Appleton & Company.

as needed. We've also added section breaks in some of the chapters to help with Lowrie's sometimes jarring tendency to switch topics without warning.

There also existed a numbering error with the original chapters: Chapters 23 and 26 were skipped over entirely. Whether those chapters were removed from the final version before print or their omission was a simple lapse in counting we cannot say barring a journey to San Francisco and burrowing into the *Bulletin* archives, so, meantime, we have inserted those chapters and left them blank intentionally.

We were also able to locate several photos of San Quentin approximate to the period of Lowrie's incarceration, circa 1890s–1910s, which we have included where appropriate. And, in addition to Lowrie's mugshots, we were able to use either direct information supplied by Lowrie throughout the text or his indirect clues and a bit of deduction to locate nearly two dozen more mugshots of inmates who populate this story, which we have placed where they seem most appropriate within the text. This is one aspect that I believe elevates and makes our edition of this book truly unique. For me, while it's sometimes incredibly disconcerting to read the words about what these individuals endured, it's something else entirely when you can actually see their faces and styled hair and dapper, early 20th century clothing (most sporting fine hats that make me nostalgic for a time I never knew) versus the dichotomy of their shaved heads and faces and those plain, bold prison stripes. Convicts assuredly—whether wrongfully or rightfully—but humans absolutely.

Finally, I will leave you with these words by Lowrie from this book's final chapter to better preface and bookend the many events of which you are about to learn:

"Much that could be written has been left unwritten, and much that has been written has been toned down

ends next p.

in order to be entirely fair, or to avoid giving offense to readers."[18]

While the historical record may cast doubt on Lowrie's version of events in the lead up to his arrival at San Quentin, I think it's no doubt that he chose to "tell it straight" after stepping through its gates. If only for the simple fact that there were too many witnesses—approximately 1,500 to 2,000 of them—to the events which he details. I also have no doubt that, as noted, he left *much* unwritten. Just how much we may never know—but what he did write sure is a doozy.

Regardless of who you are as you begin this book, I'm most certain that you won't be the same once finished.

I'm also most certain that no matter the assumptions you may have already formed concerning the character of Donald Lowrie, the words that follow will challenge all of them—for as Thomas Mott Osborne wrote (a man so passionately inspired by this very book that he chose to voluntarily commit himself to one week of imprisonment at Auburn Prison in New York), this book is "written so simply yet with such power."[19]

What was it within Lowrie that fueled that power?

Sheridan Cleland
Co-Heathen
March 2023

[18] p. 421
[19] Osborne, T. M. (1914). Why I Went to Prison. *Within Prison Walls* (p.4). D. Appleton & Company.

My Life in Prison
Donald Lowrie

1

I was broke. I had not eaten for three days.

I had walked the streets for three nights. Every fiber of my being, every precept of my home training protested against and would not permit my begging.

I saw persons all about me spending money for trifles, or luxuries. I envied the ragged street urchin as he took a nickel in exchange for a newspaper and ran expectantly to the next pedestrian. But I was broke and utterly miserable.

Have you ever been broke?

Have you ever been hungry and miserable, not knowing when or where you were going to get your next meal, nor where you were going to spend your next night.

Have you ever tramped holes in your shoes in a tiresome, discouraging effort to get work, meeting rebuff and insults in return for your earnestness and sincerity, and encountering an utter lack of an understanding of your crying necessity in those with whom you have pleaded for a chance?

Have you ever felt as though the world itself were against you and that a mistake had been made by nature in inflicting you with life?

If you have not felt each and all of these things it will, perhaps, be futile for you to read what they brought to one who has felt them, and it will be difficult for you to tolerate any thought of extenuation[1] for what happened.

Thousands of persons have felt these thoughts, have suffered these experiences, but very few have done what I did; at all events, very few have done what I did and then told about it, as I am going to tell.

Few crimes are committed from choice.

The number of professional criminals is small, amazingly small, in comparison with the number who are criminals of circumstance. But society makes no distinction; the man who steals because he is hungry, and too proud or squeamish to beg, is classed with the thug who waylays you at night and takes your money by persuasion of an ugly .44-caliber "smoke-wagon" held within an inch of your brain, and with money jingling in his own pocket at the moment.

The first is an unfortunate human being driven to commit an act which he abhors; the second a dangerous menace to humankind and organized society.

I belonged to the unprofessional class. And despite a long term in prison, I am not yet a criminal.

Every atom of my body, each vibration of my mind, revolts at the thought of crime. Yet I committed burglary; also I have a big, warm tolerance for other men who have committed burglary, or other crimes, no matter who they may be. Do not mistake me—I am not seeking to apotheosize[2] the offender against the law; far from it. But I know that all men are human—even the men in convict stripes and shaven heads.

Why shouldn't I know. Haven't I been one of them?

Didn't I violate the sacredness of a home in the dead of night, and didn't I spend long years in the penitentiary?

Who knows if I don't?

As I look back I wonder what has been accomplished by my imprisonment.

Perhaps before this series of sketches is done some of you

[1] To cause an offense to seem less serious than it appears.
[2] Glorify; idolize.

may discover what has been accomplished in my individual case. But what is being accomplished in the thousands of other and more unconscionable cases?

Perhaps you do not care; possibly you may feel that it is none of your concern; that you pay taxes for protection, and that you cannot be held accountable for the shortcomings of others or for the inhuman and illogical system that enhances the certainty of still greater violation of man-made laws.

Be that as it may, you are still responsible; and you are not protected.

I was broke and utterly miserable. True, there were thousands of others just as miserable—I realized that—but I was myself, I was no one else save myself, and I had a nickel with a hole in it in my pocket.

Never mutilate a coin of the realm. It may fall into the hands of a starving man or woman and prove the last argument in favor of crime—or suicide.

It was nearing midnight and the possibility of escaping another night in the streets growing slimmer with each passing moment. Somehow I felt that something must occur to relieve my crying necessity.

Subconsciously I had buoyed myself over three breadless days and sleepless nights with the unframed thought that something must turn up.

Put yourself in my place. What would you have done?

Suddenly, almost with the effect of an unexpected physical blow, it came upon me that hope was a chimera,[3] that I must do something for myself.

I had made every reasonable effort consistent with my individual temperament and physical capability to get employment.

I had passed display stands where a careless dropping of the hand might have yielded an apple or a raw potato. But now the time had arrived for action.

What should it be?

[3] Something hoped or wished for but is illusory or impossible to achieve.

ch. ends p. 10

Suicide instantly presented its hideous features—a vivid picture of the dock and the muddy green waters closing over a drawn human face arose before me.

I was not shocked, not even surprised; merely awed. It seemed a natural solution. Yes, that was it—suicide.

A dead man's stomach was insensate[4]—its clamorings were done—it was filled to repletion forever and forever.

Unconsciously my footsteps quickened, for such is the effect of decision of the mind on the body, and I turned toward the bay.

As I did so my fingers closed over the damaged nickel in my pocket, and a new thought occurred to me. The hole in the coin suggested crime; why I do not know.

I stopped and reflected. Yes, I would leave it to the nickel—the bogus nickel. Why not? It was a matter of life and death—essentially a gamble.

I would take the nickel from my pocket. If my eyes encountered "heads" I would commit crime; if "tails" appeared I would hurry to the jumping-off place.

I drew the coin from my pocket and looked at it unconcernedly, impersonally.

It was too dark to see. Holding it firmly so that the test might be fair, I walked rapidly to the corner and under a gas lamp.

The head of Liberty stared me in the face. I flung the coin into the gutter and buttoned up my coat.

I had suddenly become a criminal.

Why I should have decided that burglary was the only crime open to fulfill my needs it is hard to say. Looking back over the desert of years I seem to recall that I was actuated by a recollection of something that had occurred during my boyhood. Inadvertently we had left the back door open one night and a nocturnal prowler had taken advantage of it. That childhood incident came back to me, and the fact that I decided to emulate the unknown gentleman who had

[4] Without feeling.

appropriated my father's watch tends to strengthen the claim that man is a simon-pure[5] imitative animal.

Two hours after I had arrived at my decision I found myself skulking along the quiet, tree-fringed streets of the residential section. A sense of guilt permeated me. I felt that I had already taken an irretrievable step, a step from impecunious[6] respectability to impecunious dishonor.

I had no desire to abandon my intention, and yet it occurred to me that it would, after all, be more honorable to beg than to steal. But humiliation before my own self seemed far more preferable and endurable than humiliation before others, for, of course, I did not expect to be caught.

As for the penalty, that never occurred to me at all. It would not have made any difference if it had.

I walked several blocks farther, turning each corner that opened into the obscure and remote reaches of the neighborhood, but it was a long time before I mustered sufficient courage to turn and cross a lawn. When I finally did it was with startling suddenness, as though at the direction of some external agency, and this feeling was emphasized a moment later when I found myself standing before a partly raised window, concealed from the street by a friendly rose bush. It seemed as though I had come directly from my starting point to this window.

After a brief wait to satisfy myself that I had not been observed entering the grounds, I proceeded to raise the sash. Very slowly and noiselessly I pushed the sash upward until there was sufficient room to permit the passage of my body. My mind was already inside, counting returns. I stood still a moment, listening acutely. No sound broke the somber stillness. The great world was so quiet that I imagined I could hear the circulation of my own blood. A moment later I was inside the house.

---

[5] Genuine. A reference to the character Simon Pure, a Quaker preacher, in the 1717 play *A Bold Stroke for a Wife* by Susannah Centlivre (1669–1723).

[6] Poor; without money.

ch. ends p. 10

A street lamp some distance away sent a dim light through the front windows, and I saw that I was in a parlor. The piano looked inviting—that was strange, wasn't it? But instead of yielding to its lure I sat down and rested. I was quite cool.

All the burglar stories I had ever read had distinctly stated that the burglar removed his shoes and examined his "trusty" revolver before proceeding into the more menacing regions of the domicile which he entered. But I was without a revolver, and the squeak had long since been ground out of my shoes. As for a dark-lantern[7] and "jimmy,"[8] I had never seen either accoutrement of my profession and I shouldn't have known what to do with either had they been at hand.

While sitting in the parlor I saw the form of a man flit past the house. Instinctively I knew he was the night watchman for that district, and hugged myself that I had arrived just when I did. I was also surprised to find myself so much at ease. I had been more upset and fearful while on the street than I was now. Surely I would not find it terrifying to enter other rooms and seek the money and valuables that I knew awaited me. Again, my mind preceded my body. I arose and followed it.

Turning into the hall, I had an awful moment—a moment that still gives me the creeps. As I stepped forward I became conscious of another man moving close beside me. My blood seemed to solidify! For an instant I went senseless with horror, but the reaction was prompt and I sprang back with a smothered cry.

The man sprang back with me and disappeared. I stood there trembling, but could hear no sound.

I must get to the window, and quickly. As I moved I noticed a glare on my right. The next instant I realized what had occurred. I had been dodging my own reflection in the hall mirror.

After the first revulsion of feeling had passed I was

[7] A lantern with a movable panel that can be used to hide the light.
[8] A short crowbar.

thankful that I had not a "gun" on my person, for I had felt one awful moment; the thought of self-protection had been strong upon me. Had I been a professional crook I would certainly have shattered a useful and inoffensive mirror during that moment.

It required several minutes for me to regain my self-possession, and then I ascended the stairs, instinctively keeping close to the wall in order to circumvent the creakings that had heralded my use of the first three steps.

I wondered if I had ever done this same thing before—it seemed so strange that I should know just what to do.

On the upper floor I paused at an open door. The slow, regular breathing of a sleeper came from within the room. I stepped across the threshold and stopped.

It was pitch dark. I listened tensely. Presently I located an objective point—the soft, yet jubilant, ticking of a watch—a little machine at work while mankind slept.

I compared myself with the watch. Was I not working also, or was I? Was I not facing a possible ignominious[9] and sudden separation from life? Was I not—in a certain sense—earning whatever I might get—even a "package" from his Honor? Yes, indeed. Already, I considered the watch as my own property—also as my friend.

Three cautious steps, a moment's fumbling at a clothes rack and the watch was in my hands; not only the watch, but also a man's purse that was gloriously heavy.

Bending, I laid the rifled garments on the floor and slowly backed from the room.

Going downstairs I heard the parlor clock strike four and a milk wagon rattling faintly on the next street.

At midnight I had been an honest man. Now I was an outlaw, a burglar. Still, no one save myself knew it, and no one ever should know it. I felt justified in having done what I had.

On the lawn outside, in the shadow of a rustling palm,

---

[9] Disgraceful; humiliating.

ch. ends p. 10

I paused to empty the purse and count the money. There were three twenty-dollar gold pieces and some silver. Exultingly I slipped them into my pocket. The purse I flung into space.

A few steps took me to the street, and I walked rapidly away, head erect and full of vigor.

I had re-established my right to live.

While eating breakfast downtown an hour later—my first meal; in fact, the first food that had passed my lips in eighty-four hours—I reflected on what I had done. Somehow I felt that there should be a reaction, that I ought to be horrified at the thought that I had committed a crime; but the food tasted natural and I was happy, actually and unqualifiedly happy. I felt absolutely no qualms of conscience.

After all, a criminal, so-called, is not such a desperate, dangerous, despicable creature. The patrons in the restaurant did not regard me any differently because I had committed a burglary an hour before. Why? Because they did not know.

I wonder how many persons there are walking the streets, riding in the cars, sitting next to you at the theater, who are undiscovered, undetected, uncaught criminals?

Have you ever violated the law yourself? Have you ever passed a counterfeit coin that has been palmed off on you? That is a felony, you know, punishable by imprisonment in the penitentiary.

True, it doesn't stack up with burglary, or robbery, or forgery, or passing a fictitious check. But it is nonetheless a crime.

My meal finished, I bought a twenty-five-cent cigar and strolled down the street; nor did I forget to tip the waiter. Though I had been dead tired and weak for want of sleep at midnight, I now felt wide awake and alert, I seemed to be intoxicated with the success of my temerity,[10] drunk with the knowledge that I possessed nerve and initiative, proud that I had solved the riddle of my predicament and come out the winner. My fingers toyed with the watch in my pocket and

[10] Boldness; audacity.

I turned into a side street to look the timepiece over. It proved to be an eighteen-karat, full-jeweled Swiss.

"Worth not less than a hundred," I thought, "and a dangerous article for me to keep. I must pawn it."

The thought was no sooner conceived than I decided to act on it. Surreptitiously I fastened the watch-guard to my vest and looked for the familiar three balls.[11]

Five minutes later, four $20 gold pieces were grudgingly shoved toward me by the cadaverous individual behind the pawnshop counter, and I signed my name. He had looked at me very searchingly during the transaction—so searchingly that I felt uncomfortable and apprehensive. But when I reflected that the theft was only a few hours old and that he could by no possibility have an inkling of my guilt, I became reassured and said something about "cutting the poker game for a time."

"There ain't much doubt of that," he answered significantly. I did not detect the menacing sarcasm of the remark at the moment, but now—ten years later—it rankles.[12]

I remember groping my way from the place, and on reaching the street tried to hasten my steps—but the need of sleep had come over me with brutal suddenness. My feet seemed laden with lead.

Glancing at the signs about me, I discovered a rooming house and turned to enter. As I did so I felt a strong impulse to run. The next instant a hand was fumbling at my coat cuffs, and before I realized what had happened a pair of nippers[13] closed around my right wrist.

It is always the right wrist that feels the nippers. Still, policemen have been shot by left-handed men. A voice full of exultation was at my ear.

"I guess the chief wants to see you," it said.

Turning faintly, I encountered the gray eyes of a thick-set, florid-faced man, his hat on the back of his head.

Impulsively I drew back.

"Come along, kid; no fuss!" he admonished.

---

[11] The traditional symbol for pawn shops is three gold balls suspended from a bar.
[12] Causes annoyance or resentment.
[13] Slang for handcuffs.

ch. ends next p.

I wonder if you can appreciate the awful revulsion of feeling that smothered me. A moment before I had been a free being; now I was an apprehended criminal. I offered no resistance, but turned and accompanied my captor without a word. No one but he and I knew of the arrest then.

At headquarters I was led into the presence of the Chief.

"A live one," commented the man who had arrested me, removing the nippers and starting to go through my pockets.

I had not yet spoken a word. I was fighting with myself, trying to determine what course I should adopt.

Should I refuse to talk and let the police officers find out what they could—what they were paid for doing—or should I tell the truth and sue for mercy?

I decided to hold my own counsel.

"What's y'r name?" inquired the Chief.

"I wonder," I instantly replied.

Imagine my surprise when he dipped the pen into the inkwell and drew the blotter toward him.

"What's y'r first name?" he inquired. "What's the I stand for?"

"I wonder," I reiterated doggedly.

"Oh, very well," he snarled. "We've got y'r right. You're a dead one. The name don't cut much ice. You can do time under that name as well as under any other." And he wrote "I Wonder" on the record.

When he asked other questions I refused to answer. I was threatened with dire consequences if I did not "come through," but did not yield. I didn't care. I was tired and sick. At last, realizing the futility of trying to force me to speak, he desisted, and I was led away.

"You'll talk before we get through with you," commented my custodian, as he pushed me into a bare cell in the basement and slammed the barred door. "You'll talk, and be damned glad of the chance."

2

The contrast between being a free creature walking the streets and a captured criminal locked in a cold six-by-four stone cell, away from the sun and air, was awful. I felt as though the sides, as well as the bottom, had dropped out of the universe. I sank upon the board slat constituting the bed and dropped my head into my hands. At last I realized the enormity of my act. But, no, it was not the enormity of the act so much as the enormity of the consequences.

There is a glaring distinction.

I tried to delude myself that I had nothing to fear, that there was no evidence against me. I had been arrested simply because of my seedy appearance; perhaps because I looked guilty of having done something wrong.

But why should the plainclothesman have deemed it necessary to use the nippers? Why should such an air of confidence have pervaded the attitude of the Chief? And why had the pawnbroker looked at me so curiously?

Suddenly I recalled that there had been someone standing beside me while I had been in the pawnshop; also that the pawn ticket which had been taken from my pocket had been labeled as evidence. There was no use in dodging the fact that I was up against it. Even though the burglary had not been reported, it would be—and the fact that the watch had been practically found in my possession a few hours after the crime was insurmountable.

That day seemed unending. No one came near me; no one spoke to me. I could hear the rumble of street cars overhead and far away, and wondered how far I was under the teeming city. Also, occasionally, I heard the clanging of a cell door in the distance.

As evening approached the monotony was broken by the maudlin mumblings of a drunken man whom they placed in a cell opposite mine.

I tried to scrape an acquaintance with him, but he clung to the bars and eyed me suspiciously.

"Offisher," he shouted, "he's trying to (hic) pick my pockets."

The remark filled me with loathing. Somehow that stupefied brain had recognized me as a criminal—it must already show in my face and bearing.

I slunk back into the cell and sat down. I was thirsty, but could find no water. I also wanted to smoke. As for food and sleep, I had forgotten them.

At last they came after me.

It felt good to get out of the cell, even if it were only for a grilling.

I was led into a brilliantly lighted room. Several persons were present. My eyes rested upon the cadaverous features of the pawnbroker's clerk and remained there.

"Is this the man?" asked the officer at the table, nodding toward me.

"Yes, that's him. He pawned that watch this morning."

I followed the sweep of the witness's hand and saw the watch lying on the table. It did not look so friendly now, and I wished I had never heard or seen it. The officer turned to two persons who were seated at the end of the table—an elderly gentleman and a young lady.

"This is the man who burglarized your house last night," he announced. "Have you ever seen him before?"

The young lady's eyes embarrassed me and I hung my head.

"No," they replied, in unison.

"Look closely," he continued. "This is important."

"Stand with your face to the light," he added, gruffly, glaring at me.

I did as he commanded.

The witnesses shook their heads.

"No, I have never seen him before," declared the old gentleman.

"And you, miss?" asked the policeman, expectantly.

"No, I don't know him," she replied.

"Very well; thank you," said the inquisitor; "that's all."

They arose and departed with apparent relief.

Until midnight I was quizzed and threatened, pushed and jostled, subjected to everything save actual physical violence, but refused to talk. The more insistent and threatening they became the more stubborn I got. Nothing would ever make me speak unless I wanted to speak.

Back in the bare, cold cell, I threw myself on the board and slept. When I awoke it was daylight—crepuscular[1] daylight down there in that sepulchral[2] place—and I saw a tin of water and a chunk of bread on the stone doorstep outside.

I arose and drank the beverage greedily and then felt a desire to wash. My face and hands were clammy and sticky.

I could find no sign of water. With a portion of the hot beverage I wet the handkerchief which they had returned to me when I was searched, and managed to wash my face and hands.

It was at that moment that I became conscious of the fact that I had ceased to be human.

True, I had committed a crime, but had I done anything warranting society to inflict me with the horror that I saw crawling on my sleeve? It was different from any insect I had

[1] Of or like twilight; dim.
[2] Of or like a tomb; gloomy.

ch. ends p. 19

ever seen. My blood seemed to change into a slimy snake that didn't have room to crawl through my heart. Like a burning iron it came into my brain that I was—lousy. My character had been besmirched by an act of my own. My body was to be defiled also. That was a part of the consequences.

My soul went sick, for even a burglar has a soul. We all have souls. And, in essence, we are all alike. There is no difference save in manifestation. A mangy rat nibbling at the chunk of bread on the door-stone scarcely interested me. Rats are infinitely preferable to lice.

After three days of stubborn silence on my part the detectives gave me up, though not without a promise of "getting even." I have often wondered why they did not man-handle me, for I have since learned that is the common process with the suspect who refuses to talk. I can only account for their restraint on the ground that they intuitively realized that brute force would only have served to seal my lips—that in locking up my body they had also locked the doors of my mind.

On the fourth morning—unwashed and unkempt— I was hustled upstairs to the Police Court. I had not had my clothes off since my arrest, and I felt like an animated week-old cadaver.

I paid little attention to the proceedings. It matters not much what was said and done, for I already saw the future. I knew I was going to spend long years in prison.

Against the advice of counsel, I pleaded not guilty and stood trial before the Superior Court. Before the trial was half over, however, I regretted my decision and would have withdrawn my plea had it not been for my inherent defiance—and the lice.

I would maintain an attitude of indifference and unconcern to the very end.

At last the jury was instructed, principally about "reasonable doubts." They filed from the room with bored expressions predominating. In five minutes they returned.

"Guilty of burglary of the first degree," read the clerk, after taking the written verdict from the hands of the foreman.

I felt a hundred pairs of eyes focused on my face, but sat unmoved. No one should know how I felt. My lawyers spoke a few apologetic words to the judge and sat down.

"Sentence 10 a.m. Saturday," announced the judge.

Back in my cell at the jail I paced the floor in my stocking feet and smoked innumerable cigarettes. What would the sentence be?

According to the peroration[3] of the District Attorney, I was the greatest scoundrel unhung—a vicious wolf masquerading in sheep's clothing. Every burglary that had occurred during the past six months was inferentially laid at my door. If this address had impressed the judge as it seemed to have impressed the jury I could hope for nothing less than the maximum penalty—15 years.

Yes, that was it—15 years—180 months—780 weeks—5,475 days.

I had entered a private dwelling in the dead of night, "armed to the teeth and ready to commit murder," according to the People's representative. The fact that no burglar's tools had been found in my possession, nor a revolver on my person, and that I had, unprofessionally, taken only a small portion of the valuables contained within the home I had desecrated, had been overlooked entirely. Even my own attorney had failed to make capital of these facts.

During the intervening days between my conviction and sentence my thoughts were wholly occupied with what I would get. The preceding Saturday a professional "pete" man[4] had slipped into court, "taken a plea" and returned exultingly to the jail with a six-year "jolt."[5] He had been caught in the act of blowing a safe at midnight and was

---

[3] The concluding part of a speech.
[4] Peterman; safecracker.
[5] Prison slang for a long sentence.

ch. ends p. 19

already a "three-time loser."[6] But he knew "Gold Coin Mike," the boss of the ward where his mother washed clothes for a living. That made a big difference.

Saturday at last arrived and I found myself standing before the "bar of justice." I wanted the ordeal over, yet dreaded it. But at precisely 10 o'clock, even as the hour tolled dolorously[7] from the courthouse tower, his Honor bustled in from his chambers and took his place on the bench. He bowed mechanically to one or two prominent attorneys and wiped his spectacles abstractedly.

Strange to say, I liked "his Honor." Intuitively I knew he was a man with a heart. Once during the trial he had caught the smile with which I had interpreted what had been intended as a serious assertion by the District Attorney. I had endeavored to suppress the smile when I saw him observing me, but felt immensely relieved and grateful when he smiled in return.

A man who could sense that I had intended no disrespect or levity, and a man who could think in the same groove as myself certainly could not deal with me unjustly.

Immediate events did not justify this conception of "his Honor," but subsequent events did—I was not at fault in believing him to be a man of heart.

I was exceedingly interested in all that transpired. Why shouldn't I be interested? Was not I the particular delectation[8] scheduled for that morning's gratification of the rows of morbid spectators behind me?

In blatant tones the bailiff announced that the court was in session. Immediate quiescence[9] settled over the room. Only the hoarse cry of a fruit peddler on the outside violated the solemnity of the moment.

---

[6] Prison slang denoting the number of times one has been sentenced to prison.
[7] Mournfully; sorrowfully.
[8] Delight.
[9] Quiet; stillness.

The judge began speaking—something about regret and his "painful duty" and the "protection of society."

The reporters wrote rapidly.

At last came the climax, "——and the judgment of this court is that you be punished by imprisonment in the State prison at San Quentin for the term of fifteen years."

The deputy who had me in charge quickly placed his hand under my armpit, ostensibly to keep me from falling.

Next morning the papers stated that I had collapsed and had to be assisted from the room. As a matter of fact, I had been repeating "fifteen years" to myself for five days, steeling myself to hear it without a tremor, and I was elated at the thought of getting away from—the lice.

The penitentiary would be clean and wholesome, at least.

I was taken to San Quentin on the 24th day of July, 1901. The day was perfect and the world seemed to be a particularly desirable place to stay in.

People were laughing and chatting and carefree. Many of them were starting off on their summer vacation.

By holding a newspaper folded once before me I managed to conceal the manacles that pinched my wrists and prevented me from slapping at a fly that seemed determined on buzzing an insect secret into my ear.

No wonder people were gay and happy and carefree—they didn't know that I was on my way to prison for a long term of years.

I had been in jail several weeks. Consequently, I noticed everything. The visitor to a jail notices small details and carries off a composite impression from them.

The jail inmate does not see these details—they are commonplaces of his existence. But when the jail inmate goes out into the world he notices details also—the commonplaces that are unseen by free men and women.

His first impression is that of immensity—he is blinded by distance. He is also intoxicated with the pure air, so sweet and grateful after the long days and nights of chloride of

ch. ends next p.

lime, carbonized atmosphere of jail. Disinfectants are typical of jail; they are responsible for the "jail smell"; they are the mute apologies for a paucity[10] of soap and water and the absence of God's sunshine.

And speaking of God's sunshine, the man just out of jail wilts in it. At first it vitalizes and invigorates, but not for long. The contrast is too marked. In a few minutes it enervates[11] and depresses and makes the head swim.

Jail atmosphere is always several degrees lower than that of the outside world—it is always cellar-like. Long immurement[12] deadens one's sensibility to this. Consequently, upon entering the sunlight, the first thrills of pleasure and gratitude are soon replaced by discomfort and lassitude. It was so on that July day ten years ago.

The cool waiting-room at the ferry building was an oasis—it afforded shelter from the sun. A little child came running toward us in chase of a ball, but stopped and cocked her golden head questioningly. Apparently she sensed that the man with the newspaper hanging over his hands was different from other persons.

The Deputy Sheriff kicked the ball toward her and she ran happily away. A tall, graceful girl sank languidly into the seat opposite us and, munched comfortably from a box of bonbons.

The incongruity of eating in public struck home, yet made a pretty picture—a picture that has remained undimmed for ten years. She wore a plaid dress. I wonder where she is now?

On the ferry-boat we occupied one of the benches beside the space reserved for vehicles. It was noon and I watched a teamster unbridle and feed his horses. From the methodical way in which he went about it I knew he was in the habit

[10] Small quantities; scarcity.
[11] Weakens.
[12] Confinement.

of making noonday trips to Tiburon.[13] It occurred to me that he was an economist; he fed his team while in transit.

There were other teams on the boat, but none of them were at dinner. I fell to studying the horses. The bay[14] was a nervous animal and kept tossing its head in efforts to get more satisfying mouthfuls of oats. With each toss a quantity of oats spilled from the nosebag and pattered to the deck. Its mate had more sense—horse sense, perhaps. It balanced its feedbag on the neckyoke in front and had no difficulty in regulating its supply.

I speculated a good deal on those horses. The nervous one was thin and looked worried; the other sleek and contented. Two men in the seat ahead attracted my attention. One, a spare, sallow man, was talking shrilly. It was something about money. His companion placidly puffed a cigar and listened. I compared them with the horses.

The deputy who had me in charge at last became aware of my abstraction and mistook it for despondency.

"Let's go and have a couple of drinks," he suggested kindly, rising.

When I declined he seemed to be disconcerted. Apparently, with him, a "drink" was the panacea[15] for any situation.

But why should I take a drink? I had been in jail several weeks without a drink—save water and "bootleg." Why should I drink now? Certainly I did not need any "Dutch" courage to enter prison.

---

[13] Tiburon is an incorporated town in Marin County, California, located on the Tiburon Peninsula, which reaches south into the San Francisco Bay.

[14] Bay is one of the most common hair coat color of horses, characterized by a reddish-brown or brown body color with a black point coloration of the mane, tail, ear edges, and lower legs.

[15] Solution; remedy.

Birds-eye View of San Quentin circa 1890s

Birds-eye View of San Quentin circa 1913

3

My first glimpse of San Quentin prison was decidedly depressing. It looked bleak and ugly—a scar on the landscape. Somehow I thought of the black hole of Lucknow and that awful summer day in the fifties.[1] As the train wound in and out through the Marin county hills and vales, the prison, silhouetted on a bare promontory, seemed beckoning me. Presently it was hidden by intervening hills, and the train drew up at a small, barn-like station. I expected the brakeman to call San Quentin, but he said "Greenbrae!"[2]

A rickety, dust-begrimed stage awaited us. There were several other passengers. Instinctively I knew they were connected with the prison, and I dropped the newspaper. The handcuffs did not attract attention. An utter indifference characterized the passengers—they talked and laughed among themselves quite naturally. But I caught a fleeting, half-shamed glance of sympathy from the brown eyes of an

---

[1] We believe Lowrie has confused his Indian cities here and is likely making a reference to the Black Hole of Calcutta, which was a dungeon in Fort William, measuring 14×18 feet, where troops of Siraj ud-Daulah, the Nawab of Bengal, held British prisoners of war on the night of June 20, 1756, after the fall of Fort William. According to John Zephaniah Holwell (1711–1798), one of the British prisoners and an employee of the East India Company, the surviving British soldiers, Indian sepoys, and Indian civilians were imprisoned overnight in conditions so cramped that 123 of 146 prisoners of war died from suffocation and heat exhaustion.

[2] Greenbrae is a small unincorporated community in Marin County, California, approximately three miles northwest of San Quentin.

awkward, freckle-faced schoolgirl. It did me good—I still remember it.

Passing through the "patent gate" that marks the western boundary of the prison reservation, my attention was drawn to another scarification of the earth.

I gazed, appalled.

Slowly it dawned upon me that I was looking into the prison cemetery. There was no green thing near—nothing but bare, dirty-yellow earth. Rows of white boards, each with its black number staring out over the road, marked the last resting place of hundreds of men—and some women—who had passed that same spot, living, breathing entities, and they had gazed horrifiedly, just as I gazed. I shuddered.

What had fate in store for me? Would my number ever stare at future men in handcuffs on their way to the grim walls beyond? Then I thought of other aspects. How must a mother feel as she passed that sepulchral place on her way to visit her wayward boy? What emotions are evoked in the breast of the condemned man as his hopeless eyes are assailed with this horrible reminder of his fate?

What complete indifference to human sensibilities was responsible for placing this graveyard at the very entrance to the penitentiary?

My melancholy thoughts were diverted by a herd of little calves—all brown and white—which gazed round-eyed as we passed the prison ranch house. Presently a horse guard, with rifle slung across his lap, fell in behind the stage. He seemed to have dropped from nowhere.

"Yes, that's where the guards practice shooting. Each guard is required to make 30 out of a possible 50 at the yearly test, in order to hold his job," said one of the passengers in reply to a question, pointing at a rifle range.

The range was 200 yards, but I afterward learned that a number of the guards shot "forty-five" regularly. Not much chance for a fellow to make a run for it!

We were rattling under the first Gatling gun[3] post now. Liberty Post it is called, because it is the last post passed by the outgoing prisoner. At that time it had a draped statue of Liberty, the handiwork of an old German "lifer," on top. Poor old "Bismarck"![4]—he never saw his statue after it left his hands in the prison cabinet shop.

True, he passed the spot, but his "going-out" suit was of wood.

Approaching the prison I saw striped figures at work in the vegetable gardens. They did not look up as we passed. Some had dampened red handkerchiefs on their heads to keep off the sun. Yet straw farm hats are cheap!

As the stage drew up before the black prison portcullis [5]I felt relieved. The days of dread and hope were done. The moment had arrived. A new life was at hand. Henceforth I was to be a convict, and afterward—if there should be an afterward—an ex-convict. I should never again be a free and natural human being. I had made a mistake. This was the penalty.

At the main entrance to the penitentiary we were halted by the gatekeeper, who unlocked and held open a drawer in his desk. The Deputy Sheriff who had me in charge was evidently accustomed to delivering prisoners there, for he at once produced an ugly-looking revolver.

The weapon fascinated me. Until that moment I had entertained no idea that my custodian was armed. But one of the rules of the prison is that no arms of any description are permitted inside the walls, save after lockup at night, when the dog-watch go on duty in the little guard-posts close to

[3] The first practical machine gun; a rapid-fire, crank-driven gun with a cylindrical cluster of several barrels, named after its inventor Richard J. Gatling (1818–1903).

[4] A nickname for people of German descent; a reference to Otto Eduard Leopold von Bismarck (1815-1898), chancellor of the German Empire under whose leadership Germany was united from 1871–90.

[5] A grating, often of iron, that slides along vertical grooves within a gateway to prevent passage.

ch. ends p. 31

and surrounding the cell buildings, and the day watch comes off the walls and from the Gatling gun towers beyond.

As the deputy laid the gun in the drawer I saw there were other revolvers there; also a bottle of whiskey that had been left by some visitor who was making the rounds inside. The revolver filled me with loathing and resentment. It had been brought along for use on me—not on anybody else, but me.

It is not a pleasant thing to look upon a loaded revolver that has been intended for use on you. A long-forgotten picture of a thief trying to escape in a crowded city street came back to me. I recalled how I had joined in the chase, how the hound instinct had been aroused in me by the contagion of the moment, and how the man who finally ran the poor wretch down puffed out his chest and talked as if he had done something big and noble.

Perhaps he had, but the picture of the emaciated and ragged culprit, gasping for breath after his heartbreaking effort to escape, his face a study of mingled hopelessness and defiance, surrounded by the exultant mob, came vividly before me. I saw the hole in his hat as though it had been yesterday. But at the time I had felt with the mob—we had succeeded in capturing a thief. Now, however, I knew how the thief must have felt, and wondered how many of the others who had assisted in the capture had come to feel like the thief felt.

There are two sides to everything.

While these thoughts were racing through my mind the deputy deftly removed the handcuffs from my wrists, and we passed through the man-gate into the arcade[6] that leads to the prison yard. At the farther end of the arcade a prisoner opened a second man-gate, part of a massive steel portal. I observed this man closely, for it ran in my mind that his position must be the acme[7] of trust for a prisoner. I afterward learned that he was "doing it all" and had twenty-two

---

[6] A covered passageway with arches along the sides.
[7] The peak or highest point.

years' service behind him. He didn't look it—appearances are very deceptive in prison.

My first impression on entering the yard was that of surprise. I had expected to see massive bars and rigid discipline. Instead I saw a beautiful flower garden, a fountain surmounted by a figure of a white swan, in the center. Two or three prisoners, with thin, drawn faces, were at work in this garden. They were consumptives and were given this light outdoor work to prolong their lives. One of them, I later ascertained, was a "lifer," and the irony of prolonging his penance appalled me. What was the use? Still I knew it was a humane motive that had given him the place in the garden, close to God's promise of heaven—the flowers.

We were received by the Captain of the Yard—at that time an old man who had been engaged in prison work all his life. He held out his hand and the deputy gave him my commitment.

"Fifteen years," he commented, glancing at the document and scanning the endorsements. "It's about time you were bringing us somebody with more than a year or two—these short-termers are overrunning the place."

He favored me with a prolonged scrutiny, and then led the deputy into his office to make out the receipt, leaving me in charge of the turnkey.[8]

After a thorough "frisk" I was escorted to the photograph gallery and "mugged," with my prison number attached to my breast. During the preparations of the photographer I glanced down at this number. It was 19,093.

The assistant photographer noted my interest.

"Oh, don't worry," he said; "it don't add thirteen."

I was not told to look pleasant when the moment arrived for taking the picture, simply admonished to keep my eyes still. The operation over, I was bustled to the bathroom and ordered to strip.

My body was carefully inspected by the Chinaman in

---

[8] The person in charge of the keys of a prison; jailer.

ch. ends p. 31

charge—a highbinder[9] serving life—to see that I had nothing concealed between my toes or any other possible place.

I could not see the necessity and did not understand the object of this examination, and it was very humiliating. Subsequently I learned that it had to be done to prevent the smuggling of "dope" into the prison.

At last the officer in charge seemed satisfied and I was ordered into the tub.

It was not necessary for the Chinaman to tell me to "wash-ee heap lot; scrub-um good," for I had never felt happier at being in a tub of warm water. It was my first real bath since my arrest. The Chinaman was much elated at the way I took it.

"Heap good," he kept repeating; "all-ee same Chinaman; like-ee heap clean. Lots white men no like-ee water." The praise did me good. It was the first word of commendation I had received from anyone since my arrest. "How long have you been here, John?" I inquired. "Five t'ousand eight hundled fi'ty-five days to-day. To-moller five t'ousand eight hundled fi-ty-sic."

He seemed to take great pride in his statement, and I afterward learned that he kept account of his time in this way and was always primed to tell the exact number of days he had served.

At that moment another prisoner entered the bathroom with my new clothes.

"Here's your summer suit," he observed pleasantly. "No charge."

He laid the garments on the chair, dropped the shoes like two bricks, and disappeared.

Ten minutes later I was dressed, and felt very uncomfortable. The underclothing was coarse and heavy, as were the outer garments. The "top shirt" was of stripes, black and white, each about an inch and a quarter in width and

---

[9] A member of a Chinese-American secret society that engaged in criminal activities.

running horizontally. The stripes of the outer garments were perpendicular. The clothing was entirely new and sweet, but the stripes hurt. I was very conscious of them. Most prisoners get used to the stripes and forget them. I never did. I feel them yet. I found it difficult to walk confidently in the brogans.[10] They had no shape and the soles were slippery. I felt as if I had two chunks of lead tied loosely at my ankles.

Crossing the yard to the barbershop, I was the cynosure[11] of all eyes, and I felt like an arrival from some strange planet, dropped into an unknown place on this one.

"New man!" shouted my guide, half shoving me through the barbershop doorway.

I was taken in charge by one of the barbers and escorted to the chair. "How'll yer have yer hair cut?" he asked, with well-simulated sincerity. "Puff, shingle—any way yer like."

I was rather surprised to find so much of what seemed to be levity. Like the public in general, I had imagined that men in prison went around with elongated countenances and an expression of chronic gloom. Instead I found smiles and indifference—or feigned indifference. Every man realizes that self-pity, or a bid for sympathy, is despicable. The jocular sarcasm I learned was merely an effort to delude themselves and each other that they didn't mind. It was the innate, manly trait of "gameness."

Many a smiling face in prison—just as in the world at large—conceals a tortured, despairing soul.

Although I felt anything but gay or indifferent, I immediately adopted the barber's mood.

"Oh, cut it summer-style, to match my suit," I laughed.

Even as I spoke the clippers were dropped onto my skull, not gently and obsequiously, but roughly, so much so that it hurt. The man may have been a capable barber outside, but I doubt it. At all events, he would have to develop more

[10] Heavy, coarse, laced ankle-high work shoes or boots.
[11] Center of attention.

ch. ends p. 31

concern for the feelings of a patron if he expected to do that sort of work in free life again.

My hair began falling in bunches and in two minutes was all gone. The barber sarcastically held a small mirror before my face so that I might see the result.

"How does it suit?" he asked in mock concern.

I regarded myself critically. It was the first time in my adult life that I had seen my cranial "bumps."

"I'm afraid you left some of the roots," I replied.

"Yes, I miss them occasionally," he laughed, and proceeded to shave me.

From the barbershop I returned to the photograph gallery. In addition to taking a picture of the incoming prisoner, as he appears in "free" clothes, he is also photographed in stripes, front view and profile, with a "slate showing his number, name, term, crime, the county from which he has been committed and his age and place of nativity.

My next experience was with the Lieutenant of the Yard. I sat on the "mourners' bench" and he stood before me, instructing me as to the rules of the prison.

"Always fold your arms when crossing the yard. Don't talk in the dining-room and don't carry food from the table. Don't trade with other prisoners. Don't leave your work without permission. Always remove your cap when speaking to the Captain. You are permitted to write one letter a month."

There was a lot more, altogether too much for me to retain, and I was obliged to learn most of the rules by observation and by asking questions of my fellow prisoners.

Many new prisoners learn the rules by breaking them and being punished therefore, and I have often wondered why a little pamphlet containing all the rules has not been printed. By giving each incoming prisoner one of these pamphlets much trouble could be avoided, though they would have to be printed in Spanish and in Chinese, as well as in English.

Discharged Feby. 13 05

#28735Q

19093

Name C. Donald Lawrie
No. 19093
County Los Angeles
Crime Burglary
Term 5 years
Received July 24-1901
Discharged Feb. 24-1905
Remarks

C. Donald Lawrie

Burg. 5 y. Los A. age 26. Stenogra-
pher. Mass. 5f 10⅞. Cfs 151.
Received July 24. 1901.
Discharged: Feb 24 1905.

19093
C. Donald Lawrie
Los Angeles
Burglary
5 Years
Age 26
July 24th 1901
Mass.

Illiterates—and there are quite a few—would, of course, have to be instructed orally.

I remained on the mourners' bench about an hour and was then taken to the Bertillon[12] room. A group of visitors happened to be there and I was used as a subject for their edification.

The fingerprint process interested me. Each of my ten digits was inked and an impression taken, and then each hand was taken as a whole, all five fingers simultaneously. There are especially prepared blanks for the purpose, and the impression of each finger, and of each hand, is indicated by a heading printed over the space reserved for it.

There is no doubt that fingerprint identification is infallible. The records are classified so that an identity may be established readily. Also, the careless touching of a finger may be "developed." After you have handled a book or touched a table the lines of your fingers may be brought out and the classification established any time within twelve hours afterward.

With the inauguration of the central bureau of criminal identification at Leavenworth,[13] and the general adoption of the fingerprint records and classification, the time is surely at hand when the professional criminal can no longer hope to conceal his past. This is a step in the right direction and will tend to reduce the number of real criminals at large.

After my fingerprints had been taken I was ordered to

[12] Alphonse Bertillon (1853–1914) was a French police officer and criminologist who applied the anthropological technique of anthropometry (the measurement of a human) to law enforcement creating an identification system, known as the Bertillon System, based on physical measurements. It was the first scientific system used by police to identify criminals until superseded by the technique of fingerprinting at the beginning of the 20th century.

[13] The use of fingerprinting in the United States began in 1904 at the United States Penitentiary, Leavenworth (USP Leavenworth), a medium security federal penitentiary in northeast Kansas, as a result of the 1903 William West/Will West Case. After Will West was "booked" into the prison, it was noted that he bore the same name, Bertillion measurements, and a striking resemblance to the previously booked inmate William West. The incident called into question the reliability of Bertillion measurements and it was concluded that a more positive means of identification was necessary.

strip to the waist, and the turnkey proceeded to measure me for the Bertillon record. I was very much impressed by the manner in which he went at it. It looked like a complicated process, but he had learned to save time by working along the lines of least resistance, and got several of the measurements before I was aware of his purpose.

Next I was taken to the turnkey's office and subjected to a long series of stereotyped questions and asked to sign my name to the effect that I had no money or valuables on my person when received; also giving the prison authorities permission to open, inspect, retain or destroy any mail or express matter that might be addressed to me.

I was then asked if there was anyone I desired to have notified in the event of my death.

"No one," I instantly replied, and regretted it a moment later.

Returning to the clothing department, I was given two pairs of blankets and a change of underwear, labeled with my number, as were all my garments. The Chinaman then escorted me to a mattress room and I was given a mattress. I flung it over my shoulder, and with the blankets under my arm and the extra clothing dangling from my free hand, followed the celestial to my cell.

"When bell ring to-night, you come here—savvy?" he instructed.

I glanced at the number on the cell door. It was 34—34 Tank. There were five bunks in the cell, steamer-style, one of which was without a mattress. I laid my belongings in this bunk and then followed my guide to the yard, where he left me.

Prisoners in the yard at San Quentin circa 1910

4

I had no sooner been left alone in the prison yard than I was approached by a tall, sorrowful-looking man whose age I judged to be about 45.

"Wadger bring?" he asked, leading me to the board extending between the posts of the shed provided for shelter from the rain, upon which we seated ourselves.

I failed to understand the significance of this question and thought he referred to the property I might have had on my person.

"Oh, only a handkerchief or two," I replied.

He laughed. "No, no; I don't mean that. What sort of a package?"

"Package?" I asked. "What do you mean?"

"Why, what did his Honor hand you?"

"Oh, you mean the sentence?" I queried.

"Yes," he responded. "How long'd yer get?"

"Fifteen years," I replied.

"Huh, that's easy. Yer kin do that on yer head. Wadger think I'm doin?"

I hesitated before replying. If fifteen years was "easy" he must be doing a much longer period. While I was still hesitating he answered his own question.

"I'm doin' it all, an' I been here fifteen already."

He made this announcement with evident pride, as if he expected me to voice great surprise and concern.

I'll have to admit that I was shocked. I had heard and read of life prisoners, but this was the first one I had ever talked with. The remembrance has remained with me because of that fact, but long before I left San Quentin a life prisoner became commonplace and excited no wonder and not a great deal of sympathy. It all depended upon the individual's temperament. Observing this particular man during the six months following my arrival, I saw that he got the ear of every new man and then posed, made a bid for sympathy, poor fellow, the same as he had done with me.

We sat there for an hour, and he told me about his life and the act that shattered it. He had been a successful rancher and had killed his young wife because she persisted in infidelity.

I could readily appreciate that he would jar on a woman's nerves, for he was very selfish and inconsiderate, and talked about himself and indulged in self-pity almost exclusively. Still, he did not talk nor look like a man who would commit murder.

Several times I tried to interrupt his repetition of the facts concerning his own case to ask something about the conditions surrounding us, but invariably he returned to his own affairs, apparently much soothed by my expressions of counterfeit concern and sympathy.

Some years later this man succeeded in getting a parole, only to commit suicide.

I have often wondered why he did so, and can only account for it on the supposition that he could not find the human sympathy he craved—so self-indulgently. Never once during the years I knew him did he refer to his victim save in scorn, nor did he ever express any regret at the sorrow he had brought upon her mother and father.

Yet persons unfamiliar with all the facts, and not knowing the man intimately, as I did, are prone to condemn me

ch. ends p. 45

for judging him fairly. Have I the right to form judgment on any man? That is for you to answer. I know I am honest, that I see both sides of the prison system, and that I want to temper sympathy and understanding with fairness and even with condemnation of the "underdog" sometimes. I condemn myself.

I noticed a small negro, a little, thin creature, with sunken cheeks and big sorrowful eyes, who wore a red shirt.

"Why is he wearing a red shirt?" I asked.

"Fer tryin' to beat th' place," answered my acquaintance. "He's doin' 35 years an' has the T.B.[1] They put him to work outside, in the vegetable garden, on account of his health, and he copped a sneak one day. Got clear over the hill, right under the nose of 'three post.' So small I guess they didn't see him. They rang the big bell and we was all locked up while they went out to run him down. Found him hidin' in a barn 'bout three miles from here an' brought him back. They allus[2] puts a red shirt on them as tries to make a getaway."

I have forgotten the little negro's name now, but used to watch and pity him. Never in my life have I seen a human countenance with such an expression of absolute hopelessness.

About three months after I entered the prison the little negro disappeared. Inquiry developed that he had at last been taken to the "old hospital," where the incurables fret out their last weeks on earth. I never saw him again. He died some time during the following winter. I wonder how black his soul was?

And the little negro served a purpose, for his case reminds me of something important. When a prisoner is taken from a cell at San Quentin and assigned to the consumptives' ward as incurable, the cell which he vacates is not fumigated. It is merely swept out, sometimes whitewashed, and then some

[1] Tuberculosis.
[2] Always.

other prisoner, perhaps a young boy, free of any physical taint, is assigned to it.

The floors of the cells at San Quentin are never washed—the construction will not permit—and the ventilation is fearful.

Only a person who has spent a night in one of these cells can realize what it means. In the morning the outside air is such a contrast that one tastes it. Contagion is bound to linger in these cells, and many a healthy prisoner has contracted consumption[3] in this way.

In this connection I noted that Indians and negroes are more prone to consumption than are Chinese and whites. I can readily understand this as applied to Indians—they wilt and die in confinement; they are natural outdoor creatures—but I have never been able to explain why negroes succumb so rapidly.

To be absolutely fair, I recall that at one time, some years ago, an order was issued that the doctor should report all cases of consumption assigned to the incurable ward, so that the cells vacated by the victims might be fumigated, but, like many other orders, this one has long since been forgotten, and to the best of my knowledge and belief nothing is now done to prevent the contraction of this deadly disease along the lines I have indicated.

At 4:15 a whistle blew in the yard and my new acquaintance told me it was for supper, and I lined up behind him. There were only a few men in the upper yard, not more than one hundred, and my guide informed me that I would see the mill crowd come into the dining-room from the lower entrance.

I shall never forget my first impressions of the mess hall. It is partly underground, with windows on one side only, and is about four hundred feet in length. An immense building—the old sash and door factory—cuts off the light from these windows so that it is often necessary to have artificial light

---

[3] Pulmonary tuberculosis.

ch. ends p. 45

for the midday meal. An aisle extends down the center of this cellar-like place, and long tables, each accommodating twenty-two persons, run out at right angles on either side of this aisle. The floor is asphaltum[4] and is always wet or damp. The walls are whitewashed.

Of course there are no tablecloths or napkins—just the plain board table. Tinware is used exclusively and is always rusty, save when a dozen or two new pans are added to the equipment.

The place smells worse than a stable, always, but more so on some days than on others.

The prisoners file into this place indiscriminately, the only segregation being that of the Chinese, who have separate tables. Negroes, Japanese, Hindus, syphilitics,[5] old men without teeth, young boys with huge appetites, line up as they may and march in to the general trough.

Under the present warden a table has been set apart for those without teeth—it is known as the "toothless table"— and they are allowed more time to eat than is accorded the main line.

Twelve minutes is the regular time allowed for meals, and the food is served in pans, each prisoner helping himself. No service spoons or ladles are provided. Each prisoner dips into the common receptacle with the spoon with which he eats. This is especially disgusting on "stew days."

I recall one man, now in confinement for his third "jolt," known as "the Russian." His face is covered with running sores which he keeps plastered with some kind of white ointment. I have sat opposite this man, seen him help himself to a portion of stew, eat it voraciously and then dip into the service pan with the same spoon with which he had eaten.

I do not want to disgust or sicken you, and hope you will forget this picture before you get home to dinner. But if you ever wonder why a man coming out of prison is bitter and

---

[4] Latin spelling of asphalt.
[5] Persons suffering from syphilis.

San Quentin Prison Dining Room

feels revengeful, perhaps this one minor fact will help you to understand and tend to make you charitable.

If the theory of imprisonment is purely punitive why, of course, this and other horrors should not be condemned, but if there is the least idea of making the prisoner a better man, of reforming him—and I believe that is the theory—then these things should be known to the public.

As I have said before, it is only the man who has suffered them, the man who has felt them, who knows.

Even the prison officials—the subordinates who see these things every day—do not notice them. They are concerned in maintaining discipline and in an endeavor to provide enough to eat.

The food itself offers no cause for complaint. It is ample and wholesome, especially under the present warden, but there is much to be desired in its preparation and manner of serving. And this is not an insignificant detail. If a man is compelled to eat like a pig he is bound to acquire pig instincts, and he is bound to carry these pig instincts out into the world with him. True, there are a few men, who become chronic fasters, eating just enough to keep body and soul together, but are they not also irreparably injured?

In paying the penalty for crime—loss of liberty, working day after day through long years without pay, suffering the stigma of the convict brand—does not an offender expiate[6] his crime sufficiently?

Should he be reduced to the level of a brute, should he be compelled to starve his body because of higher instincts which are inherent and which he cannot help having?

Why should it be necessary?

What does it accomplish?

Does it not degrade men and fill them with bitterness?

Do they not feel that they have been cast into the public filth heap?

---

[6] Make amends; atone.

Can they be expected to become better men under such conditions?

Someone may say, "Good! That's just what they deserve. It will teach them a lesson. They will be so horrified, so disgusted, that they will never return." But if your boy, your husband, your father, committed crime, would you advocate his confinement in a pigsty? Of course you wouldn't. You might be broad enough to admit that a prison term should be imposed upon him, but you certainly would not admit that he should be reduced to the level of the lowest brute in order to "teach him a lesson."

That is merely a spirit of revenge and revenge spells HATE. Hate always breeds hate.

Sometimes the horror of these conditions dies away; the victim becomes apathetic and an apparent indifference manifests—a smoldering hate. I have seen a new prisoner sit at the table day after day, nibbling at a piece of bread and sipping his "tea" or "coffee," and then, after the lapse of a few months, I have seen this same man sit down at the table and eat like a hog.

Simply the result of the system, or, perhaps, you may prefer to call it an ability to adjust himself to conditions— which is considered a desirable trait.

I say calmly and deliberately that few, if any, men are deterred from the commission of crime by reason of the fear of the consequences, even after they know the consequences down to the last sickening detail. If I felt that anything beneficial to anyone were accomplished by these conditions—and others which I shall recount later—I should have nothing to say. But I know that degradation and a spirit of revenge, a determination to retaliate, to "get even," is frequently the result. The prisoner is not only deprived of his liberty, but also of his self-respect and whatever innate sense of decency he may possess.

I did not eat anything that first meal. I simply sipped a little "tea." I was impressed by the utter unconcern with

ch. ends p. 45

which the others at the table attacked the food—boiled beans, bread and tea.

A man wearing gold spectacles, sitting opposite me, attracted my attention. His face was a picture of chronic disgust, yet he partook of everything. Next day I learned that he was serving the last month of a fourteen-year sentence which had been imposed for forgery, and was the son of a man prominent in public life. He unburdened his soul to me before he left the prison, and was determined to redeem himself, but didn't. He is now serving a long term in an Eastern prison.

An entire book could be written about this one man. He is purely and simply a "criminal" of the system, and should be an honorable, law-abiding and industrious member of society.

But most of these things should be presented in concrete form. It is tiresome and uninteresting to read generalities. Perhaps before I finish, I may be able to convince you that a pound of flesh is not so important as a human soul. I hope so.

My first meal in the penitentiary was not a success. I could not eat and I was glad when the signal was given to march out.

It requires about twelve minutes for the prisoners to march into the mess hall, and as the last ones enter the first arrivals begin to leave, resulting in a continuous procession of striped figures along the center aisle.

Stomach trouble is common among prisoners, and I have often thought that the twelve-minute limit is responsible. Why should it be necessary for a man serving life to eat as if a train were waiting for him? I asked an old prison keeper about this one day, and he told me that most men can eat all they want in twelve minutes, and if they were waiting until the slow eaters finished they would get uneasy and disturbances in the dining-room would become common.

The prisoners are not permitted to talk while in the mess

hall, and meals seem more like a function, a part of the routine, than an occasion for refreshment. A kind of I'm-doing-this-to-stay-alive-and-not-because-I-want-to expression is characteristic on the faces of the men while at meals.

Passing the entrance to the kitchen on my way to the upper yard I noticed a sign over the clock—*Tempus Fugit*.[7] It was a pleasant, optimistic thought, but failed to stir any appreciable degree of acquiescence in me at the moment.

In the yard we had a moment's breathing spell before the bell rang for lockup and I was the center of interest for nearly two thousand pairs of curious eyes.

The new arrival, or "fish," is always an object of interest to the other prisoners, and is generally kept well occupied answering questions about the outside world—until the next "fish" drops in.

As the bell started ringing there was a stampede for the iron stairways of the four cell buildings.

"Don't lose any time," admonished a voice behind me. "It's a case of spending the night at the springs if you're not at your cell for the count."

In answer to my hurried inquiry about "the springs" he informed me that he referred to "the hole." This didn't sound reassuring, and I wanted to ask more, but was jostled away from my informant, and lost no time getting to "34 tank."

Now a peculiar incident of one's first day in the penitentiary is that one doesn't know who his cellmates are to be. I knew I had been assigned to a cell containing five bunks, which meant four cellmates, but I did not know who they were, whether young or old, grave or gay, healthy or unhealthy, congenial or uncongenial.

Arriving at the cell entrance, I found three men standing just inside the doorway. Before I had time to "size them up" one of them accosted me:

"Take off y'r lid an' face th' light," he ordered. "Th' bull 'll be goin' by f'r th' count in a second."

---

[7] Translated from Latin: Time flies.

ch. ends next p.

It was rather an abrupt and unconventioned introduction, but I did as I was told. I heard the doors slamming all about me, and presently, just as the fifth habitant of the cell dodged breathlessly in, the "bull" flitted past.

"Five," I heard him mutter as he glanced at our faces.

The next instant the door slammed violently in my face and the bolts and bars were shot into place by the trusties[8] who followed close upon the heels of the counting officer—the "bull."

Outside it was broad daylight, but when that solid steel door slammed shut the cell became dark. It was like being suddenly dropped into antipodal[9] night. One of my cellmates immediately struck a match and lighted the coal oil lamp.

"Allus look out f'r y'r fingers when dey slams dat main entrance t' dis hotel," he admonished. "A new guy got his mitt cut clean in two las' week; had it in th' crack when dey slammed th' door. Some says he did it a purpose, so's t' beat th' mill, but he wuz too green f'r dat. I'll show him t' y'r termorrer. My name's Smoky Ryan—dey all calls me Smoky."

He was the same man who had ordered me to remove my cap a moment before, and I observed his face closely as he bent over the lamp. It was not a bad face, yet was deeply seared with the marks of sensual indulgence; also, his eyes were small and a trifle too close together.

True to my inherent trait of forming conceptions of persons at first glance, however, I felt that I was going to like him.

"Make y'rself 't home," he suggested, noting that I was ill at ease and uncertain what to do. "But whatever y'r do, never put y'r lid on th' piany or muss up th' lace curtains. We never stands f'r dat, do we, cullies?" he finished, addressing the others. A general laugh greeted this pleasantry, in which I joined, and felt better.

---

[8] Plural form of trusty (a prisoner considered trustworthy and allowed special privileges).

[9] Exactly opposite.

The other three men undressed immediately and crawled into their respective bunks. None of them had spoken to me. One was a mere boy, stunted, and sickly in appearance; the others men of 35 to 40, one a very light, straight-haired blonde, tall and with pimpled face; the other a phlegmatic, heavy-set Italian.

Smoky moved the cell furniture, consisting of a small, rickety table and a slop bucket, to one side, and then dragged my mattress from the top bunk, where I had placed it earlier in the afternoon.

"Y'r can't sleep on dat as it is," he informed me. "Y'rd roll out th's first time th' ol' ship struck a high wave."

The mattress had simply been stuffed with straw and was cylindrical in shape. Placing it lengthwise on the rusty steel floor, Smoky proceeded to jump up and down upon it, inviting me to join in. I did so, and we jumped up and down for ten or fifteen minutes, until we had the mattress stamped into some semblance of flatness.

At last Smoky seemed satisfied and tossed the result of our handiwork—or footwork—back into the bunk. It weighed not more than five or six pounds. The stamping process had filled the small eight-by-ten tank with dust, and the lamp had already consumed most of the oxygen—yet we had been locked in only a few minutes.

I had already discovered that the penitentiary had many advantages over the police station and the county jail, but was appalled at the thought of spending long nights in a crowded eight-by-ten cell, with no ventilation. Already I felt choked.

5

While Smoky was arranging my bunk I peered out through the slit in the steel door. Outside it was broad daylight, the sun was still hours high, and the glare of light hurt my eyes. I saw several prisoners crossing the yard.

"Who are they?" I asked.

"Oh, cooks, an' house servants, an' office men," replied Smoky, coming to the wicket[1] and peeping out with me. "Some of 'em don't get in till 8 o'clock. There's three lockups after we come in."

Later I learned that the night sergeant, who was in charge of the prison after 5 p.m., was kept busy locking doors and checking off the count until taps. The system was to "drop the lock" of each cell not occupied at the regular lockup, so that the inmates might enter at any time after they had finished their duties, the sergeant making regular rounds and locking them in.

Of course I was interested in my other cellmates, and as we turned away from the wicket I spoke to one of them, the tall blonde.

"What did you bring?" he asked. He was lying in the bottom bunk, opposite the door.

Smoky had already addressed him as the "Count," and

---

[1] The aforementioned slit in the steel door.

I later learned that he was the renegade son of an Alsatian[2] family of some standing. He had finally been shipped to America, after many lapses and depredations[3] at home, in the hope that he might straighten up and "reform." He spoke with a German accent and proved to be a hypochondriac, and I learned that he was the proprietor of the array of bottles in the corner of the cell, some of them thick with grease, which had attracted the dust and made them look anything but inviting.

At that time prisoners were permitted to buy medicines— and some of them went the limit.

The Count imagined he was the victim of every known— and some unknown—physical ailment, and had tonics galore—codliver oil, cherry pectoral, pills, ointments and other concoctions, and took as many as five doses of medicine during the first half hour of our acquaintance.

The medicine privilege has long since been abolished, but at that time one of the prison officials had the perquisite[4] of selling all sorts of things to the prisoners, and made about 50 percent on every sale. Carpets, rugs, mattresses, sheets, towels, clocks, underwear, hats, ties, socks, shoes, handkerchiefs, medicines, and even feather pillows could be purchased—if the prisoner had the money. This lasted until the inmates of Red Room—one of the dormitories housing about forty men—clubbed together and bought six dozen bottles of patent medicine, got drunk and "whooped it up." They were transferred to the dungeons and otherwise punished.

Strange to say, the incident reached the Board of Directors, and an order was issued prohibiting prisoners from buying anything, even towels and soap. At present the men are permitted to buy necessaries, and it is so arranged that

[2] A native or inhabitant of Alsace, France (a region of northeastern France, on the borders with Germany and Switzerland).

[3] Acts causing damage or destruction; pillaging.

[4] Perk.

ch. ends p. 59

they pay the minimum price. Soaps, toothbrushes, towels, handkerchiefs, tobacco, and musical supplies are now purchased through the commissary department at wholesale prices and sold to the inmates without profit to anyone. This is but one of many minor details proving the fitness and fairness of the present warden, some of which I shall recount later.

It was a good thing to abolish the sale of medicine, for many of the men, not knowing what use to make of the money at their command from relatives, spent it for medicines that they really didn't need, resulting in harm to their bodies and a lowering of the prison discipline. There was always a great demand for such medicines as were thought to contain "dope."

Numbers of times I have seen the Count drink an entire bottle of patent medicine before breakfast in the hope that he might get a "kick" from it.

It is remarkable how far some men will go in their desire for a stimulant. I know of a recent instance where a human wreck procured a bottle of camphorated oil from the doctor, ostensibly to rub on his chest and throat for a cold, and promptly drank it. I was present in the hospital when he was pumped out, and it required heroic treatment to save his life. At first the doctor thought he had taken the stuff with suicidal intent, but on recovering consciousness the victim admitted that he had done so to get a "kick." The doctor was tempted to oblige him with another kind of kick.

About an hour after lockup I was startled by a blast of music. Smoky noted my surprise and smiled indulgently.

"Jus' a little serenade by th' band," he informed me. "Not stric'ly in honor of y'r arrival, an' yet it is—dey plays ev'ry night; dat is, dey practises an' den plays in th' yard on Sundays. Can y'r dance?" he asked, expectantly.

"No," I replied, regretting to disappoint him.

"Dat's too bad," he complained. "We has a great time dancin' Sundays under th' shed. Of course, dey ain't no dolls present, but we pairs off an' has some fun. Y'r'll have t' learn t' dance, Bill."

It was right here that I was christened "Bill," a nickname that stuck to me all during my imprisonment.

I listened to the strains of the "Olympia Hippodrome," [5] and then to a selection from "Lucretia Borgia," [6] before making any comment.

"Pretty good band," I offered, tentatively.

Smoky's face lighted up. He was glad that I had praised the effort. There is quite a little pride among the prisoners regarding the band and other purely internal accomplishments.

"Well, I've seen it a lot better," Smoky apologized. "Fifteen years ago, when 'Cornet George' had it, it was a crackerjack. Still, it ain't so bad now. Th' only trouble is dey plays too much of dat high-toned dope. I like rags an' waltzes."

I regarded him in undisguised astonishment. How long had he been in prison? He spoke of "fifteen years ago" as though it were yesterday. I wanted to ask the question, but refrained. Something told me he would impart more about himself without being questioned than would be the case otherwise. His nonchalance was remarkable.

I seated myself on the edge of the bunk and gazed at him incredulously.

"Can you play chess?" suddenly asked the Count.

"I play at it," I replied. "Why?"

"Oh, I'd like to play you a game," he said.

"Sure," I invited. "Come on."

He arose with alacrity[7]—also with a medicine bottle— and got the chessboard and men from under the bunk. Drawing up the stool, he placed the board upon it and set

[5] "Olympia Hippodrome March" (1898) composed by Russell Alexander (1877–1915).

[6] *Lucrezia Borgia* is a melodramatic opera in a prologue and two acts by Italian composer Gaetano Donizetti (1797–1848).

[7] Cheerful readiness; briskness.

ch. ends p. 59

up the pieces. He then placed two folded blankets on the floor to serve as seats.

During these preparations I studied his face and bearing. His lips were thick and greasy-looking, and every movement was eloquent of patronage, as though it were a great condescension for him to play me. After the first five or six moves, however, he looked at me questioningly.

"Why, you've played this game before," he objected. "I thought you didn't know much about it?"

"I don't," I replied. "This is my first game in several years."

"Bet him a sack he can't beat y'r, Count," urged Smoky, standing behind my opponent and winking at me. "Y'r never been beat in th' cell yet, even if dey does skin y'r in th' yard right along. Bet him y'r win th' game."

"Bet you a sack I beat you!" ejaculated the Count, succumbing to Smoky's taunting suggestion, and challenging me with his eyes, as well as with the inflection of his voice.

"A sack?" I asked. "What's that?"

"Why, a sack o' weeds—terbaccer," said Smoky. "Dat's th' coin o' th' realm here, jus' th' same's money outside. Y'r got a sack with y'r things t'day, didn't y'r?"

I remembered I had been given a sack of tobacco with my extra clothing, and promptly wagered it on the result of the game.

Smoky became deeply interested, and the Count put forth his best efforts. Twice I thought I had him mated, but he wiggled out of it, and then, in a moment of aberration— I was thinking about the vileness of the air—I blundered, and the game went to the jubilant Count.

Smoky had great difficulty concealing his disappointment, but predicted that I would win the next game.

"Don't get puffed up, Franco-Germany," he said. "Bill ain't got settled yet. He's still thinkin' about some rag 'r something outside. Wait till he's here a month an' y'r won't have a look-in."

During the chess game I noticed that the boy had a bad

cough, and wondered how long he was serving. After we had put away the chess I asked him what was the matter.

"Oh, I cough all the time," he answered disconsolately. "I guess I've got the con. My brother died with it, an' my mother is—"

He stopped abruptly and lay staring at me half resentfully, as if I had wormed something out of him that he preferred not to divulge. I did not ask him to go on, though I was interested and felt sorry for him—how could I help it? Smoky relieved us by calling to the next cell.

"We got a new boarder, fellers!" he shouted.

"Have y'r tried him yet?" came back a voice faintly, as though from the bottom of a well.

"No, he ain't broke no rules yet," replied Smoky. "He seems t' be a pretty good sort o' plug. He's doin' fifteen f'r prowlin'."

"What does he mean by 'trying me'?" I asked.

"Oh, dat's Fatty Smith," laughed Smoky. "Dey tries ev'ry new fish dey gets in dere—tries him th' first night an' sentences him t' carry th' bucket f'r a month. Fatty's a good feller, only he likes t' have fun."

"Carry the bucket?" I asked. "What's that?"

Smoky winked at the Italian before replying.

"Oh, we takes turns carryin' th' bucket. We each takes a week. When dey unlocks in th' mornin' one of us has t' empty th' bucket, an' one man is on th' broom. I bet him my turn on th' bucket f'r a month on th' lasht prize fight, an' he lost."

Developments brought out the fact that it was a common practice for the inmates of a cell to bet off their turn at the cell work, and Smoky had a faculty for winning his bets.

"How you spell-a bucket?" asked a voice from the middle bunk. It was the Italian. He had a piece of broken slate and a stump of pencil and was busy trying to learn to write English. It was the first time he had spoken.

"B-u-c-k-i-t," Smoky imparted.

ch. ends p. 59

The Italian moistened the pencil stump with his lips and laboriously drew the letters.

"How is'a dat?" he asked, proudly handing me the slate.

I regarded the letters carefully, not knowing whether to correct the spelling or not. I decided not to. It would put Smoky "in bad."

"That's fine," I commented. "How long have you been learning to write?"

"Two year," he replied, much pleased at my praise.

He hesitated a moment and then got up and impressed me into service as instructor. At first I did not like it. I wanted to learn more about the boy, but Spaghetti, as Smoky called him, was so enthused that I soon became absorbed in showing him how to figure. In the midst of the lesson the bugle sounded taps, and Smoky extinguished the light, leaving us in darkness.

"Dat's th' rule," he apologized in a low voice. "If dey ketches y'r light burnin' after taps y'r lose th' lamp, an' dat's hell. Y'r not supposed t' talk, neither, but we got so we kin tell when th' night watch is comin' an' quit."

We undressed in the dark, conversing in low tones, and I then climbed to the top bunk.

"What time do we get up?" I asked.

"Six o'clock; but sh-sh-sh-h!"

The next instant the cell was flooded with light and I heard someone fumbling at the lock. I was startled and raised up to look, bumping my head against the ceiling. I saw a bullseye at the wicket. It remained a second and was then withdrawn, and I heard a padded step, and then the noise of the pull at the lock of the next cell.

"Dat's th' night bull," whispered Smoky. "He allus comes by here right after 9 o'clock, an' it won't do f'r him t' ketch y'r talkin' or with th' light burnin'."

I wanted to ask questions, but heard Smoky turn over in his bunk and settle himself to sleep. Though I had not had a good night's sleep for many weeks, I lay wide awake,

thinking and wondering. The Italian was soon snoring—
in English. I knew it was he by the location, and the boy
coughed and sighed continually.

I wanted to talk with the boy, but it was against the rules,
and there was no telling what instant the bullseye would flash
through the wicket.

The night watch wears "sneaks," and it is only after
long imprisonment that you learn to catch the sound of his
approach. Suddenly the stillness was broken by a call—

"Ten o'clock an' all-l-l's well!" There was an interval and
then it was repeated in the distance. Another interval and
I heard it again, still fainter. Then it sounded close by, having
gone from post to post around the cell buildings—and then it
was caught up and repeated by the sentries stationed in the
lower yard, growing fainter and fainter with each repetition.

The sergeant of the night watch listens for these calls and
counts them. If he does not hear eight he investigates.

New guards are put on night duty for the first three or
four months, and many of them go to sleep. There is an
ironclad rule about this. Sleeping on post means discharge,
without recourse. Frequently the culprit denies that he has
been asleep, and it becomes a question of taking his word or
that of the sergeant. This has led to an interesting procedure.
When the sergeant fails to hear the requisite number of calls
he goes from post to post until he locates the sleeping man,
quietly appropriates his shotgun and other accoutrements
and delivers them over to the gateman before waking the
delinquent.

"Where is your gun?" asks the sergeant as he awakens the
sleeper.

Of course, the man does not know.

"You'll find it between the gates," the sergeant informs
him, "and you needn't come back."

Another guard is aroused to take the vacant place, and
the watch goes on.

In years long past attempts to escape at night were not

ch. ends p. 59

infrequent, and I know of one instance where a contemplated escape was reported by a "stool-pigeon,"[8] and the Captain of the Guard—unknown to the night watch—posted a day man with a loaded rifle at one of the windows in the guards' quarters commanding the suspected cell. When the two men emerged from the cell they were shot down without warning, like dogs. It was cold-blooded murder, pure and simple, but the newspapers didn't get it that way. The murderers have long since severed their connection with the prison.

Eleven o'clock, 12 o'clock, 1 o'clock passed, and I listened to the calls. I did not hear 2 o'clock, but was awake at 3 and heard all the other calls until morning.

In his sleep the boy kept mumbling something about work—he was evidently hard at his daily task—and coughed a good deal.

When day began to break I got up and stood with my nose at the wicket, breathing in the fresh air. The cell was foul and stifling.

Only by spending a night in one of the "tanks" at San Quentin can one appreciate what it means. Think of spending years of nights under such conditions, and then understand why many men come out of prison broken and embittered. At times when something goes wrong with the cooking, or when the water becomes tainted in late summer, the nights are nightmares—sickening to think of.

At present San Quentin prison is fearfully overcrowded. Cells that were originally built for two inmates now shelter four or five. There are less than 700 cells for nearly 2,000 prisoners, and a number of these cells, known as "singles," are so small that it is impossible to place more than one man in each, which crowds four or five into larger cells. This condition has necessitated the conversion of two large rooms in the old furniture factory into dormitories, where 300 men sleep.

[8] Informant.

Talking with a man prominent in public affairs recently and telling him of these things, he said:

"No judge should be qualified to sentence men to prison until he has spent at least one night in one of these cells."

This may be an extreme view, but so long as human beings are treated like brutes extreme views are tenable. You cannot make a saint out of a man by confining him in a church, but you can make a devil out of him by treating him like hell.

I was standing at the wicket gulping in the fresh air when the bell began ringing for unlock. In an instant all was changed. Where a moment before the softness of summer dawn had made the grim buildings and massive walls sepulchral, imparting a sense of living death, there now reigned a pandemonium of clanking keys, creaking levers, shouting warders, and scurrying trusties, emphasizing by contrast the hideous reality of the place.

My cellmates came tumbling out of their bunks and began dressing hurriedly. There was only one wash basin and a small bucket of water. I waited until the others had washed and then poured what water there was left into the basin. In doing so I noted that the bottom of the water bucket was slimy with sediment, yet we had been drinking from it the night before.

It is the duty of the "cell-tenders" to clean and fill the water buckets in the cells on their respective tiers, but most of them merely add fresh water to that which may be left. The cell inmates are not allowed access to the water faucets at the ends of the tiers, and cannot get fresh water for themselves.

I soon learned to rinse out our water bucket each morning with the residue. But the bucket has a capacity of only about a gallon, and sometimes, especially on warm nights, we would drink nearly all of it and have insufficient for washing in the morning, and, of course, none for cleaning purposes.

"Why, you haven't got a towel, and no soap," commented

ch. ends p. 59

the Count as I prepared to wash. "Here, use my soap, and here's an extra towel."

Prisoners are not furnished towels. Those without money either get along without a towel or else break the prison rules by trading their tobacco for one. In many cases men use their shirts or blankets as towels until such time as they are able to get a flour sack or piece of rag. Those having money to their credit at the office may purchase towels and other necessaries on the first of each month, but a man entering the prison early in the month, even though he have money, must wait three or four weeks before he can make a purchase, meanwhile using some other man's towel or trading, on credit, for one. The "Jimmy Hope"[9] soap furnished is such as is ordinarily used for scrubbing floors and other coarse cleaning.

There is a marked fellowship among the prisoners. Generally the new arrival sees a few familiar faces—men who have been in jail with him and have been sent "across the bubble" while he has been awaiting trial or dickering with the District Attorney for a "plea."

The day following my arrival half a dozen men, mostly strangers, offered me towels, toothbrushes, soap and other things. But the Count had a remittance from the "old country" and was well supplied with extra things. He seemed to derive a lot of satisfaction in being able to supply me and would not listen to my protestations that I could wait.

"Hurry up," urged Smoky as I began to wash. "Th' bell only rings a minute, same's at lockup. Dey'll be openin' up pretty pronto."

Hastily finishing my ablutions in the scant supply of water, I looked for a place to empty the basin. Smoky pointed to the bucket. It had a yellow foam on top, resultant from the chloride of lime that had been in the bottom the night before. This vile stuff, while serving as a disinfectant, filled the cell with a pungent odor, rasping the throat and smarting the eyes.

[9] A mixture of cockney rhyming and prison slang used for soap.

"It's full," I objected.

"No, dat's foam," said Smoky, and, grabbing the basin from me, he carefully poured the contents into the bucket.

This basin served for five men. We used it one after the other. Still, it might have been worse—the Kid didn't have syphilis—only consumption.

A moment later, when the signal was given to unlock the doors, a trusty came running along the tier, releasing the final catch of each door as he passed, and the men poured out.

I then learned what "carrying the bucket" meant. The Count grabbed ours, full to the brim, and dodged along the tier, holding the receptacle in front of him. At the bottom of the stairs at the end of the building he fell into line with hundreds of other men, all carrying buckets, and moved slowly to the sewer opening at the south end of the yard.

This opening is within fifteen feet of the south cell building, and the men confined in the cells close by and above it breathe the foul fumes all night, additional to the foulness existent in the cells themselves.

Going to the wicket for a breath of fresh air, the inmate of one of these cells is assailed with the sewer odor. On hot summer nights it is awful. I celled there once for a few days, but moved as soon as I could.

After emptying the bucket the Count rinsed it in cold salt water and then halted a moment while a crippled prisoner flipped in the allotted portion of chloride of lime with a rusty ladle. Then the Count came running back to our building and up the stairs to our cell—as rapidly as the rules permitted—in order to be in time for breakfast line.

Everything is done with a rush at the penitentiary—eating, bathing, shaving, even the dressing of the prisoner about to be discharged. I often wondered why. It seemed so absurd.

Even when a human being is hanged it is done with scientific swiftness, but I understand that—more about it anon.[10]

[10] Soon.

ch. ends next p.

Under Smoky's directions I made up my bed, and then we proceeded to the yard, leaving the Italian engaged in sweeping and "tidying" the cell. The boy had dodged out as soon as the door opened.

"Smoky," I inquired, as we joined the herd in the yard and waited for the whistle to line up, "how long is the Kid doing and what for?"

"Fifty years," answered Smoky, "and a rotten shame. Some Fresno judge soaked him—handed him th' fifty—as an example. An example, mind you! Why, it makes me jus' hanker t' git outside an' rob an' kill f'r th' rest of my life. Here I am a five-time loser, doin' twenty f'r stick-up, an' dat poor Kid gets fifty th' first rattle outer th' box. An' it was only a plain case of rollin' a drunk. He an' his pardner follered him t' a lonely place an' took three measly dollars off him. Fifty years and Rockefeller an' dem other thieves, ridin' in automobiles an' livin' in glass houses on de money wot dey robbed outer little kids' stomachs. Example! I'd do ten years on top o' dis twenty , t' git at pipe dream outer dese judges, solid ivory noodles."

"But about his mother?" I asked. "He started to say something about her last night and stopped."

"Oh, dat's nothin'; jus' a mere trifle. She's only bughouse[11]—laced up in a straitjacket in a madhouse on account o' th' Kid's sentence. Dat's part o' th' 'example' dat fat judge got off his chest when he handed out th' fifty. He sent th' Kid's partner, another kid, to Folsom f'r fifty, too."

"How long has he been here?" I asked.

"Oh, he's only t'ree years in—he ain't got a chance. He's got th' T.B. an' can't last more'n a year, nohow. His mother lives in Chicago, an' she tried t' spring him when she first found out, an' when dey turned her down she jus' give way and went nuts. But dere's th' whistle."

---

[11] Crazy.

We fell into line and crawled along toward the stairway leading to the dining hall.

"Where do I go after breakfast?" I asked.

"Come back t' dis yard an' wait till dey sends f'r y'r from th' office. Dat'll be in an hour or so, an' y'r'll be assigned t' th' mill."

Breakfast consisted of oatmeal, with bitter molasses, bread and "coffee." According to rule it was eaten in silence.

An incident of that meal is still fresh in my memory. At the tap of the guard's cane we sat down at our table—a low bench runs along either side of each table—and a man opposite us—a middle-aged man wearing spectacles, and with thin, straggly hair—reached for the service pan of oatmeal with one hand, while he bowed his head on the other.

"Dat's 'Rebel George,'" Smoky informed me in a whisper, without moving his lips. "He used t' be th' best confidence man in th' business, but he's got th' religious bug now—got it so bad he won't even eat his slop widout sayin' grace. But y'r notice he ain't got much fait' in der Lord in amongst dis bunch o' sharks, th' way he's hangin' on t' der mush wid dat big mitt!"

After "Rebel George" finished his prayer he proceeded to help himself to a generous share of oatmeal before any other man got a helping. I saw him do this same thing many times afterward, and it made me doubt his sincerity as to the "religious bug." Still, when his time expired he turned evangelist, and, so far as I know, lived an unselfish life trying to help others.

6

After breakfast I returned to the upper yard. Save a few cripples, and two or three men who had been excused from work by the doctor, I found the place deserted. Its bareness and silence were in marked contrast to the crowd and confusion of a few minutes before. I no sooner appeared at the top of the stairway than I was accosted by a one-armed man who proved to be the yard-tender.

"You'll have to help clean up," he informed me. "All new guys has to do that the first morning. Get one of them brooms over there," he added, pointing to a stack of brooms standing against one of the guard posts.

I got a broom and joined the other men. We started in a line and proceeded down the yard, sweeping the refuse before us. There were hunchbacks, blind men, men minus an arm or leg, and one poor creature with St. Vitus' dance[1] in that line. The man beside me was very talkative and seemed to derive a lot of satisfaction in posting me—a "green one."

"That's 'kid alley,'" he announced as we arrived opposite the space between the south cell building and its neighbor. "All single cells. 'Battleship Mag,' 'Clara Bell' and all the notorious characters cell there."

---

[1] Sydenham's chorea, also known as chorea minor; an autoimmune disorder characterized by rapid, uncoordinated jerking movements primarily affecting the face, hands, and feet.

We swept along to the next opening.

"'China alley,'" said my guide, "where the chinks live. Just on the ground row, same as in 'kid alley.'

"And this is 'crazy alley,' where they keep the bughouse guys. There's about thirty or forty of 'em," he imparted as we came to the third opening between the buildings. "Take a peep at that chink."

Looking through the slats of the high stockade extending across the end of the alley from one building to the other, I saw an insane Chinaman, naked, save for striped trousers rolled to his knees, fighting a desperate sword duel with an imaginary foe. His eyes were serpent-like and concentrated in deadly hate as he danced back and forth, sparring for an opening. Suddenly he uttered a weird cry of triumph and lunged forward. He stood tensely for a moment, as though over a prostrate body, and then went through the motions of withdrawing the weapon. Then his expression changed to one of fear, and he darted into a cell.

"He does that stunt every mornin' regular, and then goes into his cell and stays there all day without a murmur," said my informant. "But do you see that skinny plug with the sailor cut to his rig, the one hikin' in the strip of sunlight?"

I nodded.

"Well, that's 'Sailor Charlie.' He's been here since 1874. He's the oldest prisoner in the dump, and he's in the alley twenty years."

To say that I was appalled is putting it weakly. He had been committed there before I was born. He had been there all during my childhood, during all the time I had been attending schools, while I had been skating and coasting in winter and swimming in summer. He had been there during all the years that had passed since. And he was insane, and would never get out.

"What did he do?" I asked.

"Oh, got into a drunken fight in a sailor boardin' house and killed a guy with a whisky bottle. It was nothing more

ch. ends p. 76

than manslaughter, but he had no money or friends. He was
in the alley when I drove up seventeen years ago, and he's
been there ever since. He never speaks to anyone—nobody
has ever heard his voice. All he does is mumble to himself
once in a while."

We passed the alley and were nearing the end of the yard.
I had forgotten where I was and what I was doing—it seemed
such an awful thing that a human being should have been
in prison that long.

At the moment I could think of no crime deserving such
a fate. The words "imprisonment for life" when pronounced
in court sound terrible enough, though oftentimes such
a sentence appears inadequate for particular cases, but to
come into contact with a man who had actually been in
prison thirty years filled me with horror. There is a vast difference between words and facts.

And "Sailor Charlie" is still in confinement, though not at
the penitentiary. He is now at one of the State insane asylums.
At present a hospital for the criminal insane is being erected
at Folsom. When it is finished, San Quentin's "crazy alley"
will become a hideous remembrance—a step upon human
souls in our march toward better things.

As we arrived at the end of the yard there came a tragic
interruption. One of the inmates of the alley had crawled
through the small opening where the sewer runs under the
stockade and had escaped into the main yard. He passed
us running like mad, bareheaded, a scrawny, white-faced
human wreck, with a guard in close pursuit.

As he reached the gate opening into the outer yard and
the flower garden the guard overtook him.

I was totally unprepared for what occurred, and shall
remember it, and the guard, so long as I live.

The guard was a big, strong, vigorous man, and I thought
he was merely going to catch the puny fugitive and take him
back to the alley. Instead he raised his cane, loaded with lead

at the end, and brought it down upon the unprotected skull before him.

The runaway took a few steps forward, carried by his momentum, and then sprawled in a heap, striking the asphaltum squarely upon his face and sliding some distance before his body stopped. His legs twitched convulsively, and he made a feeble effort to rise, but sank back, the blood streaming from his nostrils.

With the assistance of a prisoner the guard lifted the inert form and they carried it back to the alley.

As they passed I came within an ace of attacking the guard. I was wild with fury. Everything appeared red, but the man beside me laughed, and that turned my rage upon him. He backed away from me in affright, and I gradually regained my composure.

I never learned what became of the man who was struck. I never saw him again, but the guard is still on the payroll, only he is no longer a guard; he is an officer.

I never think of him without a shudder, and I saw him commit several atrocities of similar character during the years that followed.

I shall recount them later.

I was sitting on the side wall at the end of the yard, still fuming at what I had witnessed, when the Chinaman came from the office and beckoned me to follow him. He took me to the captain of the yard.

"How are y'r eyes?" asked that officer. "Y'r ain't hurt 'em lookin' for work, have y'r?"

"They seem to be all right," I replied.

"And y'r haven't got any bum fingers, or a broken arm, or a lame back, or anything like that, have y'r? Let's see y'r hands."

I extended my arms and he examined my fingers critically.

"Huh, they're all right," he commented. "How old are y'r?"

"Twenty-six," I replied.

He turned to the clerk beside him.

ch. ends p. 76

"Jute mill," he ordered, laconically, and walked into his office.

"Sit down on that bench," ordered the clerk; "the runner will take you to the mill in a few minutes."

I seated myself on the mourners' bench—so called because men charged with infractions of the prison rules sit there while awaiting a hearing before the captain—my thoughts anything but pleasant. A pet parrot served to divert them. It flew from the bush where it had been perched and alighted on the railing before me, cocked its head on one side and regarded me speculatively.

"What did you bring?" it suddenly asked.

It was the same old stereotyped question, but coming so unexpectedly from such a source it certainly amused me. It also made me feel foolish. I didn't know whether to reply or not.

The parrot strutted up and down on the railing, keeping its head turned, so that it never lost sight of me, and crooning to itself contentedly. Finally it stopped and repeated its question.

I was on the verge of imparting the desired information when it spread its wings.

"All right, all right," it said, and flew away.

I was still laughing when the runner appeared and took me in charge.

"We're going to the jute mill," he said. "Come on."

The runner took me down to the lower yard and through the big double gates into the jute mill. Entering the doorway of the mill the din was deafening. It was the first time in my life that I had been inside a large factory. Hundreds of men were at work, many of them in undershirts, and the air was heavy with dust and heat. My guide took me to the office of the superintendent and left me there. Presently the superintendent came in.

"What do you work at outside?" he inquired, after looking me over with a critical eye.

San Quentin Jute Mill circa 1912

JUTE MILL

San Quentin Jute Mill circa 1919

"I'm a stenographer and bookkeeper," I replied, "and I've also been a traveling salesman."

"Well, we ain't got no use for stenographers here," he informed me, "and as for travelin' salesmen, they, ain't got no chance at all."

He turned abruptly to the man at the desk and spoke in a low voice before telling me to sit down. The man at the desk wrote something on a slip of paper and handed it to the runner attached to their office. This man went into the back room and returned with a pair of scissors, blunted at the ends, which he handed to me, and at his bidding I arose and followed him from the office. We traversed several long aisles, with whirring belts, roaring machinery and tense-faced men all about us, and stopped at the far end of the mill—at loom No. 201. The runner spoke to the man at this loom—I could not hear what he said on account of the noise—and then departed.

My new custodian was a short, thick-set German, not bad looking, and I judged him to be some years younger than myself. He favored me with a prolonged scrutiny and then went on with his work as though I were non-existent. I must have stood there ten or fifteen minutes watching him "pick the warp" and change the shuttles before he spoke to me.

"What cher bring?" he finally inquired, coming close and shouting into my ear.

When I told him my sentence his demeanor instantly changed. I did not understand why at the moment, but learned later that a prisoner's respect for his fellow is in direct proportion to the length of sentence. Lifers are accorded more deference than fifty-year men, and fifty-year men are treated with more respect than those serving twenty-five, and so on down the line to the one-year bunch, who are considered unworthy of serious notice. A year sentence is known as a "sleep."

A great deal has been written concerning the jute mill

ch. ends p. 76

at San Quentin. It has been painted as a veritable inferno, I did not find it so.

In two weeks I learned to weave so that I could do my task. True, the work is irksome and the air is charged with fine particles of dust, fatal to the weak-lunged, but the conditions are no worse than those prevailing in many of the textile mills of New England, where young girls perform the same work that is required of able-bodied men at San Quentin. I never had any sympathy or patience with malingerers nor with those who complained about the "terrible" jute mill. I worked in the mill eighteen months, worked on a loom—which is considered the least desirable work of all—and I did my task every day. Two summers passed before I was assigned to another department, and I never missed a day. I know the conditions. I am not writing from hearsay. In fact, I know all the conditions about which I am writing, and I am telling the exact facts—anything else would be absurd under the circumstances.

My object in writing is not to arouse sentimental concern for those who have been caught and are being punished for violations of the law, but to endeavor to show the futility of the present system and the unnecessary degradation to which the delinquent is subjected; also, if possible, to point out possible remedies. State institutions should not be utilized for political ends. Politics is not government; it is a business—a business which has little or no regard for the welfare of the citizen, individually or collectively.

The criticism I have to make of the jute mill at San Quentin is its inefficiency. It barely maintains itself. A plant of the same magnitude managed on an economic basis would yield a good profit. And right here permit me to digress for the purpose of emphasizing this anomaly. There are nearly two thousand men confined at San Quentin, eighteen hundred of whom are able-bodied, capable of discharging a good day's labor. Eighteen hundred able-bodied men should support a community of eight or ten thousand persons in comfort and plenty. Yet these eighteen hundred able-bodied convicts, fed on the coarsest food, clothed in the cheapest manner, and housed like dogs, cost the State of California an average of $200,000 a year to keep in prison. Not only this, but a number of them were supporting families and relatives before they were imprisoned. Who is supporting these families and relatives now?

And aside from this loss in dollars and cents there is a terrible moral loss. A man condemned to work day after day at something in which he has no interest, with no incentive to do his best, and with no remuneration, becomes mentally indolent—he gets so that he does not care. Whatever he may learn about making jute bags will be of no value to him in the outside world. He realizes that the jute mill is maintained simply that he may be compelled to do a certain amount of labor each day—labor that becomes a "task" in every sense of the word. Thousands of men have passed through San Quentin, many of them spending long years there. Nothing has ever been done to make them better nor to fit them to take up the battle of life intelligently. They have been reduced to a dead level of obedience and kept there. But at last there is to be a change. Thanks to the untiring efforts of the present warden and the generous cooperation of the labor leaders the Legislature has authorized the establishment of new industries. Hereafter the clothing, shoes, furniture, and other utensils used at all the State institutions are to be manufactured at San Quentin. This will not only afford interesting and instructive work for the prisoners, but will effect a big saving to the State. It is planned to place the prisoner on a wage basis, charging him for what he now receives gratis,[2] and thus teaching him the fundamental lesson of self-support and frugality. The plan is eminently practical and can be carried out without in the least particular interfering with free labor.

But while I had no trouble mastering a loom and doing

[2] Free; without charge.

ch. ends p. 76

my task, there are other men not so fortunate. The looms are obsolete and have been in use for many years. Some of them are "cranky" and it is a difficult matter to coax the daily task from them. Men of nervous temperament frequently break down under the strain of trying to "make good."

I know of several instances of insanity directly due to prolonged work at a refractory[3] loom. I have watched a man do his best day after day, his face drawn to a tensity painful to behold, only to meet with disaster and punishment in the end. When I worked in the mill the rule was that a man should go to the "hole" on bread and water from Saturday night till Monday morning if he failed to have his task completed at the end of the week. And then, after spending this period in the "hole," he would be brought back to work Monday morning and expected to get out his task for that day.

I recall one man in particular, a fair Englishman, who worked at a loom near mine. At first, after I had learned to do my own task, I used to help him, but soon found that it was useless—he simply couldn't master the work. If he had a "break down," due to defective shuttles or poor warp, it would require from two to three hours for him to get started again. Quite often a second "break" would occur, due to his not having made the mend properly, and I have seen him sink down behind his loom and cry. Every Saturday night he went to the "hole," and every Monday came back, each time more weakened and broken and discouraged. I noticed that his eyes were changing. They began to protrude—a sign which I have since observed frequently precedes insanity. One day when his loom broke down for the third time he seized one of the shuttles and demolished the reeds. With frenzied cries he smashed right and left until the guard in charge of the section came running to see what was the trouble.

The enraged man turned upon this guard and endeavored to strike him in the face with the shuttle. Without thinking

[3] Stubborn; unmanageable.

I rushed to the spot and threw my arms about the infuriated man. At the same instant the guard struck him in the face with his fist. I had not anticipated this and instantly released my hold. I had not struck; why should the guard?

Three days later, raving and foaming at the mouth, the little Englishman was trussed up and conveyed to one of the insane asylums, where he died a few months later.

For the part I had taken in this affair I was condemned by a number of the prisoners. It is an unwritten law that no prisoner shall ever assist an officer in subduing another prisoner. But I had not known this, and it probably would not have made any difference if I had, for I acted instinctively. Yet I know of cases where a prisoner has been ostracized and branded a stool-pigeon by his fellows for preventing a guard's murder. I was never able to reason this out. Had the man remained silent and had the murder occurred, would not the man cognizant of the plan have been a murderer? But I am getting ahead of events.

During my first month in the jute mill I learned a number of interesting things. The loom-tender in charge of the section where I worked was not only accommodating, but also willing to impart information that it sometimes requires years to absorb. I learned, among other things, that many of the weavers were able to finish their task by 1 or 2 o'clock in the afternoon and that some of them then worked on other looms, ostensibly helping friends to get through, but in reality doing it for pay. Men with money at their command in the office took advantage of this to hire other men to do their work, paying for it in commissaries purchased through the office. Everything purchasable through the office had a distinct value in tobacco, which was the medium of exchange. A cake of medicated soap, for instance, was valued at five sacks of tobacco, towels at seven sacks, hats at from fifty to one hundred sacks, according to quality, and so on covering everything that it was permissible to have.

The task on a loom is 100 yards a day, and an expert can

ch. ends p. 76

weave about eighteen yards an hour, which means that he can do his task in less than six hours. The working hours are from 6:45 a.m. to 4:30 p.m., with thirty minutes for dinner. The whistle for dinner is at 11:30 a.m., and it requires about twelve minutes for the men to file out through the arcade into the upper yard and the mess hall, each man being counted as he goes in and out of the mill yard.

This made a working day of more than nine hours, and the expert weavers had three hours each day for recreation or for doing extra work, as they chose.

The charge for weaving was twenty yards for a sack of tobacco, or more than an hour's work for five cents.

As I was without funds, and needed such necessaries as were allowed, I determined to become an expert weaver and thus have the time to earn what I wanted in the way of extras. In six weeks I was able to finish my task by 3 o'clock, and spent the other hour and a half working for a "bon-ton," the term applied to those prisoners who are able to have their work done for them. In this way I soon had what I wanted and was as comfortable as circumstances would permit.

In hurrying to get through with my own task, however, I became careless and would sometimes leave "skips" in the cloth or fail to repair a "break" as it should be. This led to my being "called to the table" and reprimanded.

Each loom has its number, and as a roll of 100 yards is finished it is labeled with the number of the loom. When this roll passes through the cutter to be cut into the proper lengths, for making the grain bags, an inspector watches each cut as it drops off, pulling out those in which he sees defects. These defective pieces, with the number of the loom, are sent to "the table," where the head weaver and an assistant examine them. If it is evident that the weaver has been careless he is sent for and the defective cloth shown him. He is warned that he must do better work, and a record of the warning, with the date, is entered on a book kept for that purpose. If this same man is sent for three times within a month he is reported to the Captain of the Yard for punishment.

At that time this punishment consisted either of 24 hours in the "jacket" or three days in the dungeon on bread and water.

I had learned a great deal about the "jacket" from my loom-tender, and also from my cellmates, and after listening to the warnings at "the table" I returned to my loom determined not to be called up again.

It prevented me from finishing my task as early as I had been doing, but it also prevented my making an intimate acquaintance with the "jacket."

I found that the "jacket" was greatly feared by all prisoners, yet this fear did not prevent its being used every day. [4]

This only goes to bear out my belief that fear has no legitimate place in the training of men. What a man fears he generally hates, and hate incites resentment and defiance.

The man who is influenced by fear in refraining from certain acts, whether positive or negative, is essentially a coward, and cowardice unmakes, rather than makes, men.

Twist this as you will, it is irrefutable.

Man is prone to fear that which he does not understand.

So when I was "called to the table" and warned that I must make better cloth I decided to do so. I did not want the humiliation of being trussed up in a "jacket" like a dangerous maniac, and I knew that I could make better cloth by being careful. True, it would cut into my extra time and prevent my working for others and earning tobacco for the purchase of necessary comforts, but not entirely so. It would merely take me longer to get what I needed.

One night about two months after I entered the mill the Count failed to appear in our cell at lockup. As soon as the door closed upon us Smoky told me the reason.

"Franco-Germany is at the 'springs' f'r the night f'r makin' bad cloth," he informed us. "I tol' him t' get next t' himself,

---

[4] Lowrie provides much greater detail of the "jacket" in Chapters 8 and 19.

ch. ends p. 76

but he kep' on takin' chances, an' now he's roped up in th' sack."

"I saw them taking him up this afternoon," commented the Kid, "and he looked like the last rose of summer. He's been flirtin' with the 'jacket' ever since he came here; now he'll find out what th' old girl is like."

There was more room in the cell with one member absent, and the Count's misfortune did not seem to arouse much sympathy.

"What-a he do for da cod-a oil?" asked Spaghetti; "He no getta da med in da hole."

"Oh, he's gettin' his medicine, all right," said Smoky. "Maybe if he spent a few days down there he'd f'rget his drug store stunt."

We spent the evening talking of the Count's plight, and I was conscious of a curiosity to have him return so that I might learn what it was like.

The next night on going to the cell we found the Count sitting on the side of his bunk, nursing a bottle of medicine.

No sooner had the door closed than he stripped off his upper garments and showed us the marks, where the ropes had bound him.

"It was terrible!" he whined. "I'll never live to get out of this place alive now!"

The marks of the ropes were plainly discernible on his pink body; red stripes showed where the bonds had held him.

"Tell us about it," I asked.

"Well, they said I made bad cloth, and I promised to do better, but it was the fourth time this month, so they sent me to the office. I tried to square it with the Captain, but he wouldn't listen, 'Take him to the hole,' was all he said.

"They took me down to the dungeon and into one of the dark cells. There was an old mattress on the floor and they told me to lay down on it, and they put the 'jacket' on me. It held my arms so I couldn't move them, but that wasn't enough. They turned me over on my stomach and laced me up. R—— put his foot in the middle of my back so as to pull the ropes up tight, and when I hollered he laughed and said: 'You'll make bad cloth, will you? We'll teach you how to make it good.'

"After they had me laced up so I could hardly breathe they went out and shut the door. It was about 3 o'clock in the afternoon, but when the door was shut it was just like night. For half an hour or so I didn't suffer much, but gradually I began to feel smothered, and my heart hurt me when it beat. I got scared and began to holler, but that only made my heart hurt more, and I was afraid I might die if I didn't lie still. Pretty soon my arms and hands began to tingle—just like pins and needles sticking in them—and this got so bad that I couldn't stand it and I began yelling again. Some guy in the next cell called me a 'mutt' and told me to 'lay down.'

"'Dis is a picnic,' he said. 'You'll soon get used to it and go to sleep.'

"But the longer I stayed there the worse it got, and I rolled over on my face and bit the mattress to keep from yelling.

"It seemed like a week before the lockup bell rang. I had forgot all about that and thought it was late at night. Only two hours since I had been laced up. That meant twenty-two hours more.

"I gave up. I didn't think I could live that long.

"Just after lockup they brought another fellow in and put him in the next cell. I screamed for them to come and let me out, and they opened the door. It was the night sergeant and a trusty.

"'What's the matter?' asked the sergeant.

"'I'm dying,' I gasped. 'My heart is weak; I can't stand this.'

"At first the sergeant laughed and turned as if to go out, but just as he got to the door he stopped.

"'Loosen him up,' he said to the trusty, speaking low, so the men in the other cells couldn't hear. 'I suppose I'll lose my job some day for doing this kind of thing, but I can't help it.'

ch. ends next p.

"The trusty seemed glad to loosen the ropes, and it was like heaven to me. Just before he went out he held a can of water to my mouth and gave me a drink.

"It got awful cold in the night and I couldn't move, but just lay there and shivered in the dark. I thought the morning would never come, but at last I heard the bell. They let me out this afternoon, and R—— was surprised to find the ropes so loose.

"'It beats hell how these stiffs manage to work these ropes loose,' he said. 'I tied this foreigner up to a fare-ye-well, and here he is wearin' a mother hubbard. But wait till I get you the next time,' he snarled."

7

One night at lockup the Kid came staggering into the cell, "all in." As soon as the door closed he sank on the stool in a paroxysm of coughing. We waited pityingly until it was over and then Smoky spoke. As usual under each circumstances, he asked a foolish question.

"Wot's th' matter, kid? Ain't y'r feelin' well?"

The boy's big, sorrowful eyes took on an expression of gratitude at the sympathy vibrant in the words.

"No, I ain't feeling very good," he gasped. "I can't stand that mill much longer. It got me today—it was so hot, and I spit blood all afternoon. I saw the croaker when I came up and asked him to give me another job, but he stuck a thermometer in my mouth and then called me a faker and gave me a dose of salts."

He stopped to cough and expectorate[1] into the bucket.

"Roll me a cigarette, Smoky, will you?" he asked, trying to smile.

"Yer oughter cut cigarettes, kid," Smoky warned him, "but I understands how y'r feel—y'r wanter have it over, don't you?"

He was rolling the cigarette as he spoke, but dropped it to the floor in consternation. The Kid had broken into

---

[1] Spit.

convulsive, abandoned weeping, his hands hanging dead at his sides and the tears rolling down and dropping into his lap, unheeded, unchecked.

"You poor little God-forsaken kid," gulped Smoky, turning his back and gazing intently at the wall. In fact, we all turned abruptly so that our faces were concealed from one another.

Spaghetti began to whistle the only tune he knew—an insidious, elusive Italian air, and the Count took four kinds of medicine with absent-minded rapidity. I confess that I was obliged to use my handkerchief—an ample bandanna.

Smoky was the first to speak. He turned and placed his hands under the boy's armpits.

"Come on, kid; y'r better go t' bed, an' I'm going t' see if I can't get y'r somethin'."

We all helped put the Kid to bed, and the Count insisted on giving him his feather pillow—an evidence of his Alsatian remittance and the only feather pillow in the cell. After the Kid was in bed and covered up Smoky gave a peculiar rap on the wall.

"Hello," came the faint response from the next cell.

"Hello, Fatty, is that you?" shouted Smoky.

"Yes; what is it?"

"Th' kid's all in. Can y'r slip me somethin'? You know. I'll t'row out a string."

"Sure thing," came the cheery response. "Glad I'm fixed to do you a favor. Smoky."

Smoky immediately got busy. Reaching under his mattress he produced a little ball of jute string, to the end of which he attached a small wire hook. He then arranged the string in the form of a lasso, and, going to the wicket, flipped it outward in the direction of the next cell. He stood tensely, for a few minutes, his eye cocked at the wicket, watching and listening for the guard. Then he uttered an ejaculation of satisfaction and began to draw in the string.

Pretty soon the little hook appeared, and caught in it was another hook, which was also attached to a piece of string.

Belatedly I realized what had occurred. One of the men in the adjacent cell had thrown out a string and hook so that it had fallen across our string, and when Smoky drew the string of course the two hooks caught. A line of material communication had been established between the two cells.

"Dis is dead against th' rules," Smoky advised me, hurriedly. "If th' bull chances t' hike along it means th' hole f'r y'r Uncle Dudley." He reached over and tapped on the wall. Presently there came an answering tap and Smoky began hauling in the string, rapidly, but carefully. Suddenly a little paper package rustled through the wicket. Smoky seized it. He didn't wait to untie it from the line, but broke the string. Then he rapped on the wall again.

"I broke y'r string. Fatty," he called. "You savvy. It's a big chance we took, an' I won't f'rgit y'r f'r it. I'll give y'r y'r hook in th' mornin'."

Much to my disappointment Smoky turned his back while he unwrapped the little package. Then he dipped some water from our water bucket and leaned down over the Kid.

"Here, take dis, quick, and den drink dis water," he ordered.

The boy opened his mouth and Smoky dropped a small pellet between the parted lips, and then held the tin cup while the boy drank.

I wondered what it was and could hardly refrain from asking the question, but intuitively knew enough not to do so.

In ten minutes the boy was fast asleep. None of us spoke. The Count yawned several times and then crept into his bunk, and he was soon followed by Spaghetti.

Smoky had a month-old copy of the San Francisco Bulletin and read it from beginning to end, including the advertisements, without saying a word, his heavy, prizefighter jaws held at a belligerent angle. He had what a "criminologist," so-called, would class as a "criminal face."

I sat there staring into space, not thinking of anything

ch. ends p. 87

in particular, just in a kind of wide-awake trance, while my subconscious mind skimmed over a thousand things.

At last Smoky folded the paper, folded it carefully, so that he might slip it to someone else—for a contraband paper is passed from hand to hand until it is worn out—and then he spoke.

"They're all asleep," he said, in a whisper, with just the slightest inflection of suggestion, as though he knew I wanted to ask him something that he was willing to tell.

I got up and looked into the faces of our three cellmates as they lay.

"Yes, they're asleep," I whispered. "What was it you gave the Kid?"

And then Smoky came close and looked searchingly into my eyes, long and steadily, until they wavered.

"I believes y'r on th' square," he finally whispered. "Are y'r?"

"You bet I am," I responded earnestly.

"Well, dat wuz—d-o-p-e—th' real thing. But dat's enough," he added, quickly, raising his hand as another question framed itself in my mind. "I'll see y'r in th' yard termorrer. Dere's a whole lot yer've got to learn 'bout dis dump. Let's turn in."

Before retiring I wanted a drink, but did without. There was no way to wash the cup.

The next day was Sunday and I sought and found Smoky in the yard. He led me around to the east side, where it was less crowded, and we stopped under one of the iron stairways of the cell building.

"About that deal last night," he began. "Ordinar'ly I wouldn't let anybody in on a thing of that kind, but the Kid was so bad I had t' do somethin'. As I said before, I think y'r on the square; if I didn't think so I wouldn't be talkin' t' y'r.

"Havin' or handlin' dope is a mighty ticklish business here. It's takin' y'r life an' hangin' it on a cobweb. They've already croaked five or six guys in th' jacket, tryin' t' make 'em squeal.

I never use th' rotten stuff myself, an' I never encourages anyone else t' use it, but once in a while it comes in mighty handy, like las' night f'r instance."

Smoky was gradually warming up to his theme, his eyes were taking on a reminiscent glow, and I knew enough to remain silent.

"A few years ago this dump was full of dope. Every other man y'r met had a heat on, an' lots o' young kids what came here strong an' healthy went out with a habit. D'y'r know what that means? It means they would be back in five or six weeks, or maybe even worse, f'r lots of 'em took t' livin' on women. I ain't no saint—I've busted th' law a hundred times, tore big holes in it, an' I ain't th' kind what t'rows bouquets at m'self, but there's two t'ings I'm proud of—no, t'ree t'ings: I ain't never used dope, I ain't never been a mack,[2] an' I ain't never robbed anyone what trusted me. Some day when I get good and ready—if I can forget that Fresno judge, and a few more t'ings—I'm goin' t' straighten up. Maybe I'll do it this time, if th' cops give me a chance. But that ain't what I started t' tell y'r. Up to a year ago th' place was full o' dope; up to th' time Aguirre (the warden) came.[3] I ain't got no use f'r Aguirre, but he's done one t'ing what no man ever did before, an' he deserves a medal f'r it—he's got th' dope out o' this prison—almost. He's killed a few guys doin' it, but there was no other way. I've seen too many young fellars go to hell here, an' if that can be stopped by sendin' a few more dope fiends out feet first, why I say send 'em out, an' a good job.

"When he first came here everybody had money, an' th' place was wide open; th' lid was off. But soon after he took charge we got an awful jolt—th' bell didn't ring one Sunday mornin', th' first time in th' history of th' prison, they say.

"Instead o' ringing th' bell they came around an' unlocked th' cells one at a time an' made us step out on th' tier in our underclothes. They frisked us that way, an' then went into

---

[2] Pimp.

[3] Martin Aguirre was warden of San Quentin from 1899 to 1903.

ch. ends p. 87

th' cell an' handed out th' rest of our duds, a piece at a time, friskin' each piece before they gave it to us. Then they locked th' cell, and we dressed out on th' tier an' went down to th' yard.

"After ev'rybody was out o' th' cells we went t' breakfast.

"All that day they searched th' cells, an' maybe they didn't make a clean-up—dope, money, knives, oil stoves, saws an' ev'rything y'r can imagine.

"'Bout five o'clock we was locked up again, an' instead o' going t' work the next day we stayed in th' cells, an' they searched th' shops an' th' mill. They came pretty near gettin' all th' dope there was in th' place.

"It was a dandy scheme, an' it worked to a T. Nobody got wise to it till it was pulled off.

"I know one hop merchant—'Willie-off-th'-Pickle-Boat,' they called him—what lost $300. They was supposed t' turn all money inter th' office t' go on th' books, but lots of it never got there.

"When they let us out o' th' cells on Tuesday mornin' there was a big notice up in th' yard sayin' that any guy caught with dope or money after a certain date would lose all his credits an' be severely punished, but that anyone could turn in whatever they had up t' that time an' nothin' would be done to 'em. Of course nothin' was turned in—leastwise I never heard of any.

"Y'r oughter seen that bunch o' dope fiends. 'Bout fifty of them had t' go t' th' hospital f'r treatment, an' I even saw two or three guys eat chloride o' lime to stop their yen.[4]

"It was awful. Guys what I never suspicioned o' usin' dope went around beggin' friends f'r a ball right out in th' open.

"Take dope away from a fiend an' y'r take away ev'rything. He ain't got no principle or nothin' left—till he's cured.

"Well, o' course lots o' guys started schemin' t' get more dope right away.

"A lot o' th' guards had been makin' good money bringin'

---

[4] Craving.

th' stuff from th' city, an' in a couple o' weeks there was a fresh supply. But it was so little compared to what had been there before that they was like a lot o' tigers after it, an' it didn't take long f'r th' bulls t' get next. Finally they caught one guy dead t' rights with the goods right on him.

"That was when they first started usin' th' jacket. Up t' that time it was hangin' by th' thumbs, or th' dungeon for a month or two. Nobody thought th' jacket was bad. But after th' first guy got squeezed a few hours he yelped—tol' where he got th' stuff, an' they pinched another guy. He squealed quicker'n th' first guy, an' then they went right down the line. Before they got through they had 20 or 30 in th' hole, all a'squealin' on each other, until they got th' one what knew how th' dope came in, an' he squealed on th' guard. He——"

Smoky broke off abruptly and a hard look came into his eyes.

"There's a stool-pigeon tin-earin' right behind us," he warned me. "Prob'ly heard me say 'dope' an' thinks he can get somethin' t' peddle at th' office. Let's go somewhere else."

Smoky had not turned around, yet, sure enough, one of the notorious stool-pigeons of the prison was standing close behind us.

Silently I followed Smoky to another part of the yard.

Arrived at the other end of the yard, Smoky and I spread our coats on the asphaltum and lay down in the sun.

"Let's see; where was I?" he mused.

"You'd just finished about the bunch squealing on one another in that dope deal," I prompted.

"Oh, yes. They all squealed—trust dope fiends t' do that ev'ry time—an' th' guard got canned. A lot of 'em lost their credits, an' when they came out o' th' hole an' told about th' jacket it put th' fear o' hell inter th' hearts of th' rest of th' fiends—that is, all but a few.

"Then th' Legislature passed a law makin' it a felony t' bring dope inter th' prison, an' that scared off th' guards. It got harder t' get dope, but some guys kept at it, an' there

ch. ends p. 87

was several squealin' bees before th' thing died down. One guy stuck it out in th' jacket f'r ten days before he hollered. He died in th' hospital twelve days before his time was up on a fourteen-year sentence. Baker was his name, if I remember right.

"Th' main trouble was that in usin' th' jacket on th' hop-heads they got careless an' got t' usin' it on other guys f'r fightin' an' things like that. There's two guys here now what was in th' jacket f'r fightin' an' got paralyzed. I'll show 'em t' y'r after a while; remind me.

"So y'r can see what a chance I took f'r th' Kid last night. If a bull had come along an' got that package it would 'a' been curtains f'r all of us. We'd a hit th' jacket, sure.

"Many an innocent guy has hit th' jacket over dope. I know one feller what had dope dropped inter his pocket by another guy what had a grudge against him. This guy tipped it off, an' when they pinched him an' found th' stuff right on him they nearly killed him in th' jacket tryin' t' make him tell where he got it. Th' doctor finally told 'em they'd have t' let up if they didn't want t' have th' guy die in th' sack.

"Another case where an innocent guy got it dead wrong was like this:

"A feller what wos goin' out promised t' send some mor-phine to his cellmate. He was t' sprinkle it between th' pages of a magazine an' then paste th' pages together here an' there an' mail th' magazine. But so's not t' take any chance, they put up a job. Th' guy what was t' get th' dope got through his task early an' came up in th' first line from th' mill, an' th' fellers in th' next cell never got through their work till th' whistle at half-past four. So th' magazine was t' be addressed t' one of these guys in th' next cell—him not knowin' it, of course—an' th' feller who was t' get th' stuff, comin' up from th' mill early, was t' go inter th' cell an' yaffle th' magazine. You know how they deliver th' magazine mail in th' cells ev'ry day.

"Well, th' guy what went out sent back th' stuff all right,

just as he promised, an' he addressed it t' th' guy in th' next
cell, but they nailed th' magazine at th' office an' found th'
plant. They sent f'r th' innocent guy an' showed it to him
an' told him he'd have t' tell who sent it t' him so they could
pinch th' party an' prosecute him. Of course, he said he
didn't know anything about it, an' he hit th' jacket an' got
nearly killed. Th' only thing that saved him was that th' guy
in th' next cell what had put up th' job got word out underground t' th' party outside what had sent th' dope, an' he
wrote t' th' warden an' explained how it happened, an' then
ducked his nut. Of course, he didn't tell who th' stuff was
really intended for.

"It was a fierce case, all right, an' goes t' show how a dead
innocent guy can get up against it, but I know a lot more
cases just as bad—even worse.

"Dope'll make a man do anything. There uster be a murder
here nearly ev'ry month in them days, an' I always carried
a shive m'self. Ev'rybody carried a shive. Y'r had t' carry
one. I got stabbed one day in th' yard. A dope fiend came
up behind me an' mistook me f'r some guy what he wanted
t' croak. Th' only thing that saved me was I got a hunch
somethin' was goin' t' happen an' turned around just as he
tried t' stick me. Th' shive struck kinder glancin' like, an'
I sidestepped and batted him one under th' ear before he
knew what hit him, knockin' him cold. Then I ducked into th'
crowd. They never found out who hit him, an' some friend
of his took th' knife away before callin' a bull.

"But that's all a thing of th' past. There ain't much dope
here now, an' it's curtains t' get nailed with it. You don't need
any advice, I guess; only look out who y'r runs with, an' allus
keep y'r mouth shut an' y'r ears and eyes open. It's hard t'
get in wrong if y'r watch y'rself, an'—

"Der y'r see that shine comin' down over there by th'
stairs?" Smoky suddenly interjected; "th' one carryin' his
hand up?"

I looked in the direction indicated and saw a medium-sized

ch. ends next p.

negro with one arm bent almost at a right angle from the elbow, and with stiffened fingers, resembling claws.

"Well, that's one of th' guys I told y'r got paralyzed in th' jacket. He got inter a fight here in th' yard with a white feller, an' th' bull what pinched 'em had it in f'r 'em an' he put 'em in th' jacket himself.

"When they came out they was both paralyzed. Th' other guy is worse than him, an' won't live long. There's some talk of takin' his case before th' Legislature. He's got friends in Frisco, but th' shine ain't got no friends."

The negro was quite close now, and I looked at him closely. His face was chalky, over his black skin, as though it had been dusted with white powder, and I saw the hideous, grinning skull of death in his tired eyes.

"For God's sake. Smoky, show me the man that did it!" I said, tensely, "I want to keep out of his way."

"I knew y'r'd ask that," laughed Smoky; "they all do. He's th' man in charge of th' cells an' th' cell yard. Come with me."

We got up and Smoky led the way up the yard, dodging through the crowd. At the south end of the shed he stopped.

"D'y'r see that bull walkin' over there with his head down an' his hands in his hip pockets? Well, that's him."

One swift glance and I turned abruptly away. It was the same man whom I had seen strike down the wretch that had escaped from "crazy alley" a few weeks before.

The negro managed to survive to the end of his sentence and was discharged—with five dollars. The other man, S——, was paroled on account of impaired health. Later he appeared before the California Legislature and stated his case, and a committee was appointed to investigate the straitjacket at San Quentin. Shortly afterward S—— died. His death was directly due to the jacketing that paralyzed him. The man who laced it is still employed. He still puts men in the jacket—occasionally.

During the years that followed I became intimately acquainted with this man. He has many fine traits and is an excellent officer in many respects. I have known him to furnish an old lifer with the funds necessary for parole; I have known him to do a number of kind and humane things. I have not the least particle of personal complaint against him, nor against any other employee at San Quentin, but I am not going to dodge facts. I know this man to be unjust, cruel, and vindictive. I have seen him strike a prisoner, which is equivalent to striking a man who is down, or with his hand tied, and which is a direct violation of the law of the State of California.

I am still a prisoner, in spirit as well as in fact—in spirit because my sympathies are with prisoners; in fact because I am merely on parole. To be clearly understood I may add that my sympathies are not with prisoners as criminals, but as human beings, each one—with possibly a few exceptions—capable of being molded into a good citizen.

I honestly believe this officer is a retarding influence. All the prisoners hate him. They do not hate the warden; they do not hate the guards; they do not hate one another, but they hate him. Why? It would require a book to tell that.

I feel every word that I have written. I feel that this man is a menace not only to the welfare of society, but to the official now in charge at San Quentin, who is my friend, the same as he has proved himself to be the friend of all unfortunates. But he does not know what I know and what hundreds, yes, thousands, of others know. It seems to be a case on a parity with that of a deceived husband whom all the neighbors regard with open-eyed wonder.

8

The legislative committee that investigated the use of the straitjacket at San Quentin made an interesting report. Almost immediately afterward the State Board of Prison Directors passed a resolution regarding this form of punishment. Since that time the jacket has been used in "modified form," the modification being a limitation of time rather than of severity. The rule is that no prisoner shall be kept in the jacket for more than six consecutive hours. Also that no prisoner shall be subjected to this form of punishment save after examination by and with permission of the physician.

I have witnessed the "examination" of hundreds of men for this purpose. It consists of applying a stethoscope to the subject's thorax. This in itself is a negative acknowledgment that the jacket is a dangerous form of punishment and liable to cause death.

But before these rules were made men were "cinched" in the jacket and left there two, three, five, ten days without attention, save that of holding a crust of bread and a tin of water to the victim's mouth, or a demand for "confession."

After the passage of the resolution fixing the six-hour limit the system changed merely in externals. Confessions were secured with the same monotonous regularity. The victims were kept in the jacket for days, even weeks—six hours in, six hours out, six hours in, six hours out.

And the victims were kept in the dungeon on bread and water in between the periods of "cinching."

The hours for changing were 7 and 1. Just think of being awakened at 1 o'clock in the morning to spend your allotted six hours in the jacket!

Sometimes I regret never having had the experience myself, for it would have given me the touch of "color" so essential to description. But I had unusual opportunities for observation at first hand. For a number of years I was employed in the clothing room, where men change their clothes before going to the dungeon, and where they change when they come back.

I saw scores of cases and I talked with dozens of victims immediately after their punishment. The marks of the ropes, the red stripes around the torso and limbs, were always visible and the skin wrinkled and irritated in between.

Quite often a man was unable to walk without assistance, and those who could walk did so uncertainly and feebly, somewhat like a man who is drunk.

A straitjacket may be so applied that it will kill a man in a few minutes. I have known it to be so applied that the victim screamed for mercy within an hour, mercy which he gained by "confessing."

The inmates of A and B rooms have often been awakened in the dead of night by the horrible cries and curses of men in the dungeon below, although the intervening partition is of solid masonry.

The jacket is still in use at San Quentin and Folsom. True, it is used very seldom, at least at San Quentin, yet with its lessened use there has been a steady improvement in the prison discipline. This goes to show how utterly ineffective and barbaric it is as a means of maintaining order. So long as it may be used, just so long may its use be abused.

It should be abolished by legislative enactment; in fact, the mode of punishing prisoners should be the direct will of the people, expressed through their Legislature. So long as

ch. ends p. 100

an individual has the power to devise punishment, so long will remain the possibility of torture and cruelty.

Fortunately, San Quentin is now in charge of an able, kind-hearted, clear-headed executive. But what assurance is there that it will be always so governed?

The straitjacket was first used in the fight to eliminate "dope" from the prisons. Used for that purpose, with all the facts taken into consideration, it was almost justifiable, as were other punishments, rules, and restrictions. But now that "dope" has been definitely and positively stamped out, why should these restrictions remain, and why should these punishments still prevail? In order to keep "dope" out? No. Conditions are not the same.

A few years ago it was an easy matter to get "dope" in almost every town or city of California. Its use was quite prevalent. Every third or fourth prisoner entering San Quentin at that time was a "hop-head." But during the past two or three years I do not know of one drug fiend being received at San Quentin. True, there have been sporadic attempts to introduce "dope" into the prison, but the majority, the great majority, of the prisoners are against it, and each attempt has been promptly reported.

The reason for this attitude on the part of prisoners is easily explained. They are human and they have a human understanding of what a terrible thing "dope" is. They also realize that their privileges and treatment depend in a large measure upon themselves. This spirit has developed to a marked degree under the present warden. He has discouraged prisoners from carrying tales for selfish reasons, but he has encouraged them to help themselves by making known such things as will tend to keep them down.

Yet certain rules and regulations devised solely for the purpose of reducing the possibility of smuggling "dope" into the prison are still in force and effect.

A prisoner may not receive any material remembrance from those who love him—not even at Christmas time.

He may not receive books, save by order direct from the prison to the publisher.

I know one prisoner—a lifer—who has a valuable set of textbooks at home, but he cannot have them. It is against the rules. But he may order the same books from a publisher. He is without money; therefore without the books.

When the present warden took charge four years ago he started to change these rules, but was urged not to do so. They are still in effect.

What does this mean; it means that every prisoner who enters San Quentin is reduced to the level of the dope fiends who were imprisoned there ten or fifteen years ago.

It means that every prisoner is reduced to the lowest moral status that has ever prevailed.

It means that home ties and loving sentiments, the fundamentals of our social cohesion, are almost completely taken out of his life.

Experience has demonstrated that prisoners are susceptible to kindness—that they respond to a recognition of the fact that they are human and have human feelings.

This being so, why should it not be extended to the greatest possible degree consistent with their safe detention and proper government?

There are some who believe that a prison should be a place of punishment—or revenge. But has not that been tried? Has it not proved to be ineffectual and uneconomical? Why not at least try the other?

I do not mean that prisons should be "pleasure resorts," but I do mean that they should be constructive—morally and physically—rather than destructive and demoralizing.

Remember, there is a permanent prison population of more than 3,000 in the State of California.

Three thousand boys now in short trousers are destined to spend years of their lives behind prison walls.

One of these boys may be yours.

A terrible thought, but they have to be somebody's boys.

ch. ends p. 100

May no boy, born or unborn, ever experience imprisonment as it is today. It is neither just nor logical that he should.
It is appalling to think that he may.

*

On Sundays and holidays the prisoners at San Quentin are permitted to congregate in the "yard," which is the
narrow space surrounding the cell buildings and hemmed
in by the prison walls. This space is much too small for the
number of men, and when the total population is assembled
there it looks very much like a cattle pen. All day long the
prisoners mill in and out and wander listlessly from one place
to another. There is not sufficient room to walk in a straight
line. Some pass the time playing chess or "Chinee domi-
noes"; others read, a few study. There are no benches. True,
there are boards extending between the posts of the shed,
but these are inadequate; they will not accommodate more
than a hundred men. One must either walk all day, jostled
on every side by others, or else sit down on the asphaltum.

A few find seats on the iron stairways leading up to the
cell tiers, but are not permitted to go beyond the fourth or
fifth step.

Quite a number spread their coats, or pieces of paper, on
the asphaltum and go to sleep in the sun—in summer.

But this must not be taken as a criticism of the prison
management. There are many prisons where the men never
get out of doors, where they are not permitted to congregate
under any circumstances.

It is interesting to note that the percentage of recidivism[1]
is just as great in these prisons as it is in San Quentin and
Folsom. Solitary confinement does not tend to make men
better. I believe the congregate system does. Under the congregate system the individual prisoner has more choice, and

---

[1] Repeated or habitual relapse into crime.

the ability to choose rightly is the only true indication of character. When this right of choice is taken away there is nothing left; the prisoner becomes a mere animal.

The fact that the prisoners at San Quentin are permitted to spend Sunday, until 3 o'clock, in the open air is a fine thing. It is a humane privilege and one which it would seem querulous[2] for me to criticize adversely.

But I am trying to present what I felt and what thousands of others feel.

At first the new prisoner, freed from the odious confinement of the county jail, finds the yard at San Quentin very refreshing. In a few weeks, however, it begins to pall. Then it becomes irksome. Finally it is maddening.

After a year of imprisonment he dreads Sunday and the yard and retires to the seclusion of his cell whenever he can get permission to do so.

To the casual visitor passing through San Quentin the yard seems to be a splendid thing, but to the average man confined there it is hell. There is no privacy, either from his fellows or from the guards.

As the day advances the asphaltum becomes filthy with tobacco and cough expectorations. On warm days a fetid mist arises, sickening to the senses, menacing to the lungs.

I never spent a Sunday in the yard at San Quentin without getting a severe headache. Three o'clock was always welcome. I preferred the close, ill-ventilated cell. It was merely a choice between two evils.

In winter, during the rainy season, it is even worse. When it rains on Sunday the men go to their cells immediately after breakfast, but when it rains on Saturday afternoon it means a wetting.

The mill closes at 2:30 on Saturday afternoon to enable the prisoners to draw books from the prison library and whatever clothing may be due them.

Supper is at 4:30. If it be raining the great majority are

[2] Complaining.

ch. ends p. 100

obliged to remain in the yard and wait patiently for lockup. I recall one Saturday afternoon soon after I entered the prison. We came up from the mill in single file, compelled to walk slowly. The rain was descending in torrents.

Arrived at the yard, we crowded under the sheds, crowded together so closely that there was not room to turn around. It was a windy rain and great sheets of water whipped in under the shed.

I had been one of the last to arrive from the mill and was on the outskirts of the crowd. There was no escape from the rain. It soaked me to the waist.

After supper, on getting to my cell, I found the Kid and Spaghetti had suffered the same experience. The cell was dark, cold and damp. The only warmth we could obtain was from the coal oil lamp. We had no way to dry our clothing, and no change.

Prisoners are limited to one suit of clothes. It is an offense, punishable by "loss of privileges," to have extra clothing, and now that the laundered underwear is no longer delivered at the cells there is no possibility of putting on dry undergarments. There remained but one thing for us to do. We went to bed.

I know men in San Quentin who have never been near a fire since their imprisonment began. This is especially hard in winter. The only time one is comfortable is while at work in the mill. Some men are more thin-blooded than others and suffer from the cold even in bed.

The bed clothing consists of two and one-half pairs of blankets; no sheets, no pillow. Someone discovered that paper makes a warm protection. Many men sew paper between their blankets during the winter months. Of course, this prevents their shaking out the blankets, and the covering stays on the bed for several months without airing. That is when the bedbugs revel.

Friday is the day on which one is permitted to hang blankets on the railings along the tiers. But in winter very few blankets are hung out. It is either raining or else the paper quilting is considered of more consequence than an airing.

On rainy days in winter the "hill gang" are obliged to stay in their cells.

The allotment of oil is one pint to each cell, with an extra portion during the longer winter nights. This supply of oil is inadequate. One is obliged to nurse the oil in order to make it last the prescribed time.

We used to do without a light until 6 o'clock on weekdays and until 7 or 8 o'clock on Sundays. If no one were reading we always kept the lamp turned low so that it would not consume so much oil.

Quite a number of the men trade for extra oil. By parting with a couple sacks of tobacco we used to get an extra pint of oil occasionally. This means that someone had to steal it. And to be caught trading is followed by punishment. It is rather hard to be punished for trying to keep normally comfortable.

After we had gone to bed that Saturday evening Smoky proceeded to dry our clothes. He rigged up a line so that it passed directly over the lamp, and then hung our garments there, a piece at a time, first wringing out all the water he could.

At 9 o'clock he was still busy and did not hear taps. A few minutes later the night sergeant poked his bullseye up to our wicket.

"What you doin' with that light burnin'?" he asked.

"Has the bugle blown?" asked Smoky.

"Oh, you know it's blown well enough. Put out that light. This is the third time I've called you fellers down for burnin' your light after taps, and it's the last time."

Smoky extinguished the lamp and undressed in the dark.

"That means we lose our lamp f'r a month," he growled.

Sure enough, on returning to the cell next afternoon (Sunday) at 3 o'clock the lamp was gone. That was the rule.

"D'y'r feel like takin' a chance, fellers?" Smoky inquired,

ch. ends p. 100

after he had finished cursing. "If y'r do I'll rustle another lamp an' fool these people."

We all agreed that we were willing to take the chance.

"It means th' hole if that night man ketches us with it," Smoky warned.

"To hell with the hole," I exploded; "let's have the lamp if you can get one."

The next night Smoky brought in a coal oil lamp under his coat, chimney and all. It cost him ten sacks of tobacco to get it, and we each assumed part of the expense. During the month that followed we kept a cloth hanging over the wicket whenever we had the lamp burning.

*

About six months after I entered prison I witnessed a murder. I am averse to the recounting of an event of that kind because so many persons imagine convicts are vicious and murderous by nature.

I did not find them so, although during the first few years of my prison experience I saw a number of assaults, and two or three murders occurred, but these were due chiefly to "dope."

True, there have been murders and assaults in recent years, but not to a greater extent than occurs in any locality—certainly not to a greater extent than is the case where 2,000 men are together, without the sweet presence and leavening influence of women—as in the army and navy.

Detractors may call this sentiment, but it is an interesting and important aspect of imprisonment and one which I hope to amplify before I finish. Men become abnormal under such conditions and tend to manifest their worst proclivities. I think the poet must have had the absence of women in mind when he wrote:

"The vilest deeds, like poison weeds,
    Bloom well in prison air;
It is only what is good in Man
    That wastes and withers there."[3]

But the murder of "Jerry"—I never learned his full name—
presented so many of the details of prison life that it made
a lasting impression upon me, aside from horror.

Jerry worked in the "cophouse" in the jute mill. He was
tally man there. The "cops" are the weft[4] of the burlap made
by the weavers, and the men who make the "cops" have
a regular daily task, so many boxes of "cops" for each man.
As a "copwinder" finishes a box of "cops" he takes them to
the "cophouse" and gets credit for the box.

Miller, the man who killed Jerry, worked on the "copwind-
ers," and in some way had aroused the deadly enmity of the
"con boss" of his section. This "con boss" was a mulatto,[5]
Thompson by name.

I do not know what the trouble was between them, but
the mulatto took advantage of his "authority" to "rub it into"
Miller. This mulatto was very generally disliked by the men.

Jerry, however, had always been considered a "square guy,"
and it was a mystery that he should have permitted himself to
be drawn into the scheme which the mulatto concocted—no
less than a plan to rob Miller of his task. The first day that
Jerry failed to tally on the task correctly, Miller thought it
was a mistake and returned to his frame and did the extra

---

[3] Absence of women, indeed! The first four lines of the 94th stanza of *The Ballad
of Reading Gaol*, a poem by Oscar Wilde, written in exile after his release on May 19,
1897, from Reading Gaol (a former prison located in Reading, Berkshire, England;
in operation from 1844 to 2014). Wilde had been incarcerated in Reading after
being convicted of "gross indecency" with other men in 1895 and sentenced to
two years of hard labor.

[4] The filling, or horizontal threads, in a woven fabric.

[5] A person of mixed white and black ancestry, especially one having one white
and one black parent.

ch. ends p. 100

work without further protest. But when a shortage occurred a second and third time he became suspicious.

By watching closely and by having a friend keep tally of his task with him as he delivered the boxes of "cops" at the window during the day he satisfied himself that he was being "jobbed." He also observed the mulatto and Jerry in consultation on several occasions, and he was forced to the conclusion that they were conspiring against him.

In the presence of witnesses Miller accused the mulatto and Jerry of "pinching" his task, and told them it would have to stop, and stop at once.

"If it don't stop I'll kill you both," he said. "This is no bluff. I'll put you both in the morgue as sure as I'm a foot high."

Despite this warning the "pinching" of Miller's task continued.

Then came the tragedy.

I was working at my loom one morning when I noticed a commotion at the "cophouse" window. Two or three weavers who had gone there for "cops" came running away with white faces.

An instant later the half-door opened and Jerry staggered out.

Never so long as I live shall I forget the look of unutterable despair on his face. His eyes were starting from their sockets and his mouth was opening and closing spasmodically.

He may have been screaming, but the roar of the machinery prevented my hearing. His hands were held against his abdomen, and I looked there. I saw a ghastly mass of red——. He swayed a moment and then started to run.

Like a mortally wounded animal, he half staggered, half flung his gaping body forward to the loom section, twisting and turning between the machinery blindly, until a whirling belt caught him as he staggered and flung him backward and down—a crumpled corpse. He had traveled nearly half the length of the mill before he fell.

Too horrified to move or think, I remained rigid, as did

all the weavers about me, and then my eyes turned to the "cophouse."

Miller had emerged and was standing in the open space between the "cophouse" and the looms, a long, bloody knife in his hand, his lips curled back from his teeth, a murderous glare in his eyes.

No one dared approach him closely. Gradually a ring formed about him—a ring of guards and prisoners—but he did not move; he just stood there glaring.

I have always felt that he was insane at that moment.

And then occurred one of the nerviest acts I have ever witnessed. A tall, young guard—I wish I could remember his name—suddenly stepped into the ring and approached Miller. As he drew near the infuriated man he threw down his cane and extended his hand for the knife, still approaching.

There was a moment of frightful intensity, as Miller turned his bloodshot eyes upon the guard, but the officer never wavered. He walked right up, reached down and leisurely loosened Miller's unresisting fingers from the knife handle. As soon as he had possession of the weapon he took Miller by the arm. Then the other guards rushed in.

After it was all over there was a deal of excitement. At noon I learned the full details. Miller had first struck down the mulatto with an iron weight, fracturing his skull, and had then sprung through the "cophouse" window and slashed Jerry with the knife.

The mulatto finally recovered, but was never again permitted to mingle with the other prisoners. The feeling in the prison was very strong against him, for everyone believed he was responsible for the tragedy.

He was assigned to work in the vegetable garden outside the walls, and was never permitted to enter the yard while the men were there, being locked in his cell after the others were in.

A number of men cognizant of all these facts petitioned

ch. ends next p.

the warden for the privilege of taking up a subscription for Miller's defense, which was granted.

At the trial, however, it was brought out that Miller was serving sentence for manslaughter when he killed Jerry; also that he had threatened to kill the deceased, and the jury found him guilty of murder in the first degree, without recommendation.

He was sentenced to death and was hanged at Folsom a few months later.

9

During the past twelve years, there has not been one permanent escape from San Quentin. Many attempts have been made, and a number of men have got off the reservation and been gone a few hours, days or weeks, but they have all been apprehended and brought back. When I arrived at San Quentin, and for some time afterward, it was the custom to put a red shirt on a man who tried to escape, and there were several such men in the yard during the first few months of my imprisonment. I became especially interested in two lifers who had attempted to escape several months before. Both were thin, nervous individuals, nearing middle age, and I always felt sorry that their bid for freedom had not been successful. I learned to know them very well, and gathered all the facts. For obvious reasons I shall not use their names, but will designate them as H—— and J——.

At the time of the attempted escape H—— and J—— were employed as nurses in the "old hospital," a building erected in 1859, the second floor of which is used as a ward for consumptives and other incurables. This building is about thirty feet from the north wall of the prison.

Working cautiously night after night H—— and J—— cut their way through the ceiling and made an egress to the roof. At that time there were no electric towers on the prison, and this roof was obscure.

The night watch at San Quentin is distributed about the prison yard, inside the walls, occupying little guard posts provided for their protection from the elements in inclement weather. There are eight of these posts, and each guard is armed with a revolver and double-barreled shotgun.

It is only after lockup that firearms are permitted inside the walls, and the bell never rings in the morning until all the firearms are back in the armory and accounted for. The day watch, also armed, is posted on the walls, and in the six Gatling-gun towers surrounding and commanding the prison on every side.

The reason why the day guards on duty inside the walls are not permitted to carry arms is that they might be over-powered and deprived of them, which would make possible the shooting of the wall guards and the men in the Gatling-gun towers and a general delivery of the prison. For subduing refractory prisoners and for self-protection the day guards carry canes loaded at one end with lead. A single blow from one of these canes usually renders a man insensible.

Beginning at 9 o'clock, at which hour taps is sounded and all cell lights, save condemned row, are extinguished, the night guards call the hours, "Nine o'clock and all's well," "Ten o'clock and all's well," and so on until five in the morning. Starting at No. 1 post, near the main entrance, the call is close and blatant, and then it is caught up by each successive guard and repeated until it reaches the man in No. 8 post, down near the jute mill.

It is a never-to-be-forgotten experience to hear these calls. From No. 1 the cry goes from one man to another, growing fainter with each repetition, until the cry of No. 8 is heard far, far away, like a voice from another world.

The hourly call assures the night sergeant that all his guards are awake and on the watch.

Also, immediately after lockup the rope attached to the prison bell over the main entrance is dropped so that the end dangles a few feet from No. 1 post. In the event of fire, or

a "break," the alarm is sounded by ringing this bell, bringing the day guards to the scene. Nearly all the guards live
on the prison reservation, which they are not permitted to
leave, even when off duty, without first getting permission
and "signing off."

Night post No. 5 is between the "old hospital" and the
north wall, and in order to reach the wall H—— and J——
were obliged to pass directly over it, and within a few feet
of the guard on duty there. On the night of the escape they
awaited the 2 o'clock call and then began operations.

First, they tossed an improvised rope—made from jute
fiber—over the wall, thirty feet distant.

There was an iron hook, padded with scraps of blanket,
attached to this rope, and it went over the wall with the first
throw, the pads preventing the hook from making any noise
when it struck against the side of the wall outside.

By drawing the rope back slowly the hook was brought up,
and caught on the handrailing that runs along the top of the
wall as a safeguard for the men who patrol it during the day.

As soon as the hook caught on this railing the men on the
roof drew the rope taut and fastened their end about one of
the chimneys, establishing a line between the roof and the
top of the wall.

Dangling forty feet above the ground J—— swung himself along the rope, hand over hand. He reached the wall
without being seen and at once threw himself flat on his
stomach to await his partner. H—— immediately followed.
Looking down as he swung along he saw the dim outline of
the guard directly beneath him, the glint of his gun barrel
plainly discernible in the rays thrown by a gas lamp some
distance away. It seemed impossible that the guard should
not be attracted by the swaying figure so close above him,
but he was humming a popular tune as he walked back and
forth, and neither saw nor heard anything.

As H—— drew close to the wall J—— whispered a tense
warning.

ch. ends p. 109

The outside watch was approaching along the wall. Each hour during the night a guard makes the rounds of the prison walls on watch for any plan of external help toward escape of those within, and also to prevent discharged prisoners from returning and tossing contraband articles or messages into the prison enclosures. Such things have been done in the past.

H—— was obliged to remain suspended until the outside guard had passed, and then he and J—— fastened another rope to the handrailing and slid to the ground, free!

But their freedom was destined to be short. Almost as they touched the ground a small dog came trotting out of the gloom and spied them. In spite of their whispered coaxing it refused to help, and barked shrilly.

Realizing that its tone would convey warning, H—— and J—— did not wait to pull down the rope by which they had descended, but ran for the obscurity of the field across the road.

The guard who had passed the spot a moment before, attracted by the barking of his dog—which, unfortunately for H—— and J——, had lingered behind its master—turned and came back. He discovered the dangling rope and fired his revolver to give the alarm. Then, guided by the dog, he took up the trail of the fugitives. In a few minutes he sighted them and commanded them to halt. They paid no heed to the command, but kept on, running toward the hills. The guard raised his shotgun and fired, hitting H—— in the legs and bringing him down, but J—— was not hit, and disappeared in the night.

By this time the alarm bell was ringing and guards were running from all directions. Several posses were immediately formed and set out to overtake J——.

After running up the hillside until he was exhausted J—— stopped to rest, secreting himself in some bushes. A few minutes later one of the posses passed close to the spot. They did not discover him, and were going on when a cow lying close by, and which J—— had not seen, took fright at the striking of a match with which one of the guards stopped to light his pipe, and jumped up. This attracted the attention of the posse and they came back.

J—— saw that he was about to be discovered and tried to crawl off, but they saw him and caught him before he could get to his feet and run.

"If it hadn't been for four-legged animals we'd a made it," J—— complained to me one day in the yard a year later. "It just seemed as if fate was against us. It was a clean getaway for both of us if it hadn't been for that dog, and a good chance for me, even with the dog, if it hadn't been for the cow. I've always liked dogs—liked them all my life—but now I don't know. That dog may mean that I'll die here. I'm certainly up against it pretty hard, doin' life, and a charge of escape against my record."

His face, seared with deep lines of care, assumed an expression of despair, and he stared stolidly at the wall before us. "And poor H——'ll never be the same man again," he continued. "They dug that buckshot out of his legs without giving him anything, and joked about it when they were doing it—just strapped him on the table like a piece of meat and cut 'em out. But there's one satisfaction. H—— wouldn't holler. The doctor tried to make him beg, tried to make him moan, but he never made a sound. Just gritted his teeth together and never winced. Of course, that kind of a deal made him awful sore. He'll never get over it. It was certainly rubbing it in, for God knows a man's got the right to escape from this kind of a life if he can.

"Of course, a man knows the penalty, but after shooting H—— down it wasn't square, it wasn't human to dig that shot out of him like that."

Several years later, by good conduct and excellent service to the State both J—— and H—— earned and were granted parole and both have "made good." Determination and grit are characteristics that may count in the fight to "make good," just as much as in any other way.

ch. ends p. 109

*

We were assembled in the yard, just before lockup, one Sunday, waiting for the bell to ring, which would permit our going to the cells, when one of the prisoners stepped over the "dead-line" and ran through the gate into the flower garden.

The guard stationed at the gate tried to stop him, as did his "con" assistant, but the running man brushed them aside and kept on. This attracted everyone's attention, making what ensued all the more spectacular and tragic.

Running to the broad stairway leading down to the lower yard, the prisoner disappeared, followed by the guard and his assistant. We all began speculating on what the runaway had in mind, what he intended doing.

"He's gone bugs," asserted one man near me.

"No, he's goin' down to 'get' some waiter what's given him a dirty deal in the dinin'-room," said another.

Suddenly there was a cry, "There he goes!" and we all turned. The fugitive was running up the steps of the old sash and blind building, two steps at a time, with three guards, two of whom joined in the chase from the dining-room, in close pursuit.

The stairway of the old sash and blind factory is on the outside of the building and in plain view from the yard. To the first landing, the second, the third and then to the top rushed the escapee without pausing.

I noted a package held under his arm—a package of lunch. Prisoners are permitted to carry a lunch from the dining-room on Sundays and holidays because there is no supper served on those days, breakfast being at 7 a.m. and dinner at 2 p.m.

Arrived at the top landing, the fugitive paused and looked over. Then he glanced swiftly behind him. The guards were close, already reaching to grab him. He laughed shrilly and then deliberately toppled his body over the low railing. He seemed to hang suspended in space for a moment, and then shot downward with frightful velocity.

A groan arose from a thousand throats. The falling body turned completely over in mid-air, and the package of lunch slipped away.

The groan died away almost instantly, and there was a hushed moment when we all seemed to cease breathing. The falling body struck the brick pavement with a kind of whack—a combined thud and crack that was awful.

Every man turned his eyes away, and just at that moment the lockup bell began to ring.

It makes no difference what occurs, the lockup bell always rings at the precise time.

With awed faces, and in silence, we made our way to our respective cells. Smoky arrived after I did, and immediately asked if I had witnessed the suicide.

"Yes. Who is he?" I asked.

"I don't know his name," replied Smoky, "but I know him by sight. He works on a breakin' carder[1] an' he's doin' seven years. I always noticed he was kind o' quiet like, an' queer, but I never thought he'd go th' Dutch route.[2] Still, y'r can never tell. I've seen some pretty good men go that way—do it all of a sudden. Chances are this guy didn't know he was goin' until five minutes ago. I noticed he had a lump (lunch) with him."

That night while he was preparing our "hash" over the lamp, with Spaghetti stationed at the wicket as lookout, Smoky again referred to the suicide.

I had asked a passing "runner" if the man were dead, and learned that he had died in the hospital an hour after they picked him up.

---

[1] A toothed implement or machine used to comb, clean, and disentangle raw fibers before spinning.

[2] The Dutch act, or to do the Dutch means to commit suicide. The expression originated in America in the 19th century when many Dutch immigrants had a reputation for attempting suicide.

ch. ends next p.

"The best suicide I've ever seen here," said Smoky, "was about ten years ago. They brought a high-toned feller in t' do a ten spot. He was a doctor, I think, an' killed some gal operatin' on her. As soon as he stepped inside th' big gate he jus' took one look around an' then put somethin' into his mouth.

"It must 'a' been morphine, er somethin' like that, f'r it didn't faze him at first, but while he was in th' bathtub takin' his bath th' chink stepped out a minute t' get somethin' an' when he came back th' new guy was clean out. He'd slipped down in th' tub an' his head was under water. Th' chink gave th' alarm an' they tried hard t' save him, but he croaked that night. It didn't take him long t' do his ten years."

While telling this story Smoky had assembled our "lumps" and had produced some grease and an onion from the cavernous depths of his "commissary" pocket. With a pair of loom scissors he cut up the meat and potatoes and the onion.

The receptacle into which he dropped the pieces was an extra wash basin which we kept concealed under one of the bunks for cooking purposes only.

When all was ready he seasoned the mess with pepper and salt, added a little water and grease, and then set the pan on top of the lamp chimney, first inserting a specially made bracket to permit the passage of air between the bottom of the pan and the top of the chimney.

In a few minutes an appetizing odor filled the stuffy cell, and I could tell by the actions of my other cellmates, as well as by my own yearning, that they were hungry and hardly able to wait for results.

It is strictly against the rules to cook in the cells, but we used to make "hash" or a "mulligan" each Sunday night. The guards in charge of the cell buildings spend a good portion of their time during week days searching the cells, hunting for contraband articles.

Anything that looks like a cooking utensil is invariably confiscated, and at one time it became so hard to keep a pan in the cell for that purpose that many of the men resorted to using their wash basin, waiting until they got to the mill before washing in the morning.

But after each "home-cooked" meal it was necessary to scour the basin in order to remove the evidence of its having been used for cooking. Finally this scheme was disclosed, and to stop it an order was issued that all wash basins be painted. After that there was very little cooking done in the cells.

But a few years ago it was quite common. By saving our meat and potatoes at Sunday dinner, and by trading for an onion and for grease, we were always able to have sufficient ingredients to make a very creditable concoction on Sunday night, and I always enjoyed the "home cooking," as Smoky called it, better than anything else I got to eat.

Had we been caught at it we should not only have lost our lamp, but would also have probably "hit the hole," for that was the penalty. But sometimes the night sergeant would be generous and would make no effort to catch men cooking in the cells; and then again, when it became too prevalent it was almost impossible to avoid being caught by him.

Of course, in passing along the tiers where cooking was in progress his sense of smell guided him directly to the cell where it was going on.

I certainly used to enjoy watching Smoky cook. He took an extraordinary pride in getting the hash done "just so," and I believe he sometimes took more time than was really necessary, just to tease us. I know we were always like a pack of ravenous wolves when it was ready, and it was fine to see the way the poor Kid enjoyed it.

And Smoky would pretend to eat a whole lot, merely that he might save and have enough to give the Kid a second helping.

Smoky was what the world knows as a "criminal," but the Kid didn't think so. Neither did I. Neither did anyone else who knew him as we did.

10

Although I had religious training as a boy—too much of it, perhaps—religion, lip-religion, the external Christianity does not appeal to me now. I attribute this largely to my experience with religion in prison.

In order to avoid giving undue offense to the readers of this narrative who believe that salvation is only secured by embracing the faith, attending church, and thanking the Omnipotent for all that befalls us, whether it be good or evil, I want to say that I do believe in the spirit of religion—the spirit of Christianity, of Buddhism, of Confucianism.

I believe that a man's religion is what he does, not what he says or professes. I do not believe that lip-religion has a proper place in prison. The money paid for a weekly exposition of the Bible could be used to much better advantage.

True, such exposition does benefit some prisoners, apparently, affording them an avenue of expression in a life of abnormal suppression, but I found that nearly all those who embraced religion while in prison were unreliable and inclined to be treacherous and self-righteous.

That is a scathing denouncement, but I make it calmly and deliberately.

One of the dormitories at San Quentin, accommodating about forty men, is reserved for those who have the "religious bug," as the other prisoners call it. They hold a song and prayer service every night and seem to be honest and sincere.

It is, however, a delusion, a sort of ephemeral ecstasy, a subtle expression of self-pity, and it is a noteworthy fact that a large percentage of them fail to "make good" when released on parole or at the expiration of sentence. And, of course, many of them are hypocrites who deliberately calculate that the "religious route" is the shortest way out.

It is difficult to separate the wheat from the chaff, and it is certainly discouraging to those who are deceived by such men and have so many cases of "backsliding" and "ingratitude."

But before entering into the recital of my personal experiences and observations in connection with the prison chapel and chaplain, I want to present a few facts that should be of interest and value to so-called penologists[1] and criminologists.

Nearly every man committed to prison for rape, or for crime involving lack of sexual balance, comes through the front gate with a Bible under his arm and is prone to break down and weep on being received at the inner office.

During the years I spent at San Quentin I always held that no prisoner had a license to execrate[2] another on account of his offense against the law, and I certainly do not want my present statement of facts to be taken as an indication that I have fallen into that error.

As Smoky used to say whenever some other prisoner "cut him" because of his slang and uncouth mannerisms, "his stripes ain't a bit wider than mine."

But the connection between the crimes I have indicated and religion is so marked, and is so well known to the old-time prison officials, that I should not feel that I had presented a true picture if I omitted it.

I got my initial insight into these things on the occasion of

---

[1] One who studies the punishment of crime and of prison management.

[2] Curse; detest; abhor.

ch. ends p. 123

my first attendance at religious service, which occurred one Sunday during the winter following my arrival.

The day was cold, raw, and foggy, and it was impossible to keep warm in the yard. The prisoners were huddled together like cattle in a storm, and when the bell rang for services at 9 o'clock there was a regular stampede to get into line.

The "chapel" accommodates about 600 men, when crowded, and possibly 500 comfortably. The prison population is close to 2,000, hence the stampede on cold Sundays.

On the Sunday in question Smoky and I were chattering (not chatting) with a circle of acquaintances when the bell rang.

"Say, fellers," exclaimed Smoky, "they say Hell is a hot place; whadger say if we take in a prelim'nary round an' get a little heat in advance—a kind o' credit from his Nobs down below f'r what's comin' to us?"

His way of putting the proposition appealed to us, and we lined up.

At that time the resident chaplain was the "Rev." August Drahms. I'm sure I don't know how I can portray this man honestly and fairly without giving offense to those who believe a minister of the Gospel should be exempt from criticism. All I can say is that I am not attacking Christianity, that I believe in the spirit of Christianity, and that I am consciously striving to imbue this narrative with conservatism.

It is only necessary to call for the testimony of others who knew him, either freemen or prisoners, to substantiate what I am going to tell. If the telling discredits me with those who are satisfied to have their thinking done for them by others, I can't help that.

I have met many spiritual Christians during my life—I am meeting them every day—and I know there are a great many men and women in the world who have the capacity to put themselves in the other person's place, to understand and feel what the other person understands and feels, but there is no sense in deluding ourselves with the idea that every professional Christian has the Christian spirit.

The "Reverend" August Drahms certainly did not have it. He stands out like an ugly toad on a marble pavement. I cannot forgive him, and I honestly believe that his influence did more to turn men away from religion than any other element that has ever obtained within the four walls of San Quentin.

One needs but to read his book, *The Criminal*,[3] to find a self-indictment more scathing than any facts I can bring to bear.

In that book he devotes chapters to the "criminal ear, the criminal nose, the criminal head." In one place he asserts that one of the surest indications of "criminosity" is the love of pets. The fact that prisoners are prone to lavish their attention upon mice, birds, or cats (dogs are not permitted), thus giving expression to the yearning that lies latent in every human breast and bids us find and love someone or something more than we love ourselves, he calls criminal.

He was the chaplain at San Quentin for nearly twenty years. Each warden tried to oust him, but couldn't do so because he had been a chaplain in the army during the Civil War and there is a law on the California statute books inhibiting the discharge of such a person from the employ of the State without a hearing on written charges.

The man held services every Sunday and seldom left the reservation. It remained for the present Board of Prison Directors to solve the problem, which they did by abolishing the position of "Resident Chaplain"—one of the best things they have done.

Mr. Drahms used to lecture in the smaller towns and cities about the bay, invariably holding that prisoners were criminals in all that the word implies and advocating that they be reduced to a still lower level.

"Work them!" he said at one of these lectures. "Work them

---

[3] *The Criminal: His Personnel and Environment: A Scientific Study* (1900).

hard and work them long, and then give them more work. Make them feel that they are despicable and that they have no place in the established order of things and when they come out of prison rest assured that they will not go back, for if there is anything a prisoner hates it is work."

These are not his exact words, but they convey just what he meant. He had then been a prison chaplain for fifteen years, and he was supposed to be a Christian. Naturally, a great many people believed he knew what he was saying and that his ideas were based on facts.

Such was the man that Smoky and the rest of us went to hear preach that cold winter morning in the year of our Lord 1902—nineteen centuries after the crucifixion of Jesus Christ "to save sinners."

Arrived at the chapel, we found seats near the door. The benches were straight-backed and hard. I never had a more uncomfortable seat in my life. The person who planned them knew very little about human anatomy.

As soon as we were seated I looked toward the rostrum. [4] I saw a weazened, yellow skinned man of about 60 years, with hard features and wisps of thin, straight hair hanging down, giving him the appearance of wearing a wig.

"That's him," whispered Smoky, nudging me in the ribs. "That's th' celebrated August Drahms, only they ought 'a' named him December 'stead of August. If there was ever a human icicle he's it. Why, he's so cold he'd—"

Smoky didn't finish the thought, for the guard stationed in the aisle close by had heard his voice and was endeavoring to locate the man who was talking. It is against the rules to talk in the chapel.

The men were still filing into the place and crowding down the aisles. When the doors were finally closed a large number were shut out. Like a huge serpent the line of striped figures reversed its motion and crawled back to its hole—the cold, cheerless yard. Those of us who had been fortunate

---

[4] A raised staged, platform, pulpit, or the like for addressing an audience.

AUGUST DRAHMS.

enough to get in were comparatively warm, though there is no artificial heat—save a small stove in the corner reserved as the chaplain's office—in the chapel. But in a few minutes the packed human bodies had emanated enough warmth to make it cozy and we settled ourselves for the service.

A middle-aged man with tragic features, serving life, arose beside the wheezy organ (an instrument bought by the prisoners themselves—the State makes no provision for such things, not even for library books. The library is supported by the prisoners) and sang "Lead, Kindly Light"[5] quite effectively. His voice was cracked and broken, but it was very apparent that he felt the words as he sang them.

I felt moved. I was carried back to my childhood. I was standing beside my fond mother—whom I shall always remember as the most beautiful young woman I have ever seen—and we were singing that same beautifully expressive hymn in a magnificent church. Little had she or I imagined that I would ever hear it standing in a prison chapel, surrounded by striped figures, in stripes myself, and with no women's voices in the chorus.

Women are not permitted inside the prison walls under any circumstances. That is the State law, I believe.

When the singer finished the verse he extended his arms invitingly and everyone sang together. I joined in mechanically—I found myself singing before I knew it. It was an awakening of my emotional nature that I had thought dead because it had been suppressed so long. Right there and then I believe a revolution took place in my soul. I felt a great pity for the human derelicts about me. I pitied myself.

It was not until the hymn was ended and we had sat down that I was struck with a remarkable fact—Smoky had joined in the singing, too. He had sung in a deep, baritone voice, resonant above all the others about us. I had not thought

---

[5] A hymn with words written in 1833 by Saint John Henry Newman (1801–1890) as a poem titled "The Pillar of the Cloud."

it incongruous at the moment, but when we sat down I wondered.

"Where did you learn that hymn, Smoky?" I whispered.

"In th' orphanage," he replied, briefly. "They used t' make us sing our li'l' heads off."

There was no opportunity to talk with him right then—it was against the rules—though I felt it was what is known as a "psychological moment." I determined to stay with Smoky after we got outside and try to learn something of his early life. The more I saw of him the more I felt drawn and the more I realized that he was a flower which had been choked by weeds. I knew his life should have been different. I also knew that it was going to be different. All he needed was a chance.

But all I had felt, all the preparation for the "seed" that had taken place within me was ruthlessly banished a moment later when the chaplain started to talk. As soon as he opened his mouth I felt as if someone had exposed a raw nerve and were operating upon it with a horse-shoer's rasp.[6]

I frequently find myself associating persons I meet with animals or flowers. The "Reverend" August Drahms always reminded me of a toad—I couldn't help it. Still, there is no rancor or hate in my thought of him. He couldn't help it, either. We should never condemn a man for being blind. But we all know that blindness is an awful thing.

He read a text from the scriptures—I've forgotten what it was—and then delivered his discourse. He spoke in a jerky fashion, biting off his words—something like the final sounds made by a dog which has been aroused in the night. First, the dog barks loudly and rapidly, then with pauses, finally half-heartedly, subsiding with gulps and growls and little snarls. That was the way the chaplain's talk impressed me.

I shall never forget that sermon. There wasn't a word of charity nor a tone of sympathy in it. We sat there and squirmed while he digressed for a moment to tell us it was

---

[6] A coarse file with sharp points instead of raised lines forming the grating surface.

ch. ends p. 123

for our "good" that we were in prison and that it was for our "good" that we had assembled to hear him say so.

After he had finished there was another hymn, not nearly so effective as the first had been—the "sermon" had deadened response—and then the chaplain called for "testimony."

Quite a number of men responded, and Smoky kept up a running commentary.

"A fakir," "A hypocrite," "He'd steal th' rings off his dead mother's fingers," "That guy's on th' square," "He'd cut y'r t'roat in a minute," were some of his expressions as different men arose.

Finally an unprepossessing man, with a sensual face, got up and talked for ten minutes, chiefly about himself and how much better he felt since the Lord had singled him out as particularly worthy. He finished with, "—but there's one thing above all others that I'm thankful for. Praise the Lord I'm not here for stealing."

Smoky squirmed in his seat and clinched his hands, and I knew he was very much wrought up, especially when the chaplain arose and offered a prayer in which he recommended the last speaker in particular to the watchfulness and favoritism of the Almighty.

When we got outside I took several breaths of fresh air. I was conscious of conflicting emotions.

"That last man who spoke," I ventured, as Smoky and I reached the yard—"what's he here for? He thanked God he wasn't here for stealing."

Smoky turned so abruptly that I thought he was going to hit me. His eyes were flashing and his shoulders heaving. He spat vigorously and bit off a chew of tobacco before replying.

"D'y'r wanter know what that guy's here f'r?" he asked. "D'y'r really wanter know?"

Of course, that only served to make me more curious.

"Well, I'll tell y'r. You an' me is angels, milk-white angels, alongside o' that stiff. All he did was f'rget that th' little 15-year-old girl was his own daughter; that's all. An' that hatchet-faced grafter gettin' up an' askin' Almighty God t' single that kind of a yeller-tail outer th' herd an' save him a reserved seat when we all bumps off. Bah! If that's Christianity, thank God I'm an honest crook."

While we had been in the chapel the sun had dispelled the fog and we found the yard more comfortable than it had been when we left it. As is the custom, the prison band assembled at 11 o'clock and gave a concert. This band is comprised entirely of prisoners, self-instructed and self-supported at that time. Instruments and music were secured by subscriptions from the prisoners.

There was a strong demand for waltzes and other dance music, and I noticed that Smoky wanted to go under the shed, where the dancing was in progress. I wanted to ask him about his early life, but refrained. I already knew him well enough to know that it would be best to wait until he was in the mood. He asked me to accompany him to the shed and I did so.

About thirty couples—ladies conspicuous by their absence—were dancing. Smoky sought and found a partner, Frisco Slim, I think it was, and whirled off. I sat and watched them.

Nearly every face that bobbed past me seemed content. There seemed to be a forgetfulness of their imprisonment, of their surroundings. I did a good deal of thinking during those two hours. While it seemed strange to see men in prison dancing, nevertheless I realized that it was a good thing.

The more abnormal a man's life is the more abnormal he becomes and the more liable he is to get out of touch with what we call civilized conditions.

The scene before me was but a safety valve—it afforded some of the men an opportunity to work off part of the repression. Better work it off that way than to have it stored up until the end and then manifest itself in utter abandonment and disregard for law and order, as it so frequently does.

People are prone to wonder when a man just released

from the penitentiary gets drunk and commits crime within twenty-four hours. The wonder to me is that this does not occur to a greater extent than it does. Let us stop and enter into the feelings of such a man.

He has been in prison for years, perhaps for a decade. During all that time he has been kept in physical and mental subjection, he has been discouraged from manifesting initiative, he has spent long hours thinking of the "good time" he will have on the day of his release. He has had nothing to make him realize that release will mean new responsibilities.

In prison he has his meals and a place to sleep, sordid as they may be. He need give no thought for the morrow; he need not practice frugality; he loses all sense of the order of things and of the fact that what each man gets is what he earns. He has no conception of the use and value of money. He has received nothing in return for his labor. In short, he has been reduced to the level of an unthinking animal, and kept there.

On the day of his release he is given a suit of cheap clothing and five dollars in money. He feels that he is entitled to have a good time—and I believe he is. If he didn't have a good time he would still be a prisoner—and the methods that have been employed to keep him in subjugation have not tended in the least to make him realize the need of self-control and temperance. Nine times out of ten he turns into the first saloon he comes to. From the saloon he goes to a worse place—and he comes out of this "worse place" crestfallen and "broke."

He has not made any provision for his board and he has no change of underclothing. Credit is entirely out of the question.

His work in the jute mill has not fitted him for hard, physical labor, and those who essay[7] hard labor at first generally "cave in." Some men manage to tide themselves along— how I do not know—and gradually become used to normal

[7] Attempt.

conditions. In time they get employment, and, if fortunate, manage to keep it without exposure.

But a great many, after their pitiful little "fling," see but one solution to their plight—crime. Some of them are caught immediately and are held up to the world as confirmed criminals.

"Only out of prison twenty-four hours and commits robbery," say the headlines.

Last week I took lunch in a place where thousands of persons congregate daily for midday refreshment. My mood was heavy, well suited to understand what I experienced before I left. I felt alone in that crowded place.

People all about me were laughing and chatting. Pretty girls nibbled daintily at their dessert, some of them happy in the presence of a male adorer at the opposite side of the table.

I wondered how many men there are in San Francisco whose lives are without the music of home ties, of a nearness to someone who knows and understands them. There is no solitude like that of a crowd. But this is aside from my purpose.

The young fellow who waited on me was an ex-convict. I recognized him instantly and he recognized me, but neither of us gave any sign. While eating I tried to remember his name and how long he had been out, but all I could recall was that I had seen his face above a suit of stripes—the rest was merged in 6,000 other striped figures, the number of men who passed through San Quentin while I was there.

Just as I finished and was preparing to leave the young fellow came and stood beside my chair.

"I beg your pardon," he said, in a low voice, "but isn't your name Lowrie?"

I replied that it was.

"Don't you remember me?" he asked.

"I remember your face," I replied, "but that's all."

"Don't you remember 'Lefty Wright'—I used to run with him?"

ch. ends next p.

Instantly I recalled the period; also the man beside me. 'Lefty' Wright had been a conspicuous figure in the prison and had been in the "hole" a great many times for fighting.

"Yes, B——, I remember you now. How are you getting along?"

"I'm doing fine," he replied, proudly. "I've held this job two years now, and I'm all right. But at first I had a hard time of it. I left that dump with my mind made up never to go back, but do you know what I had to do? I had to commit four burglaries before I got my head above water. I couldn't get a job at first, and nearly starved. If I'd got pinched any one of those times nobody would have understood; thy'd have all said I was no good. But I was only fighting for a start and I made it. But I must go. Come in again some time. I'm on this section at this hour every day."

After he left I sat there and pondered. Two ex-convicts had met and conversed in the crowd, and no one was the wiser. If it had became known that we were ex-convicts there would have been a drawing aside of skirts, perhaps an exodus—yet we were both living right lives, earning what we got, and we had both paid the penalty for the wrong of the past.

Perhaps I should not have made this digression now, but it was so vividly real that I couldn't help it. On every hand I see ex-prisoners, most of them at work. The other day I saw a man who spent twenty years at San Quentin—twenty years that made him an old man. He was driving an ash cart[8] in Oakland. The horse was old and decrepit, the cart was old and unpainted, the driver was old and broken. We recognized each other and he pulled the horse up short. His face broke into a great smile.

"Hello," he said, cheerily.

"Hello," said I; "how are you?"

"Well, I used to be a family man and had a good home of my own. Now I don't even own old Ben here," referring to the horse. "That jolt robbed me of everything. I'm just

---

[8] A cart in which ashes and other refuse or trash are carried.

worrying along, trying to get ahead of old age. But it's better than that life over there."

He chuckled to the old horse and moved on. Again two ex-convicts had met and entered into each other's feelings. After all, it is only the man whose soul has been in the depths that can put himself in the other fellow's place, though the self-righteous may say it is "birds of a feather."

11

"An' y'r really want t' know who I am an' where I come from an' where I'm goin'?" queried Smoky, in response to a direct question from me after he had finished dancing.

"Yes, Smokes"—we called him "Smokes" sometimes instead of Smoky—"I'd like to know," I rejoined earnestly. "Not out of curiosity, not because I want to pry into your affairs, but because—well, because I like you; because I think you're a better man than I am, even if you have crushed into the pen four times."

I blurted this out in one breath. It was just what I felt.

Smoky was visibly affected, although he tried to conceal it.

"There ain't much t' tell. Bill," he said, with a quaver in his voice, "but y'r th' first person I've met in my life that asked me. As to who I am, I don't know; as to where I come from, I don't know; as to where I'm goin', I don't know that, either, an' I don't care a hell of a lot.

"They tol' me at th' orphanage that I was found in a pasteboard box in th' middle of a vacant lot, with not'in on but m' skin an' hollerin' t' beat th' band. Many a time I wish I'd been one of them dummies what talks with their fingers—me an' th' pasteboard box wouldn't 'a' separated then.

"Durin' my kid days at th' 'sylum I was a holy terror. I was always in trouble an' I was always fightin' back when they tried t' make me behave by beatin' me or puttin' me t' bed without supper. Many a night when I was a li'l' bit of a kid less'n five years old I went t' sleep hungry, with m' li'l' breadbasket feelin' as if my li'l' t'roat had been cut. But I'd never give in; I'd never let them know that it hurt. Maybe if I'd had a mother it might 'a' been different.

"I come near havin' a mother once. I never tol' anyone about it before, but I'll tell you. It was after I finished my last bit in prison. I was younger then, an' I went out full o' good res'lutions—so full o' them that it hurt. Th' first couple o' days I had a hard time keepin' clean—I wanted t' go an' have a time, take in th'—oh, you know.

"But I won out, an' th' third day I shipped as waiter on a boat goin' north. Luck seemed t' be with me, f'r I got a job 's soon 's I landed, workin' as handy man around a big boardin' house. Th' lady o' th' house treated me fine from th' start. No bossin', no orderin' me around 'r not'in' like that. She jus' tol' me what she expected me t' do an' I did it, an' I ate at th' table with th' rest of 'em. She took care o' me jus' th' same as if I belonged t' her, helped me buy some decent rags, an' never asked a word 'bout who I was 'r where I come from. An' maybe I didn't work—I enjoyed workin'; I was always lookin' f'r somethin' t' do, somethin' that needed fixin'.

"Pretty soon me an' th' girl—that was her daughter; Rose was her name—got so we was always lookin' at each other, an' I began t' feel like there wasn't anybody but us two in th' world. I f'got ev'rything that ever happened t' me, an' after a time it got so bad that I couldn't think o' not'in' else. If she touched me 'r brushed again' me I used t' feel 's if my skypiece[1] was cut off an' flyin' up t' the stars. It was great. An' one Sunday when she washed her hair—say, I wish y'r could 'a' seen that hair! It was red, th' beautifulest red y'r ever saw, an' long an' thick, an' she had big gray eyes what looked good t' drink, an' her——"

[1] Head.

ch. ends p. 132

Smoky suddenly stopped and looked foolish. Then he broke into a hard, harsh laugh.

"Say, y'r must t'ink I'm simple," he said, with that peculiar inflection inviting a negative answer.

"Simple!" I made haste to reply. "Why, Smoky, I know all about it. I had a girl once myself. She was the most——"

I stopped as abruptly as he had, just in time to save myself from usurping the place of leading man.

"Put it there!" I said, impulsively, extending my hand.

Smoky put his hand about mine and gave me a great squeeze.

"Well," he continued, "you know how I felt. I was in love with th' gal, that's all; clean daffy over her, an' that Sunday when she washed her hair an' was sittin' on the back porch with it hangin' down behind her chair she let me brush it t' help get it dry—an' what d'y'r t'ink I done? I yaffled th' end of it an' kissed it an' she pinched[2] me. I'll never f'rget it 's long 's I live. I don't know how she knew, but she turned round quick 's a flash an' caught me dead in th' act, with th' goods right on me, an' I was so rattled I jus' stood paralyzed, with her hair up against my kisser, like a great big boob.

"At first she looked kind o' mad, then she gave a quick look toward th' windows, an' then she laughed.

"'Well, that's a nice way t' brush hair, I must say,' she says, kind o' shy like.

"'You bet it's nice,' I shot back at her, gettin' bold all of a sudden, 'an' I'd like th' job of takin' care o' it all th' time, an' what goes with it.'

"At that she jumped up an' looked at me steady, her big eyes meltin' soft an' kind o' troubled like, but she never said another word, but went inter th' house.

"I stood around a while, feelin' sheepish, an' then moped t' th' woodshed an' cut up about ten cords o' wood before night. But th' more I thought about it th' better I felt, an' when I saw her at supper that night she blushed, an' neither

---

[2] Caught.

of us would look at each other; that is, every time I looked at her t' see if she was lookin' at me she was lookin' at me t' see if I was lookin' at her—you know what I mean.

"Well, her mother got on t' th' play an' it seemed t' please her. She treated me better'n ever, an' lookin' back now I can see how she used t' fix it so's me an' Rose 'd be together a whole lot.

"Natcher'ly, I f'rgot all 'bout th' crooked game an' got ambitious—an' that's where I broke my neck. If I'd been satisfied t' keep on workin' there it would 'a' been all right, but I wanted t' do better. So I got a job at one o' th' hotels as a kitchen helper. Y'r know, I learned cookin' when I made that trip t' Australia.

"Things went along fine f'r a time, an' I got a raise in wages, an' used t' help around th' house nights—me an' Rose used t' wash th' dishes—we was crazy t' do it—an' we had it all fixed up t' get married when th' crash' came.

"A dick (detective) what knew me down here happened t' stop at th' hotel an' spotted me. He tol' them at th' office, an' I was called up an' fired. I begged f'r a chance, but they said they was sorry, but they couldn't keep an ex-con in th' hotel.

"Maybe I wasn't hostile. At first I thought o' croakin' th' dick, but that wouldn't 'a' got me not'in', only th' rope, maybe.

"There was another feller workin' at th' hotel what boarded with us, an' he was so hot that he went home an' tol' Rose an' her mother. When I got there they treated me th' same as if not'in' had happened, an' when I said I was goin' away they both broke down an' begged me t' stay, but I wouldn't listen.

"I wish I had now. But I jus' packed my duds and skinned out. She got mad an' called me a coward an' a lot o' other things, but I wouldn't listen. I tol' her I'd get a start somewhere else an' let her know. But all th' time I knew it was all off—that it had all been a mistake. She was too good f'r an ex-con like me.

"Y'r see, I'd f'rgot all that while I was there—th' thing

ch. ends p. 132

happened so easy like an' I got to think o' her so much that I f'rgot who I was. But that dick exposin' me showed me jus' where I stood. I couldn't marry Rose, not even knowin' what my name was, an' an ex-con t' boot. That wouldn't be fair t' her.

"But sometimes I think I made a mistake, that I oughter stuck it out an' took her, f'r she wanted me f'r just what I was t' her, not f'r what I had been.

"An' I ain't never wrote. That was sixteen years ago, an' I don't even know if she's alive, 'r what's happened. I came back down here an' got t' drinkin' an' runnin' with skirts, an' th' first thing I knew I was in th' can ag'in, up against it f'r robbery, an' got this twenty-year jolt."

That night when we went to the cell the Kid did not appear. As soon as we were locked in I asked Smoky where the boy was.

"Oh, they've taken him inter th' hospital at last," he replied, "an' th' chances are we'll never see him again."

The next day I asked one of the hospital attendants about it.

"Oh, the Kid's got the T. B., an' got it bad. He's in th' old hospital, an' th' chances are he'll come out feet first. Once he gets up there with that bunch of incurables he'll give up like nearly all of them do."

I asked if there was any chance of my getting permission to see him, and learned that it was against the rules. I reported the result of my inquiry to Smoky that night and learned that such was the case—prisoners were not permitted to visit friends who might be in the hospital.

"Why, I remember a case only las' month," Smoky informed me. "Two fellers got kicked in here f'r robbery— got ten years apiece. One of 'em took sick about two months ago, an' his partner tried t' get up t' see him, but couldn't. Y'r see, they didn't give their names when they was pinched, an' they didn't tell anybody here who they was. So th' feller in th' yard wanted t' get to see his partner so's t' find out if he wanted his folks tol' about his bein' sick. But they wouldn't let him go up, an' th' young feller died. They planted him out there where they put Charlie Bryce. I was talkin' to his partner in th' yard this afternoon, an' he don't know what t' do. He don't know whether t' write an' tell his partner's mother what's happened, 'r keep still an' never let 'em know he died in th' pen. They was raised together in th' same town, an' ran away from home. Down there in Fresno they rolled a drunk an' got seven dollars off him, an' th' judge soaked 'em with ten years each because they wouldn't tell who they was an' where they belonged. The feller what's left says he'll never be able to look his partner's mother in th' face if he ever goes back home. An' it seems there's some girl back there what was stuck on him, too. They thought they could get a start here in Californy an' then go back all dogged up an' cut a figger. But this is what they got."

"It seems to me," I suggested, "that it would be better to tell the boy's mother what's happened. If she isn't told she'll worry and fret all her life. It would be best to have it over with, bad as it is."

"Well, I never had a mother," rejoined Smoky, "but it seems t' me it is best not t' tell her. She'll go on hopin' an' imaginin' all kind o' good things; an' jus' think what a blow f'r her t' find out that he died in th' pen, a con. No, it's better f'r her never t' know. Of course, if his partner had got t' see him an' found out what he wanted him t' do in case he bumped off, why, it would 'a' been diff'rent."

I remained silent a few moments, thinking of the boy who had been our cellmate.

"Where is the Kid's father, Smoky?"

Smoky turned to me in pleased surprise. "Now, that's funny; I was thinkin' o' that very same thing m'self. His father is a policeman in Chicago, an' he's tried ev'ry way t' get th' Kid out, but it ain't no use. Th' law says he can be paroled in one year, but th' board has their own rules, an' they say he mus' serve half time. Of course, in his case, with

ch. ends p. 132

fifty years, they don't make him serve half time, but he's jus' th' same 's a lifer; he's got t' serve eight years before they'll listen t' parole f'r him. I've thought 'bout that law and them rules a whole lot. It seems t' me that they passed that law at Sacramento f'r jus' such cases, so's some o' these sentences from roughneck judges could be evened up. You know how it is. T'day some four 'r five time loser 'll drive up with a year, an' t'morrer some poor kid, 'r a farmer, will come f'r fifteen 'r twenty, an' f'r th' very same kind o' crime.

"Take Lefty Wright's case, f'r instance. They caught him blowin' a pete right in th' heart o' th' city in th' dead o' night—caught him right in th' act. But he happened t' have fr'en's in politics, an' even with three jolts t' his credit he got off with four years. And th' very same day a young feller got kicked in from Los Angeles f'r breakin' inter a boxcar at night an' got twelve years. Both cases was burglary, first degree. Lefty had 'soup' an' tools with him an' was a professional prowler, same's me, an' all he gets is four years. The young feller was an accident, an' he gets twelve. That ain't right. It ain't square. Once in a while an old-timer gets jolted, but more oftener he knows enough not t' fight th' case, slips inter court, gives th' judge a hard luck tale an' gets off light; while th' green one, not bein' onter th' ropes, tries t' beat it by standin' trial, an' gets th' limit. That's what th' parole law oughter work on—cases like that. There's lots of 'em. Why shouldn't that kid go home t' his father an' maybe be th' means o' gettin' his mother out o' th' bughouse?"

I did not reply to the question. There wasn't any reply to make.

"Mind you, I ain't kickin' about m'self," Smoky went on. "I got just what was comin' t' me. An' lots of th' judges are good men an' use discretion. Take Judge M——, 'r Judge R——, 'r Judge B——. They wouldn't send no boy t' prison f'r fifty years, an' even after they sends a man here they take an int'rest in him. But there's bad judges 's well 's good judges, like ev'rything else. It oughter be fixed some way so's ev'ry man would get a square deal—get jus' what was comin' t' him."

"You mean the indeterminate sentence?" I asked.

"Well, yes—pervided it could be fixed so's a man would always get a square deal here. It wouldn't work th' way things are now. A man like th' one I pointed out t' y'r in th' yard, what holds in f'r a feller an' lays f'r a chance t' cinch him, could keep y'r here forever. But if they had it fixed so's ev'ry man would have t' go out on parole, an' give him a fair start, I think it would be a good thing. Maybe if that had happened t' me when I drove up th' first time I might not be here now. I like t' work—I ain't lazy—an' I know this game don't pay—there's not'in' in it.

"A man startin' out on parole, with th' prison officers backin' him up an' seein' that he gets a square deal has it all over th' guy what does his time an' goes out without knowin' where he's goin' t' sleep th' first night. I been watchin' th' game a whole lot lately. There's more men comes back after doin' their time an' being discharged with five dollars, an' not knowin' what they'll do when they get out than there is men what have been paroled. Five 'r six second-timers blow in t' each guy what violates parole. Don't that go t' prove that parole is a good thing? An' ain't ev'rybody th' gainer when a guy straightens up an' does th' right thing? What good does it do t' keep me f'r a twenty-year sentence an' then turn me loose t' do as I please, an' not knowin' where I'm goin' 'r what I'm going' t' do? An' most fellers feel sore, especially if they've done a long jolt. Not only that, but I knows lots o' guys what has families. Some o' 'em do time awful hard; they do more time in a month than us fellers do in a year. Why? Because they keep thinkin' an' worryin' about th' wife and kids. What good does it do t' keep a man like that penned up jus' so long, simply because some judge had a grouch on an' handed him five 'r ten years? It's no wonder so many guys go wrong again. I've talked with lots of 'em what have gone out sore. An' lots o' homes are broken up jus' on that

ch. ends next p.

account. Th' woman struggles along, tryin' t' keep her head above water, hopin' she can wait f'r her man t' get out, but it's too much, an' she has t' give up. Lots o' divorces happen jus' that way, because th' woman can't keep herself an' has t' get another man jus' f'r that reason.

"But 'make 'em serve half time,' says th' board. No matter who they are, 'r what they done, 'r who suffers, 'make 'em serve half time—let's have revenge.'"

12

Shortly after my first attendance at chapel, an event occurred which served to clinch my impressions and turn me, with many others, still more decisively against religion as then exemplified at the penitentiary.

Before recounting it, however, I want to say that the present chaplain is a hardworking, conscientious man. During the time he has been chaplain he has established a school for illiterates and for teaching English to those who are unable to speak it. Also he has improved the prison library, though it has not yet been brought up to the state of efficiency practically possible. There are no printed catalogs, and the men do not have opportunity for getting to the library as they should.

It would seem to me that each prisoner should be furnished with a catalog and arrangements perfected by which books would be delivered at the cells. At present the men desiring books are obliged to rush to the library in the early morning or wait until Saturday afternoon, when there is a big crowd and poor service.

Until quite recently there was no fund for the purchase of new books, but, thanks to the persistence of Warden Hoyle, arrangements have been perfected by which the interest from the prisoners' and parole funds, a sum aggregating $22,000, is available for that purpose. Prior to that arrangement the moneys in these funds were held in trust by the bank, without interest.

Also, under the present chaplain the prejudice against religion has been softened to a great extent. It was not religion itself that the men repudiated and condemned so much as the man who professed to expound it during the twenty years that August Drahms was chaplain.

Prisoners are quick to "size a man up," and they are keen, exceedingly keen, in detecting insincerity and lack of human sympathy.

But before relating the one incident that stands out above all others in my knowledge of Drahms, I must say a few words for the visiting chaplains from the Roman Catholic diocese at San Rafael. These good men make regular semi-weekly (sometimes more frequent) visits to the prison hospitals, hold services each Sunday and take a genuine interest in the work. They help many men to redeem themselves by personal effort, and I know of dozens of cases where they have made the $25 deposit and furnished the work and clothing necessary for a man's parole.

Also, it is a noteworthy fact that nearly every condemned prisoner embraces the Roman Catholic faith before being taken to the scaffold and dropped through the awful little square hole without any bottom.

This was especially true of the two score human beings who were executed at San Quentin during Drahms' incumbency, and in one case a condemned man's final request of the warden was that Drahms be excluded from the execution room, which request was granted.

It was the only execution that Drahms missed during his term of office. He attended even when he did not officiate.

It was no wonder to me that he succeeded in bringing religion into disrepute, and I feel sure it will be no wonder to you. I could fill pages with incidents concerning him, some of them so unconscionable as to be incredible, but one will suffice.

Charlie Bryce, a lifer who was very popular with all the prisoners, died suddenly one night from the effects of a hemorrhage. At the time of his death the friends of a deceased prisoner were permitted to attend the burial at the prison cemetery. This attendance was limited to fifty, however, and Charlie had been so popular that a petition was made to the warden asking if there might not be a funeral service in the chapel. Such a thing had never been done before—and has not been done since—but the warden gave the desired permission.

The band men—of which organization Charlie had been a member—had a tasteful musical program arranged, and all went smoothly until the chaplain delivered his oration. He started in well, but before he had proceeded very far he forgot the sacredness of the occasion by endeavoring to drive home the "moral" of Charlie's death in prison. He pictured the deceased prisoner's ignominious end and predicted a similar fate for a great many of us if we did not accept his teachings and example.

The audience became audibly and visibly impatient, but the speaker paid no heed. As he went on there was a murmuring and a shuffling of feet. But, entirely oblivious of the fact that he was addressing the dead man's friends, the men who had known him as a "square guy," the chaplain persisted.

I began to get nervous, sensing that there would be some sort of disgraceful demonstration before he finished unless he paid some attention to the uneasiness he had aroused, nor was I mistaken. The climax came dramatically.

Visibly annoyed at the way the men were behaving, the chaplain suddenly stopped. So did the noise. Then, pointing a long, bony finger at the face of the corpse lying in the black-painted pine box before him, Drahms took two measured paces forward and said:

"There lies the wages of sin. Gone to the judgment of his Maker with blackened soul. But the Almighty is merciful. He may have mercy on this man, for, even though he was

ch. ends p. 142

a criminal, there may have been some good in him. The Lord——"

I do not know what he said about "the Lord," for his words were drowned in hisses and cat-calls. The guards arose and made a half-hearted effort to restore order—half-hearted, because they, also, had known and liked Charlie Bryce—but the men were inflamed, and each time the chaplain tried to continue they hissed and scraped their feet.

Finally, with a sneering expression, he resumed his seat, and the men at the organ immediately began singing "Nearer My God to Thee."

I shall never forget the scene, nor my emotions. I was torn between regret that such a disgraceful demonstration should have occurred and a desire to go up and lay violent hands on the man who had caused it.

After the hymn we were permitted to form in line and march after the coffin. As I passed beside it I was glad that the shell before me had not been conscious of what had taken place a few minutes before.

When we had all passed the spot the turnkey took a long look at the dead face to assure himself that it was really a corpse in the box, and then the lid was screwed down in his presence. Fifty of us had permission to attend the burial outside the walls.

As the cortège[1] passed across the yard one of the gardeners stepped furtively from his work and laid a bunch of violets on top of the coffin. It was one of the most human acts I have ever seen, and yet he seemed half-ashamed of himself for doing it. Afraid of being considered sentimental, I suppose. So many of us fail to differentiate between what is human and what is sentimental.

There was no hearse, and when the six lifers who were acting as pallbearers got to the front gate they were obliged to maneuver to get the coffin through the little man-gate. The front gate at San Quentin is so arranged that but one person

---

[1] A solemn procession, especially for a funeral.

can pass through at a time, the big double gate, of which the man-gate is a part, never being opened. All teaming is done through the back gates, down by the jute mill.

By dispensing with the crossbars and placing a man at either end, the coffin was shoved and twisted through the small opening. I could not help but feel that there was something sacrilegious about it. It looked so much like handling a box of freight, or something like that.

We were counted as we passed out behind the coffin, and on getting outside armed guards took up positions on either side of the procession. Immediately I forgot all about the funeral. I was so interested in the scene before me—the bay and the distant shore lines. It was the first time I had been outside the four walls since my arrival.

Arrived at the cemetery, we stopped at an open grave. The chaplain was already there; he had ridden out in a conveyance. We all had our hats off, but he kept his on. He stepped up to the grave to say the last words, but one of the men began singing before he could speak, and as soon as the hymn was finished the gravediggers began shoveling the earth in hurriedly. But the chaplain was persistent and managed to mumble something about "dust to dust."

Then, slowly and with great feeling, the cornetist,[2] who had been Charlie's "bunky" in the band room, sounded taps over the grave. He seemed to put his whole soul into it, and we were all deeply moved. That sounding of taps touched holes in our breasts that the words and songs had failed utterly to reach.

Someone had taken the little bunch of violets from the top of the coffin before it was lowered, and after the grave was filled laid it on top.

---

[2] One who plays a cornet (a brass instrument resembling a trumpet but shorter and wider).

ch. ends p. 142

Sydney Lanier[3] says a violet is God.[4]

And then, even as we stood there, waiting the signal to march back, the gravediggers placed the white board at the head of the grave—just a white board with a black number painted on it—the dead man's prison number.

The chaplain had referred to Charlie Bryce as a criminal. Was he a criminal? He was sentenced to imprisonment for life because he killed another man during a heated altercation and after the other man had attacked him. For one moment of anger he paid with his life, yet every characteristic of the man clearly demonstrated that he was a normal human being, kind to his fellows and peaceable. There are many such men whom the unthinking regard as "criminals."

✱

During the first eighteen months of my imprisonment I bathed outdoors. The only provision for bathing was a shed, open on all sides, in which there was a primitive shower arrangement running down the center. Two afternoons each week the water—warm salt water—was turned on, and those who desired to do so were excused from work for twenty minutes to take a bath. There was no compulsion about it, and a surprisingly small number of men took advantage of it, especially during the winter, when the air was cold, or damp, or foggy. Sometimes there would be a comparatively warm day during the week when a bath might have been taken in the open air without a great deal of discomfort, but Wednesdays and Saturdays were the regular days, and it made no difference whether it were rainy or windy or cold, they were the only days that the water was turned on.

---

[3] Sidney Clopton Lanier (1842–1881) was an American musician, poet, and author, known for his adaptation of musical meter to poetry, and was hailed in the South as the "poet of the Confederacy."

[4] Likely a reference to an outline Lanier had written for a poem, "I know that thou art the word of my God, dear Violet," found in his *Poem Outlines* (1908).

A great many of the men did not bathe at all during the winter months, and no record was kept to show whether a prisoner bathed or not. Of course, I caught a severe cold which I was unable to cure, and which came close to developing into pneumonia once or twice. But during the entire eighteen months that I worked in the jute mill I never missed a day at my task, though there were several occasions when I worked all day while suffering from the effects of fever.

And there were times when I did not dare take a bath for two, even three weeks. Going out from the warm mill and undressing outdoors, with no protection from the cold wind blowing off the foggy bay, was an ordeal even when one was healthy, but to one suffering from a cold, or with fever, it was positive torture. True, the hot shower was refreshing, and comparatively comfortable, so long as one remained under it. The menace was afterward, during the interval of drying the body and dressing in the cold. Imagine taking a hot bath in midwinter and then going out on the porch or in the back yard to dry and dress yourself. But it was a case of taking the chance of catching cold or going without a bath. Many of the men chose to take the chance.

Smoky used to heat a wash-basin of water over our lamp and take a "sponge bath" in the cell on Saturday night, and he persuaded the Kid and the others to do likewise, but I only tried it once. There was not sufficient water, and I felt sticky and uncomfortable afterward. I determined to get used to the open-air bath in the jute mill yard. Among those who did likewise quite a number became seriously ill and were taken into the hospital, where several died of pneumonia or sank into chronic lung trouble.

Additional to the physical danger of bathing without protection from the elements, there was the utter lack of privacy to endure. One had to undress and bathe in the presence of hundreds of men, frequently in the presence of visitors who were being shown through the prison. Of course, some of the men didn't mind that, but quite a number did. It used to

ch. ends p. 142

embitter me to hear the different guards in charge of visiting parties descant[5] on the "fine" bathing arrangements.

"Here's the bathhouse," one guard used to exclaim. "Fine hot shower bath, salt water; almost as good as a hotel."

Of course, very few of the visitors stopped to think of the inhuman method of making men come from under hot water and dress in the open air. And this method of bathing prevailed at San Quentin for many years. It has only been within the past year that a large, airy, modern bathroom has been completed and put into operation. This bathroom has about forty booths, each with its swinging half-door, and with hot and cold salt water, additional to fresh water, in each compartment. The bathing has been systematized so that every prisoner is compelled to take a bath at least once each week unless excused by the doctor. A check is kept on each individual as he passes into the bathroom and gets his change of underclothing. This is but one of the many humanizing and much needed improvements that have been made, or are being made, by the present warden.

There is a swimming tank in the upper yard, but it is small and is not used save by the few men whose work permits them to get to it just after it has been filled with fresh water. But sometimes on a hot Saturday afternoon in summer this tank is crowded. The jute mill closes at 2:30 on Saturday and the prisoners congregate in the upper yard.

Saturday is the day of events at San Quentin. The rule is that the men may be passed into the jute mill yard on that day as soon as they have completed their tasks and cleaned the machinery. There are signs posted all over the mill warning the men not to clean machinery while it is running, but in spite of punishment if they are caught at it, a great many men persist in cleaning up while the machinery is in motion. Scarcely a Saturday passes without some man, frequently two or three, being caught in the machinery and losing fingers and limbs. I witnessed several horrible mutilations of

[5] Talk tediously or at great length.

human beings in the massive "breaking carders" at the back end of the mill.

Quite frequently a man is caught by no fault of his own. I know of several instances where men have shut down their machine, and while at work cleaning the cogs at the far end or underneath, the machine has been started by someone else, the same as if a fireman started a locomotive while the engineer was underneath it repairing a break or hunting for one.

It has been claimed that this dastardly crime has been committed intentionally more than once, the enemy of some man watching for the opportunity to "get" him in that way.

Of course, accidents occur during other days also. New men get caught in the machinery or in the belting through inexperience or lack of proper instruction and caution as to the danger. There is not a single shield on any of the cog mechanism that I ever saw on the hundreds of machines in the jute mill at San Quentin—certainly not on the looms.

An examination of the resident physician's official report for the year ended June 30, 1909, discloses nineteen amputations during the year, and this does not include those who were caught in the machinery and escaped without losing bone matter. Probably not more than one-fourth of this number would have suffered had the cog machinery been provided with shields. And the man who is maimed while in prison goes out into the world with $5, hopeless, friendless, and crippled.

It has been claimed that men sometimes "jim" themselves intentionally; that is, deliberately place a finger in the cog wheels in order to "beat" a loom. I know of one instance where this occurred. The man worked on the loom next to mine and was suffering with tuberculosis. Every instant of the day was a physical torture to him. One day, just after we returned from dinner, he called to me, and when I looked toward him he smiled, a wan, sickly smile, and then deliberately placed his left index finger in the cogs. The smile froze on his face as the finger went through and he turned deathly white. But he recovered almost instantly, wrapped a piece of jute about the crushed member, leisurely got his coat and reported at the office. He was hurried to the hospital and the finger was amputated at the second joint. He never came back to work in the mill. But two years later, when I was in the hospital with typhoid fever, this man occupied the cot next to me. He was in the last stages of consumption and coughed almost continuously. His relatives learned of his condition and succeeded in getting him paroled. They came after him in an automobile. It was the first automobile that had ever been inside the penitentiary walls, and was an object of great wonder to the lifers and other men who had been in prison for years. I was convalescent[6] at the time and watched the crowd that craned their necks from the yard to see the machine. I also saw poor P—— carried out and deposited in the back seat beside his weeping sister. He died in San Francisco three weeks later.

[6] Recovering from illness.

13

Life in the penitentiary is not without its humorous aspects. In fact, a great many prisoners buoy themselves along by striving to see the bright side of things, and many of them never miss an opportunity to create a laugh. Smoky had a keen sense of humor—possibly some of you have discovered that—and I recall one incident which came very near resulting in serious trouble for him.

We had come up from the jute mill in the first line one afternoon and found the upper yard comparatively deserted. We used to "make" the first line whenever we could get through with our tasks because the upper yard was a pleasant place to walk in when the crowd was not there. While we were walking up and down together on this particular afternoon we saw a "fish" coming across the garden from the office. The Chinaman who had him in charge took him to the mattress room, and then up onto one of the tiers to show him his cell. As was his habit, Smoky "sized up" the new arrival critically as he went by.

"Jus' fell off a load o' hay outside th' front gate," he observed, "but he looks kinder forlorn; I'll bet one of them alfalfa judges has handed him a ten-spot, 'r somethin' like that. Wait till he comes down an' we'll see if we can't cheer him up."

Presently the Chinaman reappeared, followed by the new

prisoner. They stopped quite close to us and the Chinaman gave his final instructions.

"You no forget, when bell he ring you lun to cell. You no lun, no ketchum count. No ketchum count, ketchum hole."

It has always remained a mystery to me why they had a Chinaman as guide for new prisoners. He was trying to tell the new arrival that he must be at his cell promptly when the lockup bell rang, under penalty of spending the night in the "hole" if he failed to be there for the count.

As the Chinaman walked away Smoky and I approached the new man, or rather I should say the new boy, for the first thing I noticed was that he had not been shaved in the prison barbershop. There was no need; his face was like a woman's and his upper lip had the same downy growth as may be seen on nearly any woman's face if you observe from the right angle. His eyes were big and limpid, but without expression. Looking at them I was instantly reminded of a cow. But he had a man's physique—nearly six feet of it. The earmarks of the country were unmistakable. His feet were large and he moved awkwardly. He turned in a half-frightened way when spoken to.

"Let's see y'r breadhooks, kid," said Smoky, reaching for the boy's hands and turning the palms upward. "Jus' as I thought," he added, turning to me. "Look at them corns."

The hands showed plainly that the boy had been at hard work.

"What's them from, th' plow?" asked Smoky.

"Yeh," replied the boy; "I worked on th' ranch ever since I was old enough t' walk."

"An' what did y'r get kicked inter this dump for?"

"Oh, I stole a set o' harness belongin' t' th' Jones' ranch. I wanted t' take Cynthia Bell t' th' circus at Oroville, but I didn't have no money, spent all I had at th' fair a couple o' weeks before, so I sneaked over t' th' Jones place at night an' broke inter th' barn and got a set of harness. Bill Starchly, him that lives in Oroville, he told me there was a man there who would buy anything like that and say nothin', but when I went there t' get the three dollars they arrested me."

"An' whadger bring—er, I mean, how long did y'r get?" asked Smoky.

"They called it burglary first degree, and give me twelve years," replied the boy dolorously. "Jim Peters 'll get Cynthia sure now."

"Well, y'r up agin it pretty hard, kid," said Smoky consolingly, "but take my advice, f'rget th' skirt. There's lots more of 'em, an' I guess there'll be two 'r three still left when y'r get this jolt in. Skirt-itis is a bad bug t' do time with, an' y'r wanted f'rget y'r ever saw one." A sparkle of mischief came into Smoky's eyes and he winked at me.

"Whadger get in that sack y'r brought over with y'r blankets an' mattress?" he asked.

"Extry clothes," replied the boy.

"I s'pose y'r looked t' see that y'r got ev'rything that's comin' t' you. Y'r sheets, an' towels, an' hairbrush, an' ——"

"I didn't get no sheets," interrupted the boy, "only these——"

"Y'r didn't get no sheets!" exclaimed Smoky incredulously. "Are y'r sure?"

"Sure I didn't," replied the boy.

"Well, whadger think o' that?" asked Smoky, turning to me. "That bunch o' thievin' trusties in th' clothin' room oughter hit th' mill; robbin' a feller what's just blowed in f'r twelve years." He turned to the boy again.

"D'y'r see that old codger walkin' up an' down over there on th' porch with his mitts in his back pockets?" he asked, nodding toward the office. "Well, that's th' Capt'n, th' best ol' chap what ever cut a throat. You hotfoot it over an' tell him them stiffs did y'r out o' y'r sheets. He'll see that y'r get 'em, an' he'll make it warm f'r th' dirty robbers."

"But I don't want to get anybody into trouble," protested the boy, his inflection showing that he wanted to get what

ch. ends p. 156

was due him, but at the same time did not want to do anything that would bring punishment on others.

"Oh, that's all right, kid. Make 'em come across with what's comin' t' y'r. They'll jus' say it was an oversight; y'r needn't worry about them. Go ahead. Leave it t' me not to steer y'r wrong."

The boy hesitated a moment and then started for the office.

Incidentally, I may say that sheets are not furnished prisoners; just a straw mattress and blankets.

"Here's where we see a circus," chortled Smoky, seizing my arm. "Let's go over here under th' shed an' have a reserved seat. I hated t' run that ear o' corn up agin a play like that, but he was so green I couldn't help it. Gee, but Johnnie 'll go straight up."

At that time the Captain of the Yard was an old man. He had been a prison officer nearly all his life, and was what is known as "con wise." With advancing years his nature became very crabbed, and, like nearly all prison officers, he had a nickname with the inmates. He was known as Johnnie. He was a man of strong prejudices. If he fancied a particular man he favored him; likewise, if he took a dislike to a particular man, he missed no opportunity to reprimand or punish him. During half a dozen administrations he remained as Captain of the Yard. The present Captain of the Yard was his chief lieutenant at that time—an apt pupil.

As the new prisoner drew near the office porch the Captain saw him and stopped walking. Smoky could hardly contain himself, "Gee, but I'd like t' hear that confab," he exclaimed. "But there's Happy Jack standin' in the doorway, he'll hear it, an' we'll find out t'night."

For several minutes the Captain and the boy remained in conversation, the former glancing under the brim of his hat toward the yard where we were crouched and watching. Presently he and the boy stepped off the porch and entered the clothing room together. Smoky became concerned at once.

"Gee, I hope he ain't goin' t' put him in th' hole," he muttered. "If he starts anythin' like that I'll have t' go over an' square it."

But when the boy stepped out of the clothing room he did not turn toward the path leading to the dungeon. He and the Captain remained standing in conversation for a moment and then the boy started for the yard where we were waiting. He had something under his arm, something white.

Suddenly Smoky broke into a fit of laughter; good, hearty laughter that it was a joy to hear.

"Well, whadger think o' that?" he exclaimed. "If that o' codger didn't give him a pair o' sheets. That's certainly one on me. That's one time that Johnnie slipped it over all right."

The boy was quite close now, and Smoky unthinkingly rushed up to meet him.

"Well, I see y'r got 'em," he greeted, "but what did he say?"

"Oh, he asked me a lot o' questions, an' I told him a kind-hearted feller in th' yard sent me over t' get my sheets, an' he asked me who it was. I told him I didn't know, but he wanted t' know what you looked like, and so——"

"An' o' course y'r told him?" interrupted Smoky.

"Yes. An' he scratched his head, an' looked me all over, and then he took me in and give me th' sheets. After we come out he told me t' be careful who I talked with, an' then he says, 'Look out you don't lose these sheets, an' when you get back to the yard you tell that kindhearted feller to come over and get his.'"

Smoky was still laughing at the humor of this invitation when he was "pinched."

"Did this guy chip in and get y'r t' come after them sheets, too?" inquired the guard, laying his hand on my arm and looking at the boy.

"No, he didn't say anything," was the puzzled response. "What's the matter?"

"Oh, nothin'," replied the guard. "Just a case of this smart aleck spending a night 'r two at th' springs, I guess."

ch. ends p. 156

In spite of his predicament Smoky burst out laughing. "Well, this is certainly a fine pickle," he observed. "The next green one what drives up an' don't get his sheets 'll have t' do without 'em. No more Good Samaritan stunts f'r y'r Uncle Smokes."

Much concerned, I watched proceedings on the porch when Smoky arrived there in the custody of the guard. He and the Captain held a long conference, with many absurd gesticulations, waxing warmer and warmer, and then Smoky saluted and came back.

"Well, I had t' talk like a Dutch uncle, but I beat it," he exclaimed as he approached us. "At first he was strong f'r havin' me try th' springs over night, but I tol' him I knew he had a sense o' humor, 'r I wouldn't 'a' done such a thing, an' after dilly-dallyin' with me 's long 's he could, t' keep me guessin', he let me go. Th' only thing I'm sorry f'r now is that I didn't ask him f'r a pair o' sheets, too, before I left."

We were lined up for breakfast one morning when an amusing incident occurred. The "line-up" takes place at the blowing of a police whistle a few minutes before meal time, and owing to the narrow limits of the yard the line forms in convolutions; part of the men are under the shed, but the great majority stand in the open. On the morning mentioned the weather was threatening, and just after the line had formed there was a sudden shower. Those men who were without protection of the shed did not wait for permission to break ranks, but immediately rushed for cover.

A new guard, fresh from the bucolic regions "up State," was standing at the top of the dining-room stairway when this rush occurred. He had been on the job only a few days, and, like a great many of the men who secure employment as prison guards, imagined that we were a lot of murderous thugs. He had not been there long enough to learn otherwise.

When he saw that horde of striped figures break ranks and rush in a body toward the shed—toward him, as he thought—discretion instantly became the better part of valor; it was better to be a living farmer than a dead guardsman. He flung his cane at the advancing cutthroats, presumably in the hope that it might serve as a morsel upon which they might stop to spend the first fury of their thirst for blood, and then flew down the stairs to the dining room. Some wit in the crowd immediately took in the situation and shouted:

"There he goes! Head him off! Stick him in the back, and strike high!"

This gentle remark served its purpose. The fleeing man cast a despairing glance behind him and then took the last eight steps in one supreme leap, disappearing into the dining-room. The guards on duty there saw him coming and tried to stop him, but he brushed them off, managing to gasp the word "break" as he passed each one. Apparently the "heading-off" process was uppermost in his mind, for he went through the long dining-room hall as if intent on reaching the Oregon line before noon. He gained the other stairway, ascended it in four spasmodic leaps, rushed across the flower garden and "escaped" through the front gate. It was the only "escape" that "stuck" during my prison experience. True, he came back and gave himself up, but the warden was charitable and refused to take him in.

By shouting "break" as he passed through the mess hall he succeeded in stirring up quite a commotion. The mess hall guards imagined that some kind of a riot or "break" was in progress in the yard, and came rushing pell-mell[1] up the stairs, prepared to put up the fight of their lives. They found the men crowded under the shed and watching the rain. It required a great deal of explaining to straighten matters, and then everybody laughed.

And while writing about guards I want to say that nearly all of the men I saw acting in that capacity at San Quentin were fair and conscientious men. Of course, there were exceptions; that goes without saying. I recall one guard who reveled in his "little brief authority" and seemed to take

[1] In a confused, rushed, or disorderly manner.

ch. ends p. 156

a delight in insulting prisoners. He never missed an opportunity to reprimand a man, and always with abusive language. One day he called "Cockey" Hines a "dirty bum."

"You never did a day's work in your life," said the guard. "You're nothin' but a dirty bum outside, and it's me that knows it. And you call yourself a thief! Huh! You couldn't lift a lead nickel out of a barrel."

"Cockey" worked in "sack alley" and was a fairly industrious man. He had done nothing to deserve a "calldown," certainly not such a one as this. And he was recognized as one of the cleverest pickpockets in the business. When the guard sneered at his ability as a thief "Cockey" was hurt. Nothing hurts a professional crook so much as to be regarded as a "mutt" or "dub." So "Cockey" brooded over the insult and determined to "get even." All that morning he attended to his work assiduously, though it was noted that he was particularly deferential to the guard who had reprimanded him. On the slightest pretext "Cockey" sought this guard and asked for instructions, buzzing about the man obsequiously.[2] Early that afternoon, however, "Cockey" ceased these attentions. He asked and received permission to leave his work for a few minutes and was "passed" to the superintendent's office at the farther end of the mill. Returning from there, he sneered openly at the guard, so openly that the guard decided to "run him in."

"You come with me," he ordered; "I'll teach you a thing or two."

"Cockey" made no protest; in fact, he obeyed with alacrity and accompanied the officer willingly.

Arrived at the office of the superintendent, the guard registered his complaint with that officer.

"This guy is altogether too fresh and keeps giving me the dog eye," he complained.

"But didn't you call him a bum this morning? Didn't

[2] Obediently to an excessive degree.

you tell him he wasn't even a good thief?" asked the superintendent.

"Sure I did," replied the guard; "and what of it?"

"Only this," said the superintendent; "I don't believe you or any other man has the right to talk that way to a prisoner. It's like hitting him with his hands tied behind him. You wouldn't talk to a man like that anywhere else and expect to get away with it, would you?"

"Oh, of course, if you want to stick up for a 'con' against an officer, why, all right," was the reply; "but I'll see the Captain about it."

"Very well," returned the superintendent, "and while you're seeing him you might ask him to get your watch and purse for you."

"My watch and purse?" asked the guard. "What do you mean?"

But even as he asked the question his hands sought his pockets and he discovered that he had been robbed.

"They're gone!" he ejaculated. "My watch and purse are gone!"

The superintendent smiled. "Perhaps the Captain will find them for you, so long as you want to go over my head."

This was just enough suggestion to arouse the guard's curiosity.

"What do you mean, Mr. B——?" he asked. "I've certainly been touched for my watch and purse. Do you know where they are?"

"How much money was there in your purse?" asked the superintendent.

"I don't know exactly, but I'd say about eighteen dollars," was the reply. "Why?"

"Oh, nothing. Just look this over and see if it's all there."

The superintendent drew his hand from his coat pocket, where he had been holding it, and handed the guard his watch and purse.

The man was so astonished that he couldn't speak, but

ch. ends p. 156

stood gulping and looking from one face to the other. Presently he recovered sufficiently to say: "I'm certainly much obliged to you, Mr. B——, but how on earth did you get them? Some 'con' muster 'touched' me for them, and I certainly thought they were gone for good."

"Can't you guess how I got them?" asked the superintendent.

The guard looked perplexed for a moment, and then his eyes changed. He regarded "Cockey" questioningly.

"Yes, 'Cockey' dipped you for them," said the superintendent. "Of course, I can report him for it and have him jacketed, and of course you can do it if you want to, but if I were you I'd think this thing over and see if you can't treat the men a little better from now on. I've had more trouble from your section than from any other part of the mill, and I don't believe the men are any worse there than they are anywhere else."

The guard swallowed two or three times, struggling with the impulse that had assailed him. Finally he turned to "Cockey."

"This is a new thing for me to say to a 'con,'" he blurted out, "but I got to hand it to you; you're all right. We'll see if we can't get along better after this."

Of course, the story was too good to keep. It got out and the guard was subjected to a great deal of chaffing. He took it good-naturedly, however, and from that day he was "Cockey's" friend, and when "Cockey's" term expired he got him a position on a steamer sailing for Australia, where he belonged.

This incident is not without displeasing features, but it occurred just as related, and the guard, without sacrificing a particle of dignity or respect, was the friend as well as the keeper of the prisoners from that day.

Smoky had been in the habit of coming to the cell at night with a sack of choice tobacco, and I had frequently wondered where he got it. The prisoners receive a ration of cheap tobacco each week, and are permitted to purchase a limited quantity through the commissary, if they have the money to their credit. But the regular issue, as well as the purchased article, is a standard brand, and to have any other kind of tobacco is a breach of the rules, indicating crookedness.

Although I wondered at Smoky always having this choice brand of tobacco, I knew enough not to ask him where he got it. That is the one unpardonable offense in the penitentiary, asking another man, "Where did you get it?" when he shares a contraband article with you. But one night Smoky voluntarily told me where he was getting this tobacco.

"A funny thing happened in th' mill t'day," he began. "Of course, y'r've wondered where I was gettin' this weed. Well, I've killed th' goose what laid th' golden egg, an' I'll have t' rustle up some new leak now. Y'r know big Jim S——?" he inquired, naming one of the guards, a big, good-natured fellow.

I nodded.

"Well, he was in th' habit o' carryin' his terbaccer in th' side pocket o' his coat, an' I was in th' habit o' helpin' m'self t' it ev'ry two 'r three days. I often wondered why he didn't get next. He'd come inter th' mill in th' mornin' with a full sack o' weed in his pocket, an' at night it'd be gone.

"But he never seemed t' get wise. Th' next mornin' he'd have another sack an' act 's if he never missed th' one I got. Him an' me 're great friends, y'r know, an' it used t' hurt m' conscience at first, but after a time I got so that when I saw him come in in th' mornin' with a fresh sack I considered it as mine, an' before noon it would be. But it's all off now. I queered th' game m'self.

"This mornin' Jim came up t' me an' says, 'Say, Smoky, I jus' got hip t' somethin'; there's some guy touchin' me f'r m' terbaccer right along. I been wonderin' where it was goin'. I knew I didn't smoke it, but I never thought I was bein' 'touched' f'r it. Yesterday I tried a scheme. I came in with a new sack in m' pocket on purpose, an' at noon it was

ch. ends p. 156

gone; an' I didn't have m' coat off all mornin'. So it's a dead shot somebody's touchin' me f'r it. Now, I don't want t' git nobody in trouble, but I would like to ketch th' feller what's gettin' it, an' I've got a pretty good scheme.'

"Of course I listened t' all this sympathetic like, an' said it was a dirty shame, an' all that, an' then I asked him what his scheme was.

"'Well, I'm goin' to put this new sack in m' coat pocket an' leave th' string hangin' out, so's ev'rybody can see it. But I got a safety pin here, an' we'll pin th' string t' th' linin' of th' pocket, an' of course when the guy tries t' get th' sack he'll get th' surprise o' his life instead, an I'll nail him.'

"'Fine,' I says, pretendin' t' warm up t' th' plan. 'Some mutt 'll fall f'r that, sure's y'r born.' But o' course I was laughin' up my sleeve all th' time.

"Well, th' funny part o' it was I helped him pin th' sack o' weed inter his pocket. But instead o' pinnin' th' sack itself I pinned th' string, lettin' th' end hang out so's ev'rybody could see it. He was tickled t' death, an' put his hand down an' felt th' sack, an' then started hikin' up and down th' aisle. Ev'ry once in a while he'd go an' stand close t' some feller's loom an' throw his side pocket up toward th' guy an' look th' other way. Then he'd go back in th' aisle an' walk a few steps an' take a side glance down t' see if th' string was still there. Th' play was too good t' keep t' m'self, an' I put most of th' gang next. Ev'rybody was pretendin' t' work, but they was all watchin' Jim.

"Say, it was great. He'd go up t' a guy an' rub all around him, an' bump him, an' look th' other way, an' leave his coat hang loose on that side, an then he'd mosey off an' take a gander t' see if th' string was still there. This kept up f'r a couple of hours, an' I began t' see that Jim was gettin' desperate. Gener'ly a man don't want t' be 'touched,' but Jim was jus' dyin' t' have somebody try t' lift that sack o' ter-baccer. I was afraid m'self that some mutt 'd try it an' spoil ev'rything, but nobody did. Along 'bout 11 o'clock I went over t' 'Roguey' Smith's loom an' put him next. 'When he comes around again, 'Roguey,' I says, 'get it; it's pretty near dinner time.'

"Pretty soon Jim strolled up t' 'Roguey' an' stalled around, lookin' at th' ceilin' an' all that, an' 'Roguey' goes inter th' pocket with his loom scissors an' cuts th' string below th' pin an' yaffles th' sac. 'Nice day, ain't it, Jim?' he says, an' then shoots round back o' his loom. Jim hung around a few minutes and then walked off. When he got in th' aisle he glanced down, an' there was th' string still there. Of course, we all knew what had happened, an' was watchin', hopin' he'd put his hand down an' feel f'r th' sack. I guess it must 'a' been one o' them cases o' mental telegraphin' 'r somethin' like that. Jim walked t' th' end of th' aisle an' then started back, twirlin' his cane an' whistlin' an' lookin' innocent like, an' then all o' a sudden he puts his hand down t' feel f'r th' sack.

"Say, I wish y'r could 'a' seen th' look on his face when he got wise. But I'll give him credit f'r presence o' mind. He tumbled in a second, smiled t' himself an' walked right on. Th' gang had been hopin' that he'd do th' clown act, turn his pocket inside out, an' all that, but he didn't. Pretty soon he moseyed up t' where I was. I pretended t' be workin' 's if I was gettin' wages.

"'Say, Smoky,' he says, 'how much longer have y'r got?'

"'Thirteen months,' says I. 'Why?'

"'Well, I'm goin' t' throw up m' job when you go, an' we'll open up a detective office, f'r we're certainly th' candy kids when it comes t' that kind o' work; we've got Sherlock Holmes backed clean inter th' river.'

"'How's that?' says I, all innocent like.

"And then he took me t' one side an' showed me th' cut string. I looked at it close, an' then I looks up at him an' says: 'Cut with a pair o' scissors by a man with two hands an' dressed in a striped suit. Call in Watson at once; but whatever y'r do don't let th' perlice department know. I'll dispatch

ch. ends next p.

a telegram t' Paris immejiately, an' we'll leave on th' next train f'r th' city.'

"He took this all right an' seemed t' see th' joke. After he was gone I went over t' 'Roguey' an' got th' sack o' terbaccer, an' at noon I gave it back t' Jim.

"'Where'd y'r get it?' he asked.

"'Never mind,' I says, 'only y'r won't be 'touched' no more, Jim.'

"This afternoon I passed th' word t' th' gang t' leave Jim's terbaccer alone, so it's up t' me now t' look up another mark."

While Smoky had been beguiling us with this tale I had heard a whistle. It sounded like a boat whistle, and as soon as he finished I asked him about It.

"Did you hear that whistle a few minutes ago, Smoky?" I inquired. "I have heard it several times at night. What is it?"

"Oh, ain't y'r got next t' that yet?" he replied. "Why, that's th' *Caroline*, th' boat that brings th' beans an' things here. An', say, th' guy what owns her, Cap'n Leale, is a prince. Ain't y'r never heard of him? He's always doin' somethin' f'r us cons—gettin' fellers jobs when they go out an' helpin' 'em along afterward. An' don't y'r remember th' fresh fruit we had five 'r six times las' summer? Well, he brought that. He gets it from th' commission merchants on Saturday nights, when it 'd spoil before Monday, an' brings it over here. There is one right guy that y'r certainly ought t' know. But what gets me is how he stays with it. He's been thrown down by twenty dif'rent guys, an' yet he comes right back an' helps th' next feller that asks him.

"But it's nearly 9 o'clock. I can tell by th' way things are quietin' down; let's turn in. I'll tell y'r more about th' Cap'n some other time. I wonder how th' poor Kid is t'night? Jim S—— was awful good t' him in th' mill, an' he'd 'a' enjoyed hearin' about him."

14

After eighteen months in the jute mill I was sent for by the turnkey one morning and assigned to work in the clothing room, where incoming and outgoing prisoners are dressed, and where those undergoing sentence draw their supply of clothes. The assignment was a complete surprise to me. I had not asked for a change of work, not because I did not want it, but because I did not think there was any chance of my getting it. There were too many men who had been in prison much longer and who were more deserving than I. I knew scores of men in the jute mill who had worked there year after year, some of them for ten or twelve years, and many of whom had applied for other work.

Theoretically, a man is supposed to get a "job" after he has given faithful service in the mill for a number of years and if his record has been clean otherwise. But seniority in point of service did not seem to have much weight in those days. Men were given the choice positions indiscriminately, and prisoners with a "pull" did not go to the jute mill at all, but were assigned to the dining rooms or other "soft" places. Of course, this led to ill-feeling.

Men who had worked hard and faithfully for years quite naturally resented seeing a new prisoner given easy employment and mollycoddled by the officials. At present each prisoner must spend at least six months in the jute mill, and

The San Quentin Clothing Room circa 1919

a consistent method of giving the "old-timers" the first chance at other work is followed. This is no more than right, and it certainly tends to make the prison discipline better. Once the body of men feel that the officials play no favorites they respect and have confidence in them accordingly.

Of course, there are exceptions. Certain individuals imagine they are more deserving than the others and think they are dealt with harshly because they are compelled to work in the jute mill. But so long as the jute mill is there, save when a prisoner is sick, I believe every man should do his share of work in it.

At the time I was assigned to the clothing room, it was under the supervision of the turnkey, a small, spare man who chewed a cigar all day and didn't say much. In a few brief sentences he acquainted me with the nature of my duties. I was to keep account of all supplies received and issued and remain on duty in the clothing room all day.

"You will get up half an hour before the bell rings in the morning, and you are now on the second lockup," he informed me. "You will also move into a single cell and eat in the 'Red Front.'"

There were a number of other perquisites that went with the job, and the contrast to my previous way of living was marked. It was almost like getting a pardon. At the same time I regretted leaving Smoky and my other cellmates. True, it had been miserable and unhealthy in that small "tank" with four other men, and a "single" cell was considered a great privilege, but I had grown attached to them, and familiarity with the discomforts of the "tank" had bred indifference.

But when I went to the "Red Front" at noon and ate better food, served on "outside" tableware, with a tablecloth and with permission to talk during the meal, I could not help feeling elated. Still, there was no element of self-glorification in my feelings.

It is a peculiar fact that a great many of the men who succeed in getting office or bon-ton employment at San Quentin

ch. ends p. 170

immediately hold themselves superior to their fellows, some of them even going so far as to strut and patronize.

I made up my mind that first day that the fact of my promotion should not alter my relations with anyone, a resolution to which I easily adhered during all the years that followed, and which can be attested by the thousands of men who came and went subsequent to that time—without exception.

I deem this explanation necessary at this point, because a few persons who don't know anything about the facts—how often persons of superficial knowledge or no knowledge of certain conditions are prone to assume the right to judge—have been inclined to criticize adversely. I have been accused of self-righteousness. Nothing could be more galling.

The first "fish" who came in after I went to work in the clothing room was No. 19723, a condemned prisoner from Sacramento. As he stepped into the room in charge of the turnkey's assistant I was instructed how to measure him for his clothes. The man whose place I was to take—he had three days left to serve on a three-year sentence—then asked the new arrival how long a sentence he had received. The man made no reply, but smiled wanly.

"He's for over across," said the officer who had him in charge, nodding toward the condemned row.

At first I did not comprehend what was meant, but when I saw the serious look which replaced the smile that had wreathed my predecessor's face as he had asked the question I knew. To say that I was aghast is putting it mildly. It was like a sudden blow in the face.

I had given no thought to the fact that I should come into such close relationship with men who were destined for "the rope," and it seemed an inauspicious beginning in my new duties. By what strange freak of chance had it come about that I should be assigned to the clothing room just in time to measure and give a condemned man his prison clothes? I didn't like it. It made me uncomfortable. I felt

#19723

18861

19723

Aug 10th 1902
Age 21
Death
Kentucky
Second Term
Same as S.Q. 18861

19723
Chas Wardrip
Murd 1st Deg.
Sacto

18861

January 27th 1901
Age 19
1 Year
Elaine

18861
Fred Clark
Burglary
Modera

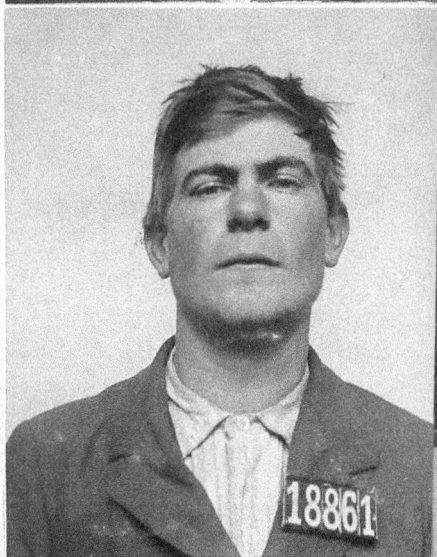

Name   Chas Wardrip
No.   19.723   2 T.
County   Sacramento
Crime   Mur 1 Deg.
Term   DEATH
Received   Aug 10-02
Discharged
Remarks

resentful. Somehow I felt like a *particeps criminis*[1]—a cog in the murder machine. I remember a slight nausea and an impulse to "throw up the job." But it passed—that "Red Front" meal was still undergoing the pleasing process of assimilation, and it had been the first approach to a "square meal" in eighteen months.

This is merely the old, old story. One man's meat must ever be another man's poison. I deluded myself with the moth-eaten sophistry,[2] "If I don't do it someone else will; and I'm not to blame because they have sent this man here to be hanged."

After he had gone to the bathroom, still in charge of the officer, who watched every move, I turned to the short-termer.

"Does this happen very often?" I asked.

"Oh, no. Maybe once a month. We get ten or twelve men for 'the rope' in a year, but most of 'em beat it on appeal; they don't hang more than three or four out of every twelve. You don't want to mind a little thing like that; you'll soon get used to it, and you'll see lots worse. Wait till some of these guys come up out of the dungeon after a week in the jacket. Seeing a condemned man is nothing alongside of that."

Later that day I learned what the condemned man had done.

In company with a boy he had burglarized a residence at Sacramento, the boy being left outside to watch. The man of the house came home unexpectedly and caught the boy on the front porch and tried to hold him while calling for the police. Wardrip—the condemned man—had heard the scuffle and had rushed to the boy's assistance. The property owner had paid no heed to the command that he desist, and Wardrip shot him, both he and the boy escaping in the dark. When the police arrived they found the wounded man lying on the porch. He made a broken statement of what had

---

[1] Translated from Latin: An accomplice in crime.
[2] A plausible but misleading or fallacious argument.

occurred and then died. The city had been scoured for the culprits, but in vain.

About two months afterward a man undergoing a sentence of thirty days at Salt Lake City for vagrancy told his cellmate that he was the man who had committed the murder at Sacramento a few weeks before.

It is surprising how frequently this occurs. Men with a price over their heads have done this same thing time and time again, and always with the same result. There seems to be something in the deadly monotony of a cell that unlocks the innermost recesses of a man's mind. Wardrip told his cellmate, a stranger, a bird of passage, what he had done. The cellmate promptly told the jailer. Communication was had with the Sacramento officials and a man was sent on with requisition papers. Too late, Wardrip tried to deny that he was the man, but he had divulged little details that only the murderer could know. Other evidence was gathered against him—some of the proceeds of the burglary were found in his possession, I believe. The officials tried in every conceivable way to make him tell who the boy was, but he remained mute on this point to the end. He was tried and convicted and sentenced to be hanged.

But I also learned that his case had been appealed. It would be several months at least before the sentence could be carried out, and there was a possibility of a reversal of the judgment. That made me feel better.

My first week in the clothing room was an interesting experience. I learned many new facts concerning the prison and made a number of new acquaintances. While working in the jute mill I had frequently endeavored to learn what the population of the prison was, but had never been able to get anything closer than an estimate. The men in the mill have no means of knowing such things.

But the clothing room was directly connected with the turnkey's office, where the official records are kept and where the "census chart" is revised each night. There were 1,450

ch. ends p. 170

prisoners on hand. This was in the fall of 1902. At present the population is close to 2,000.

The method of "receiving" new prisoners interested me at first, but I soon became indifferent to it. The Sheriff, or Sheriffs—sometimes two officers accompany a prisoner to the penitentiary—first delivered the commitment to the captain of the yard. This officer, upon satisfying himself that the papers were in order, would authorize the turnkey to receive and "put through" the new arrival.

But when two or three new prisoners arrived coincidently the Sheriff or Sheriffs would be called into the turnkey's for the purpose of identifying their respective charges. This is necessary to prevent exchange of identities. Prisoners have been known to adopt each other's names while on the way to the penitentiary.

An interesting case of this kind occurred some years ago in Pennsylvania. Two men were on their way to prison, handcuffed together and in charge of a deputy sheriff. While on the journey they concocted the plan of exchanging identities.

The deputy who had them in charge merely knew that he had John Smith and William Jones; Smith to be confined for ten years and Jones for two years. When they arrived at the prison Jones answered to the name of Smith, assuming the ten-year sentence, and it was taken for granted that the other man—the real Smith—was Jones. At the expiration of two years Smith, who had been committed for ten years by the court, was discharged. Then Jones, who had been entered on the register as Smith, ten years, protested that his time was up, that a mistake had been made in entering him as Smith, and that he had received a two-year sentence.

While in prison he had kept himself as inconspicuous as possible, and had been known exclusively by his prison number. Investigation proved his contention to be correct, and it was impossible to establish collusion between him and the real Smith. After a short litigation the prison authorities were compelled to release him. Meanwhile the real Smith had disappeared and he has never been captured.

After the new arrival has been identified he is subjected to a thorough "frisking." Everything which he may have in his pockets is placed on a desk before him, the money and valuables by themselves, and he is then required to sign an "inventory" which states the amount of money and the nature of the valuables. He is then escorted to the clothing room, where he is measured to ascertain what size clothing he requires. While this clothing is being branded he is taken to the bathroom, where he is compelled to strip in the presence of an officer and is subjected to further examination, first to see that he has no contagious skin disease, second to make sure that he has nothing concealed in the crevices and hollows of his body. In case of eczema the physician is called to examine him, and, if necessary, he is taken to the hospital.

If his clothing is worth saving it is taken to another room and thoroughly searched. If it is not worth saving it is stuffed into a sack and carried to the furnace and burned. A great deal of care has to be exercised to see that no "citizen's" clothing gets out of the possession of the proper custodian.

Experience has made it imperative that all clothing taken from new prisoners and placed in stock shall be very carefully examined. Some years ago the "dope" fiends learned that the clothing of incoming prisoners was not subjected to close scrutiny; that it was merely taken to the supply room and placed in stock to be given to some discharged prisoner in lieu of a new suit. Many discharged prisoners prefer secondhand clothing; it does not make them so conspicuous.

A clever case of smuggling resulted from this lax system. One of the bushelmen in the tailor shop sent word, by an outgoing prisoner, to a friend who was in the County Jail at San Francisco, awaiting sentence for grand larceny, telling him to get a supply of morphine and sew it into the pads at the shoulders of his coat. This was done, and when the man arrived his coat was sent to the supply room for the usual

ch. ends p. 170

renovating process. The bushelman was on the watch for it and cut open the seams and got the "plant."

This occurred some time after "dope" had been "stamped out" of the prison. In a few days the old-line officers detected the presence of the poison—it was apparent in the actions of the men who were using it.

Arrests and squeezings in the jacket followed. "Confessions" were secured and more arrests were made. Finally the "investigation," through repeated "squealing," narrowed down to the man who had brought in the "dope." He was forced to divulge the plot. He was then sent to the "incorrigibles," where he remained for about eighteen months, and the State Board of Prison Directors forfeited his credits—that is, he will have to serve his sentence of seven years "solid."

The bushelman, who was serving twelve years, was deprived of two years' credits and otherwise punished. The other men involved were also punished. The portion of the morphine still unused was located, through "confessions," and destroyed. Since then all clothing taken from incoming prisoners is subjected to a very careful examination, and its identity as having belonged to a certain individual confused, by delay in sending it to the tailor shop and otherwise, as much as possible.

On the second Sunday of each month the men who are to be discharged during the following month are sent for and are permitted to have their choice of this secondhand clothing. Those desiring new clothing are measured by the tailors and have a suit made to order from the cheap cassimere[3] which is bought by contract. Additional to secondhand suits there are secondhand hats and shoes and underwear. A great many men prefer a complete secondhand outfit. Men committed for one year may have their own clothing saved for them if they so desire.

A discharged prisoner's outfit costs the State less than

[3] A plain or twilled woolen or cotton cloth used for suits.

$7. If secondhand clothing is chosen the cost is reduced accordingly.

On the day of discharge the prisoner receives $5, and transportation by the cheapest route to the place from which he was committed. If he has twenty dollars or more to his credit at the office he does not get the $5. This rule has resulted in some clever manipulations on the part of prisoners about to be discharged.

I know one case, of recent occurrence, where a man had $23 to his credit at the office. Knowing that he would not receive the $5 provided by statute, he went to the prison dentist a few days before his term expired and had $4 worth of dental work done. This reduced his account to $19, and on the day of his discharge he received $24, and left with his face wreathed in smiles—happy over the dental work, I suppose.

Several times in the course of this narrative I have had occasion to mention the solitary ward, known as "the incorrigibles," at San Quentin, and as I go on I shall have occasion to mention it again. It will be of interest to you to know something about this place.

Twenty or thirty years ago the inmates of San Quentin were employed in the manufacture of furniture, principally of window and door sashes and blinds. A special building was constructed for this work, a building 400 feet long and four stories in height. This building is now used for various purposes. The ground floor contains the laundry, the new bathroom, the machine and carpenter shops and the tin shop. The second floor is used for storage and general utilities. On the third floor, the tailor and shoe shops are located, also the dormitory, known as "7 room," where 100 men, most of them "short timers," are confined at night. Owing to the overcrowded condition of the prison it became necessary to establish this dormitory—there are only 650 cells at San Quentin for nearly 2,000 prisoners.

The top floor of the "sash-and-blind" building is the place of tragedies. At one end is the "death chamber" and

ch. ends p. 170

execution room, where the hideous gallows stands gaunt and terrible, the dangling noose ever ready for the next victim—and incidentally for the edification of morbid visitors. Next to this somber place, and separated from it by a wall of masonry, is "8 room," another improvised dormitory, and at the extreme southern end, overlooking the walls and the jute mill roof, is the "incorrigibles."

Although I gained access to every nook and cranny of San Quentin prison during the years I remained there, especially after I went to work in the office, I have never been inside the "incorrigibles." In fact, save the men who have been confined there, I do not believe more than ten or twelve prisoners have ever been admitted to the place. Occasionally a plumber or carpenter is called up there to make repairs, but he is kept under guard, and is hurried through with the work as rapidly as possible. Even the man who delivers the meals does not go inside, but leaves his basket and cans on the door sill.

The ward consists of a room about forty feet long, with two rows of cells running down the center. These rows are built with their backs to each other, so that a prisoner confined in one of the cells cannot see his fellows. The windows are painted, so that it is impossible to see through them, and are heavily barred with timbers on the outside. Each cell has its individual toilet accommodations, and the men confined there are never permitted to leave the cell save for a bath, once a week. At different times there has been a system of giving the men exercise—that is, each man has been permitted to walk in the corridor alone for a short time each day. A special watch of three guards, working in eight-hour shifts, has charge of the ward, and the rule is that two of them must be there at all times. These men sleep and have their meals where they work, and the one on duty always has a fellow guard within calling distance, though he may be asleep. The third man has eight hours off duty meanwhile.

By talking with men who have been confined in the "incorrigibles" and by comparing the different statements

I believe I have authentic knowledge of some of the conditions that have obtained there, also some of the atrocities that have taken place. Under a former warden reading matter was denied, and the men were never permitted to come out of their cells. Their hair and beards ran riot, and they got a bath when it suited the vagarious[4] fancy of the jailer to give them the opportunity to take one. Men from whom it was desired to secure confessions were taken to the "incorrigibles" and jacketed, squeezed, and abused in various ways until they "came through." The reason for this was that men under torture in the "hole" could be heard screaming and pleading for mercy by the other prisoners. The "incorrigibles" is remote from the other parts of the prison; what takes place there is never known, and can always be denied if the victim tells of it. Only this week I talked with a man who underwent this form of torture in the "incorrigibles" less than three years ago. Upon meeting him I instantly recalled the occasion and the fact that he had been jacketed "upstairs." But I shall get to that story later.

For certain offenses, such as attempting to escape, murderous assault, continued insubordination, or certain unmentionable offenses men are sentenced to this solitary confinement for periods ranging from six months to ten years. Sometimes men have been taken to the "incorrigibles" and kept there for long periods without any of the other prisoners learning why. I recall such a case of recent occurrence. The man was taken from his cell in the dead of night and hurried away. Speculation was rife for a few days, but no one knew what he had done, and then he was forgotten. I believe he is still there. A man who was confined in "solitary" for five years told me that he only kept his reason by living "mentally." He spent his days thinking about everything save his condition, and perfected a life-saving device—perfected it mentally—which he subsequently had patented. One man, a lifer, was confined in the "incorrigibles" for many months

[4] Erratic and unpredictable.

ch. ends next p.

because he was insane. He was finally transferred to one of the asylums, where he now is.

Of course men undergoing this kind of punishment become very bitter and ugly, and several attempts have been made to escape. One man cultivated the acquaintance of his guard until they became quite friendly, and then tried to hang his custodian to the cell door. By some method of persuasion he succeeded in getting the guard to stand with his back to the door, whereupon he reached out and passed a cell-made garrote[5] around the man's neck and quickly twisted the ends about the bars of the door. The guard succeeded in crying out for assistance before his strangulation began, however, and was succored by his colleague before the prisoner could accomplish his purpose. The plan had been to choke the guard into insensibility, reach out and get the keys from his pocket, unlock the door and then release the other prisoners confined in the ward. Then the second guard, who was sleeping, was to be captured and bound. By removing the bars from one of the south windows the desperate men hoped to throw a line to the wall and escape over the heads of the night-guards in the yard below. It was a wild and stormy winter night when this attempted escape took place, and had not the guard succeeded in crying out before his voice was choked off, it is barely possible that the plan would have succeeded.

Occasionally innocent men are sentenced to solitary confinement, but not often. This is made possible by reason of placing credence in stool-pigeons—something which a wise warden will avoid. In the course of subsequent events I learned of one such case where the victim remained in the "incorrigibles" for five years. I shall recount it later.

---

[5] A cord or wire used for strangulation.

15

A Gubernatorial election occurred, resulting in the election of a new Governor. Of course, this meant a complete change in the prison management. The various offices at the State prisons are regarded as legitimate spoils for such supporters of the "party" as are in need of "jobs" after election, the Wardenship being the largest and juiciest of the "plums."

One morning about two months after the new Warden had taken charge I was busily engaged in marking clothes when a step sounded on the asphaltum pavement outside and a form darkened the doorway. I thought it was one of the "runners" or perhaps an unfortunate being brought in to "dress" for the "hole," and did not look up. But when I heard the voice of the Lieutenant of the Yard say, "Give this man a complete new outfit," I became interested. The order was an unusual one. I glanced up in response and experienced a decided shock.

Human beings are ever prone to the inevitable—there are some things that seem to be preordained. Some call it "the will of God"; others "kismet"; still others "karma." I prefer the latter term.

Certain moments, certain meetings in each of our lives stand out clear and distinct, marking a revolution in our thoughts and acts and outlook. Sometimes it is the meeting of a man and woman who see future worlds in each other's eyes; sometimes the initial contact of two men who are destined to fight out an instinctive hatred; sometimes two women who are to make or mar each other's future; or it may be the inception of any one of a score of tragedies or blessings. The fact remains that such moments, such meetings, come to all of us in some degree. This meeting of two convicts in the sordid clothing room of an antiquated and inhuman prison was such a moment. It was fraught with tensity.

Instantly, intuitively, I knew that I was gazing into the countenance of a man whose soul I was destined to understand, and from whom I was to receive, as well as to give, friendship and help. I did not think all this at the moment, but in a confused, nebulous, tentative sort of way I knew and felt it; a kind of super-conscious knowledge, such as we all experience at tense moments, though we seldom realize it. Though we were physical strangers, it seemed as if I were meeting someone whom I had known for ages.

One swift, penetrating glance and we had measured each other. Without a spoken word we had become intimately "acquainted." It bothered me for days. I did not understand it.

He was a thin young man of medium height, with long, straggly blonde hair and beard. He was garbed in a ragged suit of dirty stripes. His steel-gray eyes blinked as though the light hurt them, and yet they were very alert, and there was a defiance, an indomitableness in their depths. They protruded slightly, as the eyes of persons who have suffered so frequently do. The lines radiating from the corners bespoke mental as well as physical distress, as did the spasmodic twitching of his mouth. His skin was akin to the color of a thirsty road and his garments looked as though he had not had them off for months—the knees and elbows bulged and the frayed edges of the coat curled under. I was conscious of a warring within me. I had not yet learned who he was, and still I knew I was gazing at a human creature who had been through hell.

All the concentrated blindness, indifference, and horror

of "man's inhumanity to man" was standing before me. My own punishment paled into insignificance—it was nothing. This man was an evidence of what others suffered.

I did not regard him as an individual, but as a composite, a composite of all that was cruel, heartless, and unjust. All this passed through my mind like a flash. I did not think it; I suffered it. I seemed to have had a moment of travail. Something had been born within me, something new and strange and powerful. I knew from that moment that it had been necessary for me to live. I had never felt it before.

And then, like a ghost from the past, a picture of Rip Van Winkle flashed upon me. Poor old Rip, coming back to find himself an anachronism, a man who had been dead and buried for years.

"This man will fit you out," said the Lieutenant, turning to his charge. "When you're dressed report around at the Captain's office. That is, if you remember where it is," he added with a grin.

"Treat Morrell right," he admonished as he withdrew from the room and left us together.

Morrell! The notorious "Ed" Morrell about whom I had heard so much, and who had been confined in the "incorrigibles" for five years!

The majority of the prisoners, as well as the freemen, believed him innocent of the offense with which he had been charged and for which he had been subjected to such awful punishment. So this man was Ed Morrell! No wonder I had been agitated.

As the Lieutenant disappeared, Morrell smiled wanly and sank wearily into a chair. It had fatigued him to come across the yard from the place where he had been buried for so many years, away from the sun and air and human companionship.

"So they have let you out at last," I said, removing the clay pipe, which I had been smoking, from my mouth and extending my hand. I did not know I had the pipe in my

ch. ends p. 182

mouth. I have no recollection of it. Morrell told me about it afterward. He said it looked so "funny" after his long siege in the semi-darkness of "solitary."

"Is there any chance to get a bath?" he inquired, eagerly. "I feel as if I'd like to wash off some of the hell."

He spoke in a whisper.

"What's the matter—a cold?" I asked.

I stepped close to hear his reply.

"No. There ain't much chance of taking cold where I've been. I don't know what it is, but my voice has gone back on me. I can't talk out loud any more. It's been getting worse for the last two years. I tried myself out on the guard once a month or so. If I had stayed up there much longer I'd have lost it entirely. But I'll get it back, now that I've got a chance to use it again."

I looked at him, appalled. "You don't mean to say you've lost your voice?" I inquired, incredulously.

"It speaks for itself, don't it?" he rejoined, a sparkle of humor lighting his tired eyes.

My first impression had been more that of surprise than anything else, but as the full significance of the truth burst upon me I felt as though I had come upon the greatest horror of my life.

Here was a man who had suffered for five years, innocent of the offense charged against him, and solitude had stolen his voice. The condition might be chronic. It might grow worse. Perhaps the day was not far distant when he would be a mute. Yet it was apparent that he was eager to talk, that the suppression of the years was boiling for vent. Again I felt that I had entered upon a new epoch of life. The future loomed big and beckoning.

"Well, do I get that bath, or have you fallen asleep?" asked the man with a stage-whispery voice.

The question aroused me from my abstraction.

"You bet you do," I responded; "but first let me measure you for some new rags."

He arose from the chair and stood dejectedly while I took the necessary measurements, and then I led the way to the back room, where the bathtub was located. I started to return to the front room for the purpose of marking his clothes, but he stopped me.

"Wait a minute," he urged. "Wait and see what a man looks like after five years in hell. I was a husky when I went up there, hard as nails and full of red blood, but look at me now."

While speaking he had dropped off the outer rags, and a moment later stood nude beside the tub of warm water. The enormity of what he had suffered could not have been more forcibly demonstrated. His limbs were horribly emaciated, the knee, elbow, and shoulder bones stood out like huge knots through the drawn and yellow skin, while his ribs reminded me of the carcass of a sheep hanging in front of a butcher's establishment. The hollows between them were deep and dark. I thought of the picture I had seen of the famine-stricken wretches of India.

"I weighed 160 pounds five years ago," he remarked, bitterly. "What do you suppose I weigh now?"

"About 95, I should say, judging from your looks," I replied, dropping my voice to a whisper to conform with his. "If they'd kept you up there much longer it 'd been curtains."

"Curtains!" he flashed back at me, clinching his thin fingers, his intensity so strong that the whisper in which he uttered the word took on a note of ordinary speech—like a momentary struggle between his natural voice and the ghost that was left of it—"Curtains! Not on your life. I made up my mind from the first day that they wouldn't get me. I'd 'a' lived it out if it 'd been twenty years instead of five."

He was getting into the tub as he spoke, but stopped and turned toward me.

"Maybe I oughtn't to talk this way to you," he said. "God knows I've seen enough human treachery to last me a lifetime, and you may be a spotter for the bunch, feelin' me out. But no, I know you're not, and I'll prove it by saying

ch. ends p. 182

that I've lived with one idea, an idea that I'll carry out if it takes the rest of my life. Every man responsible for what I've been through has got to pay for it. No violence, mind you; no bloody 'Diamond Dick' revenge; but I've just willed that way. I've dreamed and dreamed, day after day and night after night, that they get all that's coming to them, and as sure as mud is dirty they will. You wonder why I'm so thin. The rest of the bunch up there ain't that way—in fact, most of them get fat. The only one that don't is Jake. I'll tell you lots about him that they don't know when we get a chance. He's just like me; he don't live with his body at all; he's just alive mentally up there. That will make any man grow thin."

Dramatically Morrell laid the tip of his forefinger against his temple, bending the first joint backward and holding it there in the intensity of his feelings.

"The rest of me has been dead for years. I've been living from my neck—yes, from my ears up. Sometimes I've been living even higher. I seemed to be out of this broken-down carcass entirely, damn them!" He ended in a kind of gurgle, with a minor sound like that of escaping steam. Then he stepped into the tub.

"What are those scars on your back?" I asked as he sank onto his knees in the water.

"Scars," he laughed, sardonically, "Scars? Those ain't scars. They're only the marks where the devil prodded me. I was in the jacket, cinched up so that I was breathing from my throat when he came and tried to make me 'come through' and when I sneered at him he kicked me over the kidneys. I don't know how many times he kicked; the first kick took my breath away and I saw black, but after they took me out of the sack I couldn't get up, and I had running sores down here for months afterward. I ain't right down there now; I've got a bad rupture, and sometimes it feels as if there was a knife being twisted around inside of me. It wouldn't be so bad if they'd got me right, but to give a man a deal like that dead wrong is hell, let me tell you."

I remained silent. There was nothing to be said. But I did some thinking. I wondered where God had been—and then laughed. Sacrilegious? Call it that if you wish. It's just what happened.

Morrell floundered in the water, splashing it over the sides of the tub and laughing like a schoolboy.

"This is great!" he exclaimed; "it's almost as good as being free again."

I left him laughing and returned to the clothing room to mark his clothes. A few minutes later he had them on, and I helped him dry his hair and beard. His hair hung down on his shoulders and had a tendency to curl, and his beard covered the second button of his shirt. When he was all ready I escorted him to the barbershop for the "shearing" which the Lieutenant had mentioned.

As we stepped into the barbershop there was a noticeable air of expectancy. The word had passed through the prison that the new Warden had released "Ed" Morrell from "solitary." All but one of the half dozen barbers were strangers to Morrell. They had been committed to the prison after his siege of solitary confinement had begun. The one exception was old Frank, a lifer with twenty years' service behind him, and the owner of the parrot which had scraped an acquaintance with me the day I arrived. "Old Frank" was the "boss" of the barbershop. He was not required to shave any of the "customers"; his duties were to see that the other men did the work properly and to maintain order. But when Morrell stepped into the shop he arose from his chair and extended his hand.

"Hello, Ed," he exclaimed; "I'm glad to see you back. How is it up there on Mars, anyway?"

And then, without waiting for a reply, he continued: "I claim the honor of fixin' you up. I ain't shaved a man for two months, but I sure want to shave you and cut that wool."

When Morrell made a terse response in a whisper "Old Frank" stepped back and regarded him with amazement.

ch. ends p. 182

"What's the matter with your bazoo?" he asked.

"Oh, I've got a cold," replied Ed, winking at me. "Let's see what you can do with this wool."

The old barber got out a fresh cloth and tucked it in about Ed's neck. Then, quite suddenly, he stepped out in front of the chair and regarded his man excitedly.

"Say, fellars!" he exclaimed, "come here a minute. Who does Morrell here remind you of?"

The rest of the barbers came with alacrity and stood before the chair. They had a natural curiosity to see Morrell at close quarters, anyway, and "Old Frank's" query had aroused their curiosity.

"Before I spoil it, who does he look like?" repeated the old man, standing on foot in his impatience.

A number of guesses were ventured, but "Old Frank" only laughed. I found myself regarding Morrell with renewed interest. Something in the way the light fell on his face and the light-colored cloth tucked in under his chin made him look ethereal. His features are of the refined type, anyway, and I found an elusive answer to "Old Frank's" question dancing back and forth in my brain, but I was unable to put it into words.

The old barber waited a few minutes smiling down at the face before him.

"What are you laughing at, Frank?" asked Morrell in a tragic whisper, an effort to be patient apparent in his inflection.

"Do you want me to tell you?" rejoined the old lifer, becoming serious.

"Certainly I do," replied Morrell. "You're making me feel like some kind of a freak on exhibition. Let's have it."

"Old Frank" took a step backward and a hush fell over the little group.

"With all due respect, Ed, you're the finest living picture of Jesus Christ that I've ever seen, so help me God. And, Ed," he added, hastily, his voice breaking, "we're all Jesus Christs, if we'd only remember it. This ain't no time to preach. I know what you've been through, but you don't look the part of a bad man, and I know you're not. Let's all get together and see if we can't play the game better."

I was moved. I wanted to "beat it." But a voice behind me served better than retreat.

"'Old Frank's' got 'em at last," it said. "The religious bug has crawled into his skypiece and found good feedin's. Poor old Frank! And I thought he was an ironclad."

The circumstances which led up to Morrell's conviction and his sentence to prison for the term of his natural life were both romantic and unique. While still in his teens he met and became infatuated with the daughter of "Chris" Evans, chief of the well-known Evans and Sontag band of robbers which terrorized the central counties of California some years ago. At the time of this meeting Morrell was impressionistic and full of big ideas. And even after all the years of tragic vicissitudes that have since elapsed he is still young in spirit and still an impressionist. He is distinctively of the Golden Fleece type. With him the future ever holds the possibility of earthly Nirvana.

But during all my intimate relations with Morrell I have never been able to prevail upon him to relate the story of that part of his life. Whenever any mention is made of his adoration of Miss Evans he abruptly changes the subject. It seems to be a closed and sacred chapter with him. All I know is that she was young, beautiful, vivacious, and had a love for her father that almost amounted to worship. And this filial attachment was not without good reason. Evans worshiped her in turn, and was a good and kind father.

At the time Morrell met this girl her father was confined in the County Jail at Fresno, convicted of murder in having killed one of the posse which pursued him after he had committed train robbery, and under sentence of life imprisonment at the Folsom State prison.

When Morrell learned this fact he immediately

ch. ends p. 182

determined to hold up the jail and effect Evans' release. By watching the jail Morrell learned that Evans was getting his meals from a restaurant, and this instantly suggested a plan whereby he could gain access to the place and carry out his intention. Waiting for a dark and rainy night, Morrell put on a waiter's apron and hurried into another restaurant also close to the jail. He ordered a tray of food, which was hastily prepared for him, and then made his way to jail.

It was a few minutes before the regular waiter was due with Evans' evening meal, and upon seeing a man in a white apron with a tray in his hands the jailer immediately opened the door. Morrell had two loaded revolvers on the tray, covered with a napkin, and his plan was to have Evans seize these revolvers as the tray was presented to him and then hold up the jailer. But as they advanced toward the corridor where Evans was confined the jailer suddenly discovered that it was a strange waiter and stopped to make inquiries. Morrell instantly realized the gravity of the situation. Should the jailer lift the napkin and discover the revolvers the plan would not only fail, but he would be caught in a trap. So, even as the jailer stopped, Morrell dropped the tray, whipped a revolver from his pocket and ordered the jailer to throw up his hands.

Completely surprised, the man did as he was ordered. Morrell then made the jailer turn his back while being relieved of his weapons and keys. He marched the man to the corridor where Evans was waiting and unlocked it. Then, taking the jailer with them to prevent an alarm, they passed out of the jail.

There were more than 100 prisoners confined in the jail at the moment, under sentences ranging from one day to life, but there was no thought of turning a horde of wrongdoers upon the public. This was certainly a mitigating circumstance in Morrell's favor, but he was never given any credit for it.

On gaining the street Morrell went on a few paces ahead, leading the way to where he had a team in waiting. Evans, with the jailer in charge, followed. A short distance from the jail they met the Chief of Police, accompanied by another man. Something made the chief suspicious and he endeavored to stop them. Without any parley[1] Morrell instantly held the chief up. At this moment Evans and the jailer came up and a brief struggle took place, the friend who was with the chief joining in.

The chief had managed to get his arms about Morrell's body and was holding him and calling for assistance. Evans ordered the chief to release his hold. He would not do so and Evans shot him. The two fugitives then made their way out of Fresno on foot, held up a team on the outskirts of the town and made for the hills, thirty or forty miles distant. They managed to elude the posses that were started out immediately behind them, and after two days of awful hardship gained the safety of the mountain.

Then commenced one of the most celebrated manhunts of modern times. After many skirmishes and fights in the mountains they were lured into a trap near Visalia[2] and surrounded. Evans parleyed for hours, but finally consented to surrender. The next day he was hurried to Folsom, where he had already been sentenced to life imprisonment. Morrell was placed in solitary confinement in the Fresno jail, and after two months of persistent efforts to sweat him, during which he suffered the various tortures of the third degree, the officials carried out their threat to railroad him for life to Folsom.

They had believed that he was cognizant of the detailed history of the Evans and Sontag gang and were determined that he should tell it. But he remained mute. His trial lasted three days, resulting in a conviction for robbery, and he was sentenced to imprisonment for life.

"How did they convict him of robbery?" you ask. Nothing

---

[1] Discussion or conference between enemies or opposing sides.
[2] A city situated in the San Joaquin Valley of California, about 230 miles southeast of San Francisco and 43 miles south of Fresno.

ch. ends p. 182

more simple. He had "robbed" the Chief of Police of his revolver while the chief had been holding him. He had reached down and taken it out of the chief's back pocket. True, he had not taken the weapon because of its intrinsic value—he simply wanted to prevent the chief from using it. The fact remained, however, that he had taken it, and with violence. He had also "robbed" the jailer.

The penalty for assisting a prisoner to escape was only ten years, while the penalty for robbery might be anything up to life. Therefore he was tried for robbery.

Morrell was taken to Folsom prison heavily ironed. The officers who delivered him told the prison officials that he was a very "bad man" and that he would be scheming to escape from the first day. This led to an especial espionage, and for the least little infraction of the rules he was reported at the office, called up and punished. For two years he alternated between the dungeon and the office, and then it was decided to transfer him to San Quentin. It is a peculiar fact that whenever it becomes necessary to transfer prisoners from one prison to the other the officials invariably pick out the worst characters they can find, or at least those whom they judge to be the worst characters. The opportunity to get rid of them is too tempting. It makes no difference that they will be a source of trouble at the other prison. And in my own experience I have seen a dangerous dement[3] transferred in this way and no word passed to the officers. Such a man transferred from Folsom to San Quentin killed two of his fellows before he was found to be insane and transferred to an insane asylum.

In being transferred to San Quentin "Ed" Morrell met the greatest tragedy of his life.[4]

[3] A person suffering from dementia.

[4] Ed recounts his own version of these stories in his 1924 book *The Twenty-Fifth Man: The Strange Story of Ed Morrell, the Hero of Jack London's "Star Rover."*

DISCHARGED 3-27-93

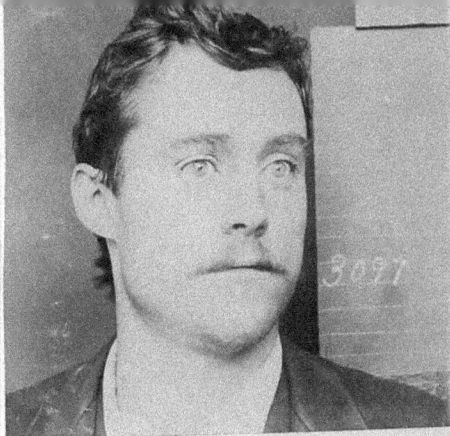

No. 3097
Name Ed. Morrell
County Fresno
Crime Robbery + prior
Term Life years.
Received Apl 17-94
Discharged
Remarks: 2d Term

May 18th 1896
Age 24
Life
Term dates from
April 17th 1894
Transferred from
Felton

16766
Ed Morrell
2d Term Same as
#14486
Robbery & Prior
Fresno

Height 5.6½
G'h Head 22½
B't Templ 5¾
L'h Nose 2
" Head 7⅝
McFing 4½
" Foot 10¾
"F.Arm 18½
"th Hand 3¾
G'h Ches. 35

14486
Edwd Marti
Grand Larcen
2½ years
San Bernard
Age 20
Pa.

Name Edward Morrell 2 T.
No. 16766.
County Fresno.
Crime Robbery + priors.
Term Life
Received May 18. 1896.
Discharged
Remarks transfd from Folsom #3097

16

During the first week following his release from the "incorrigibles" Morrell was permitted to remain in the yard and was not required to work. Then, greatly to the astonishment of everyone, the new Warden assigned him as head key-man, one of the most trusted and responsible positions which it is possible for a prisoner to hold. Such a thing was unheard of and speculation was rife.

It had always been the custom when a man came out of solitary confinement to assign him to the jute mill and keep him there. Only after a long service in the mill, with a perfect record, could a man who had been in the "incorrigibles" hope to get a trusted position, and even those who earned that consideration were always looked upon with a certain degree of suspicion and apprehension, and seldom got positions of any great trust.

The head key-man is the night sergeant's chief assistant. His duties consist in carrying the keys to the various tiers of cells after lockup and accompanying the sergeant on his rounds for the purpose of unlocking and locking the cell doors of such prisoners as may be on the second or subsequent lockup, the sergeant checking off each man on his "lockup board" as he enters his cell for the night and is locked in. The key-man also accompanies the night sergeant to the dungeon at regular hours, and is supposed to be available for any emergency that may arise, such as fire in any part of the prison, a fight in the cells, or a call to the hospital for the removal of a deceased prisoner to the morgue. No matter at what hour a man dies in the prison hospital his body is immediately removed to the morgue.

At 9 o'clock, when everyone save the lamplighter and one or two others is supposed to be locked in for the night, the key-man's duties are ended for the day, and he goes to his cell. But he must be up before the ringing of the bell in the morning to distribute the keys to the "unlock crew" and to see that each key is returned to its proper place afterward.

During the day he is on duty at the Captain of the Yard's office, assisting the Lieutenant of the Yard in taking prisoners to the "hole," running messages when the regular messengers are busy, helping to receive new prisoners—one of his duties being to search the new man in the presence of the turnkey—and otherwise making himself generally useful. It is an arduous position, requiring a man of good physique, and balanced mentality.

The opportunities for "lording" it over his fellow prisoners or doing "dirty work" for the officials are almost limitless. A good man in this position can accomplish a great deal toward making life more bearable for the unfortunates who break the prison rules; likewise a bad man can make life well nigh unbearable.

When it became definitely known that Morrell had been given this place—the incumbent having been paroled to leave in a few days—there was a flurry throughout the prison. The general verdict of the freemen was that the Warden was a "mutt" and that he would rue the day he had trusted a man like Morrell, while that of the prisoners was that Morrell had "stooled" his way out of "solitary" by divulging some contemplated "break" and had been given the key-man's job as an additional reward.

None of these conjectures and predictions proved true.

In my position at the clothing room, adjacent to the office,

I came into daily and nightly contact with Morrell, and I can say without qualification that I have never in my life met any man more kindly in heart, more fair in his estimates of others, or more capable of carrying out whatever his sense of justice tells him is right.

His own sufferings had made it possible for him to appreciate fully the sufferings of others, and time after time I saw him take chances that would have cost him his position, which even might have resulted in his being returned to "solitary" had they been known—invariably for the sole purpose of relieving the misery or extremity of a fellow-prisoner and without any possibility of selfish return.

Also he was, and still is, a thinker. A prisoner is not supposed to think, especially out loud. Thinking is always, or nearly always, taken as an indication of "criminosity" or an unbroken spirit.

To break a man's spirit seemed to be the principal object in those days. It is yet, to a large extent, though the present Warden at San Quentin is an exception. His treatment of prisoners indicates that he believes in developing, rather than crushing, them; that such traits as independence, initiative, and self-respect should be cultivated, not strangled.

Probably I learned more from "Ed" Morrell than from any other prisoner with whom I ever came in contact. True, I learned a great deal from Smoky, and in many ways Morrell reminded me of that "rough diamond." But Smoky was negative, while Morrell is positive.

In a few days after his assignment at the office Morrell began to take on flesh and regain his strength, and before the regular key-man's date of parole rolled around he had grasped every detail of his duties and was ready to step into the vacant place. His voice began to get stronger also, and although even now—after five years—it is still husky, in a short time he was able to carry on a conversation at a distance of ten or fifteen feet.

It was not until I had known him several months and we

had learned to understand and confide in each other that he told me the facts which had resulted in his being confined in "solitary" for five years. I had heard many versions of the affair—"the big night break," it was called—but had never been able to dovetail it together. There always seemed to be an absence of motive, a lapse, an element of impossibility, a missing link. I knew that "Sir" Harry Westwood Cooper,[1] a clever forger who had duped some of the best business men of San Francisco into believing he was an English nobleman before he was caught and committed to San Quentin, had been the arch traitor, and that his treachery had resulted in a dozen prisoners—many of them "lifers"—being charged with conspiracy to escape, for which they had been placed in solitary confinement and otherwise tortured, Morrell among them; but I had never been able to understand why Cooper himself had been likewise punished and deprived of his credits. It didn't seem plausible that a man who had exposed such a gigantic conspiracy for wholesale escape should have been punished along with the men whom he had "given away." I had never seen Cooper, at least not at that time, though he was subsequently returned to San Quentin for another forgery, or, rather, perjury growing out of a charge of forgery, and somehow I felt that he was unjustly accused, that there was a "darky in the fuel," as Smoky used to put it, that he had been made a scapegoat and that some other man concerned in the plot had been the real informer. But Morrell certainly disabused my mind of this charitable delusion. Gradually he gave me the history of the entire tragedy. But even then it was so complicated, confused, and incredible that I often found myself doubting. The story worried me and I sometimes found myself looking at Morrell with a certain degree of distrust. At last he seemed to sense this, and also the cause, so one night when everyone was locked up and we were in

---

[1] We have corrected the text using Cooper's real name. In the original, Lowrie used the fictitious (and not-too-dissimilar) name "Harry Eastwood Hooper," likely to avoid a libel or slander lawsuit—for reasons that will soon be made clear.

ch. ends p. 197

the office alone he recounted the affair from beginning to end. I shall endeavor to tell it just as he told it to me, using his own words as closely as memory permits.

"You must remember that when I was transferred to San Quentin from Folsom a lifer had little hope of ever getting out. Of course, there was the parole law, but you know how that was worked in those days. Maybe half a dozen men with the right kind of a pull would get out in a year, and a life-termer—well, he had about as much a chance of getting a parole as he had of becoming King of England. Naturally, I wanted to get out. I didn't want to stay in prison until I was an old man with one foot in the grave. I wanted a chance to live a man's life, as God, or whoever put me here, intended.

"On the way down from Folsom I did a lot of thinking. I knew there would be a strong knock registered against me here, but I made up my mind if they gave me half a chance I'd do the right thing and try to earn my way out on the square.

"Of course, I didn't feel as if I had done anything to deserve life—and I don't feel that way yet. If I'd gone into jail and released a prisoner in time of war I'd 'a' been a hero, but being a time of peace made me a desperate and dangerous criminal. Did you ever think of that?

"I had a friend in jail and I took the quickest and surest way to get him out, and that made me an outlaw, a man to be shot down on sight. I've tried to see the other side of it, too, and, of course, I know there has to be law and order, but if I was a judge I'd take a man's motives and all the circumstances into consideration before I handed a man life.

"God, just think what that means. It don't do anybody any good. I look around me every day and see young fellows doing it all, some of them for getting a few paltry dollars when they were up against it for a feed and a place to sleep, and—well, I'm surprised more of 'em don't jump off the tiers. But I'm getting away from my story.

"The day after I got here they sent to the mill after me and the captain took me into his private office. He sat down on the lounge and spread out a piece of paper on his knees, leaving me standing in the middle of the room.

"'Morrell,' he says, 'you might as well understand what you're up against from the start. Here's your punishment record at Folsom. You may think you're a bad man, but I want to tell you right now that the first time you bat an eye you'll think Folsom is a paradise alongside of this place.

"'No, no! Never mind,' he says, jumping up as I tried to speak. 'I'm doing the talking now. All you got to do is listen, and listen damn close. We're putting a special watch on you, and the first move you make you'll hit the hole so hard you'll think a cyclone's struck you.'

"I tried to speak again. Even after what he had said I wanted to tell him that I'd made up my mind to try to get along without trouble, but he stopped me again.

"'Go on back to your work,' he snarled. 'Cons don't do any talkin' here until I let them; understand?'

"Even after this I still wanted to talk, but I choked it down and just gave him one long look. Then I turned and swaggered out on to the porch, and right there and then all my good resolutions turned red. If that was the way he felt I'd meet him on his own grounds. I'd show him that if a con couldn't talk he could act, and I made up my mind to beat the place, or get killed trying it.

"Well, for a couple of weeks everything went along all right. I was lying low, studying the situation and feeling my way along with the other cons. Of course, I knew cons pretty well, and I knew I'd have to be damned careful who I talked to or who I took into my confidence. One day, I guess it was about a month after I got here, a guard pinched me for crowding in line and ran me up to the office. I hadn't done any crowding; it was some guy behind me, but he landed on me and wouldn't listen. As soon as the captain saw me he got excited.

"'So, here you are!' he said to me before the guard could speak. 'You can't behave yourself, hey? What has he done?' he asked, turning to the guard.

ch. ends p. 197

"'Pushing and shoving and making a disturbance in line,' says the guard. 'He's a bad actor, Captain, and I've had my eye on him for several days.'

"And then, without a word to me, the Captain turned to the Lieutenant, who was standing close by with his cane:

"'Dungeon; 48 hours,' he says, turning his back and walking off.

"Well, I knew it was no use resisting, and I went down meek as a lamb, but with hellfire bubbling inside of me. They slapped me into the dungeon, chained to the wall, and I stayed there two days on bread and water. All for nothing, mind you, and without a chance to defend myself.

"Of course, when I got out I had it in for the guard, and I never lost an opportunity to show him how I hated him. Every time he came around I glared at him and tried to show how much I despised him. Of course, that didn't get me anything, and finally it got so raw that he pinched me again.

"'What's the trouble now?' asked the Captain, as we came up on the porch.

"'Oh, this stiff is trying to stir up trouble all the time, and he keeps dog-eyeing me. He's the worst character on my section, Captain.'

"I knew it wasn't any use saying anything. In fact, I wouldn't have said anything for myself if I knew I was going to be hung the next minute. Johnnie noticed I was looking sullen, so he asked me for an explanation. He could tell by looking at me that I was raging inside, and I suppose he thought he'd get me to tear loose and get myself in worse. But I was onto his game, and just stood there without saying a word.

"'Well, an officer's addressing you,' he nagged, 'and when an officer speaks to you, you answer; understand? What you got to say for yourself?'

"Of course, that only made me hotter, and I knew if I opened my mouth I'd call that guard every name ever invented by a pirate sea captain. So I just stood and looked at him, pretending to smile, as if I was bored to death. I knew that would get the Captain's goat, and it did. He lifted his little cane as if he was going to hit me, expecting me to cringe or dodge, I suppose, but I just kept on smiling. With that he ordered the Lieutenant to put me in the hole for a week—'and see that he don't get too much bread and water,' he added, as I was led away.

"Well, this kept up for two or three months, and I spent most of the time chained to the wall in the dungeon, and then I got a tip that opened my eyes. A friend of mine, a guard who knew me before I ever got into trouble, was over in San Rafael in a saloon one night when this other guard, the one who had it in for me, came in.

"'How's things going at the prison?' asked the bartender.

"'Oh, pretty well. But we've got some mean customers over there now. I've got one of the —— —— —— —— in the hole right now. He's one of that Evans and Sontag crowd, and they killed a cousin of mine in the mountains, at least the gang did, a few years ago. My cousin was in a posse that was hunting them, and I'm taking it out of this fellow's hide.'

"When my friend came into the mill the next morning he looked me up and took me to one side and told me what he had heard. Of course, it made me crazy mad. At first I thought of getting a hammer or something and killing the guard who had dogged me, but I didn't. I made up my mind to give them a show first. So that afternoon I got passed to the Captain's office. He tried to stop me from talking to him, but I paid no attention and finally got him interested. That was one peculiar thing about the Captain—he imagined he was always giving everybody a square deal. I don't remember exactly what I said, but I told him what I knew, and how this guard had boasted that he was taking it out of my hide, and wound up by saying that the next time he bothered me I'd kill him so dead that the crack of doomsday wouldn't faze him.

"The Captain spoke kindly to me for the first time, but it was too late. He'd treated me like a dog, and what he'd done

ch. ends p. 197

couldn't be wiped out by one kind word, especially when I knew it wasn't from his heart and that he was eager to expose the guard and take the credit of having given a con a square deal. Oh, I read him like a book.

"The upshot of the whole thing was the guard was transferred from the mill to one of the outside posts, a Gatling post, and he never got another chance at me. But I was full to the neck with hate, and I was more determined than ever to make them dance to my music instead of me dancing to theirs. I felt as if I could stand alone against the whole world, and win out.

"And it was this feeling, brought on by having it thrown into me unjustly, that paved the way for the 'Sir' Harry Cooper deal.

"I was introduced to 'Sir' Harry Cooper by a forger that did time with me at Folsom. At first I took a dislike to him. There is a phony note in his voice and a kind of sizing-you-up expression in his eyes, something like you see in a pawn-broker's eyes. He's a slick one, and he fooled me. But he taught me one lesson, and that is always to follow the first impression I get of a man. Ever since that deal I've done that. If my first meeting with anyone tells me to look out, I look out. But his soft ways and his pretended interest in me got under my skin. Besides, he was thin and peaked looking, and you couldn't help feelin' kind of sorry for him. He had that I'm-a-gentleman-doing-time-hard air about him. You know the type.

"Well, for a few days he had me going south, and then I got his measure. A little chance remark dropped when he wasn't thinking put me wise to him, and I put him down as a guy that would do anything to get himself to the front and out of prison before his four years were up.

"That set me to thinking, and I made up my mind to use him. I had already hatched a scheme for beating the dump, and I needed a good forger. I'd show him how we could both beat it and I'd get him mixed into it so bad that he couldn't

14592

Jan 15. 1898.

Age 30.

3. Years

Eng

17592

H.W. Cooper

Forgery

San Francisco

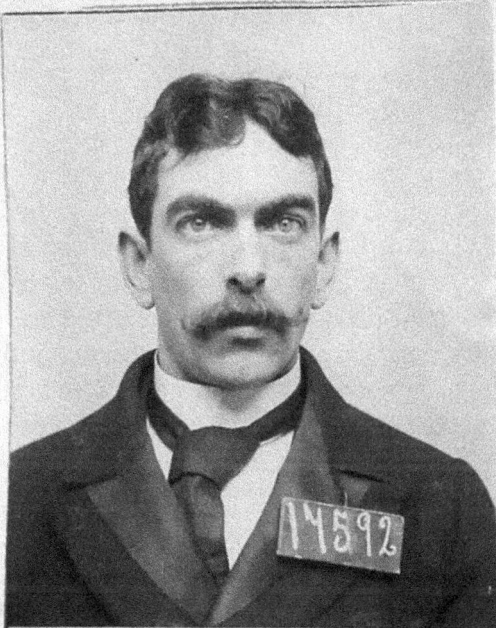

Name Harry Westwood Cooper
No 17592
County San Francisco
Crime Forgery
Term 3 years
Received Jan'y. 15 - 1898
Discharged May. 15 - 1900
Remarks

possibly squeal without giving himself away too. So what did I do? I started in to get 'Sir' Harry a job in the Captain's office. That sounds funny, don't it? I, supposed to be one of the worst characters in the prison, deciding to get one of the best forgers in the place into the Captain's office!

"But it was dead easy. I watched my chance and dropped a hint to him, showing him how he could do a little stooling and land. I knew he was itching for a chance to peddle something to the Captain, and he fell for my plan like a house afire. He was using dope at the time, and by hustling I managed to keep him supplied. And every two or three days I'd slip him a piece of change. Every time I got a chance I'd bait Harry with some flattering remark about what a swell guy he was and how much I thought of him.

"In less than two months after I started in on him he got a job in the office as the Captain's private clerk. That was just what I wanted, and I lost no time in telling him the scheme. It was getting close to the end of Hale's administration,[2] and my plan was to have Harry get hold of my commitment and his own and three others, make counterfeits in place of them, giving us all less time than we had, change the books, and then when the new bunch of politicians came in we'd walk out discharged.

"My commitment was to be changed from life to nine years. That would put me out a few months after the new crowd got here. The others were to be changed the same way, so we'd all go out at the beginning of the new administration. When I explained all this to Harry he was tickled to death, or seemed to be, and got busy right away. In a few days he handed me four commitments, but his own wasn't there. That made me kind of suspicious, and I asked him how about himself.

"'Oh, I'll fix my own,' he says.

"You see, I had worked another forger into the scheme since I'd started, and this man was to do the work in his cell.

---

[2] William E. Hale was warden of San Quentin from 1891 to 1899.

I let it go at that, and that's where I made a mistake. I should have insisted on having all the commitments changed by the same man.

"Well, after a day or so, Harry gave me the blank commitments, and I handed the whole bunch over to the man that was to do the changing.

"Two days later I had them all back, and I wish you could have seen them. The forgeries were perfect, seals and all. How he did it I don't know, but I compared the counterfeits with the genuine commitments, and exceptin' that the time had been changed you couldn't tell the difference. All the handwriting and the signatures were exactly like the originals.

"Maybe it didn't make me feel good to see a commitment with my name on it giving me nine years instead of life. And, of course, the other fellows in the game were just as tickled.

"When I had made sure that everything was all right I burned up the original commitments one night in my cell, and then I handed the bunch of counterfeits back to Harry. He looked them over and said, 'Fine! Fine! Almost as good as I could have done them myself. You ought to see mine; it's perfect. I've only got one year instead of four, and I'll be going out in five months. I'm changing all the books as I get a chance, but I'll have to leave the main books, the ones the Captain is liable to see, until after the new bunch comes. I can make all the final changes in one night when the time comes.'

"I carried the word to the gang, and we all chirked up and began to feel like somebody. We were all short-timers, you see, and that makes a fellow feel pretty good. I settled down to behave myself so's to keep out of trouble, and I was so good it hurt. Every day I'd manage to see 'Sir' Harry. He'd slip over to the yard at unlock, or at night, and I'd hand him a ball and a piece of change.

"But all the time he was double-crossing me. He was playing me for the livest sucker he'd ever patted on the back. That's where the complication comes in. I wish I could tell

ch. ends next p.

you the story just as it happened, because I was in the dark as to what he was doing until the big pinch was pulled off and I found myself in solitary. It wasn't until several months after the whole thing was over that I got it straight, but in order to make it plain to you I'll have to tell it the same as if I knew just what was going on inside that devil's noodle all the time.

"He knew, for one thing, that I was about seventeen miles off the track when I imagined I could beat the dump by changing my commitment and expecting to have all the books changed. He knew it was impossible, because every man's time and the county he comes from is sent to the Governor's office in Sacramento when he comes in, and nobody can get out until the Warden sends to Sacramento and gets a discharge signed by the Governor. And, of course, they never make out these discharges until they look up their records. I didn't know all that, but 'Sir' Harry did, and yet he got the commitments and put the phony ones back in their places.

"But he was scheming along a separate line all this time. He was laying the train to spring 'Sir' Harry and leave us suckers marooned on Damn Fool Island.

"Well, he came up to me one day in the yard and said, 'Say, Ed, I'm going to leave the office. I've already played the nervous breakdown gag on Johnnie, and I've got him thinking I'm the sweetest candy kid that ever happened. I'm going to throw a fit for a stall, and when I come out of it I'll ask him to assign me to the night job in the Red Front. That will be a good change of employment for me, and I guess I can carry the lunches around to the night guards without hurting myself much.'

"'But how about the books you haven't changed yet?' I asked, flaring up.

"'Tut, tut, man!' he says, patting me on the back and laughing that slick, oily laugh of his. 'My, but you'll be run over by a hearse when you get out, you're so slow. Don't you see how this move strengthens the game? I know that office from A to Z now, and I'm going after a night job that permits me to go anywhere in the prison. All I've got to do is slip over there some night when everything is nice and quiet, and the time is ripe, and make the few little changes that are left. And then there's something else you haven't thought of, either. In case, by any chance, they should spring those commitments, I'd be clear. Of course, some other guy will get my place over there when I land this night job, and they'll never be able to say who did the trick. Of course, there ain't one chance in a thousand that they'll spring them, but if they do we're all in the clear; savvy?'

"This certainly looked like a slick move, and I told him so, but somehow, down underneath, I caught a false note. I couldn't make out how I could get nailed, and he seemed to be mixed into the thing so much himself that it didn't seem possible that he could do us dirt. So I refused to let myself doubt him. What a sucker I was!"

17

"A couple of days later 'Sir' Harry threw the fit on the office porch. They packed him to the hospital and made a great hullabaloo over him, and then, after three days in bed, he came out again, and the Captain give him the night job in the Red Front. And what do you suppose? Throwing the fit and getting the job in the Red Front was all part of a little by-play, a nice little frame-up between him and the Captain.

"You see, Harry had told the Captain that there was a big plot on foot for a night break, that he was in touch with some of the leaders, and that they wanted him to help them out. They had come to him and proposed that he try to work the Captain for the night job, so that he would be where they wanted him and give them the necessary help.

"The Captain saw a chance to do a good turn for himself and Hale. It was near the end of Hale's administration, and if they could nip a big scheme like that in the bud it would give them a boost, and they might manage to hang on for another term.

"As a matter of fact, Harry had sprung a plot on two or three lifers, telling them he was sorry for them and was willing to go the limit himself. He told them that he'd have to get the night job in order to carry out the plan, and then he told the Captain that he'd have to make some kind of a grandstand play to get out of the office and into the night

job without arousing the suspicion of the guys that was supposed to be hatching the scheme. Do you get the drift?

"The poor suckers that he had roped in knew he was going
to throw a fit so's to fool the Captain, as they thought, and
the Captain knew he was going to throw a fit so's to fool
the guys that were in on the plot. As for me, I didn't know
a damn thing about it. I thought 'His Lordship' was getting
into the night job so's to cover up his tracks on the commitment deal.

"Talk about psychology! Talk about wheels within wheels!
I certainly have to take my hat off to that guy. There he was
playing half a dozen different schemes, making suckers out of
everyone, and laughing up his sleeve all the time, I suppose.
But he had one grand idea. When all the smoke cleared away
he expected to find himself outside the front gate, dressed
up in glad rags, and with a pardon in his pocket.

"As soon as he got the night job he began carrying reports
to the Captain every day. He told the Captain that the gang
had fallen for the fit scheme, and imagined that they were
handing the Captain the slickest package of his career. Also
they had told him their entire plot, and they wanted him to
play the chief part in it. Should he go ahead?

"The Captain studied it over for a day or two and then said
to let her ride. Harry told him that the plan was to have him
drug the coffee of the second watch when they came into
the Red Front for lunch before going on duty at midnight,
and then when they had all gone to sleep at their posts he
was to go up to a certain cell and unlock it, and the party
in that cell had skeleton keys that would unlock the cells of
all the other men that were going—there'd be about thirty
altogether, but most of them wouldn't be let in on the play
until the last moment.

"He also told the Captain that probably some guy that
was in the scheme would turn traitor before it was pulled
off, and come to him with it. Then he turned right around
and managed to get the scheme to the ears of a guy that he

ch. ends p. 210

knew would carry it to the office. Of course, this was just what he wanted. It would make the Captain think he was on a hot trail.

"I never heard of a more diabolical case of double-crossing in my life, and yet I have to laugh when I think of it. The Captain and the Warden were hobnobbing from morning to night, and 'Sir' Harry would mosey over to the office with his face all drawn, pretending that the strain was telling on him, and report progress. They patted him on the back and urged him to stay with it. He pretended it was too much, that he couldn't stand it, and wanted to quit. He urged them to make the arrests right away. Of course, he didn't want them to, and he knew they wouldn't. He knew they wanted to take the conspirators red-handed. All he did this for was to work the thing to the boiling point and make himself out a kind of martyr in their service.

"And then, in order to get the guys that were going to make the getaway worked up, too, Harry decided to get the drug and try it some night on a guard.

"'I'll dope a certain guard's coffee next Sunday night,' he told them, 'just to make sure that the stuff will work.'

"You know that when a guard goes to sleep on post he gets canned, and everybody in the place hears about it. Well, Harry figured if he could put some guard to sleep the gang would drop the last vestige of suspicion and come to him like a lot of sheep.

"He was something of a doctor, you know, and he had been tending the wife of one of the officers. They believed he had studied medicine and knew more than the regular prison physician. This officer used to take Harry out to his house to doctor his wife. She had nervous prostration or something, and he did have a magnetic treatment all right. I learned after it was all over that he used to have an office somewhere back East as a specialist.

"Well, he told this officer that a certain kind of medicine would help cure his wife, and he wrote out a prescription, addressed to some druggist he knew in San Francisco. The officer got the stuff for him all right, thinking it was medicine for his wife, and Harry got him to bring it inside to him, claiming that he had to add a couple of homemade ingredients, or something.

"A couple of nights later he doped the coffee of a night guard, some fellow that he didn't like, and this guard went to sleep on post and was fired. Do you see the deviltry? He not only convinced the gang that he had the stuff that would put the guards to sleep when the proper night came, but he also got revenge on a guard that had called him down. Gee, but he certainly was a demon.

"Of course, the Captain didn't know anything about this part of the game. He imagined the guard had gone to sleep on the square, and as they were watching for the big break, why, of course, that made them all the stricter. The guard tried to save himself, but they wouldn't listen.

"Then 'Sir' Harry went to work on the next part of the plot. He had told the Captain that there were to be a bunch of guns come in, and that he was gradually working up to the point where he could get them. I've never been able to figure out why Harry did this. The scheme was all right without guns. But I suppose his imagination ran away with him.

"At any rate, he told the Captain the guns were going to be brought in by one of the night guards, and that the guard was to get $500 for it. Of course, this night guard didn't know anything about the drug stunt. He was to be a victim of that himself, but without knowing it. In other words, Harry made the Captain think this guard was being double-crossed.

"There was an old feller cooking in the Red Front that used to be a Chief of Police somewhere back East. He came out here and got ten years for killing a man over a claim. Having been a policeman, he naturally had a nose for any kind of crooked work, and Harry knew this. So, to strengthen his play with the Captain, he acted suspiciously around the cook, so that the cook got to watching him.

ch. ends p. 210

"That was what Harry wanted. He would stop the night guards as they came in and take them over in a corner and speak low, asking some simple question, or commenting on the weather, and the cook got it into his head that 'Sir' Harry was dealing with the guards. He tore over to the Captain with this information, and he told him to keep an eye on Harry and report everything he saw. But this was not because the Captain suspected Harry, or because he wanted to put a watch over him. He simply didn't want the cook to get in on the big game, and told him to watch Harry so that he'd think he was doing the Captain a service. Harry knew that this would happen. It was part of his plan.

"Have you been able to follow all this?" Morrell suddenly asked me.

"Yes," I replied; "I think so. Go ahead!"

"Of course, as a matter of fact, 'Sir' Harry was dealing with the guards, and he knew the cook was watching every move he made. He knew that the cook had cut a slit in the screen between the kitchen and dining-room so that he could see everything that took place. As I said before, this was what Harry wanted. His game was to have the story he'd peddled to the Captain look as if it was all on the square. If the cook saw him hobnobbing with certain guards and ran to the Captain, thinking he was doing a service, why, of course, the Captain would think the plot was working out.

"So Harry told one of the guards he'd give him $20 for a five-pound box of choice tobacco, and one night the guard brought this box of tobacco inside with him as he was going on duty at midnight and slipped it to Harry. The cook was rubbering through his peephole and saw the move, just as Harry intended.

"The next morning 'Sir' Harry waited until he saw the cook go to the office and report, and then he went over himself and took the Captain in.

"'Well, I've got the guns,' he said. 'They came in last night, and Morrell and I have just planted them in the lower yard. The break comes off next Sunday night.'

"'You've done what?' fairly shrieked the Captain. 'Planted the guns with Morrell? God, man, are you crazy? Go get 'em. Get 'em as fast as you know how. Planting guns with Morrell! I gave you credit for having brains, Harry! You should have brought 'em straight to me.'

"At this Harry pretended he was scared.

"'I'm sorry. Captain. I thought that was all understood. They knew the guns were coming last night, and if I hadn't produced them they'd have got suspicious right away.'

"'Oh, rats!' replied the Captain. 'You could have stalled 'em along for a day or two. But never mind now, Harry; it's too late. Still, the damage may be undone if you hustle. Go and dig up that plant and get it up here as fast as you know how. What in hell were you thinking of, anyway, planting guns in the lower yard?'

"'Sir' Harry pretended to be completely overcome at the terrible blunder he had made, and tottered from the office and down to the lower yard. Of course, he didn't find the plant—there wasn't any to find, except in his fiendish imagination. He came back with his face all white.

"'My God, Captain,' he quailed, 'they're gone! Don't punish me; I didn't mean any harm. And we'll get 'em again. They'll have 'em next Sunday night when the pinch comes off, and it'll be easy to get them.'

"The Captain went straight up in the air. He came very near tearing into Harry, he was so mad. But he quieted down after a bit and reasoned the thing out. He knew he was helpless and that it would be impossible to get the guns, because a move like that would put the gang wise and also give away the fact that the plot was known. Then he went into a second rage and abused Harry worse than at first. It was right there that 'Sir' Harry made one of his master strokes. Talk about Rodin or any other arch-crook—they were never in it with Harry.

ch. ends p. 210

"In the middle of the Captain's rage Harry stopped him, pretending to be sore, pretending that his dignity was hurt.

"'I'm through with the entire business,' he said. 'After all I've done for you people all I get is abuse. You can do what you like with me, but I wash my hands of the whole thing right here. If you'll leave me alone I'll get this entire bunch for you, guns and all, but if you think you're so wise, why, go ahead and finish the thing up. This is a fine way to treat a man after what I've done for you. Why, man, they'd kill me like a dog if they knew. You people ought to be protecting me instead of handing me this kind of a deal.'

"It was a great grandstand play, and, of course, the Captain fell for it. He apologized and crawfished, and had a hard time getting 'Sir' Harry quieted down and persuading him to go ahead with the plot.

"'I'll go ahead on one consideration,' said Harry, 'and that is that I get a pardon as soon as this thing is over. My life won't be worth a snap of your fingers if I stay here, and what I'm doing means a whole lot to you people.'

"The Captain consulted the Warden, and Harry was promised a pardon.

"'All right,' he said, as soon as he got the promise. 'I'll go ahead, but leave me alone. If you people keep on meddling you'll queer the whole thing. Even as it is the gang may be on. Someone may have piped me looking for that plant this morning. It was a mistake to go down there and look for it.'"

Morrell stopped and got a drink from the pitcher of ice water in the corner of the clothing room before continuing.

"Have you been able to follow me?" he asked, as he turned to resume his seat.

"Yes, I think so," I replied. "But I never heard a more devilish thing in my life, and there are some parts of it that I don't quite savvy, but go ahead, I want to hear the finish. I can get you to explain afterward."

Morrell hitched his chair closer and tapped me on the knee.

"Well, the stage is set. Now we'll have the hair-raiser. But keep one thing in your mind. I didn't know a thing about all this at the time—not a solitary thing. I didn't even know there was any talk of a break.

"I was asleep in my cell that Sunday night when the door suddenly banged open and two guards rushed in and pounced on me. Ordinarily I hear the least little out of the way sound at night, but they unlocked that door so easy that I didn't hear them, and it was only as they flung it open and rushed in that I woke up.

"You can imagine how I felt. I didn't know what was up. The first thing that flashed into my mind was that it was some kind of a scheme for killing me. Naturally, I put up a fight, though they had all the best of it, and I was so badly tangled up in the blankets that I couldn't do much. I don't know what it was that hit me, but all of a sudden everything went black, and my head felt as if it had gone down into my stomach.

"It only lasted a minute, and when I recovered I was weak and dizzy, and they had no trouble handling me. One of them held me while the other searched the bunk. He was all excited and tore the mattress to pieces. I wondered what he was looking for, but didn't say anything. Finally the one who was holding me said, 'Let's take him below. We've got to get a few more, and we can lock the cell and come back afterward. They may be in the ventilator or some place.'

"Without even letting me put on my clothes they pulled me out of the cell, took me along the tier and then across the yard to the dungeon. I saw other men being brought along, too, and I couldn't make it out. When I got to the dungeon the Captain and Warden were there.

"'Well, did you get a gun on this —— ——?' asked the Captain as I was shoved in.

"'No; no sign of a gun yet,' replied the guard who had me by the neck.

"The Captain snorted and helped shove me into one of

ch. ends p. 210

the cells, and they banged the door on me. I heard quite a lot of commotion for the next half hour or so, as they kept bringing more men down, and then everything got quiet. Then I heard a man swearing and recognized the voice of George S——, a lifer that I knew pretty well.

"'Hello, George; is that you?' I called.

"'Yes; who are you?' he called back.

"'Ed Morrell,' I answered. 'What does all this mean?'

"'Why, it means that we've all been double-crossed. Somebody's tipped the whole thing off and we're all up against it; and up against it good and hard.'

"George was one of the men in on the commitment deal and I thought that was what he was talking about.

"'Well, all we've got to do is keep mum,' I told him; 'but I don't understand that talk about guns.'

"By this time the others were talking, and as near as I could make out there were ten or twelve men in the dungeon, all in different cells, and all trying to find out what it meant.

"I tried to get George to talk some more, but he said it was risky.

"'They may have a spotter locked up down here,' he warned. 'You can never tell.'

"Well, all that night I lay mum, afraid to talk for fear there might be a spotter in one of the dungeon cells, as George S—— had said. But when day broke we all got calling to each other and found out who was in each cell. Every cell was full and there wasn't any chance of a spotter being down there.—You've been down there, haven't you?" Morrell asked.

"Yes," I replied. "I went down one day with the turnkey, the day that fifty-year Chinaman in the tailor shop cut that fellow over by the gate at No. 1 Post. The turnkey wanted to get a statement from the chink, and he took me along to take it in shorthand, but the Chinaman wouldn't talk."

"No, I don't mean that," Morrell replied. "Have you ever

been down there yourself; that is, have you ever been in the hole?"

"No," I answered. "Why?"

"Well, I just wanted to tell you that it never really gets light down there in the daytime. Just a kind of dusk, something like you see in a long tunnel with a curve in it when you first get near the mouth; you know what I mean.

"It was long before the bell rang that we all got talking and found out who was down there. That was the first I learned about the break that was supposed to be pulled off the night before; how the guards were to be drugged and all that; how 'Sir' Harry was to go up and unlock the first cell and let the poor sucker out that had spent weeks making skeleton keys for unlocking the cells of the other guys in the plot.

"By making these keys he had been taking awful chances. He might have been nailed any time and had it thrown into him.

"Well, George and I got to talking, and the other fellers were talking from cell to cell, and that helped to cover up what we were saying. You really don't talk down there; you have to shout back and forth so's to be heard. It ain't like solitary, because they don't stay in the cells next to each other in the dungeon long enough to learn a code. Up in solitary we used to talk back and forth by tapping on the wall.

"'What was that talk about guns I heard last night?' I asked George.

"'Damned if I know,' he said. 'I don't know anything about any guns. The first I heard of guns was when they pinched me. I was standing at my cell door, waitin' to be let out for the break, as I thought, when the bulls sneaked up and unlocked the door quick and nailed me. They nailed all us fellers with our clothes on, all ready and waiting. That's what makes it so bad. We can't explain what we were doing all dressed at that hour of the night.

"'I got the word in the yard at lockup last night that my cell would be unlocked about 1 o'clock, and to be all ready.

ch. ends p. 210

It certainly is a fierce deal. Whoever gave it away was on the inside, for they knew just what cells to go to, and they caught us dead to rights.'

"'But how about the guns?' I asked. 'Do you know anything about guns?'

"'No,' he replied, 'That's what gets me. They asked me for a gun the first thing. I don't understand it.'

"Well, to make a long story short, they started in trying to make us tell where the guns were. They didn't have any jacket in those days, you know. The jacket was the invention of Aguirre. They hung us to the walls of our cells in the dungeon. Of course, none of us knew anything about any guns, so we couldn't tell them if we'd wanted to. They cut our rations down to a little piece of bread and a cup of water every twenty-four hours, and kept us chained up to the wall about fourteen hours each day.

"At night we had nothing to sleep on but the stone floor; no mattress or blankets or anything. About the third day some of the guys began to scream and curse and beg for mercy, but they paid no attention. Then it got to be a regular hell, with screaming and cursing and crying all the time. You can imagine how they felt.

"Some of them were lifers like me, and from high hopes of beating the place they suddenly found themselves with everything lost, and being tortured to tell something they didn't know. I wouldn't go through that again for anything in the world, not even for pardon. Not alone on account of what I suffered so much myself, but to hear those others praying to God to kill them—God Almighty! my blood turns to ice every time I think of it.

"After a week they began to let some of them out. I didn't know what became of them, but every little while they'd come down and take some guy away. And every time they came down to get a guy they'd come to my cell and open the door and ask me if I was ready to tell what I knew about the guns.

"Looking at it the way they did, I can understand a little. They thought there were guns in the prison and that some of us knew where they were. As long as those guns were not found there was danger of a break and some killing. They thought they had the men who knew where the guns were, and they made up their minds to make them tell. But it was on me especially that the most suspicion fell.

"You see, 'Sir' Harry had told the Captain that he had planted the guns with me in the lower yard, and then he'd pretended that the plant had been lifted. Naturally, they, thought I'd done the lifting.

"I found out afterward that they got the guard that was supposed to have brought the guns in, and charged him with it. At first he denied bringing anything in, but they brought the cook who had seen him slip the package to 'Sir' Harry, and 'Sir' Harry claimed that he understood that the package contained guns. He said that was the understanding, and that when he got the package he hadn't opened it, but planted it in the lower yard with me.

"As soon as the guard found out that he was suspected of bringing in guns he got scared and told the truth—told them that it was a package of tobacco. But they wouldn't believe him. He'd denied bringing anything in at first—you see, he didn't want to lose his job—and then when he learned how serious it was and told the truth they wouldn't believe him. They thought he was claiming it was tobacco because he knew it was a felony to bring in the guns.

"But when he found that they still believed he had brought in guns he got sore and told them it was up to them to prove it. The only way they could prove it was by getting the guns. Do you see how hellish it all was?

"And then, to make matters worse, the guard got cold feet, thinking they might railroad him anyway, and beat it while his shoes were good. Of course, that made things look all the worse. They imagined he'd disappeared because he was guilty.

ch. ends next p.

"Finally, after torturing some of the other boys for a month, they concluded that they didn't know anything about the guns, and that I had kept them hid to produce at the last minute. So the whole thing simmered down to me. Just stop and think of the fix I was in. I was charged with knowing where guns were concealed inside the walls, and they were going to make me tell where.

"I kept telling them that I didn't even know there was to be a break, and the strongest point I made was that I didn't have my clothes on, but was asleep in bed when they pinched me, but they took that as a sign that I was slicker than the rest of the bunch, and that I had stayed in bed so's not to take any chance of being caught up.

"I don't know just how long I stayed in the dungeon, chained to the wall, but think it was thirty-three or thirty-four days, and then I was handcuffed and taken up to solitary in the dead of the night.

"All but two or three of the rest of those that had been pinched were back in the yard, wearing red shirts and with their credits gone, but I went to solitary."

18

"I've never been able to understand why 'Sir' Harry played me this trick. The only way I can figure it out is that he was sore because he knew I had tried to use him on that commitment deal; that it hurt his pride to think I took him for such a sucker, and that in working up this other scheme he expected would get him a pardon he landed on me as the fall guy in the gun fairy tale.

"But now comes the funniest part of the whole thing. When they found out that they couldn't get the guns, what do you suppose they did? They pinched 'Sir' Harry himself, and instead of giving him a pardon they threw him up in solitary.

"I remember the day he came up. They put him in the cell next to me. When I heard the noise at the main door, and the low talking, I got up to my door and rubbered, and I saw 'Sir' Harry led by. He looked like skimmed milk—his face was blue-white—but he didn't see me. And he was in the cell next to me for several days before he found out I was in the next cell to him.

"You must remember I didn't know then that he was the cause of my being up there. I had heard from George S——that he was in on the big break scheme and that he was the man who was supposed to drug the coffee and unlock the first cell, but I didn't know that he was the man who had named me as being mixed up in the scheme, and the first thing that came into my head when I saw him was that he had been nailed on the commitment deal.

"It was not until two weeks later, when I was taken out to appear before the board and was confronted with the evidence against me, that I learned that 'Sir' Harry had roped me in. I was all excited at the moment, trying to convince the board that I was innocent, and it nearly floored me. As soon as I recovered I demanded that they bring Harry out and have him face me. They refused to do this, and then I went in the air. I don't know what I said. I was so mad I just tore loose, but I do know one thing, and that was that I was sentenced to go to solitary confinement and stay there until I told where the guns were concealed.

"I leave you to imagine how I felt when they took me back. I threw myself on the mattress and tore it with my teeth. It's the only time in my life that I went to pieces that way. I didn't get normal for three or four days, but was in a kind of trance, and every time the guard came near my door I abused him. Of course, that got me in bad with the guards up there, and they made my life a regular hell.

"And I had made up my mind to kill 'Sir' Harry the first time I got a chance. I hope I shall never have the same feelings toward any other man as long as I live.

"I used to lie awake nights and listen to him breathing and think how I'd fasten my nails in his neck and choke the life out of him. I'd choke him until he was almost unconscious, and then let go. Then, after he had got his breath a little, I'd choke him again, and then let go. Then I'd do it again and again, making him weaker and weaker all the time, until finally I'd get him into such a state that he'd die a thousand times. Oh, don't look that way," Morrell exclaimed as my expression changed to one of horror. "That wasn't me that was thinking those things—it was an insane man. I was dippy, clean bughouse. That's why I understand Jake Oppenheimer so well. You know he was up there with me those five years, and I know that he got just such deals from men that he took into his confidence. They'd pretend to be his friends and get some plans of his for a break from solitary—and that was the only hope he had of ever getting out, remember—and then peddle it to the guards so's to get out of solitary themselves.

"Just stop and imagine how you'd feel if you got that kind of a deal. Wouldn't you have murderous thoughts, and wouldn't they grow on you until you felt as if the whole world was against you?

"It took me two years to get under Oppenheimer's shell, two years of tapping on the wall—he was in the cell on the other side of me—with a note passing between us once in a great while, and then he got to trust me. But after I had known him for three years he still had moments of doubt. One day he rapped and asked me why I didn't get out of solitary.

"'All you've got to do,' he said, 'is tell them that I've got some new scheme for beating them. I'll stand in with you. I'll pretend I'm working on a scheme and you give it away. There's no use of us both staying up here, and this will get you out. And you can do me more good then than you can do me now. We can fix it up so's you can smuggle something up here to me—something worthwhile that I can cut my way out with.'

"But I didn't fall for it. I knew he was giving me the final test; he was trying to see if I was willing to profit at his expense. For over a week he kept urging me to do as he suggested, but I wouldn't listen. The temptation never even occurred to me. I've thought a good deal about it since, trying to figure out what it was that was strongest in me—my sympathy for Jake or my hatred for the guards. You see, by adopting his scheme I'd have had to serve the guards, and before I'd have done that, especially at the expense of another poor con, I'd have rotted by inches from my toes up.

"That's how I got solid with Oppenheimer. Always after that we were close friends, and I got his entire life from him. Some day I hope I can get it into print. Talk about a tragedy!

ch. ends p. 223

Talk about being born under a hoodoo![1] Jake Oppenheimer is the hardest luck man I've ever known. It's no wonder to me he's done some of the things he has. He's insane, except with persons he likes. Anyone else that comes near him he takes for an enemy, and the only code he knows after what he's been through is that a dead enemy is a good friend. But I'm getting away from my own story. I'll tell you more about Oppenheimer some other time.

"Well, I got a good many doses of the jacket after that and it looked as if they were going to kill me by inches. Many a time I thought it was curtains. But the day I got kicked gave me a new lease on life. Those kicks hurt my body, hurt it so that I still feel it down here, but they set my mind afire. I determined to live it out and get back at them if it took the whole of my life.

"One day while I was lying in the jacket Aguirre came up and made a final effort to make me 'come through.' He stuck his finger close to my eye and made motions as if he was going to jab his nail in and tear my eyes out. Of course, I closed my eyes instinctively, but I remember how I watched his fingers, hoping that he would get them close enough to my mouth for me to grab them. I was in a frenzy, lying there helpless, not able to move, and if I'd ever got his fingers in my teeth they'd have had to kill me before I'd let go.

"But after I'd been up there six or seven months they gave me up. They decided that I would never tell where the guns were. We were not allowed any reading matter, and to keep from going crazy I started working on my invention—that is, working it out in my head. I didn't have any pencil or paper; that wasn't allowed, either. I've made the drawings since I got out and sent them on to Washington, and I ought to hear from them any day. It's a life-saving device.

"I also killed some of the time learning the telegraph code we had up there. We had a system of tapping on the wall from one cell to another, and that was the only way we had of

---

[1] A run of bad luck.

talking, though Jake had a piece of lead that had dropped out of the point of a pencil—you know how a pencil point breaks off sometimes—and he'd send me a note once in a while. He kept the little piece of lead hid in his cell. Of course, it was hard for him to get paper to write on, but once in a while he'd manage it and get a note to me. It was risky, and, of course, he had to nurse the little piece of lead, for he couldn't tell when he'd ever get another piece.

"They used to search our cells every week. That always seemed funny to me—searching the cells of men in solitary confinement, with guards walking up and down in front of the doors all the time.

"But still we used to get contraband things, just the same, and they knew it. Of course, Jake's little piece of lead was so small they never found that. It was Jake that they were most afraid of. I never saw a man with more determination in my life. They say hope springs eternal in the human breast. His breast must be awful deep. I don't see how he can hope.

"But he's always scheming for a getaway. It don't make any difference how often he's caught, he starts right in on some new plan.

"Solitary confinement never did any man any good. Repression don't reform a man any more than chaining up a dog makes him gentle.

"I remember a horse I had once in the mountains. He was a wonder for traveling. He could go all day and all night on the remembrance of a handful of oats. But he was a regular demon; he'd kick or bite you if you gave him the least chance, and his sides were raw from where the spurs had been dug into him. I made a hard trip with that horse. We were alone with the sky and the rocks. At first I had to be awful careful with him, and he nearly got me three or four times. But I never hit him, I never stuck the spurs into him, and every chance I got I would pet him and talk to him and hustle something for him to eat.

ch. ends p. 223

"Before the three weeks were over I had him following me around like a lamb and when the time came for us to part it was one of the toughest things I've ever done. I often think of those three weeks and how we got to know each other. I think I thought more of God in those three weeks than I ever have in my life.

"Well, men are just like that horse. I don't care how bad a man has been, he can be got. But solitary confinement, with the jacket and kicks and abuse, will never make a man better. I'm not as good a man as I was before I went up there."

"But you're going to keep straight now and do the right thing, Ed," I interrupted, "and before you went up there you were what they call a hard character and always in trouble. How do you explain the change?"

Morrell half closed his eyes and regarded me searchingly.

"You don't believe that," he said. "You don't really think I'm being good because I'm afraid of solitary, do you?"

"But what else am I to think?" I asked.

"Well," he responded, an inflection of disappointment in his voice, "I'll wind up the 'Sir' Harry story and tell you a few more things, and then you can judge for yourself.

"Some time after we were put up there they discovered the commitment deal, and they came up and accused 'Sir' Harry of it. He was a total wreck by that time. He'd collapsed like a balloon with the gas leaking out through a big wound. You see, he'd never been up against hardships like some of us. He'd never slept out under the stars, or climbed over the ranges with twenty or thirty sharpshooters on his trail a-thirsting for his blood. He was of the dry goods variety, the kind that tip their hats to their knees when they meet a woman, but funk like a yellow-tail when it comes to protecting her from actual danger. He had the gift of gab and a Little Lord Fauntleroy nicety,[2] but his backbone was rubber and he couldn't stand punishment. He was continually begging the guards to let him see the Warden, and when he found out that they wouldn't do that he begged them to see the Warden for him.

"When the commitments were sprung he belched everything he knew. They had quite a time getting new commitments—I learned that underground.

"Then he came through with the truth regarding the gun story. He told them it was all a fake, and that the box the guard gave him that night in the Red Front was a box of tobacco, but they wouldn't believe him. He did every day of his time in solitary, and was discharged from there.

"Well, for five years I lay up there and I finally got so I wouldn't talk to anyone. Whenever the Warden or anyone else came up I used to turn my back when they came to my cell. Drahms, the chaplain, used to blow in about once in two months, and it was amusing. Some of the guys imagined he could help them get out and used to talk with him; and then when he'd show up again he'd stop before the same cell of some guy that he'd talked with for half an hour the last time he was up and say:

"'My! My! What are you up here for? What is your name?'

"One day a Mexican was brought up and put in the end cell, right where the guard sits outside. I don't know what happened, but this guard got it in for the Mexican. He found out that it annoyed the Mexican to have him in front of the cell, and what do you suppose he did? He used to put his chair right in front of the door and swing back and forth on

---

[2] Wildly popular in the late 19th century, *Little Lord Fauntleroy* is a novel by Frances Hodgson Burnett (1849–1924) about an American boy who turns out to be the long-lost heir of a British fortune. First serialized in *St. Nicholas Magazine*, then published as a book in 1886, the young heir was characterized by his charm, intelligence, and extremely good and innocent nature. So popular was the title that it soon became a cliché and came to be used to identify one who is spoiled, conceited, and characterized by a pompous air of decadence, intellectualism, and moral superiority—as used here by Morrell.

ch. ends p. 223

the hind legs, smoking a cigar and watching the man in the cage the same as if he'd been a wild beast.

"We all felt that there was something wrong—it was in the air—and one day while the guard was sitting there swinging back and forth in his chair, humming a song, the Mexican went bughouse. He crouched back against the end of his cell and then took a running leap at the barred door, at the same time letting a yell out of him like a tiger. When he hit the door it buckled, and the whole building shook. The guard happened to be swinging back when this happened and he kept on going.

"I rushed to the door of my cell to see what was the matter and I saw the guard's face when he picked himself up. He was on his hands and knees looking at the cell and he was trembling all over. His watch had slipped out of his pocket and was dangling underneath him, and his eyes looked as if they were paralyzed. The poor Mexican was lying in a heap inside the cell. He'd knocked himself out.

"When he came to he screamed and snarled and clawed, and they had to send for extra guards to get him into the jacket. He kept us all awake for a week and then quieted down. About two weeks after that they found him eating his hand one night—just tearing big chunks out of it with his teeth and snarling like a hyena. That settled it. It dawned on them that he was crazy and they took him to the asylum. I've been told he died of blood poison in a couple of weeks.

"But it changed that guard. He used to go around with a kind of scared look after that and was always asking us if there was anything he could do for us. It all goes to show that a man has got to have his heart pulled out by the roots sometimes and dangled all bloody and dripping before his eyes before he finds out he's human like the rest of us. That happened before 'Sir' Harry's time was up and every night after that I used to hear him praying, and—well, I know I ought to be ashamed of myself for saying it, but hanged if I didn't feel sorry for him.

"It's an awful thing to see a man go crazy like that Mexican. I know I began to get a creepy feeling, and it used to keep me busy fighting it off. I used to wake up in the night with a boa constrictor winding itself about me and squeezing my life out, and when I'd find out it was only a dream the guard would come sneaking to my cell to see what was the matter.

"Not being but half awake I wouldn't hear him, and when he'd suddenly pop up in the doorway it used to throw me into a cold sweat sometimes. In the daytime it didn't make any difference how much they sneaked—they wear felt slippers, you know—we always heard them coming.

"But when a man's half awake in a bad dream his hearing ain't so good. I suppose it was the squeezings in the jacket that used to make me dream of that snake, and I have the same dream yet, only not so often.

"The years dragged along and I seemed to be forgotten. One day is so much like another up there in solitary that it is hard to keep track of time. But on Christmas and Fourth of July we got a holiday dinner and were given a little tobacco, and I got so I measured time that way.

"It was five years after I was dragged out of my cell and thrown into solitary, and I was shuffling up and down my little cage one afternoon when a strange man came along the corridor and stopped at my door. He was stoop-shouldered and had a white mustache, and his voice wasn't bad. I had got so I never paid any attention to anyone, and when he stopped at my cell I didn't pay any attention to him. I was moving toward the door when he showed up, and when I got there I turned and started back.

"'Here, my man, I want to talk to you,' he said.

"'But I don't want to talk to you,' I answered.

"'What's the matter; have you got a cold?' he asked.

"I didn't make any reply, but kept on walking, and every time I walked toward the door I glared at him. But it didn't seem to bother him; he stuck right there. Presently he started off on another tack.

ch. ends p. 223

"'I'm the new Warden,' he announced. 'I don't know you and you don't know me, but I want to do the right thing by every man. Let's get acquainted.'

"I was still defiant, but something made me stop at the door and talk with him. I soon saw that I had him interested, and I told him the entire story and about being charged with knowing where there were guns concealed in the prison. He listened to every word and asked a lot of questions. Then he declared himself.

"'I believe you're innocent,' he said. 'I know you're innocent and I'm going to prove it. What will you do if I take you out of here and give you a trusted position?'

"Even then my pride would not let me seem eager—the wound was too deep for that—so I said: 'What will I do? Why, I'll throw you down cold. I'll double-cross you the first chance I get. I'll start scheming right away for getting a ton of dynamite smuggled in and blow up the prison.'

"This kind of staggered him—I could see that—but he smiled.

"'Oh, I know better than that,' he said. 'But suppose I take you at your word? Remember, I'm the Warden. If I feel inclined to believe what you say I can go away with a clear conscience and leave you here. Come, now, what will you do if I give you the chance?'

"I didn't like that. It was too much like trying to break my spirit. Rather than knuckle down I was bitter enough to throw away the chance of my life. Of course, I was a fool to act that way, but I couldn't help it.

"'I've been throwing people down and cutting their throats all my life. I'm no good. I don't know what honor is. But if you want to give me a chance to cut your throat, why, all right.'

"At this he flared up and started to walk away. But he only took a couple of steps and then came back.

"'I'm going to turn you out of here tomorrow and I'm

going to give you one of the best jobs in the prison. You're not going to throw me down, either. That's all,' and off he went.

"That was my introduction to Warden Tompkins,[3] and you know how he has kept his word. As long as he lives, and as long as I live, we're going to be true to each other. I'll stand up for him no matter what he does. He's my friend and he gave me this chance. It means that I'll be able to work my way out in a few years, and that means my life.

"Now do you understand why I'm behaving myself, why I'm not giving them any trouble? Do you still think it is because I'm afraid of solitary?"

"I beg your pardon, Ed," I apologized. "This is all new to me. You know nearly all the prisoners believe you did some kind of dirt to get out of solitary and into the job you've got. I never believed that, but I often wondered how it came about. I see it all now. Tompkins got puffed at the way you treated him, and he said to himself, 'I'll show this fellow that I'm just as game as he is. Instead of letting him defy me, I'll defy him.' Am I right?"

Morrell scratched his head before replying.

"I don't know about that. Don't you give him credit for wanting to do a kindness, for wanting to right the wrong that had been done me?" he asked.

During the years that followed Morrell proved his worth in a thousand ways. He not only did his work thoroughly, but he was always optimistic. There seems to be a general opinion that a man who has gone through severe punishment must be pessimistic and bitter. My experience tends to establish the contrary. I find that persons who have suffered most, especially persons of intense nature, are softened and broadened by it. There wasn't any silver spoon in the manger at Bethlehem.

After several years as head key-man Morrell succeeded in getting a commutation of sentence.[4] Very well, indeed, do

[3] John Tompkins was warden of San Quentin from 1903 to 1906.
[4] In law terms, the reduction of a sentence or other penalty.

ch. ends next p.

I remember the night it arrived. The Lieutenant-Governor visited the prison in person and brought several pardons and commutations with him. At previous visits to the prison he had met and learned to know Morrell personally, and that night he and the Warden came inside after lockup to break the good news to the various beneficiaries.

Morrell took it quite coolly. True, he had been expecting a commutation, but it seemed to me that he should have displayed more joy than he did. But I have since come to understand this seeming indifference on the part of the men who have been in prison a long time when they suddenly learn that they are to be released. They have become so inured to suppression that the emotions are lethargic. By long disuse the emotional nature has seeped away, so that the capacity for responding to sudden good or benefit is gone.

Men of this type have what I call the prison face—a kind of settled, melancholy expression of which they are totally unconscious. I have seen men of jovial, lighthearted nature sink into this state of chronic gloom, and it is not a pleasant thing to see.

Instead of rejoicing at his good fortune, Morrell thanked the Governor in a few brief words, and then took him to one side. I happened to be standing within earshot and heard what he said.

"Governor, there's an old soldier up in the hospital, an old chap that fought for the flag before we were born, or while we were shaking rattles and saying 'goo-goo.' He can't live long, and he don't want to die in prison. He killed an old comrade, while they were both drunk. He says he didn't mean to do it, and I believe him. He's doing twenty years for it, and he's got six years left. There's no chance for him to live it out. Will you come up and see him?"

"Get the keys," replied the Governor, "and you come over with me."

They went across the flower garden to the hospital and up into the ward, where they remained half an hour. When they came back the prison band was playing and there was a happy expression on the Governor's face. Three days later when he returned to Sacramento his first official act was to sign pardons for the old soldier and another man whom he had discovered in a nearby bed, a man whose wife and children needed him more than did the bolts and bars of San Quentin.

All this happened four years ago. Morrell has been a free agent during that time and he has "made good." I saw him the other day. The gloom has lifted from his face and his eyes are animated. He does not look like the man I knew behind the prison walls—certainly not anything like the corpse-like creature they brought down from solitary confinement the first time I saw him.

19

While talking with Mr. H. B. Warner of the "Alias Jimmy Valentine" company, a few days ago, he recounted an incident that occurred while he was visiting the State Penitentiary in Pennsylvania.

"I was on one of the tiers with the Warden," he said, "when a fellow in a straitjacket came walking toward us in charge of two guards. He was ———"

"Walking in a straitjacket?" I rudely interrupted. "Walking? What kind of a straitjacket was it?"

"Why, the ordinary kind," replied Mr. Warner. "His arms were fastened, but he was moving his elbows, and he was very eager to see the Warden."

Mr. Warner continued the story, but I did not hear him. I was thinking of what he had said about the straitjacket he had seen.

I have been mentioning the "jacket" in this narrative from time to time, and I shall have occasion to mention it as I continue. I am wondering how many of you have a true conception of what the jacket used in the California prisons is like. Probably you imagine it is the ordinary straitjacket, such as Mr. Warner saw, and such as is generally used in insane asylums for confining the arms of violent patients. You are wrong. The San Quentin jacket is something different. It certainly should be described. It is a form of punishment and torture that the people of California are negatively permitting. You are entitled to know something definite about it.

The jacket consists of a piece of canvas about four and one-half feet long, cut to fit about the human body. When spread out on the floor it has the same shape as the top of a coffin, broad near one end, for the shoulders, and tapering either way. Big brass eyelets run down the sides. It is manufactured in various sizes, and is designed solely as an instrument of torture.

Upon being sentenced to the jacket, the prisoner is first taken to the clothing room, where he is stripped of the clothing he has on and is given an old suit, consisting of shirt, trousers and worn-out shoes.

A guard, armed with a loaded cane, then escorts him to the dungeon, where a straitjacket that will fit snugly is selected. This jacket is spread out on the floor and the prisoner ordered to lie face down upon it. The sides are then gathered up over his back and a rope about the size of a window cord is laced through the eyelets.

If the word has been passed to "give him a cinching," the operator places his foot upon the victim's back in order to get leverage as he draws the rope taut, and when the lacing is finished the remnant of rope is wound about the trussed body and tied. Then the victim is rolled over on his back and left to think it over. He is left in one of the dungeon cells, where there is no light and where it is cold and damp.

Several years ago it was no uncommon thing for a prisoner to be rolled in old blankets before the jacket was applied. This was done for two reasons. First, if the prisoner were thin the blankets eliminated any possibility of the jacket fitting him loosely; second, when it was desired to give the victim a "sweat" as well as a squeeze, the blankets served that purpose.

At that time there was no limit to the duration of this punishment. Twenty-four hours was the ordinary sentence, but I know many cases where men were kept "cinched up" for a

ch. ends p. 233

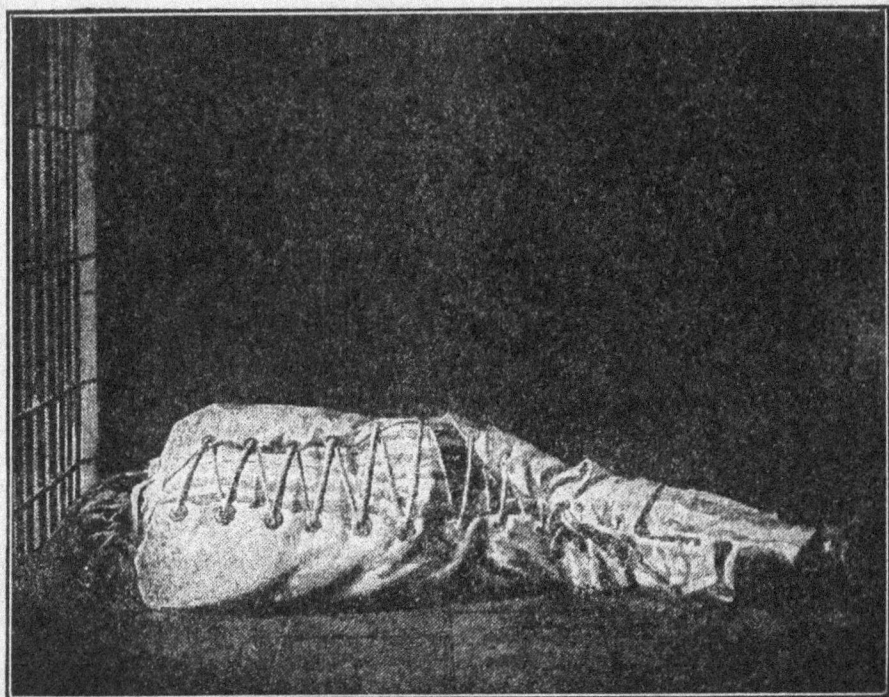

Ed. Morrell, Jack London's "Star Rover."
in the San Quentin Strait-Jacket.

Chapter 19

week, and in one instance for ten days. Just stop and think what that meant. Bound in a coarse, heavy canvas so that the hands and legs were held rigid, and left to lie without relief for days. Trussed up on Monday and not untrussed until the following Sunday. During that time the victim must remain recumbent, without moving, and could only vary his position by rolling over on his side or upon his face on the stone floor.

True, an old mattress was provided, but most men, in their terrible misery, rolled off it and could not get back. Meantime bodily excretions could not be denied—there is a limit to such repression—and the victim was compelled to suffer the added horror of near-mortification. Once each day, in the evening, attendants used to go down and hold a tin of water and a crust of bread to the victim's lips. This was known as "feeding time."

When the jacket was laced brutally, as was frequently the case, the victim could scarcely breathe. His hands and feet would "die," they would become cold and inanimate, and he would suffer the pins-and-needles sensation that one gets if one holds the feet or arms in one position for any length of time. Quite often when the jacket was removed the victim could not stand, but was obliged to grovel and wriggle on the floor like a snake to restore circulation. And when the blood began to return to the deadened parts the torture was excruciating.

I have talked with men who claimed that they got to their feet while in the jacket. One man told me that it took him half an hour to accomplish it, but by rolling over to the corner of the cell and working inch by inch in the angle of the wall he managed to rise.

"But after I got on my feet I was sorry," he said. "There I was standing in a corner, with my feet bound close together, and I didn't know how I was going to get down again. If I let my feet go out in front of me I'd go down with a crash, even with my back against the wall and, of course, I didn't dare go down on my face.

ch. ends p. 233

"I stood there for half an hour, I guess, not daring to move, and then I decided to jump for the mattress. I couldn't see it, but I thought I knew where it was. I'd been in the jacket three days when this happened, and I was weak. When I made the jump I must have got excited, for I tried to spread my feet as I came down and I fell forward. My face scraped the plaster off the wall on the other side of the cell as I fell, and I had no way to stop the blood.

"I lay that way until the next night when they came in to 'feed,' and then I got bailed out for what had happened. They thought I'd deliberately rubbed my face against the wall to make it bleed."

Other men have told me that while being laced in the jacket they would extend their elbows and double up their fists and hold themselves rigid in an effort to keep from being bound too tightly, and then, after the jacket was on, relax and be comparatively comfortable.

This trick had its danger, however. If the officer who was adjusting the jacket discovered this effort on the part of the victim to "beat it," he would pull and tug at the ropes all the harder. If the victim did not relax he would be caught and bound in the rigid condition and would be unable afterward to relax. Then his punishment would be doubly horrible, resulting in paralysis.

I have already recounted two instances of men who were taken from the jacket in a paralytic condition, one of whom died shortly afterward.[1]

These facts, and others equally horrible, finally got to the ears of the Legislature. A committee was appointed to investigate and spent a number of days at each prison. But instead of finding that the jacket was inhuman and injurious, as the evidence disclosed it to be, they recommended that its use be regulated.

Acting on this recommendation, the State Board of Prison Directors adopted a resolution to the effect that a prisoner

[1] Refer back to Chapter 7, p. 86.

should not be kept in the straitjacket for more than six consecutive hours. Since then the jacket has been, and is at the present time, used in both State prisons under this regulation. It is applied for six hours; then the victim is permitted the freedom of the cell for six hours, and then he spends the next six hours in the jacket.

There is no regulation limiting the period of time that this alternation—six hours in, six hours out—may be continued. Not only this, but realizing that as a means of extorting "confession" the torture of the jacket has been reduced by the six-hour limit, it is "cinched" with much greater severity. I know of instances of comparatively recent occurrence where the victim has screamed and begged for mercy within the hour, after being "cinched up."

A trusty, known as the "dungeon man," has a little shack just outside the dungeon door, and I have seen him come up to the office and report that a man who had been jacketed for half an hour was ready and eager to "confess."

From no viewpoint can the straitjacket be defended. It is purely and simply a relic of barbarism. It accomplishes no good. I have never seen one man who has suffered punishment in the jacket who was not filled with bitterness and who was not a worse man by reason of the humiliation and torture he had been through. As a means of discipline it has absolutely no value.

Under the present administration at San Quentin, the jacket has been used sparingly. At the present time it is scarcely used at all; yet the discipline of the prison has steadily improved. Under the Warden now in charge there is little danger of any prisoner being abused, and yet there is always the possibility. A Warden cannot know everything that transpires within the walls. His duties are numerous, and he must necessarily, as a matter of expediency and dignity, delegate the disciplining of the prison to a subordinate. So long as this is so, injustices may and do occur, as I shall show later.

Again, there is no assurance that the prisons will always

be governed by fair and capable men. Death and politics are both uncertain factors. The straitjacket as a method of punishment should be abolished by legislative enactment. It was introduced by a truculent[2] Warden. Why should a humane one continue to use it, even only on rare occasions?

I will recount but one flagrant case of torture and injustice connected with its use.

The victim's name was Brown, a common name that I will make use of, as I have done with other names, in order not to bring unpleasantness upon the persons involved, many of whom are now free agents and some of whom I have met since I began this narrative.

Brown was accused of having dope or of knowing where it was concealed inside the prison walls. When arrested and confronted with this charge he denied having any knowledge of it. In some way, probably through the malevolence of a stool-pigeon, the officials believed they had the right man, and Brown was placed in the jacket and told that he would be kept there until he "came through."

Poor Brown had nothing to tell—his case was on a parity with Morrell's in that respect—and he suffered days of torture as a consequence. He was kept in the jacket 130 hours—136 hours it may have been; I am trusting to memory, and am not quite sure—and was then released because the doctor said he could stand no more.

This punishment left him a physical wreck, and he never recovered. It was subsequently established beyond doubt that he was innocent, and the facts were presented to the State Board of Prison Directors, who addressed a letter to Governor Gillett recommending Brown to clemency on the ground that his health had been permanently impaired by his having been tortured in the jacket on a charge of which he was innocent.

On the strength of this communication Governor Gillett pardoned Brown. This letter must be on file at Sacramento,

---

[2] Savage; cruel.

and constitutes the most damning indictment against the system. The directors knew what had occurred, the Governor knew what had occurred, and yet the jacket remained in use.

Only a few weeks after Brown had been pardoned another man was subjected to the same torture and for the same reason. He was the telegraph operator in the Warden's office, and was accused of having introduced opium into the prison. He also strenuously denied the charge, and was "cinched" in the jacket to make him confess. Having poor Brown in mind, he gave up after 83 hours' torture and "confessed." I met this man on Market Street the other day, and he told me the story anew.

"Why did you confess when you were innocent?" I asked.

"What could I do?" he replied. "I didn't know any more about the charge they had against me than Brown knew about his charge, and I made up my mind at the start that I'd die rather than say I was guilty. But the more I suffered and the more I thought of what Brown looked like the day he left, all broken up, so that he would never be any good again, the weaker I got, and finally, after I could stand no more, I told them I did it.

"You know what happened. The same old story. I was sent to the mill when I could hardly walk, and when the board of directors met it took them about three minutes to take my credits. That's a great stunt of the board of directors. It takes four of them to grant a parole, but three of them can forfeit a man's credits in a couple of minutes.

"And another thing you don't want to forget is how they used to make a man go to work as soon as he got out of the jacket. I've seen men thrown into the jacket on Saturday afternoon for not having their tasks done for the week, stay there on bread and water until Monday morning, and then be run to the mill and expected to get out their tasks for the next week. If they failed it was a case of the jacket again over the next Sunday. A couple of fellows went crazy under this kind of a deal.

ch. ends next p.

"Talk about the Spanish Inquisition and people being monsters in those days! Huh! I guess the world's just about the same, only things were done in the open then, and now they're done under cover.

"I went through that torture, and I've never been the same man since. I'll never be the same man again, and you can see that for yourself. Yet I'm not a criminal, and never was. I got in there because I took a chance when I was driven into a corner, and the eight years they gave me was certainly punishment enough.

"And now here I am eking out an existence, working nine or ten hours a day, and the very man who put the jacket on me and had the say on how long I should stay in it is drawing his little $165 a month for that kind of work.[3] Isn't that enough to make a man turn bitter and tempt him to fight back? Of course it is, and it's just thoughts like those that make many a man persist in going wrong. You and I may have sense enough to know that it's a sucker game, and keep from butting our heads against a stone wall, but lots of them don't.

"And there's no telling what day some other unfortunate will get the same kind of a deal, is there? All this talk about improving prison conditions and making the prisons serve a good purpose instead of a bad one makes me tired. I'm not saying that a man shouldn't be sent to prison when he breaks a law. I've got sense enough to see both sides of it.

"Take my own case, for instance. Here I am working hard for what I get. Suppose someone breaks into my room or holds me up on the street and takes away what belongs to me, what I've worked hard to get. I'd be sore; I'd want protection; I might even want revenge, although after what I've been through myself I'm not so sure about the revenge part. But I can understand other people wanting revenge; it's human nature. But that's the spirit that kills all the good. I don't say that the prisons should be made summer resorts, or that the life should be one continual round of pleasure, but I do say that when it is necessary to send a man to prison he should

[3] Adjusted for inflation, $165 a month in 1912 would be equivalent to approximately $5,000 a month, or $60,000 a year, in 2023.

be treated as if he was almost human, and then maybe after a while they'd find out that he really is human.

"Plenty of fresh air, a good place to sleep, clean food, work that he'd take an interest in, with pay for what he did, and, above all, no torture. What would you think of a mother or father who wasn't sure that one of their children had swiped jam from the closet, and landed on the first one they got hold of and tortured it until it confessed? And if that child went wrong afterward, who would you blame? That's a fair question, and the case is parallel.

"A man commits a crime, gets kicked into the penitentiary, and then a lot of self-righteous people call it sentiment when someone has the intelligence to ask that he get a square deal and be given a chance to learn something and redeem himself, so that when he comes out he will be a better man and do the right thing.

"This old system has been tried a good many years, hasn't it? Why not try something else and see how it works. If it don't pan out there wouldn't be anything lost, and they could go back to the old scheme again.

"But I know what I'm talking about, and I believe you see it the same way. I don't see how you can help seeing it that way. It's up to you to make other people see it that way, and don't fall down; don't show the white feather. If certain people that never do any thinking above their waist, or only through a dollar sign, call it mush, let them. But the time is coming when people are going to think about these things. Lots of them are thinking that way now.

"Remember, Lowrie, there's several thousand of us fellows keeping tabs on you. Stick to facts. Tell all the good things you can, but for the love of Mike keep your mitts out of the soft soap. [4] And don't forget to show that chaining and muzzling a dog, and kicking him whenever you feel like it, never makes him a fit subject to go loose, especially when he's hungry. So long."

---

[4] A popular idiom of the 19th century. Essentially, Brown is telling Lowrie not to flatter himself or sweet talk his readers.

20

There is a band at San Quentin which practices every night, but the night before a man is hanged the instruments are mute. There isn't any rule about it—the band could practice on hang-day eve if they wanted to—but the throes of the human soul in the death chamber above will not permit. In one instance a condemned man sent down word that he would like to have music for his last night. The death chamber is some distance from the bandroom, and the blatancy of the brass instruments is mellowed into harmony when it gets there.

The band has a custom of playing a short concert the night before a "long-timer" or a popular prisoner is discharged; also on the night preceding the day when a "bunch" of paroled prisoners are to leave, but this was the first and only instance of a serenade for a man who was to "go out" through the little square hole, and with a broken neck. The band played for him, but there were many false notes, and the music was a wail.

The effect of an execution upon the prisoners can scarcely be put into words, especially the effect upon the prisoners who pass through it for the first time. Men who remain in prison a number of years become more or less accustomed to the thought that a fellow creature is to be killed at precisely half past ten o'clock on Friday morning. With each additional execution they become more indifferent.

Passing through a slaughterhouse for the first time—and with most persons it is the last time—one is horrified to the point of nausea at the cold-blooded way in which life is gashed out, but the men who work there, and those who work in the vicinity, become inured to the horror, and finally reach a state where they think nothing of it. It is so, to some extent, with those who take human life and with those who are compelled to be nearby.

Men who turn faint at the sight of blood have been known to become the most truculent soldiers, eager and ready to kill human beings wholesale. Man may accustom himself to anything, but in becoming accustomed to some things he loses in manhood. This is true of those who hang human beings, and it is true in degree of those who are compelled to be contiguous to hangings. In this way many men who have been sent to prison, some of them for taking human life, come to regard human life as cheap. On the other hand, there are a few men who suffer renewed tortures with every execution, making their punishment doubly severe.

In passing sentence the judges do not say anything about this kind of punishment. It is an injustice to prisoners that they should be made to suffer it, and it is, of course, a blot on civilization that this kind of cold-blooded murder occurs at all. The cry is that those who commit murder must be murdered in turn in order that society may be protected, the theory being that capital punishment acts as a deterrent to murder. Yet, doing it for the sake of a deterrent influence, it is done in a sneaky, shame-faced way.

It requires from twelve to eighteen seconds from the time a condemned man is started from the death chamber until he is dangling at the end of the rope. Why this scientific swiftness? Why the electric chair which is supposed to snuff out life in a flash? If the murder really is a deterrent, why not torture the victim? Why not strangle him to death slowly?

ch. ends p. 249

Why not do it in the marketplace, where men and women may come and see? They used to have public executions. Why have they ceased to be public? Because it was found that the sight of a fellow creature being murdered in cold blood hardened those who saw it done. It was realized that such a sight was not good for human eyes and hearts.

And after all is said and done, it is the poor man for whom the gallows waits. During all the years that men have been murdered by the State at San Quentin, but one man with means has been hanged. Chinese, Indians, negroes, cholos, cripples, and dements have died in mid-air, but only one man who had money. The man with money, or with friends willing to spend money for him, gets off with "life" or a term of years.

Comparing the crimes of those who have been hanged with those who are serving terms for murder, the comparison is all in favor of the men who died. In murder trials where high-priced lawyers are engaged it is the opposing lawyers, not the defendant, on trial. The jury, unconsciously, perhaps, decides the case on the strength of the lawyers.

Not so many years ago there were five cases of uxoricide[1] in San Francisco within a period of two weeks. One man shot his young wife as she lay in bed. He got twenty years. Another went half way across the city to where his wife was living and shot her to death in the presence of their little children. He got life. Another, a streetcar conductor, cut his wife's throat. He got ten years. Another shot his paramour on the street, and while she lay on the sidewalk, begging for her life, emptied the revolver into her writhing body. He was sentenced for life. The fifth man was found lying in a drunken stupor beside his wife's dead body. He had a revolver clutched in his hand, and could not remember what had occurred—both had been drinking. He was hanged.

As the time approached for his execution nearly every prisoner was miserable. A strenuous effort was made to get the condemned man a commutation to life imprisonment.

[1] The act of murdering one's wife.

One of the best lawyers in San Francisco was induced to take an active interest in the case. Warden Hoyle went to Sacramento to interview the Governor. But the man had been guilty of being too poor to hire an attorney at his trial. He was hanged.

Some condemned prisoners try to commit suicide, but such a close watch is kept over them that they seldom succeed. The only man who has accomplished it at San Quentin rushed out of his cell when the door was opened in the morning to pass in his breakfast, darted past the guard, ran up the stairway to the roof of the cell building and dived off to the asphaltum pavement below. After gaining the roof of the building he made three separate starts to jump off before he finally did so. He kept running back and forth from the apex of the slanting roof to the edge, and it was not until Captain Randolph, who had rushed over from the office, was about to grapple with him that he threw his body over. When they picked him up he was conscious. After lingering in the hospital about ten weeks, during which he suffered several amputations, and terrible agony, he died.

The day before Siemsen and Dabner were executed I had occasion to go up to the general utility room. Calmly, as though decorating a Christmas box, two striped men were tacking cheesecloth inside a coffin. Close at hand was another coffin, already finished. These coffins were being prepared for two human beings who at the moment were alive and in good health.

That night when the prisoner who had charge of the execution room came down to the office I asked him how the two condemned men, or, rather, the man and the boy, were taking it.

"Oh, they're all right," he replied. "But I've had a hard day of it. I was hung six times this afternoon. You see, they're going to hang them together, and some green guards will have to be used to do the work. They don't want any delay or slips, so they had me act as a dummy for the guards to

ch. ends p. 249

practice on. I went through the whole performance six times—stood on the trap, had my legs strapped and the blackcap and rope over my neck. Ugh! It was fierce."

Later, talking with the barber who shaved the condemned men the afternoon before they were executed, he told me that Siemsen asked to have his mustache taken off because it would make him "lighter."

A few days before the execution Dabner's mother tottered out of the prison gate for the last time. The boy's father had died a few days before. This mother was unable to come and see her boy on the fatal morning—her caged child, the being she had suffered for and with from his first wail of infantile bewilderment. He was less than 20 years of age when hanged.

If the deterrent effect of example be worthy of consideration, why should an atrocious murder have been committed in the big community where this boy had lived, within twenty-four hours after his expiation of his crime?

Up on the top floor of the old sash and blind factory at San Quentin there are two gruesome rooms. They are large, airy rooms, in which the echoes of one's voice are lost in the white-washed rafters. In the center of one of these rooms are two cages, separated from each other by a solid plank partition. The cages themselves are constructed of 2x4 timbers set a few inches apart. Inside each cage is a mattress, blankets and a bucket—nothing more. They are known as the death chambers. They are used solely for the purpose of keeping human beings who have been condemned to "hang by the neck until dead" where they may be closely watched during their last days on earth.

As a general rule a condemned man is taken from "Death Row" and imprisoned in one of these cages on the Tuesday preceding the Friday when he is scheduled to "swing off." Once he enters this cage he never comes out, save with hands lashed behind him for the few steps into the adjoining room, where he is to be the central figure in the greatest of earth's tragedies.

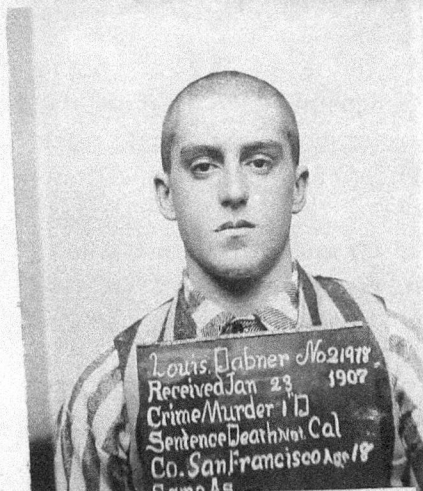

Louis Dabner No 21978
Received Jan 23 1907
Crime Murder 1 D
Sentence Death Not Cal
Co. San Francisco Age 18

John Seimsen No 21985
Received Jan 26 1907
Crime Murder 1st Deg
Sentence Death Not Hawaii
Co. San Francisco Age 28
Same As 6158 Folsom

Name *Louis Dabner*	Name *John Seimsen 2T*
No. *21978*	No. *21985*
County *San Francisco*	County *San Francisco*
Crime *Murd. 1st Deg.*	Crime *Murd 1st Deg.*
Term *Death*	Term *Death*
Received *Jan. 23, 1907*	Received *Jan 26 1907*
Discharged	Discharged
Remarks	Remarks *Same as 5158 Fols.*

In one or two instances during my life at San Quentin condemned men were taken to this chamber a week or ten days in advance of execution. A study of their temperament while awaiting the final decision in "Death Row" had convinced the officers that they would cheat the gallows by going the "Dutch route" if not closely watched during the last fortnight.

Leon Soeder was confined in the death chamber two weeks before he was hanged. He had repeatedly asserted that he would never die on the gallows.

Adjoining the death chamber is the execution room, the place where human beings are turned into loathsome corpses with scientific swiftness, the place where more than two score living, breathing men—some of them mere boys—have "paid the penalty" exacted by the law of the people of the State of California.

Prior to 1893 each county did its own hanging, but at that time a law was passed designating the State prisons as the only places where "legal executions" should take place. Since then more than forty have been executed at Folsom, an average of three each year.

Stand these sixty men in an imaginary line and take a good look at them. They are yours, you know.

What do we see? First, we see a number of boyish faces, for we are bound to be attracted by the faces of children. Then as we sweep along the melancholy line we see old men with gray hair and tired eyes. Sandwiched indiscriminately along the row are negroes, Chinese, and Indians. There are men of intelligent countenances and there are men in whose eyes the light of reason is absent. There are fat men and lean men, tall men and short men, handsome and ugly men. But they all have ceased to breathe. They are all dead; and around the throat of each is a little purple mark.

In taking up this subject I am awed. I am distraught with the fear that I may not do it justice. I am filled with a great desire to tell what I know, what I have seen and felt, and what

Taken out on order of Sup
Court of S. F. County Dec 16-06
Returned Jan 28-07
Executed March 29th 07

Leon Soeder

20791. 2nd Term

Murder 1st Deg
San Francisco
Death
Age. 38. Yrs
Cook
France
Rec Sept 15/04
Des

SEPT-15-1904
AGE 38
DEATH
GERMANY

20791
LEON SOEDER
MURD. 1ST DEG 2T
SAN FRAN. CO
SAME 16079°

20791

20791

other persons have seen and felt, so that each and every one of you may realize to its fullest extent just what the execution of a fellow being means. Those of you who are squeamish, those of you who do not want to be shocked, those of you who do not feel that capital punishment is of sufficient gravity for you to read of the effect it has upon the prisoners who are compelled to suffer close contact with it must not read what follows.

By a fortuitous, though distressing, circumstance, it fell to my lot to learn more about the gallows and the "technique" of hanging a man that occurs ordinarily with prisoners. As a matter of fact, probably not more than twenty prisoners, exclusive of those who have been hanged, have ever seen the gallows at San Quentin.

Prisoners are "not permitted in the execution room, nor are they permitted to go to that floor of the furniture factory. Only those who cut down the dead body and lay it in the black pine box are allowed to enter the place.

But several years after I entered San Quentin—at which time I was employed as history and statistical clerk in the turnkey's office—a newly elected Sheriff in one of the counties of Nevada found himself with a hanging on his hands. A man had been sentenced to death, and the Sheriff was to be the official executioner. The Sheriff had never hanged a man in his life.

Not knowing how to proceed, he conceived the idea of writing to the Warden at San Quentin for "pointers." The letter stated that he had a man to hang and wanted to know how to do it. The letter was sent in to the turnkey's office by the Warden, and I was delegated to write the desired information.

Now, as I had never hanged a man either—it is surprising how many of us have never hanged a man, isn't it?—there was but one course to pursue. That was to go up to the execution room and learn how it was done. So I went to the Captain of the Yard and got a pass, and the entire process was explained to me by the trusty in charge of the death chambers.

I confess to a feeling of morbid curiosity as I drew near the place, and entering the room my eyes were instantly drawn to the ghastly murder machine before me. I saw a double gallows, painted pale blue. It fascinated me. As I walked toward it my eyes remained staring, and I did not look to see where I was going.

The platform was supported by four heavy uprights, one at each corner. At either side of this platform were other uprights, and across the top extended a massive beam, with another upright at the middle running down to the platform and separating the two "traps." The crossbeam was notched over each trap, notched for the rope, and dangling suggestively from each notch was a gaping noose, the huge and cruel "hangman's knot," looking for all the world like a coiled snake. At the rear of the platform was a rather broad flight of steps, and back of the gallows platform was a little booth, extending clear across, but closed in so that one could only see into it from the front and only part way down from the top. It reminded me of a Punch and Judy booth[2] more than anything else, and I wondered what it was for.

The trusty led me to the stairs and we started to ascend.

"Count 'em," he suggested, as we went up. I did so and found there were thirteen.

"Was that done purposely?" I asked, without thinking.

"Naw," replied the trusty; "it just chanced that they needed thirteen steps, that's all. But it makes a good point to tell visitors. Of course, when a guy goes up to be topped he don't count steps. The chances are he couldn't count 'em if he tried. But here we are, and I'll explain the whole thing to you," he added, as we reached the platform.

"In the first place, when a guy comes in to be stretched

[2] Punch and Judy is a traditional British slapstick puppet show performed by a single puppeteer featuring Mr. Punch and his wife Judy.

ch. ends p. 249

they measure him in the Bertillon room.[3] They measure
from the bottom of his ear to the top of his head, and then
they deduct that from his height. Say a man's five feet ten
inches tall and he measures seven inches from the base of
his ear to the top of his skypiece. You take seven inches from
five feet ten and it leaves you five feet three. That's his hangin'
height. You see, they don't hang a man's head; they just hang
him from the neck down, and to get the right drop they
have to know just how many feet and inches he is from his
tootsie-wootsies to the place where the chicken got the axe.

"All right; we've got a guy whose hangin' height is five feet
three inches. Next comes the question. How old is he—are
his bones soft or brittle? You see, an old man's bones are kind
of glassy; his neck snaps like a match when the old knot here
cracks him under the ear, and if they dropped him too far,
why, it would tear his head off. The whole idea is to drop
a man far enough so's to be sure and break his neck, but not
so far that the shock will tear his head off.

"Suppose, for instance, a man jumped out of a second or
third story window with a rope tied around his neck. When
he got to the end of the rope, what would happen? You don't
know? Well, I'll tell you. The chances are ninety-nine out of
a hundred that he'd hit the ground in two pieces and leave
the rope danglin'. His head might not get there as quick as
the rest of him, but it would sure come down alone. That's
what they got to be careful of. They cut one guy's head off
here once, and it was awful. The place looked like a slaughterhouse when we came in to get the stiff, and everybody in
the room was sick."

Keen to the value of dramatic effect, the trusty slowly
swept his arm from one side of the room to the other, as if
calling my eyes to see the horrible picture he had described,
and then he paused a few moments to allow my imagination
plenty of time.

"So, you see, they have to be mighty careful how far they

[3] Refer back to Chapter 3, p. 30.

drop a guy. First I'll explain how they decide on the drop. We'll suppose a man is five feet ten inches, as I said, and his hangin' height is five feet three. He weighs one hundred and sixty pounds and is thirty years old. The hangman comes up the day before the bumpin' off is to take place and has a long talk with his meat. But instead of bein' interested in what the man has to say the hangman is observin' his neck to see if it is thick or thin, tough or soft, or if he has any deformity. If the man has an ordinary neck, the drop should be about five feet eight inches for a man of his height and age and build. All right. The hangman comes in here and selects one of these ropes that has been stretched for a year.

You see that row of ropes over there with the little tags tied on 'em and the big weights at the end?"

I looked in the direction indicated and nodded.

"Well, some of them ropes have been stretchin' for a year. It's a special made rope, seven-eighths of an inch thick, and hard as a rock. They never use the same piece of rope twice. He takes this rope and makes the hangman's knot and the noose in one end. Then he takes this little round block and puts it in the noose and pulls it up tight. You'll notice this round block is only two inches in diameter. Well, that is supposed to be the size of a man's neck when he's hangin'. His neck stretches after its broke, and the rope sinks in so that there is only two inches of flesh in the noose. After he's put the block in the noose the hangman throws the other end of the rope up over the crossbeam, and I climb up there and hold it.

"Now, before I go any further I want you to look at these scales here on the posts."

The trusty pointed to the three uprights that supported the crossbeam of the gallows. I saw that the outer face of each post was divided into feet and inches, beginning at the floor.

"We've decided to drop this feller five feet eight inches. Well, here's five feet three inches from the floor, and we tie a string across to the other post at that height. Naturally,

ch. ends p. 249

when this string is tied it will be five feet three inches from the floor of the trap. Then—oh, I forgot something.

"After the hangman has put the little round block in the noose he lays the rope on the floor and measures up it, startin' from the bottom of the noose until he gets five feet eight inches. He ties a piece of white string around the rope at that place. Then I climb up on the crossbeam and draw the rope up till this piece of string is even with the cord that is tied across the scaffold five feet three inches from the trap, and when they're even I tie the rope to the crossbeam. Do you get the drift? The string tied across the scaffold is the man's hangin' height, and the rope is tied to the crossbeam so that it drops exactly five feet eight inches below this hangin' height. Have you got that clear?"

I replied that I had, but I was marveling that he should have explained it all with so much unconcern and indifference. He might have been describing the proper way for killing a steer, so far as any feeling was concerned. Also he seemed to be proud of his knowledge and glad of an opportunity to show it off.

"Now, if you'll come in here I'll show you this box," he continued, opening a little door at the side of the Punch and Judy affair at the back of the gallows platform and leading the way in.

Inside the box was a board shelf built against the front wall, and about a foot above this shelf was the opening, extending clear across the front, from which the scaffold and the room beyond could be seen. By reaching out through this opening I could almost touch the rope dangling from the crossbeam.

"You see these three little holes here," my informant went on. "Well, there's a string comes up through each of them. The first string runs across the board and is tied to this first eyelet. The second string goes to this second eyelet here in the middle, and the third string goes to the eyelet at the other end. Two of these strings are dummies, and the other does the trick.

"When they are all ready to top a guy three guards come into this box and stand in front of these three strings. Each one has a sharp knife and holds the point down on the board on the outside of his string. When the signal is given they all draw the knives across the strings together. See! Look at the marks on the board where the knives have cut!"

I looked and saw the scars, black with dirt, where there had been repeated knife cuts across the pine board.

"You don't mean to tell me there's been that many hangings?" I asked, incredulously.

"Oh, no. We often set the trap and go through the whole performance for big visitors. That's what makes all those cuts.

"When the strings are cut a weight is released, and falls, and when this weight gets to the end of the rope it is tied to the bolts under the trap are jerked back like a flash, and the trap flies back with a powerful spring and catches on a clamp that keeps it from swingin' on its hinges—somethin' like the top of a matchbox when you press the button. It's just exactly the same as if the floor was suddenly pulled out from under you right now, only the man with the rope around his neck drops 5 feet 8 inches and then stops. Everything stops for him then, and no chance for appeal. It's off.

"Of course, the three guards don't know which string does the trick. The only man who knows that is the man who sets them, and he never tells. But all three strings have to be cut, just the same. If one man failed to cut his it would hold the key string from releasin' the weight, so, practically, they all do the job."

He paused for a moment to flick some dust from the board with his cap.

"As long as you're here I might as well describe just how a guy is topped, if you want to hear it."

I was half sick at the way he had described the murder process, but determined to learn all I could, and told him to continue.

"Well, when all is ready and the witnesses are here they

ch. ends next p.

step into his cage in the other room and tie his hands behind him. Then they lead him in here and up the thirteen steps, with the priests praying at his sides, and stand him on the trap. In case he weakens in the knees and can't stand up they have a board to strap from his heels to his shoulders—but they've never had to use that yet. As soon as he gets on the trap one man buckles a strap around his legs just below the knees, and another pulls the blackcap over his head. Then the hangman drops the noose over the blackcap and draws it up tight around his neck, holdin' his fist against the knot to keep it from slippin.' As soon as all this is done the hangman raises his other hand, and that's the signal.

"When the guys in the box here see that hand go up they cut the strings. The hangman gives a kind of push against the knot just as the trap is sprung. The man falls through the little hole like a flash and there is a kind of crunching crack that turns your stomach inside out if you're squeamish. That crunch is the whole trick.

"You see, the big knot acts just like a sledgehammer. It hits the feller under the right ear just like a club, breaking his neck like a pipestem. His head flops over and falls on his shoulder or down on his chest, and the knot takes the place where his head ought to be. Of course a feller never knows anything after that knot hits him. He just hangs there swingin' until his heart stops beatin' and the croakers announce that he has kicked in.

"They never waste any time on the job. Sometimes it is only a minute from the time they start tying a feller's hands in the next room till he's through the trap and danglin' like a rag, and out of his misery."

"And he doesn't suffer; he doesn't strangle?" I asked.

"No, not a bit," was the reply. "The instant the trap is sprung it's curtains; he's as dead as he ever will be, so far as feelin' is concerned."

"But he must have one supreme moment, one awful instant, that cannot be described in words," I insisted.

The trusty looked at me speculatively before replying.

"Well, I'll tell you what I think. If it wasn't for the days of waitin' and watchin' the hour draw near, I wouldn't want any quicker way to bump off, myself. The trouble is, a man dies a million times before he sets foot on the trap. I don't believe in topping a guy."

"And what do you believe?" I asked.

"Well, I'd let the guy think he was goin' to be bumped off, let him die the million times in his cell, and then commute his sentence at the very last moment, just as they were putting the necktie around his neck. Who ever heard of a guy killin' anyone after being commuted from the rope at the last moment? The only drawback is that the hangman wouldn't get his twenty-five bucks, and of course that would never do."

As I passed out I did a lot of thinking, especially about the three guards cutting the strings. Why should they have three guards, and why should they make a secret of the key-string? And then I knew. It was the effort to escape responsibility, an acknowledgment that they were engaged in a dastardly and inhuman act. But why should they feel that way? If hanging a man is right, why should everybody concerned want to point to the other fellow and say, "He did it"?[4]

---

[4] We Heathens can't help but see the symbolic link between the three guards cutting the strings and the Fates, or Moirai, of Greek mythology, and the Parcae of Roman mythology, who presided over the birth and life of humans. Usually portrayed as three women, each Fate had a different task: Clotho spun the thread of life, Lachesis measured its allotted length, and Atropos cut it off with her shears.

21

I recall a story that was once told me of two men who were shipwrecked. After days of hardship in an open boat they landed on what appeared to be an uninhabited coast. But on reaching the crest of the first hill they found themselves confronted with a gallows. Whereupon they clasped hands fervently and exclaimed: "Thank God we've landed in a civilized country."

There is a gallows at San Quentin, as I have told, and my duties in the clothing room brought me into close contact with a number of the men who were hanged on it. I suppose I should have felt thankful to God, but I didn't. To me a gallows stands as an indictment of Christianity, and prisons as monuments to 2,000 years of Christian blindness.

They are now busily engaged in building new cell houses at San Quentin, designed to hold 1,600 prisoners. It is called a model of "modern" prison construction. I shall have a good deal to say about these new buildings later, but the thought that such construction should be in progress in the Year of Our Lord Nineteen Hundred and Eleven certainly strikes a discordant chord.

Of course, there are many who hold that prisons are necessary, and that men who commit crime—and are convicted—should be "punished." They give no thought to the causes that may have led up to the crime, nor do they feel that the offender is worthy of any effort to make him better, save by punishing him, and thus, perhaps, filling him with the fear of similar punishment if he commits crime again. These are chiefly the self-righteous, those who have never felt the pinch of want nor the spirit of toleration and mercy that comes only by having suffered or by having come close to the suffering of others.

There had been executions while I worked in the jute mill, but aside from the general gloom and silence observable in most of the prisoners who worked there, we knew very little about it. All we knew was that some man was taken up to some place in the old furniture factory and put to death at half past ten.

On such days when we came out of the jute mill to go to dinner at noon we all spoke in subdued tones, and as we passed across the lower yard to the mess hall we all looked up at the four whitewashed windows of the execution room and imagined what had occurred there a short hour and a half before.

But after I went to work at the clothing room the horror of the thing struck me poignantly. When I had received Wardrip the day he came in I had felt that I was a party to the process that was taking him closer to the gallows, but now I found that I was to take an active part—I was to be a *deus ex machina*[1] in earnest.

With the exception of Saturday and Sunday, and holidays, the condemned men are permitted to walk on the asphaltum before their cells from 12 o'clock to 2 each day. On Tuesday, half an hour before their exercise time ends, they are escorted to the barbershop to be shaved. It is when they are on the way back from the barbershop that the move is made indicating that the dread noose is near. If a man is scheduled to hang on Friday he is cut out of the line as he comes back from the barbershop on Tuesday afternoon and guided into the clothing room.

---

[1] Translated from Latin: a god from a/the machine.

ch. ends p. 263

I shall never forget the first time I saw this done. The string of condemned men were walking toward me on the way from the barbershop to their cells, and just as they were passing the door of the clothing room two guards stepped up and tapped two of them on the shoulder. No word was spoken, yet these two men knew what it meant.

I can still see their faces as they turned and came into the room. I had only had a few minutes' warning myself. The turnkey had stepped into the clothing room while the condemned men were in the barbershop and informed me that two of them were to "swing" on Friday, and that they would be brought in to be dressed when they came back. He remained there with me to receive them.

As they stepped into the room, with the guards close behind, I observed their faces. One was a mere boy, not yet 19 years old; the other a man of about 24. They were both Mexicans and had killed an old man and then burned his body, after taking his money. Both tried to appear brave. The older man succeeded in keeping a stolid countenance, but the face of the boy was a fearful thing to see. Bravado and fear, courage and cowardice, defiance and terror, hope and despair, chased each other from his heart to his eyes and back again in rapid succession as he was ordered to take off his clothes.

When both men were stripped they were herded into the back room, where the bathtub was located, and compelled to get into the tub together. While they were bathing I selected new clothing, under the direction and watchfulness of the turnkey, and he proceeded to cut off the buttons and buckles. This was to prevent the condemned from getting anything— even a button—by which he might wound himself.

Presently the two men came back and dressed themselves in the new stripes. Then, under heavy guard, they were escorted across the yard—the "Garden of Death"—and up the stairs of the old furniture factory—the stairs run up the outside of the building—and into the death chamber.

I never saw either of them alive again.

Wednesday and Thursday dragged their leadened minutes by. Late on Thursday night, when all was still, the guards came to the clothing room and got the two black suits and the shirts, but no collars. On Friday morning, when the two condemned men arose from their troubled sleep, they found their suits of stripes gone, and in their stead the suits of black, and white shirts. But there were no collars—collars would interfere with the rope.

Having seen these two men, having talked with them, I could not keep my mind from their horrible plight. How must they feel? How must they count each moment of that fateful morning?

The sun was bright, there was not a cloud in the sky. Life was sweet and desirable, and they were full of red blood. Yet before the sun reached the zenith they would be two clods of lifeless clay. I believe I suffered every pang that boy suffered, for my thoughts persisted in remaining fixed on him. I saw his young face and his terror-stricken eyes again and again.

At 10 o'clock the front gate was opened to let in the "crowd." Immediately the "witnesses" began to pour in. Many of them were smoking cigars and most of them were laughing as they hurried across the yard for fear they might be late, or that they might not get in the first row before the scaffold.

I counted them as they entered, but I have forgotten the exact number. I am positive it was more than 400. By twos and threes they scudded across the open space and disappeared in the human murder place.

Over in the cell buildings the doors were locked, and white faces peeped from the wickets. An hour before they hang a man all the prisoners working in the upper yard and shops are locked in their cells. But there is no way to close the wickets.

An awful silence had fallen over the prison. Even the birds in the pine trees before the clothing room had ceased

ch. ends p. 263

to chirp. The very air seemed to shudder. The several men who worked in the office building, and were exempt from the lockup rule, had assembled in the clothing room, without concerted understanding, but no one spoke. Ever and anon we glanced furtively at the clock, but our eyes scarcely saw the hands, for the scaffold and two doomed creatures intervened.

"Happy Jack," a lawyer serving ten years, tried to whistle but broke down miserably, and mumbled something under his breath. The silence was emphasized when he ceased. It seemed as though every man were listening for the thud of the traps.

And this was to be a double execution. Two men were to be dropped into eternity at the same time. They were to stand side by side as the nooses were adjusted. It was horrible. It is impossible to put it into words.

There had not been a "double" execution at San Quentin for years, though on one occasion three men had been hanged on the same day. Two had "swung off" together, while the third listened tensely in the nearby chamber. I have often thought that this third man must have suffered the tortures of the damned.

The execution was to be at 10:30. At 10:29 I could stand it no longer, and started to add a long column of figures. But instead of figures I saw ropes and coffins dancing before my eyes. And then "Happy Jack" came to the rescue. He told a funny story—something about a darky captured by the Union troops during the Civil War, who, when asked why he did not join the Union forces and help fight for his own cause, said:

"Well, colonel, I've seen two dogs fightin' for a bone, but I'se nebber seen the bone fight!"

We all laughed uproariously, almost hysterically. And yet the story had been unintentionally apropos. While we were still laughing the "witnesses" began to come back. They passed across the garden briskly. I expected to see serious, even tragic faces. Instead I saw smiles and heard heartless comment. I could not understand it, save on the theory that they were trying to conceal what they really felt. I believe that was the case, for at all the executions that occurred during the years that followed the "witnesses" always came back laughing. More than 400 had witnessed this execution, and a large number had arrived too late to get in. It had been made a kind of festive or gala occasion.

Under the present Warden at San Quentin the number of witnesses is limited to twelve, which is the number required by law. But the Warden is besieged with requests to see each execution that occurs. A condemned man has the "privilege" of having five friends or relatives witness his execution if he so desires. Only two men have availed themselves of this "privilege" to my knowledge.

At 10:55 all the "witnesses" had passed out, and the silence that had prevailed a few minutes before, while the State had been engaged in murder, was broken by grating keys and clanging doors as the men poured out of their little "separate hells" and returned to their unremunerative work.

Presently I saw the trusty from the execution room coming across the yard with an armful of striped clothing. He entered the clothing room and threw the garments on the table.

"Two men discharged," he commented grimly, as he wiped his forehead with a red handkerchief.

Instantly I knew it was the clothing I had furnished to the two condemned men three days before, and I drew back so that it might not touch me. I turned into the next room—the turnkey's office—and asked what I should do with it. The turnkey had just returned from the execution room, where he had adjusted one of the blackcaps—shutting out the light of God's sun forever from a human face. I looked at his hands, expecting to see them covered with blood. He was chewing a fresh cigar and seemed quite cool.

"Have buckles sewed on and put 'em in stock," he said,

ch. ends p. 263

tersely. "They're practically new. They've only been worn three days."

It had not occurred to me that this clothing would be put back on the shelves. That meant that two incoming prisoners would be garbed in it. I got the Chinaman who helped about the clothing room to take the things to the prison tailor shop, and when they were returned that afternoon they went back onto the shelves, though I was particular to mix them with the other clothing so that I should not be able to identify the pieces. I wanted to dodge knowing to what particular men these garments would subsequently be given.

And then a horrifying thought came upon me like a stark, staring corpse. Perhaps the clothes I had received the day I came in had been imbued with the fearful agony of a condemned man's last hours. I hurried to the records to see if a tall man had been hanged at any time within a year of my arrival, and breathed easier when I found that there had not. But that did not alter the fact that two men were doomed to wear the clothes I had just put on the shelves. It seemed criminal. Such clothing should be burned.

I was not a psychometric[2] crank, but the thought of dressing a new prisoner in clothing that had been taken from the body of a man about to die on the gallows seemed heathenish. There was something unspeakably horrible about it. You smile! It is "maudlin sentiment?" Very well. How would YOU like to be compelled to wear such clothing? How would you like to have your son, or brother, or father compelled to wear it?

When "maudlin sentiment" strikes home it becomes intensely human.

Half an hour after the hanging I saw a ghastly cortège coming up the road past the dungeon. There were eight striped figures carrying two black pine boxes. The eight

[2] Psychometrics or psychometry is the supposed ability or art of divining information or facts about an event or person by touching inanimate objects associated with them.

striped figures seemed to advance blindly; their faces were tragic; they were ashamed of the light of day. At the corner of the photograph gallery they turned and went to the morgue.

The "bridge of sighs" had not been built in those days, and coffins from the execution room had to be flaunted in the eyes of the prisoners in order to reach the morgue. I gazed at the horrible, cheap black boxes through maddened eyes. It had suddenly seared into my brain that the two human beings whom I had seen alive and full of health three days before were stretched in those boxes—two corpses whose souls had been sent crashing into eternity.

I cared not what they had done. It made no difference. Murder had been committed in retaliation for murder. This being so, why should not the murderers of the murderers be called murderers? I felt that way. So would you if you had looked into a Mexican boy's brown eyes and seen the awful hopelessness, the terrible fear, the mute cry for mercy that I had seen. It was murder to me—murder and nothing else. No good example had been set. No deterrent influence had been created. Society had merely revenged itself by committing murder. That's what the cave men used to do.

The visitors, the "witnesses," had laughed as they scudded away from the terrible thing, but all that day I watched in vain to see a prisoner smile.

And afterward I learned that a "witness" who had succumbed to active nausea when the traps were sprung was obliged to take a party of "friends" to the saloon at San Quentin Point and "treat" as a bribe to keep his name out of the newspapers.

Yet there are many who wonder why a prisoner goes wrong the second time.

At the last session of the Legislature a measure had been introduced for the abolition of capital punishment. It had received the support of one House, but was defeated in the other. Yet for several weeks it looked very much as if the bill would pass, and the condemned men at San Quentin spent

ch. ends p. 263

tortured days gazing through the narrow slits in their cell doors, watching the front gate for the Warden.

Every few days the Warden would come inside the prison while the condemned men were exercising and talk with them individually. He did not talk with them as Warden to prisoner, but as man to man, and there has yet to be a poor wretch executed under his administration who does not feel that Warden Hoyle is his friend.

And it was not only while the condemned were exercising that the Warden came in to chat with them. I have seen him stand on the tier before a cell in death row and talk for hours to the eyes that peered out at him, especially at night, when all is still and the condemned are alone with their thoughts— face to face with the grim specter of approaching death.

I observed Warden Hoyle closely during the days preceding and following the executions at which he has been compelled to officiate. I do not believe it possible for a man to suffer more keenly than he has suffered. Not that he lets it be seen—to the average person there is no noticeable change in him at such times—but to me—well, I don't lay claim to any degree of occult power—still I know what he goes through.

And so when the bill was introduced for the abolition of capital punishment Warden Hoyle told the condemned men about it and kept them informed as to its progress. At each step toward its realization he went inside and carried the good news. But when the measure was defeated in the Upper House he did not go in to tell them. He couldn't.

The great majority of the men who suffer the death penalty do not suffer it because of particularly atrocious or aggravated crimes, but because they are poor and are not "defended" in the way that money defends. To prove this statement one has but to investigate the trials for murder in any county. An examination of the evidence will disclose that deliberate and premeditated murder is frequently visited by life imprisonment, or even a term of years for the defendant, while unpremeditated, even unintentional, killings are often paid for by exacting the life of the offender. It is all a matter of how the defense is presented and conducted. This being so, it being possible for the man of greater culpability to escape, while the man of lesser culpability is hanged, capital punishment, as a just measure, is farcical. On this ground alone it should be abolished.

Again, chief executives are sometimes inveigled[3] into extending clemency in the least deserving of cases, while men comparatively, or wholly, guiltless of premeditation are allowed to die on the gallows. Two cases of the former kind have been on my mind for a long time. I knew these beneficiaries of a former Governor's clemency very well, indeed, and liked them both, but that shall not deter me from telling the facts, omitting names and places, of course.

John and Caesar C——, brothers, rented a ranch. They worked hard and raised a good crop on it and then went and paid the rent to the old man who owned the place, getting his receipt. That night they returned to the old man's hut, killed him, and stole the money they had paid him.

When the murder and robbery was discovered they promptly produced the receipt to show that they owed nothing for the rent of the ranch. They not only produced the receipt; they flaunted it—flaunted it to such an extent that suspicion fell upon them.

Evidence was gathered against them, and through the testimony of a Mexican ranch hand they were convicted of murder and sentenced to be hanged. Influence was brought to bear on the Governor, and after hearing the case he agreed to commute the sentence of one of the brothers to life imprisonment. It is claimed that this man rejected clemency for himself unless it was also extended to his brother, and the Governor finally commuted both sentences to life imprisonment. One of the brothers subsequently went insane, and is now confined in the criminal ward of one of the State hospitals. The other brother served about fourteen years and

---

[3] To obtain or acquire by coaxing, flattery, or deception.

ch. ends p. 263

Caesar Cummings   John W. Cummings

16507   16508

Caesar Cummings   John W. Cummings
Murder 1st degree   Murder 1st degree
To be executed Dec. 3/95 To be executed Dec 3/95
Riverside   Riverside
Case appealed to Supreme Court   Case appealed to Supreme Court
Resentenced to be executed   Resentenced to be executed
Sept 23/96.   Sept 23/96

Commuted from death penalty   Commuted from death penalty
to Life Imprisonment Mch 9, 1897. to Life Imprisonment Mch 10, 1897.
Transferred to Insane Asylum   Paroled July 15, 1908
Jan 10, 1907

was paroled. Remember, this was a premeditated murder, committed for the purpose of robbery.

Here is the other case:

Frank D—— insisted that his young wife should become an inmate of a house of ill-fame. Protesting against the horror, she yielded, but was unable to stand it. She escaped, made her way to one of the interior towns and went to work in a factory. He succeeded in locating her, went to the factory, called the girl outside and ordered her to return with him. She refused, whereupon he drew a revolver and shot her. She tried to run, and he fired again.

Then, while she lay screaming for mercy, he stood over her poor, bleeding body and fired three more shots into her. And even as she gasped out her young life at his feet he said, "I'm glad I killed the ——."

The Sheriff had a hard time to prevent a lynching. D—— was tried, convicted, and sentenced to be hanged. On the merits of the case it looked as though nothing could prevent his execution. Powerful influence was brought to bear on the Governor, however, and word was passed to D—— that he must feign insanity.

The Governor appointed a commission to examine the man as to his mental condition, and this commission found him to be insane. On the strength of their report the Governor commuted the sentence of death to life imprisonment.

I saw D—— in the jute mill yard the very day he had been commuted from "the rope." He was surrounded by a group of prisoners, to whom he was imparting the information that he was no more insane than they were, and that he had simply stuttered and looked foolish, according to instructions.

For nine years I saw D—— nearly every day. I have never seen or known a saner man in my life. At the time he entered the prison not an officer but felt that if ever a man deserved the death penalty he did. But with the passing of time and the manifestation of good characteristics D—— became

ch. ends next p.

popular, so popular that those who had at first condemned him did not hesitate to express the hope that he would some day "beat it."

At the end of eight years D—— applied for parole. The same influence that had saved him from the rope was brought to bear, and he was paroled, to leave the prison when he had served nine years' "solid time." Exactly nine years after he entered San Quentin, D——, who had committed a deliberate and monstrous murder, was freed on parole. Yet I have known many men who have served longer than that for taking a few dollars.

Why have I told these two stories, both of which are absolutely true? Certainly not to injure the men involved. They are both making good, and long acquaintance with them won my friendship, along with that of many others. I have told their stories merely to emphasize the inequalities and glaring injustices that exist under the present system.

I could go on and tell the circumstances of other cases where men have been hanged for offenses lacking entirely in premeditation or brutality, but enough has been told to prove that so-called justice is a very uncertain quality.

Sometimes murders occur that seem to demand the life of the offender. Death seems to be the only adequate punishment. I can readily conceive of acts which, were I to commit them, I would surely be compelled to admit that I had forfeited the right to live. So can you. But the infliction of death does not accomplish any good; it is not in accord with the nature of man's soul; it is a yielding to his very lowest instincts.

What shall be done with men who commit awful crimes? I say let the jury decide the penalty, and when the jury feels satisfied that the circumstances warrant it, sentence the offender to imprisonment for life in a separate and remote prison maintained solely for such cases, and without recourse. When the jury feels that there are mitigating or extenuating circumstances, a different penalty can be imposed. Of course, under this system the same injustices that obtain today would still exist—poor men would get the worst of it—but it is infinitely preferable that a poor man should suffer life imprisonment, even without recourse, than that he should be murdered by the State because he is poor and friendless.

22

About six years ago a boy named H—— B—— was dropped through the little square hole without any bottom that is always kept in readiness at San Quentin. Just before the trap was sprung a little bird alighted on one of the window ledges and chirped saucily. But when the boy's body shot down and his neck broke with a horrible crunch the little bird flew away in affright. A group of pale-faced men stood and watched the boy's body—the inert head in the black bag hanging down over his heart, as if listening to hear himself die—while it swayed slowly back and forth. The hanging body was only 18 years old. How old the soul which was being strangled out of it was, no one knows.

And while this 18-year-old human body swung back and forth—like a pendulum of civilization—another boy, a boy with a squint in his eyes, also 18 years old, was hopping about a loom in the prison jute mill, engaged in weaving jute for making bags destined to hold wheat in transportation to other human bodies.

This cross-eyed boy was the partner of the boy whose body was swinging back and forth in the execution room above. Both boys had been guilty of the same crime, but only one had been sentenced to hang. The cross-eyed boy had "turned State's evidence." For doing that he had "escaped" with his life; that is, he had "escaped" into the penitentiary to serve "it all."

These two boys had been at the reform school together. Afterward they killed an old man for his money. The crime was a horrible one, almost as horrible a crime as the hanging of the boy. The boy who was hanged had been pronounced a "bad one" by nearly everybody who came in contact with him.

While at San Quentin awaiting execution he had made a dagger from the handle of the slop bucket in his cell and tried to stab the guard. That was what made him "bad." Of course, a boy waiting to be hanged should be meek and lowly, he should be like a lamb going to the slaughter. It should make no difference that he doesn't understand, that he fails to realize his outlawry, that he feels defiant and inclined to regard the human beings engaged in the preparations for his murder as no better than he is.

Neither of these boys had a home training; neither of them was entirely responsible for nonconformity to the laws of the society in which they found themselves. To them there was no law higher than that of the stomach, and they had hunted and killed in response to their law. For doing so they had been snatched out of the world and confined in cages. Then one of them had been sentenced to "hang by the neck until dead," while the other, in reward for putting the rope about his partner's neck, was let off with punishment for life.

While at San Quentin I had ample opportunity for observing men who turn State's evidence. Invariably such men are shunned and execrated by their fellow prisoners, as they should be. Of course, I am aware that the words "as they should be" will startle, perhaps antagonize, many persons. But why does a prisoner turn State's evidence? Because he is interested in the welfare of society and actuated by a desire to see society's laws upheld? Not once in a thousand times. Almost invariably the man or woman who turns State's evidence does so under the promise or in the hope of leniency.

ch. ends p. 289

The man who turns State's evidence is on a parity with the man who will trample upon women and children in order to be the first one in a lifeboat, or who would throw a child to wolves in order to save his own carcass. He is the nearest thing to a criminal that I know of. By "criminal" I mean one who will, under any circumstances, and at any sacrifice to others, act on the fallacy that self-preservation is the first law of nature. To me, soul-preservation, not self-preservation, is the first law—the law of all laws.

In cases where men turn State's evidence with absolutely no thought of immunity from suffering the consequences which are to be expected in return for their own culpability, but solely and honestly because they feel it is right and unselfish to do so, no adverse criticism can be made. But these cases are so few as to be almost negligible. Almost invariably men who turn State's evidence become stool-pigeons while in prison, and manifest in the same way for the police after they get out. They are despised alike by those whom they serve and by those upon whom they prey. As a general rule judges are inclined to extend leniency to those who turn State's evidence, but some judges do not. I recall a very interesting case in point.

A man whom I will call Smith (he is still in prison and I have not the right to use his name) served a term at Folsom. While there he learned the fact that ten or fifteen thousand dollars was carried across a comparatively deserted stretch of country each month by two men in a buggy to pay off the employees of a large quarry. He and another man who was released from Folsom at practically the same time determined to get this money.

But while they were perfecting their plans the other man committed a burglary and was caught and lodged in jail. A few days later the community was startled with the news that two masked men had held up two men in a buggy and taken ten thousand dollars from them. Although immediate and diligent search was instituted, no clue of the robbers could be secured.

The man in jail naturally inferred that the crime had been committed by Smith and an assistant, and he determined to use this knowledge, or pseudo knowledge, in an effort to free himself. So he sent for the officers and informed them he would tell them who had committed the robbery if they would "do the right thing by him." Of course, the officers were eager to catch the robbers, and promised that they would see to it that he got off.

They were then informed that Smith was the man, and that he could be found in a certain place. The officers went to the place indicated, where Smith lived, and arrested him. He denied being guilty. No trace of the stolen money was found in his possession, and it has never been recovered. But Smith was taken to the county where the crime had occurred and placed on trial.

It would have been impossible to convict him but for the fact that a girl residing in a ranch house a mile from the scene of the robbery testified that she had been looking through a telescope and had seen the two men waiting for the carriage, and before they put on their masks. She identified Smith as one of these men.

The men who had been robbed testified that Smith's build and height corresponded with that of one of the robbers. Smith was convicted and sentenced to forty-five years' imprisonment at San Quentin. To this day he protests that he is innocent. He says he planned to commit the robbery, but gave it up after his partner was arrested and lodged in jail for burglary. He also argues that they did not find any money in his possession, and that they failed to establish that he had spent any unusual amount of money between the date of the crime and his arrest.

But I am not so much concerned as to Smith's guilt or innocence as I am with what happened to the man who was satisfied to send him to forty-five years' imprisonment in

ch. ends p. 289

order to escape the consequences of his own crime. It was a matter of general satisfaction to all the prisoners who were familiar with the facts of the case that the judge who sentenced him ignored the "service" he had rendered the State and gave him twenty years at Folsom.

As a general rule prisoners are inclined to look askance[1] upon a fellow prisoner who claims to be innocent of the offense for which he has been sentenced to the penitentiary. Quite often such claims are not entitled to serious consideration, but there are some innocent prisoners, and I can conceive of no greater human suffering than that of a man who has been sentenced to prison for a crime which he did not commit, who finds that even his fellow prisoners—whom he expects to be sympathetic and credulous—are inclined to doubt his word. Personally, I know of a number of cases where I have been thoroughly convinced of the innocence of men who have been convicted and sentenced to prison on the strength of their criminal records. It is no unusual thing for the police to arrest and make a scapegoat of an ex-convict, especially during such periods as are known as "waves" or "carnivals" of crime.

During such times the police feel that they must arrest and convict someone to appease public clamor. Only the other day I learned of an instance where a man entirely innocent of crime narrowly escaped going to the penitentiary.

He was a young man, and a stranger in San Francisco. The day before his arrest he threw away an old notebook which he had been carrying in his pocket. It chanced that he threw this notebook into the basement of a building in course of construction. That night someone entered this basement, broke open a locker, and stole a quantity of valuable tools. When the police were notified the next morning, detectives were sent to the scene and the first clue they found was a notebook containing names and addresses. Quite naturally they concluded that this notebook had been lost by the thief,

[1] With doubt or suspicion.

and that noon they arrested the man who had thrown the book away. The detectives did not acquaint this man with the nature of the offense of which he was suspected nor of the evidence they had against him, but questioned him closely, especially as to his movements on the previous night. He accounted for himself as best he could, but they smiled derisively, and that afternoon they took him to the scene of the crime in the hope that some of the workmen might be able to identify him as the man whom they had observed loitering in the vicinity when they had locked up their tools the night before. When the accused man reached the place he was worried by a sense of having been there before—and then he suddenly remembered having thrown away the old notebook. As soon as this occurred to him he told the detectives about it. At first they took it as a clever ruse evolved by the prisoner to discover if they had the book and to head them off, but his earnestness was so intense and the truth of his statements so apparent that they finally listened to him and eventually let him go. But so sure as the sun shines, had he had a criminal record, had he been an ex-convict, he would have been convicted and sentenced to prison for burglary. The detectives had evidence enough to hang an ex-convict.

An instance within my own experience, which can be authenticated by the officers involved, will also show how an innocent man may be convicted. I was in jail at the time, and was thankful that I was. A robbery had been committed, a man about 45 years of age, and his niece, aged about 20, had been held up and robbed at the point of a revolver while on their way home on Sunday night. The following Sunday the Sheriff arrested two men on suspicion and brought them to jail. He telephoned for the man and the girl to come and see if they could identify the suspects. When they arrived seven or eight prisoners were called out and lined up in the office. The man came in alone and the Sheriff told him that he had arrested two men who, he had reason to believe, might be the ones who had robbed him.

ch. ends p. 289

"Take your time," said the Sheriff, "and look at these men. If you recognize any of them as the robbers, point them out."

The man looked from face to face several times, and then turned and spoke to the Sheriff.

"The man on the end?" said the Sheriff. "You think the man on the end is one of the robbers? Look again. We don't want any mistake on this. Take a good look at him, and make sure."

The man looked again and then nodded his head.

"Yes, Sheriff, I'm quite sure he is one of them."

"Very well," said the Sheriff. "Now look and see if you can pick out the other."

The man looked us over once more and shook his head.

"That's too bad," remarked the Sheriff. "Now you step into that side room a moment and we'll have the young lady come in."

She swept the line with a timid and terrified glance, and quickly dropped her eyes.

"Don't be frightened," urged the Sheriff. "Take your time and see if you recognize any of them."

She looked at us again and much to my embarrassment, halted her glance upon me. Like her uncle, she turned and spoke to the Sheriff in a low voice.

"Are you sure?" asked the Sheriff. "Would you swear to it in court?"

She hesitated a moment, looked at me again—and I looked as murderous as I could—and then said she would. Whereupon the Sheriff called in her uncle and said:

"Mr. ——, the man whom you have identified as a robber is my chief jailer, who was on duty here last Sunday night at the time you were robbed. And the man whom you have identified," he continued, addressing the young lady, "was also on duty here last Sunday night, only in a different way. He has been in jail for some time."

But—suppose I had been one of the young men who had been arrested on suspicion? The Sheriff is still in office, and

I have always felt a respect for him because of the absolute fairness of the test to which he put the witnesses. Frequently, when a man is arrested on suspicion the police bring him out to face the injured party or parties alone; and quite frequently, owing to the attitude of certainty that they have the right man which they assume, the complainant is hypnotized into making an identification. And then having made an identification, pseudo or real, the witness is afraid to withdraw it. Still other police officials go through the pretense of standing the accused in line with other men, but manage to indicate the suspect by some trick. For instance, one police inspector used to stand with his back to the line, and, facing the complainant, would point his thumb over his right shoulder—point directly at the suspect, and say:

"Don't you see him there—in that line—there?"

To avoid being pointed out in this way men have been known to change their places in the line as soon as the inspector's back was turned.

Another trick is to tell the complainant or witness how the suspect is dressed so that upon seeing the line of men the accused is readily picked out. Of course, this information is not given directly, but in the form of conversation between the officers and in the presence of the witness before he or she is brought before the line of men. To "beat" this duplicity on the part of the police, prisoners resort to methods of their own. When it is known that an identification is to be made they exchange clothing at the last moment. An accused man who wore a blue flannel shirt made such an exchange some years ago, and the man who wore the shirt at the "identification" was identified as the offender. Subsequently the real owner of the shirt was identified, but at his trial it was adduced[2] that the original identification had been of another man, and he was acquitted.

The most unconscionable case that ever came under my personal observation of an innocent person being sent to

[2] Cited as evidence.

ch. ends p. 289

prison was that of a man whose name eludes me at this moment, but who was sentenced to San Quentin under commitment for 50 years on a conviction for robbery. A physician returning to his apartments one night surprised a man in the act of looting the place, and a tussle ensued. The robber managed to break away, however, and escaped, but the physician had a good look at him. Shortly afterward a man was arrested with part of the stolen property in his possession. The physician was sent for, and identified the man as the one whom he had surprised in his apartment. This man protested vehemently that he was innocent, but when it was learned that he was an ex-convict, that he had served a term at San Quentin years before, the last vestige of doubt was removed from the minds of everyone. He was tried and convicted and sentenced to San Quentin for fifty years. When this sentence was pronounced he uttered a cry of impotent rage and threw an inkwell at the judge. He entered San Quentin protesting his innocence—just as many other men have done before him—but no one believed him. From day to day he became more dejected and morose until it was evident that he was losing his mind, and he was assigned to "crazy alley." Some months later Seimsen and Dabner[3] were arrested for murder committed for the purpose of robbery, and when Seimsen learned that there was no hope for him to escape, he confessed that he had committed the crime for which an innocent man had been sentenced for fifty years. At first the police were skeptical, believing that Seimsen merely wanted to get the other man out of prison, but when Seimsen confronted the physician and recounted details of the encounter in which they had engaged, details that it would have been absolutely impossible for him to know were he not the genuine robber, and when he also disclosed the whereabouts of the rest of the stolen property, it became evident that he was telling the truth. As soon as the police were convinced that such was the case they exerted every effort

[3] Refer back to Chapter 20, pp. 237–239.

for the innocent man, who was pardoned by the Governor a few days later. But unfortunately it proved to be a case where the pardon came too late. The victim was released from San Quentin with the monotonous $5 and cheap clothing, but was arrested for vagrancy and dementia a few days later. He was subsequently adjudged insane and committed to an asylum. I have never heard whether he recovered or not.

Another case just as terrible in many respects was that of a man whom I will designate as Charlie Sparks. Charlie was a bright, clean-looking young fellow residing in one of the small towns not far from San Francisco. By inheritance, I believe, he had a few thousand dollars in his own name, and when he evinced an interest in a girl about fifteen years old, who lived in the same town, her mother determined that it should be a "match." Another girl caught Charlie's fancy, however, and he ceased his attentions to the first girl. One night he received an invitation to call at this first girl's home, and never dreaming of the tragedy in store for him, he went there. The mother maneuvered until she got the young couple into the parlor where there were no lights and left them there. The girl made advances, and Charlie, being young and human, took her in his arms and kissed her rather violently. As soon as he did so she began screaming. Before he realized what was occurring two husky men rushed into the room, tore him from the girl—who had dragged him to the floor and was clinging to him—and administered an unmerciful beating. Bruised and bleeding, he was dragged off to jail, charged with rape. A few days later he was approached by an attorney and urged to compromise. If he would pay the mother of the girl $5,000 the case could be *nolle prossed*,[4] and the girl would escape the humiliation of testifying in court.

But Charlie was not only innocent but very much incensed, and he directed the legal emissary to go to the place where

---

[4] Translated from Latin: to be unwilling to pursue. In legal terms it means to abandon or dismiss the charges against the accused.

ch. ends p. 289

ice is supposed to be worth several million dollars per cubic inch. Several overtures were made subsequent to this, but Charlie would not listen. He was innocent and he'd prove it in court. Being innocent, he surely could not be convicted.

When the case came to trial, the girl gave the most damning testimony, and a physician testified that he had been called immediately after the occurrence and that the act had been accomplished. It required about six minutes for the jury to find Charlie guilty, and he was sentenced to San Quentin for twenty years. After he had appealed to a higher court, and lost, he came to prison. The lawyers had got all his money and his fate was sealed—apparently.

But nine years afterward, during which time Sparks became a prematurely old and broken man, the truth came to light. The girl had grown up, married, and had children, when suddenly, of her own volition, she confessed. The occurrences on the night of the "crime" had all been prearranged by her mother. The two huskies who had rushed in and administered the beating had been in waiting outside, prepared to get busy as soon as the girl screamed. The plan had been either to force Charlie into a marriage with his "victim" or else get his money in compromise. When the woman made this confession, Charlie's friends had her make an affidavit,[5] and the case was presented to the Governor, who at once issued a pardon. Of course, the question arises, "Why were not the witnesses tried for perjury or conspiracy?" Because the statute of limitations rendered them exempt from prosecution after three years, and the exposé[6] occurred after Charlie had been in prison nine years. I also hear the question, "How about the physician's testimony? Did he commit perjury also?" No, he didn't. It wasn't made a part of the affidavit; but one of the huskies, acting in accordance with the program, accommodated himself to the situation so that the physician could not report otherwise than he did.

---

[5] A written statement confirmed by oath for use as evidence in court.

[6] A revelation or formal report of facts.

I shall never forget Charlie Sparks' face. I never saw a more tragic and protesting pair of gray eyes in my life; and yet, until his innocence was established, I was always dubious as to the truth of his claim that they had him "dead wrong."

Another interesting case was that of John H—— and Ed C——. They were ex-convicts and had been arrested in one of the northern counties for murder. Although innocent, the evidence was strongly against them, especially as they would not account for their whereabouts on the night of the crime. Finally it became apparent that they could not possibly escape conviction, and in order to clear themselves of the capital offense they were compelled to confess to a burglary which they had committed in a town some miles distant, but in the same county, at the time the murder occurred. In order to prove that they had committed the burglary they were forced to divulge the hiding place of the loot, and upon going to the place indicated the officers found evidence connecting the men with a score of burglaries. All these charges were preferred against them and they pleaded guilty. C—— got thirty-nine years, and S—— got twenty-seven years. Both men grew old before they had another taste of liberty, and C—— went out on crutches, hopelessly affected with locomotor ataxia.[7] I never looked at these two men without thinking about the wages of sin.

Another interesting case is that of John Ward, who is serving thirty years at San Quentin for robbery. He has been there eight and one-half years, and I believe he is innocent. I first saw him when I worked in the jute mill some years ago, but at that time I did not know his name. He was a quiet and industrious man, and seldom laughed. He hasn't learned to laugh yet. Probably he will never learn to laugh. Thirty years is no laughing matter.

The other day I heard a man talking to a friend:

"Everybody should keep a laughing countenance all the

[7] Also known as tabes dorsalis; progressive degeneration of the spinal cord and nerve roots, especially as a result of syphilitic infection.

ch. ends p. 289

time," he said. "If everybody would be light and gay and laughing, the world would be much better off. The trouble nowadays is that people go around with long, tragic faces, and we all feel more or less blue as a result."

The speaker was stout and sleek. He looked as if he had never known a want in his life.

His friend did not look so prosperous. There were deep lines in his face. I took him to be the father of a large family. His manner bespoke responsibility.

"If everyone kept a smiling countenance," he replied, "how would we ever know of the misery of others?"

The two men passed beyond hearing, and I was sorry. I was interested. I liked the reply of the second man.

I have seen innocent men serving long years in prison. I have seen guilty men led to the scaffold to have their lives snuffed out. The other day I went into one of the large department stores to make a purchase. The young girl who waited on me was worn and pale. I saw other young girls standing wearily behind the bedecked counters. Some of them stood with one hip lower than the other, just as tired horses stand. I have also seen tense-faced waitresses, who walk many miles every day on the hard floors, carrying food and soiled dishes back and forth. Yesterday I saw a little newsboy on crutches. Today I saw an old, old man working with a pick and shovel in a trench.

And yet that big, fat, well-fed man said that everyone should keep a smiling countenance. He may like the smiling faces, but the sad ones with the haunted eyes are nearer the truth. They are the living monuments to man's greed and heartlessness. Were it not for them the world would, indeed, be a sorry place in which to live. There would be nothing to do but eat and sleep, and any human being who is satisfied with that has no business being alive. It is the ones who suffer, the staggering penny populace, the people of deep understanding and rich human sympathy, that are worthwhile.

Yesterday I looked into the face of a woman whose life is

devoted to humanity—did she have a gay and lighthearted countenance? And yet her face was beautiful. Her eyes were soft with compassion when she spoke of the children who are wasting their young lives away in money-making factories.

A few months ago I looked into the face of a prison warden who has learned that life is no laughing matter. Four years ago he had a gay and lighthearted countenance. Today he seldom laughs. Why? Because he has seen human suffering. And yet, though he doesn't laugh so often, he is a bigger and a better man and is doing more good with each passing day. I never watched anything in my life with greater satisfaction than I did the waning of his smile. He still radiates cheer and confidence, but in a different way—the way that counts. He still laughs sometimes, but the laugh is subdued.

I repeat that John Ward, serving thirty years for robbery, seldom laughs. He would be a monster if he did laugh. The world is better because he doesn't laugh.

About two years ago I prepared John Ward's application to the Governor for a pardon. When he came to me and asked me to "get up his papers" I had no idea that he was innocent. I knew that he was a two or three time loser, and they are never supposed to be innocent. When he told me that he wanted the proposed application based on a claim of innocence I tried to dissuade him. Experience in preparing other applications had convinced me that such a claim was prejudicial and would surely militate against success. But John wouldn't listen.

"What good would it do me to claim I'm innocent if I'm not?" he asked. "I'm no fool. I know the game. I know it would be better for me to say I'm guilty and throw myself on mercy, but I tell you I can't do it. I'm innocent, and that's all there is to it. May I drop dead right here if I'm not. It certainly wouldn't do me any good to talk this way to you, would it?"

So the application was prepared on the ground of innocence.

ch. ends p. 289

5019 FOL
20122 SQ

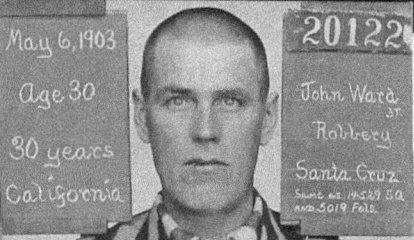

11529

20122

14529

20122

May 6, 1903

Age 30

30 years

California

20122

John Ward Jr.
Robbery

Santa Cruz

Same as 14529 SQ
and 5019 Fols.

Height 5.5¾
Gth Head 22
Blw Templ 5⅞
Lth Nose 2
" Head 7¾
Xth Fing 4
" Foot 16⅞
" F Arm 17½
Wth Hand 4
Gth Ches 32½

14529
Jno Ward
Burglary Second Deg'
3 years
Monterey
Age 20
Cal

Name	Jno Ward	
No.	20.122	3 T.
County	Santa Cruz	
Crime	Robbery	
Term	30 yrs	
Received	May 6-03	
Discharged	July 6-21	
Remarks		

John was in bed when he was arrested at 7 o'clock in the morning, charged with having robbed an intoxicated man in an alley about five blocks away. The robbery had occurred about 4:30 a.m.

The officers knew that John was an ex-convict, and he had been seen on the street at midnight. They searched his room and his person, but found nothing to connect him with the crime. The persons living in the house testified that he had come in about 12:30 and gone to bed.

The man who had been robbed of $22 while drunk testified that John Ward was one of the men who robbed him. John testified in his own behalf, but on cross-examination the questions of the District Attorney were chiefly in relation to his previous convictions. One of these convictions was for carrying whiskey to a man in jail, for which he served one year in the penitentiary. The other conviction was for burglary of the second degree, for which he served three years. A night watchman testified that he had seen the complainant drinking in a restaurant with four or five other men at 3:40 in the morning, but that the defendant was not one of them. John was represented by attorneys who were appointed by the court. They did not come to the jail to see him until the afternoon preceding the day which had been set for his trial, too late to subpoena witnesses for the defense who had moved to a different part of the county.

John asked for a continuance of the case until he should have time to reach these witnesses, whose testimony had been given at the preliminary examination and which was very much in his favor. No transcript had been made of this examination, and it was vital that he should have the witnesses for his trial before the Superior Court. But the request for a postponement was denied, and the trial proceeded. The jury found him guilty of robbery, and he was sentenced to thirty years.

The application stating these facts were sent to the Judge and District Attorney of the county whence Ward had been

ch. ends p. 289

committed. This was in accordance with the rules governing applications for pardon. The Judge and District Attorney both signed the statement, but added: "We do not admit any of the above stated facts to be true."

In preparing his application Ward made repeated efforts to get a transcript of the evidence on file in the county records, but was unable to do so. He contends that this evidence is substantially the same as the statement he prepared. After his conviction he wanted to appeal to a higher court, but he was without funds and helpless. I have a copy of his application before me as I write. It is a very convincing document. It has never reached the Governor. After it was prepared, and all the requirements fulfilled in accordance with regulations, it was given to the Warden with the request that it be presented to the State Board of Prison Directors for their recommendation. That was nearly two years ago, and no action has ever been taken. Meanwhile John Ward has been doing his daily work, obeying the prison rules, and hoping. It is a well-known fact that prisoners are the best judges of their own kind. I have never spoken to a prisoner about John Ward's case who didn't say that he believed John innocent; also that he would make good if he ever got out. The case is worthy of serious investigation, and John is worthy of a chance.

Among the thousand or more stories of men whom I met and with whom I became more or less intimate while in prison, the story of Tom is one of the most interesting and remarkable. Tom made no claim of innocence. He had been caught almost in the very act of committing burglary. But what transpired while he was in jail awaiting the action of the courts is certainly worth telling, and serves to illustrate how a prisoner may be subjected to the rankest kind of injustice.

I was talking with Tom in the lower yard one afternoon and asked him how he came to get fourteen years for a first offense. As nearly as I can remember, this is his story as he told it to me:

"I was pinched for burglary for breakin' into a store at —— in the night time. They had me dead right, and I made up my mind to plead guilty and take my medicine and get started on my sentence as soon as possible. But they only hold court in that county every three months, and after the preliminary I had to wait in jail until the next session of the Superior Court.

"About two weeks after they got me a Deputy Sheriff came into the jail one day and got to chewing the rag with me. He talked about a lot of things for a while, and then started telling me about a post office robbery that was pulled off about fifty miles from where I was pinched two or three nights before they got me. It was in another county, and besides a post office comes under the United States Court and I wondered what he was drivin' at. Pretty soon he started hintin' that the job was done just like the one they had on me.

"'Of course, you know the limit for getting a post office is only ten years,' he said, 'and the charge we've got you cinched on here calls for fifteen, if the judge wants to give it to you. If I was you I'd cough up about kicking in the P.O. and take your chance with the U.S. people. We're willing to drop our case to accommodate them, and we'll boost to get you off with a light jolt—we'll get it cut to five years.'

"'But I didn't do it,' I said. 'I don't know anything about it. I'm up against enough as it is without that.'

"'Oh, very well,' he shot back at me. 'If you want fifteen years, why, that's your business. I'm simply putting you wise to how you can get off with five. I'm just trying to do you a favor. You better think it over.'

"With that he blew and left me alone. Naturally, he had me guessing. I studied the thing over, but I couldn't imagine what his game was. The only thing I could see was that he wanted to get me to admit kickin' in the post office so's he could make a rep for himself.

"At first it made me pretty hostile, but the more I got to studying over it the more it bothered me. If I could be sure

ch. ends p. 289

that the U.S. people would let me down with a five-spot and that the people who had me dead to rights on the job that I'd really done would dismiss it, why, I'd be a sucker not to grab it. But, you see, it might be a case of double-crossing. They might be working me for their own interests and then soak me on both charges. Before I went to sleep that night I decided I wouldn't take the chance.

"The next day the same deputy came into the jail again and asked me if I'd thought the thing over, I told him I had, but I had no way of being sure that he was on the square, and then I asked him point blank what his game was.

"He looked around to make sure there was nobody within hearin', and then spoke low.

"'Of course, I ain't makin' this proposition to you for love,' he said, 'and I'll give you the straight goods. It's just as I told you yesterday—the limit for a post office is ten years, and we can get you off with five.'

"He stopped and sized me up close for a minute, and then he let the cat out of the bag.

"'I'll tell you what it is,' he said, taking another squint behind him. 'There's a reward of $600 for the guy that blew that post office pete, and the dough is pie for us if you'll say you did it; savvy? On the square, we can get you off with five, and I'll see that you get a cut to boot. What do you say?'

"All that night I hiked up and down my cell in my bare feet. It looked like a pretty good proposition, and if he had been any other man I'd probably 'a' jumped at it, but there was something about him I didn't like—there was a phony note in his bazoo that I couldn't get away from. And then I didn't know anything about the law. I had no way of telling for sure that the limit for a post office was ten years. And the more I got to thinking about my own case the more I thought the judge would let me down easy.

"There wasn't anybody sleeping in the place I broke into, and it was the first time I'd ever been arrested, though I ain't saying I'd been an angel. Besides, I was going to plead guilty and save the expense of a trial, and all that. The most they ought to give me was five years, and I could even get off with one year if the judge wanted to do it. I'd put up a good talk when I got into court, and lots of things ought to count in my favor. So I decided to pass the proposition up, and the next day when the deputy came in and gave me some cigars I told him there was nothing doing—after I got the cigars.

"I thought he'd fly off the handle, but he didn't.

"'Oh, all right,' he said. 'If you want to be a sucker go ahead. But let me put you wise to one thing—the judge in this county is a crackerjack, and he's death on burglars. Not only that, but a little word from us and you'll get the whole package. I don't say we'll go to him, but you better think it over some more.'

"The way he said this made me mad, and I told him to go to blazes. You see, I thought it was all a bluff about the judge being hard and their going to him with a knock—just a bluff to make me come through on the post office proposition. He went away puffed, but he came back the next day, and every day for two weeks, and he brought me cigars every time. I tried to turn down the cigars but he wouldn't have it, and pretended to be quite friendly. Every once in a while he'd say:

"'I know you're not going to be a sucker, and I'll make it an even hundred for you that you'll get the day you come out.'

"But I'd made up my mind, and one day he got me so sore I told him to beat it and not come back or I'd knock his head off.

"With that he called in the jailer and they sloughed me up in my cell. I'd been having the run of the corridors up to that time and getting pretty good grub.

"Well, they kept me sloughed up until I went into court. I made my little spiel to the judge and asked for mercy, and then I got mine for a fare-ye-well. When he said fourteen years it made me see red, and I wanted to fight. All I got that fourteen years for was because there was a reward of $600

ch. ends p. 289

that I wouldn't put into that stiff's pocket. I'd probably got off with five or six years only for that."

Tom stopped and regarded me seriously.

"What would you 'a' done if it'd been you?" he asked.

"What would you do if you had it to do over again?" I answered.

"Why, I'd grab at it," he instantly replied. "Wouldn't you?"

"I certainly would," I responded. "The chances are he'd have seen you through as a matter of self-protection."

"I only hope I never meet him if I ever get out," said Tom.

✱

One Sunday several months after I had been assigned to the clothing room I went over to the yard to hunt up Smoky. I had been seeing him nearly every day as he passed in the line on the way from the jute mill, but he had never once looked toward me. I had been promising myself the pleasure of going over to the yard to see him each Sunday, but something had always occurred to prevent it.

Somehow I sensed that he had ceased to regard me with the same spirit of fellowship as had prevailed while we were in the cell together, and it hurt me to know it. One of the penalties of getting a "good job" at San Quentin is that one forfeits the regard of certain men. There are many of the inmates who believe that no prisoner can get a "job" without having done something underhand to secure it; also that he cannot hold such a job without being a stool-pigeon. Not all the prisoners take this view, and I was confident Smoky did not. Nevertheless, I felt a coldness from him, even though we had not spoken for months. That is another peculiar condition of prison life.

One may be confined to the prison enclosure for months, perhaps for years, and suddenly see some prisoner who is a total stranger and yet who has been in confinement there all the time.

Worming my way through the crowd, I finally descried[8] Smoky and nodded to him. He understood and broke away from the group of listeners who were always gathering about him. We walked along toward the shed where the band had already started on its Sunday concert, and some of the men were dancing. I knew the dance sent Smoky's blood coursing toward his feet, but he made no move to join in. Instead, he led me to an unoccupied seat where we sat down. He had not uttered a word since we had started for the shed and I wondered how he would break the ice, for there certainly was a frigidity in his manner. For several minutes we remained silent, ostensibly watching the dancers, but in reality engaged in a telepathic sparring match. I knew without being told that he was very much piqued about something, and it made me uncomfortable and nervous. I felt that I would sacrifice the regard of any other man within the four walls rather than that of Smoky. My mind went racing over what he had told me of his life and I took a furtive glance at his freckled face. I remembered that at my first meeting with him I had thought him unprepossessing, even ugly, but now as he sat there gazing before him, a sad, faraway look in his eyes, he looked actually handsome. How often a plain face becomes glorified when we have learned something of the soul which it conceals, and how often a face that is unattractive when eyes meet eyes takes on force and character when seen in profile. It was a combination of these two conditions that suddenly made me see Smoky as a new creature.

"Haven't you ever heard from Rose, Smoky?" I finally ventured, taking the initiative.

He grunted an ungracious negative. I realized that I had blundered.

"What's the matter, anyway, old man?" I blurted. "You seem to be sore about something. What is it? Have I done

---

[8] Caught sight of.

ch. ends p. 289

something you don't savvy, or are you worrying about something I don't know about?"

"Well," he replied, turning toward me with a hard look in his eyes, "the whole thing is that I don't like the idea of y'r bein' a bon-ton. I don't say y'r ain't all right, I know y'r are, but since y'r got that job at th' office y'r ain't noticed me, n'r th' other guys y'r used to talk with. Maybe it's just as y'r say—y'r ain't had time t'come over t' th' yard an' see a feller, but y'r got a long stretch ahead of y'r yet, an' if y'r ain't careful y'r'll get a swelled skypiece, like all th' rest of th' guys what get good jobs, an' f'rget all about us common ones what ain't got no ability, 'r nothin' but muscle." He paused for a moment, as if choosing words, and then went on: "Y'r got a good many years ahead of y'r, Bill, an' I hate t'think that y'r may get stuckup an' cut ol' friends. I've only got two months an' a butt left now, an' it already hurts me t' think of going out an' leavin' some of these poor, helpless fellers what act like lost sheep behind. I'd rather like t' go out feelin' that y'r the friend of all th' fellers in th' yard, an' that y'r'll never go back on th' gang. I don't mean that y'r oughter run after them, 'r nothin' like that, but always stick up f'r th' underdogs. If ev'ry feller in here would do his part toward helpin' some other feller, and if ev'ry guy would keep from snitchin' and trying to get ahead at th' expense of someone else th' cons could make this place a whole lot better.

"No—no! I ain't accusin' you of doing anything like that," he interrupted quickly as I half arose and started to speak, "I know y'r all right, only, as a favor t'me, remember this little talk, an' ev'ry time y'r got a chance t' do some guy a favor, do it. A man over there where you are can do a whole lot f'r other fellers if he's a mind to, an' I'd like t' look back an' remember that I know a square guy in an office job. I've done a lot of thinking lately, and I'm going out t' do th' right thing. This kind of a life don't pay at no stage of th' game. I've been drillin' that int' all th' young fellers lately th' same as Charlie Thorn and Buck English, an' ol' Kelsey an' all th' other old timers are doin' ev'ry chance they get. It ain't us old crooks, it ain't us 'hardened criminals,' as they calls us, that steer th' young fellers wrong, you know that. Why, half of these kids that blow in nowadays know more in a minute about th' business than I ever knew, an' more 'n I'd ever know, even if I was goin' back at it. It's these reform schools that do that. Get a bunch of kids together an' they'll learn more about th' crooked game in a week than they'd get in ten years here. Kids think it's smart to know all th' ins and outs—but what's th' use of talkin' t'you, you know what I mean. You've seen it y'self. But I keep tellin' 'em it don't pay; that it's a sucker game, an' that we're a lot of mutts.

"Have y'r ever stopped t' think what a losin' game it all is? Take St. Paul Blackie's case f'r example. He got pinched prowlin' a shack in th' dead of night. They didn't get him in the act, but afterwards. What happened? In th' first place th' owner of th' house lost a measly $17. Then when they tried Blackie th' guy that lost the $17 had t' come to court as a witness, an' lost three days' work. There were four or five other witnesses, an' of course they lost their time, too. It cost the county over $500, an' that's puttin' it light, f'r the trial. Then Blackie got ten years, an' lost his liberty. He came here and worked in th' jute mill year after year, all th' time losin' the pay that a man ought t' get f'r his work. Yet all th' time he was losin' this pay it cost the State 30 or 40 cents a day t' keep him—that's more'n a hundreds dollars a year f'r one man, an' there's close t' 2,000 here, not t' mention Folsom. Not only this, but Blackie was gettin' older all th' time, an' losin' in character every day. When his time was up he went out sore, with his mind made up t' get even. You know how he got even. He was out three weeks an' then got fifteen years at Folsom f'r holdin' a man up and getting ten dollars off him. An' while Blackie was doin' his ten-spot here his mother went t' th' poorhouse, where th' State had t' support her, an' she died there. S' y'r see, all th' way through, from start t' finish, it was a dead loss all around. Th' only

ch. ends next p.

ones that gain is the people that make a livin' on th' misery of others—th' police, an' the court guys, an' th' guards here. Of course, lots of people think that society gains somethin' by sendin' a man here an' makin' life a hell f'r him. They think th' example keeps lots of others from breakin' the laws; but I don't. Neither do you. What I can't get through my nut is why two thousand able-bodied men cost the State $100 a year apiece. If we had a little town of our own outside we'd have our families and children, an' good food an' decent clothes, an' theaters an' fire department and everything else, an' we'd all be comfortable, an' some of us would have money in th' bank' an' we'd send our kids t' school, an' all that. By workin' ev'ry day we'd support five 'r six thousand people besides ourselves, an' yet in here, livin' like dogs in kennels, an' eatin' th' cheapest grub they can get, it costs th' State a quarter of a million dollars a year t' keep us. There's somethin' rotten somewhere. If they'll let us guys work an' pay us f'r it, an' make us pay f'r what we got, y'r'd see a big difference. Y'r wouldn't see men comin' back, an y'r'd see lots of 'em go out and take their proper place in th' world. They'd have th' work habit then, because they'd know that work brings a man all that makes life worthwhile.

"I tell y'r th' time has got t' come when these places 'll be sensible. This ain't no mush, it's good common sense. My life is gone now, I'm vergin' on old age, but my life wouldn't 'a' been wasted if they'd had th' right system th' first time I got kicked inter this dump. Courts an' jails an' prisons are necessary, I know that. I know that people have a right to keep what belongs t' 'em, an' that when a man takes a life, or when he takes what ain't his by right of his work, he's got t' be cut out of th' herd an' put over th' jumps, but when they do that why don't they try to make a better man of him instead of treatin' him like a brute? All these people that write about how to run prisons and how to treat prisoners make me tired. I know all about it, I been through it, but as soon as one of us guys tries to say anything they all give us th' dog eye; they think we've got an awful crust—we're supposed t' be different from other people; we ain't supposed t' think.

"Well, ol' man," Smoky finished, rising, "I didn't intend to say all this when I started, but I've said it. Keep y'r eyes open an' take it all in, an' when y'r get out perhaps y'r can do somethin.' It's got t' be some guy like you, that can write letters like y'r used t' write f'r th' kid, what's got t' do it. I'm goin' out soon, an' I'm goin' t' take th' straight an' narrow f'r mine from now on, but let me tell y'r one thing—it ain't because I'm afraid, it ain't because they done anything t' make me feel this way. It's because I've worked it all out myself. I c'n sum th' whole thing up in a few words, an' that's this: I'm goin' t' do right because it is right, an' not for any other reason.

"An' now y'r better get back t' y'r work. I am goin' t' have a dance."

I sat there and watched Smoky whirl off in the crowd, and then walked slowly back to the clothing room. I have never forgotten that Sunday, I never shall.

23 [1]

[1] This chapter or its number was omitted from the original 1912 edition. Research ongoing . . .

24

Working at the clothing room I had an excellent opportunity for observing incoming prisoners and the methods employed by different sheriffs and deputies in bringing them to the penitentiary. Of course when a man is on the way to prison for a long term of years—perhaps for life, or to be executed— he is liable to be more or less desperate; at least the majority are, I make the qualification because I have known prisoners to deliver themselves at the prison without escort. Quite recently a man on the way to San Quentin from one of the extreme southern counties got separated in a crowd from the deputy who had him in charge. Instead of escaping he inquired how to get to the penitentiary and came there alone. As he did not have his commitment the Warden could not receive him as a prisoner, but permitted him to remain on the prison reservation until telephonic communication was established with the lost officer, who finally arrived with the necessary papers. I did a lot of thinking about that particular case. It seemed so absolutely unnecessary and inhuman to dress such a man in stripes and crop his hair. Of course, it is unnecessary, inhuman, and degrading in all cases, but I have never had it come home to me so forcibly as it did in this instance.

I also know a lifer at San Quentin who had a similar experience. He was being brought to the prison from a northern county. The officer who had him in charge did not handcuff him, but put him on his honor. At San Francisco they had a few drinks together and got separated. The prisoner searched diligently for his custodian, found him intoxicated, took him to a hotel to sober up, and then they finished the journey together. Several years later, and long after he had first told me these circumstances, I asked this lifer if he would do the same thing again. He hesitated a moment, tempted to prevaricate,[1] and then said:

"No, to be honest, I don't think I would. Many a night I've lain awake and kicked myself for not beating it when I had such a chance. But Bill Suthers trusted me, and at that time I wouldn't throw a man down."

This lifer has been before the State Board of Prison Directors and his parole has been authorized to take effect when he has served eleven years. He need not have served a day had he not had a keen sense of honor. I saw him change from a bright and rather handsome young man to a prematurely old one. His face is now haggard and drawn. He has lived and suffered twenty years in the ten years that he has spent behind prison walls in a striped suit. His crime was more accidental than intentional in its nature, and it is really hard to see what good has been accomplished by keeping him in prison. His sense of honor is certainly not as high as it was at the start, and he is impaired in every way. But he has been a model prisoner. A "model" prisoner is one who drops normal manifestation and becomes a mere automaton— something on the order of a model or dummy in a clothing store. Under the present system that is what is meant by the term "model prisoner."

But not all men on the way to prison would deliver themselves at the gate. I have seen loose cayenne pepper taken from a prisoner's coat pockets when searched upon being received. He had secured the stuff in the hope that an opportunity might occur for him to throw it into the eyes of the

[1] Speak or act in an evasive way.

officer having him in charge and make his escape. Such men are decidedly dangerous, and it is the fact that there are such men that makes officers take every precaution in bringing prisoners to the penitentiary. These precautionary measures have resulted in barbarities, however, and as a consequence nearly all prisoners en route are treated as if they were wild beasts. It has resolved itself into what might be adopted as the slogan of transfer officers: Treat every prisoner as if he was the most desperate criminal that ever existed.

There are two southern sheriffs who never bring a prisoner to the State prison without an "Oregon boot."

An "Oregon boot" consists of a lead collar that fits about the ankle. It weighs, I should judge, between twenty and thirty pounds. It is either riveted or locked about the ankle and while there it is utterly impossible for a man to run. In fact, he can only walk by dragging the weighted leg behind him. But even this barbarous and shameful thing is not sufficient for some officers. I have seen a mere boy come through the gate of San Quentin not only wearing an "Oregon boot," but shackled and handcuffed also. I distinctly remember the first time I saw this. As the deputy came up the walk to the office we all thought the boy at his side was being brought to the penitentiary to be hanged.

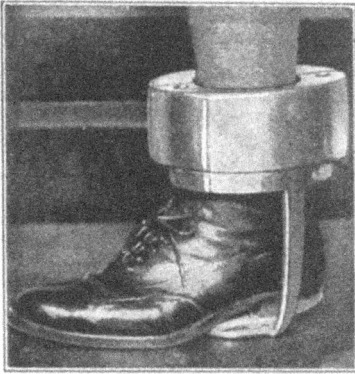

Prisoner Wearing Metal Boot Can't Escape

DANGEROUS criminals, shackled with a metal "Oregon" boot, have little chance to escape during long railway journeys. The boot, a modern adaptation of the old-fashioned ball and chain, consists of a steel framework fitting over the shoe, with a 50-pound collar above the ankle.

The prisoner who wears it can walk slowly with a fair degree of comfort, but should he attempt to run, or move quickly, the heavy weight will break his leg.

(1922, August). *Popular Science*, p. 65

ch. ends p. 303

Imagine our surprise and indignation when we learned his sentence was one year.

Several years ago an officer from one of the southern counties was nearly mobbed in San Francisco for having a prisoner manacled and weighted in this manner. He arrived on a steamer and was dragging his victim along the water-front to catch a ferryboat. A mob collected about them and forced him to remove everything from the boy save the handcuffs.

And many times I have seen lame or one-legged prisoners brought in handcuffed. Imagine a big strapping officer, with both hands free, and a loaded revolver in his hip pocket, walking beside or behind a one-legged man with hands cuffed together.

Quite frequently officers lose the key to the handcuffs or shackles and the victim is utterly helpless. An assortment of keys is kept at the prison for the purpose of removing the manacles in such cases, but I know of several instances where the cuffs had to be cut off, there not being a key on the place that would unlock them.

Some years ago a parole violator was apprehended at Memphis, Tenn., and an officer from the prison went there to return him. I shall never forget the night they arrived at San Quentin. Before leaving Memphis the officer had locked an "Oregon boot" on the prisoner's leg, and it was not removed during the journey westward. They had been several days on the road. Instead of sleeping on the train, they got off each night, the prisoner being lodged in a jail or police station, and the officer at a hotel. The "boot" was removed from the prisoner's leg in my presence, and he started for the clothing room to take a bath and don his stripes. As he did so everybody burst out laughing. He walked exactly like a sprung horse—the leg that the "Oregon boot" had weighted down for a week refused to act naturally. With each step it flew up as if pulled by a spring. Of course, it was no laughing matter, but it was really impossible to see the grim side at the moment, especially as the victim laughed himself, and went off holding both hands on the knee of the refractory limb and ordering it to "stay down, darn you."

Although I made several efforts to learn why this device is called an "Oregon boot" I never found out.[2] Aside from the discomfort—and in some cases the torture—of the thing, it is to be condemned because of the shame which it brings to the man who is compelled to wear it. I have never seen a man dragging an "Oregon boot," without feeling it a horror and a disgrace that he must feel in his very soul. Surely, no man who has ever worn an "Oregon boot" can ever again respect the law that inflicted it upon him.

*

Prisoners at San Quentin are not allowed to have anything in their cells save the "furniture" prescribed by the rules. This "furniture" consists of a bunk, a small deal table, a stool, a water can, a coal oil lamp, and a lime-encrusted slop bucket—an outfit well calculated to turn a man toward higher things and make him feel that imprisonment is for his good.

But in spite of rules prisoners persist in taking contraband things into their cells. Homemade chairs and boxes, picture frames and shelves, toilet accessories, and mats, cooking utensils, light reflectors, book racks, and many other things are persistently introduced into the cells and are just as persistently confiscated by the officials. There is a perpetual warfare between the prisoners and the guards in charge of the cell buildings, a warfare fostering resentment, animosity, and hatred.

Today, after much risk and patience, a convict manages to get a little toilet rack into his cell. In it he proudly puts his

[2] The Oregon Boot, or Gardner Shackle as it was properly known, was patented July 3, 1866, by J.C. Gardner, warden of Oregon State Penitentiary.

ch. ends p. 303

little piece of soap, his toothbrush (if he has money to buy one), and a few pictures. It has cost him much scheming to get this piece of homelike furniture. He falls asleep better satisfied with himself and his lot, more tolerant toward his keepers.

Tomorrow the cell guard discovers the bit of contraband furniture. Ruthlessly he tears it from the wall and smashes it to pieces. The convict returns to his cell thinking of the new comfort, anticipating the pleasure it will give him during the long hours before taps—and finds it gone.

Perhaps he has been reported at the office and "lost his privileges"—he won't know that "for sure" until Sunday, when the tobacco man will pass his cell without stopping, or until he writes his monthly letter home and has it returned to him marked "Lost Privileges."

The method employed by the present management of the inner prison in this respect rankles with injustice. A prisoner may be reported at the office and be deprived of his privileges without having a chance to explain or to defend himself. In taking privileges the Captain of the Yard has appointed himself supreme arbiter. He inflicts this "punishment" as he listeth, and there is none to say him nay.

"Privileges" consist of a ration of tobacco each week, the receiving of letters (opened and read at the office), and the writing of one letter and one visit each month. When a prisoner's correspondence and visits from relatives are suddenly cut off it is as though he smashed into a stone wall in the dark. It leaves him dazed and impotent. He cannot write even one letter to let his relatives know what has occurred.

The letters that arrive for him are filed at the office and kept until such time as the Captain of the Yard sees fit to restore his privileges, or until the Warden's general amnesty at Christmas.

Not hearing from the prisoner, his wife, or mother, or sweetheart, or whoever it may be, imagines all kinds of calamities. If they live at a distance they cannot visit the prison to ascertain the cause of the silence. They write three or four times, each letter more urgent than its predecessor, but get no response. The prisoner does not get the letters. Finally they write to the Warden, perhaps after two or three months of torturing anxiety, and learn that their boy has "lost his privileges."

Sometimes a prisoner's privileges are forfeited while his wife or children are seriously ill, and for weeks, perhaps for months, he has no way of finding out if they are alive or dead. He may possibly send a message to them by an outgoing prisoner, but he has no way of getting a reply, and must remain in ignorance of their condition until his "lost privileges" are restored. This is certainly not the "blissful" ignorance the poet had in mind.

Of course, a prisoner should be careful not to do anything that will bring a forfeiture of privileges upon him, but it seems to me that no prisoner should be subjected to this form of "punishment" without a hearing, especially as forfeiture of privileges destroys his eligibility for parole until six months have elapsed.

Not long since a prisoner eligible for parole had his privileges "taken" without his knowledge. A pair of jute slippers had been found in his bunk in one of the dormitories where there were nearly 100 men. It is against the rules to make slippers—even out of old rags—but in this case it happened that the slippers did not belong to the man in whose bunk they were found. They were the property of another prisoner occupying an adjacent bunk.

The Captain of the Yard did not make any investigation; he did not send for the man in whose bunk the slippers had been found, but peremptorily[3] ordered that his privileges be forfeited.

When the Board of Directors met to take up parole applications this man was scratched from the list of eligibles because he had been "punished" within six months. Not

---

[3] Conclusively or absolutely; subject to no debate or dispute.

ch. ends p. 303

understanding why he had not been called before the board
for consideration the prisoner went to the office on the following morning to make inquiry. It was not until then that
he learned that he had been "punished" for having a pair of
contraband slippers in his bunk.

He strenuously maintained that he knew nothing about
the slippers—that he had never seen them—that they were
not his. But that was an "old dodge" and he got no satisfaction. It was not until the Warden had time to take up the
matter personally, in response to the prisoner's written complaint, that the injustice was straightened out. Meantime the
prisoner had lost two months' tobacco and correspondence
and his chance for parole. According to the scriptures, the
sun and rain fall alike upon the just and the unjust,[4] but
according to the dictates of an individual subordinate prison
official the scriptures are wrong.

In the effort to keep contraband articles out of the cells
the guards make regular "raids," and when they get through
searching a cell it looks like a scrambled egg. I shall never
forget the first time I found my cell in this condition. I had
left it spick and span when I went to work in the morning,
and when I arrived at the door that night I found everything
on the floor. Mattress, blankets, letters, books, table, stool,
and lamp were all together in an indiscriminate heap.

At first I did not understand what it meant, and while
I was still contemplating the wreck the counting officer flitted
past and the door was slammed upon me. Presently I heard
the man in the next cell cursing vigorously, and from the
nature of his blasphemy I knew that his cell was in a condition similar to mine, and learned that he had been "frisked."

I had been working at a loom all day and was tired. In
a very bitter frame of mind I preceded to straighten things
out as best I could in the narrow space. Instead of reading
or studying that night I walked up and down—three steps
each way—and fumed. I had not lost anything, so far as

[4] Matthew 5:45

I could determine, but the next morning I learned that men all about me had lost some of their most treasured belongings.

As there are no printed rules concerning such matters I was at a loss to understand it, but with the passing of time I learned that there have to be restrictions placed over the men in this regard to keep them from filling their cells with "junk." Of course, the "junk"—little comforts—doesn't do any real harm, but there must be discipline. It will never do for prisoners to make their cells comfortable. A bare and cheerless cell is a part of the discipline.

*

Prisoners are discharged from San Quentin in the early morning. I shall never forget the day Smoky left. I saw him coming over from the yard to the clothing room as soon as the unlock bell ceased ringing. He had his mattress and blankets rolled together, and was carrying them on his back like a pack peddler. One of the prison rules is that a prisoner whose term has expired must bring his mattress and blankets to the clothing room on the morning of his discharge.

The turnkey has the bundle untied in his presence, and looks to see that there are two and a half pairs of blankets in the roll. As the bedclothing supplied to prisoners is insufficient in winter, men about to be discharged are besieged for their blankets. If a man is not posted as to the rules and gives one of his blankets away it is discovered when he arrives at the office, and he is not permitted to dress until he has returned to the cell buildings and recovered the donated blanket.

Sometimes a prisoner whose blankets are comparatively new exchanges with an old lifer, because, after a number of years, the blankets wear thin, and a short-term man's blankets are still in fairly good condition when his term expires. But I have known of prisoners being kept at the prison until late in the afternoon on the day of discharge while they searched for blankets which they had given away.

When the blankets are properly accounted for the prisoner is taken into the clothing room and compelled to strip in the presence of an officer. He is not given the opportunity to bathe on the morning of his discharge, but as soon as the officer has inspected him to see that he has nothing concealed about his body he is handed his discharge clothing, a piece at a time. Every precaution is taken to see that he does not smuggle out a note, or any article. If he has letters, or anything he wishes to take with him, he must bring them to the office the day before his discharge and leave them for the inspection and censorship of the Captain of the Yard.

Quite a number of men about to be released make promises to those whom they leave behind, agreeing to look up friends or relatives, or attend to other commissions. But in order to obviate[5] the possibility of forgetting addresses a man of poor or treacherous memory is obliged to resort to some method for getting the desired information out with him. Some of these methods are really clever, I have known a man to be stripped and carefully examined to see if he had any message for the outside world on his person, passed as not having any, and yet have half a dozen names and addresses in plain sight all the time.

The method is so startlingly original, and clever, that it is difficult for me to refrain from telling it. But, of course, I cannot tell anything that will serve to harden the lot of prisoners, especially prisoners who take a chance in order to do a favor for some other unfortunate. Of course, all prisoners do not know the method I refer to.

I have seen some very blundering attempts to smuggle money or notes out of prison. I recall one old man who had a five-dollar gold piece in his mouth. He did not know he would be compelled to open his mouth going out, the same as he had been compelled to open it coming in. The five

---

[5] Avoid; prevent.

dollars was confiscated and applied to the "library fund."
I have also seen a ball of tissue paper covered with fine writing taken from the ear of a prisoner about to be released.

But, as I started to write, Smoky's time was "up," and he dropped his roll of bedding at the clothing room door with a sigh of relief. It was half an hour before the regular dressing time, and I asked him if he were not going to breakfast.

"Not on y'r life," he answered. "No more prison swill f'r y'r Uncle, ever again. I start this day clean, an' it's th' clean way f'r me from now on."

We fell to talking, and the conversation by some strange twist turned to the two men who had been hanged a few days before.

"I've seen a good many men hung in my time," said Smoky, "an' I've tried t' see both sides of it, but f'r th' life of me I can't see what good it does. In th' old days, when a guy named Jeffreys used t' hang 'em in England f'r stealin' a loaf of bread, they kept on stealing loaves of bread, an' in these days when they hang 'em f'r murder they keep on murderin'.

"That proves that it don't scare anybody off, an' if it don't scare 'em off, what's th' use of doin' it? If hangin' a guy stopped some other guy from killin', there might be some use in it, but I tell y'r it's just th' savage in man—th' cravin' f'r revenge—th' thirst f'r blood—that keeps it goin'. Men like to see blood, an' y'r can't get away from it. Some day people 'll look back an' call us a lot of heathens, an' that's what we are.

"An' some day, when women get a say in makin' th' law, y'r'll see a big change in all these things. Th' only days that stand out in my life are days when I met women. Th' only kind things I ever had done f'r me was by women. If it wasn't f'r them, what would us men do? We'd be out killin' each other like a lot o' beasts in no time, an' you know it. I'm a great believer in women, an' I don't care who knows it; an' that ain't mush; it ain't any weepy dope; it ain't nursin'-bottle philosophy; it's what I know. Who stands by a guy when he's down and out? Who helps him to get up when he tries to? An'

ch. ends next p.

who pats him on th' back an' 'preciates th' struggle that goes
before success? Why, th' women. Give me a bunch o' skirts
an' a fair chance an' I'll bet I could make th' wise guys look
like a lot o' lead nickels in no time.

"A woman struggles along, raisin' th' kids, an' then what
happens? It ain't when th' kid's at home that he goes wrong;
you know that. It's when he begins t' feel his oats and gets
t' nosin' around town. First thing y'r know he finds out that
th' law—th' law made by th' wise guys, mind y'r—gives him
a chance t' drink booze, an' see prize fights, an' do other
things that he wouldn't think o' doin' before his mother, an'
things that he wouldn't get a chance t' learn if his mother had
a say on how things oughter be run. I've thought a whole lot
about it. Suppose things had been started th' other way, an'
it was us wise guys that had no say. An' suppose th' young
girls went out nights an' got tanked up, and did all th' other
things we do, while we stayed at home and wondered why
they did it. An' suppose it was because we didn't have any
say. Wouldn't we be sore? Wouldn't we want t' do somethin'?

"I've met all kinds of women, good and bad, but mostly
what are called bad, an' I've talked t' lots o' 'em, an' d'y'r
know, it's us men, it's us wise guys havin' th' hand, an' makin'
starvation laws an' givin' licenses t' red hellholes that makes
most o' 'em go wrong ? But never mind, old man, there's
better times comin', an' we're goin' to live to see it. All we
got t' do is remember that men are th' sons of women as well
as th' sons of men."

The officer came to dress Smoky in his "glad rags," and
a few minutes later he shook hands with me and passed out
of the front gate—and out of my life. I have never heard of
him since that day. As we turned to wave goodbye before
ducking through the man-gate the Lieutenant of the Yard
sneered and said:

"I wonder how long before that rotten crook will be back?"

The words were like a blow in the face. Here was a para-
site, without education, without trade, utterly incompetent to

earn a living save by manual labor, yet under pay by the State of California, deliberately sending vicious thoughts after a man who had expiated his crime by "doing" a twenty-year sentence, and who had more gold in his little finger than the officer had in his whole body—though it happens that this particular officer once took the Keeley cure.[6] Not only this, but he was indicting the entire prison system without realizing it. He was admitting that twenty years in prison had not—according to his belief—effected any benefit to the man who had suffered it.

Looking back to that last conversation with Smoky, I am struck with the clearness of his vision. That was several years ago, and yet he, a common, ordinary, supposedly ignorant person—a "thug" according to the police—had seen that man's ultimate salvation is in the soft hands of womankind. At that time I did not believe in "woman's rights," but now I do, and I am hoping that every woman who reads this account of Smoky's homely prediction will strive to vindicate him. Smoky brought a great deal into my life without my knowing it at the time. Perhaps he may bring a great deal more into yours.

After all, no life is wasted, and we should never know about the mire were it not for the men and women who have risen from it. For:

> "In the mud and scum of things,
> There alway, alway something sings."[7]

---

[6] The Keeley Cure or Gold Cure was a commercial medical operation that offered treatment to alcoholics from 1879 to 1965.

[7] The final two lines of the poem "Music" by Ralph Waldo Emerson (1803–1882).

25

At the time that the power for running the jute mill was changed from steam to electricity, the man who had been engineer of the mill for years found himself without a job. Although he was a Democrat, and the new administration strongly Republican, he succeeded in getting the appointment as Captain of the Yard.

The running of a steam engine does not seem to be a particularly accordant vocation for fitting a man to govern his fellows, yet this appointment proved to be a happy one. Of course, engineers have to be men of intelligence and judgment, and they are generally men of heart and courage, so perhaps a man from that walk of life wasn't such an arbitrary choice after all. At any rate, Mr. Harrison was fair-minded and was liked generally, by officers as well as prisoners.

The turnkey—he of the cigar-chewing habit—was succeeded by a big, good-hearted, but blundering man who had worked strenuously in the gubernatorial campaign, and got this appointment in recompense for his services. I came to know him very well, and while he had grave faults, he was also fair-minded, so far as his nature would permit.

Shortly after he took charge he changed me from the clothing room to the turnkey's office, and I was placed in charge of the records, beginning with the first man received, in 1859, when San Quentin prison consisted of an old ship anchored off the shore, down to the last man who had been received.

There are eight or ten different registers in which the records of men who have been confined at the prison are segregated in a number of different ways; also classified indices[1] of names for ready reference.

I soon learned that many requests for information were received. In many cases the data contained in these inquiries was very meager, and the segregated records valuable accordingly. There was a standing rule at that time that no information should be furnished concerning prisoners save to the Warden's office, and the Warden's office never furnished information save to qualified officers of the law who stated for what purpose they desired it.

At one time in the past, information concerning men who had suffered imprisonment at San Quentin was supplied indiscriminately to anyone who asked, resulting in the exposure of men who were striving to make good, or even in blackmail. That was before Mr. F. W. Reynolds became the Warden's secretary. He took the stand that a discharged prisoner is entitled to the protection of the prison officials as much as other people are entitled to know about him. I mention him because he is one of the men at the penitentiary who earns his salary, and because he has always been the friend of all prisoners who are friends to themselves.

The turnkey's office is situated between the Captain of the Yard's office and the clothing room, and the only entrance to the "female department" is through that room. Owing to this fact I saw a good deal of the matron and the women prisoners.

One of my duties was to question all incoming prisoners in the presence of the turnkey and have them sign an inventory of the property taken from them when received, and an order permitting the prison authorities to open their mail.

---

[1] Indexes.

ch. ends p. 333

Women prisoners are no exception to this rule, so I saw them, too. Also when a woman prisoner has a "reception" (a visitor) she is obliged to pass through the turnkey's office on her way out and back.

Shortly after I took up my duties in this new position I saw a woman carried into the prison under sentence of fourteen years. The exact facts of the case are nebulous in my mind now, but she had been accused and convicted of having shot a livery stable man in one of the southern counties. From the moment of her arrest she stoutly protested her innocence. It was proved, however, that she had a grievance against the wounded man, and circumstances were against her. When she learned that she was to be tried she refused to come out of her cell in the jail. She even refused to dress. The law had never coped with a situation of this kind before, but proved equal to it.

The woman was covered with a robe and carried into court on a stretcher. She was tried lying on this stretcher. She was convicted lying on this stretcher. She was sentenced to fourteen years' imprisonment lying on the stretcher; and when the time came to bring her to the penitentiary two Deputy Sheriffs, accompanied by a matron, carried her to the train.

Arrived at San Francisco, they carried her to the ferry. At Sausalito she was carried to another train, and at Greenbrae she was carried to the stage. When the stage drew up before the prison portcullis she was carried inside.

Her refusal to walk had, of course, made the case more or less notorious; and her arrival at the prison had been anticipated. When the man-gate opened and a Deputy Sheriff stepped inside backward, with a woman's feet in his grasp, we all knew what was coming.

The poor, wretched body was pulled through the opening, and then came the second man, supporting the woman's shoulders. He was followed by a smug matron with her nose in the air. As they came up the walk to the office veranda we all "rubbered"—as you would have done. We all wanted to see what "she" looked like.

It was not until they brought her into the turnkey's office and laid her on the floor that I saw her face distinctly. The outline and the features have escaped my memory, but I recall that it seemed as though I were gazing into the face of all the suffering that one human being could endure and live.

Before her arrival, there had been a division of opinion regarding her. Some of the men at the office held that she was a fool; others that she was probably innocent and felt the injustice so keenly that she had taken the only possible way of expressing her protest and anguish of mind.

But when I looked at her face my sympathy was all with her. She was nearing middle age and had a good, womanly face.

Mr. Sullivan, the new lieutenant of the yard, a man who had more real influence with prisoners than any other person on the reservation, drew up a chair beside the prostrate woman and tried to reason with her. He told her gently that it was not the fault of the prison officials that she had been brought there; that they were not responsible for it, and that they wanted to treat her kindly and take good care of her, and asked her if she wouldn't get up. A suspicious moisture gathered in her eyes and for a moment we thought she was going to respond, but just then a superior official came bustling into the room.

"Come, madame," he said; "the time for this nonsense is past. You're in the State prison now, and we don't carry anybody around here. Get up!"

Whatever the lieutenant might have accomplished had he had a few more minutes must be left to conjecture. I believe he would have succeeded in breaking the woman's determination, and that she would have got up and walked into the "female" department without assistance, but with this harsh and unfeeling command it was "all off." A hard look came into the woman's eyes, and she made no reply.

ch. ends p. 333

The officer, now realizing that he had made a mistake, changed his tone and tried to coax her to rise. She simply lay there and stared at the ceiling. Finally he lost patience.

"Open the door and take her inside," he ordered.

The matron, who had arrived meanwhile, promptly opened the door leading into the yard of the "female" department, and the woman was carried in.

"Lay her right down here," ordered the officer.

The woman was laid down on the asphaltum just inside the doorway.

He went and stood over her.

"Now, madame, you're in San Quentin prison, in the women's prison, and your commitment is for fourteen years. We are not going to carry you any further. You can lie here as long as you like, but you're going to get up yourself. If you don't you can lie there until you rot."

Turning to the matron he told her to see that this order was carried out to the letter, and then we all stepped back and the door was closed.

All afternoon the woman lay on the asphaltum. When night came the other women prisoners carried her upstairs and into a cell. For several months she never came out of the cell, never got up from the bed, so far as anyone knew. Her meals were carried to her and her other wants attended to by her fellow prisoners. No one seems to know just when she first got up and began to wait on herself, but after a year or so she gradually began to come out of the cell, and finally resumed normal use of her faculties. That was several years ago. The woman is still a prisoner at San Quentin, nearly forgotten.

The "Female" Department!

A nice, pleasant, human designation, isn't it? I have heard it claimed that imprisonment is not nearly so irksome to women as it is to men—that indoor life and confinement are natural for females. In passing through menageries, however, I have never been able to detect it. The female animals in the narrow, barred cages are just as restless and have the same pained expression in their eyes as is the case with the male captives. The only exception I remember was a tigress with three roly-poly cubs which I saw at the San Francisco Chutes some years ago.[2] She seemed to be wholly contented, and when she held one of the cubs between her paws and licked its soft coat her purr almost shook the building.

Of course, I never had the opportunity to roam in the "female" department of the State's human menagerie, but I saw the women individually, and I am quite sure the "natural confinement" and "indoor life" did not make them happy. Instead they always looked miserable and discontented, and, above all—with some exceptions—keenly conscious of their awful disgrace. They are "female convicts"—a nice, pleasant combination of two atrocious words.[3]

There is something about the thought of a woman in prison that bothers the coldest of men. Even the men who are used to it, who see it day after day, are conscious of the incongruity of the thing—thick, iron doors and heavily barred windows with women behind them.

California has thirty "female convicts." There is no "female" department at Folsom. They are all confined at San Quentin. One of my keenest recollections of the "female" department is the case of a young Indian girl committed for a year from Modoc county.[4] She had been employed as a servant and had stolen from her employer. I believe I know why she stole. Perhaps you will, too, when you learn the story.

The judge who sentenced her was ignorant of the fact that there is no "female" department at Folsom, and sent the girl to that place, and the sheriff, also in ignorance, took her

[2] The Chutes was a popular amusement park that opened on Haight Street in San Francisco on November 2, 1895. Its main attraction was a water ride featuring a 300-foot chute beginning atop a 60-foot structure with boats that could reach 60 mph before sailing into the man-made lake below. Due to its popularity, a theater and circus were soon added to the location, which featured lions and tigers.

[3] Wait, what?

[4] California's most northeastern county, bordering Oregon to the north and Nevada to the east.

ch. ends p. 333

there. The Board of Prison Directors ordered her transferred to San Quentin.

I was working at my desk the night they brought her in after lockup. She was in her teens, and her brown eyes were full of terror, but worse than that, worse than all else, she was enceinte.[5] It was apparent even to us who were unused to such things. It must have been apparent to "His Honor," the judge, but he had sent her in her shame to this shameful place. But then we must not forget that she had committed the offense of stealing a few dollars. For this offense the judge had been lenient; he had only sentenced her to a year in the State prison—her and her unborn child.

In pity the night sergeant took her into a side room before telephoning for the matron. At lockup time the matron of the "female" department counts her charges into their cells and then goes home for the night. When a woman prisoner arrives after lockup, or when an inmate of the woman's ward becomes ill in the night and the trusty—or trustess—rings the call bell for the night sergeant, the matron is called by telephone.

While waiting for the matron the night sergeant spoke to the girl kindly, and she replied in broken English with a little lisp. No wonder the judge had sent her to prison— she couldn't speak good English and she lisped when she talked. When the matron arrived she took the girl by the hand and led her into the place that was to be her prison. It was apparent that the girl—the near-mother—was almost at the breaking point, but she held herself together and passed into the gloom without a sound.

Steps were immediately taken to secure her pardon, but pardons are wrapped up in miles and miles of red tape, and the child was born before the Governor acted. The matron arranged with the Warden so that the birth occurred outside the prison walls—at one of the guards' cottages—but a few days later the mother and child were locked up together in

---

[5] With unborn child; pregnant.

the "female" department. The baby was the first male ever imprisoned there.

A few weeks later a pardon arrived for the mother and some philanthropic ladies who had heard of the case provided for her.

Perhaps you may think this is an exceptional case, but it isn't. A few months later a young woman was committed from San Francisco and became a mother while in prison. Her child was born inside the prison walls, though the authorities did not intend that it should be. At first this girl would not talk, and it was not until accouchement[6] was imminent that she disclosed the facts. I acted as stenographer in taking her deposition. A deputy sheriff who had taken this girl to court was responsible for her condition, and, according to natural law, she must have been in jail at San Francisco at the time of conception. This deposition and the other papers were being hastily prepared for the Governor's consideration, when the birth occurred, in the night, and prematurely.

Nothing further was ever done toward fixing the responsibility upon the deputy sheriff. The child thrived in the prison air, and the mother was discharged at the end of her term—also one year. She, too, had offended against the sacredness of property—a few dollars' worth. Again kind ladies undertook the care of mother and child, but the little one died within a year.

Men are brought to the penitentiary to have their lives snuffed out. Women are brought there and other lives are ushered in. The State is both executioner and godparent.

✱

The "female" department at San Quentin is a terrible place for a woman of refinement or culture. A large number

---

[6] The process of giving birth.

of the unfortunates confined there are wrecks from the underworld who have become lost to all sense of delicacy. Their speech and actions are of the lowest order.

When a woman like Mrs. Botkin is forced to live in such an environment her punishment is trebly[7] severe. It makes no difference what her crime may have been, it is not right that she should be compelled to live and eat with persons whom she instinctively shrinks from. Young women klepto-maniacs[8] have been sent to San Quentin and forced to live in these surroundings month after month, year after year. I know of several instances of women who would rather die than defile their bodies, sent to San Quentin because they had stolen property rather than take the other alternative, and compelled to live day after day with the very class which they had fought to avoid. Even young girls in their teens have had this experience. It is certain that no young woman can pass through such an ordeal and come out with ideals unlowered.

The women's yard is surrounded on all sides by high walls. It is covered with asphaltum, and the sun strikes it only during the middle of the day. Their confinement is far more unendurable than that of the men. They are employed in making the underwear of the male prisoners and at other sewing. For years and years they never came out of their quarters. Under Warden Hoyle and the new matron this has been changed. One Sunday each month the "female" prisoners are taken outside the prison walls and permitted to roam over the Marin hills in the fresh air and sunshine. They never come back without wildflowers and bits of green. For years and years the women prisoners were unnoticed by the parole board. Under the present matron a number of them have been paroled, and, needless to say, they have all made good.

I recently received a visit from a woman who had served

---

[7] Three times as much.

[8] Persons characterized by an irresistible impulse to steal even though no imme-diate personal or financial need exists.

two years at San Quentin. In view of the fact that there are but thirty women prisoners in California, and that they could be easily provided and cared for outside of the penitentiary walls, and as the picture in detail which this woman drew of her life in San Quentin not only substantiated my own experience, but amplified it, I am going to tell it.

It must be remembered, however, that the matron whom she depicts and the conditions which she describes were those which obtained when she was a prisoner. She was discharged two or three years ago. As she has asked that her identity be kept inviolate[9] I shall not even describe her. The reader can imagine a composite woman and not be far wrong.

She asked me first if I had not heard about a "woman who couldn't walk, or wouldn't walk, being kept in the dungeon for eighty-three days. Just think of it! Kept in the dark for eighty-three days on bread and water!"

"Are you sure of that?" I said, fearing that she was exaggerating.

"Sure of it?" she rejoined, tensely. "Sure of it? Why, every woman there at the time kept track of the days and wondered if the victim would ever come out alive."

"Tell me your impressions of San Quentin," I urged. "Tell everything just as it was. Don't exaggerate. That doesn't pay; it doesn't get you anything, and it will never bring results. But tell of the life just as you lived it."

"Good," she responded. "I'll describe the bear-pit just as it is; I'll tell you just what I felt.

"When I entered the front gate I was pleased with the trim garden, the beautiful flowers, the playing fountain. My heart was cheered by the sight. 'It isn't such a bad place after all,' I thought. But alas! When I stepped into the yard of the women's quarters I realized that the flowers and the garden were not for me. The place reminded me of the bear-pits where the poor, captive animals stand so forlornly and silently begging for liberty, and before I left I learned that

[9] Free or safe from injury, violation, or disturbance.

ch. ends p. 333

the bears are treated better than we were, for they are given peanuts and not abused.

"The pit at San Quentin is ninety feet long and about sixty feet wide, but in this area are the buildings. The walls, some twenty feet high, are the same dull color as the buildings. And there, where mother earth can never be felt, and nothing seen but a bit of sky, live thirty women, some of them there for life, and such a life!

"On the hill is a guardhouse with a frowning Gatling gun, and on foggy days an armed guard patrols the wall close at hand. On either side of the courtyard are the cell buildings, with outside stairways leading up to the cells. Near the center of the court is a dwarfed pear tree. The barred windows of the cells open to this court, and the poor creatures confined there have in the windows a few sickly plants, growing in old rusty cans, around which they tie paper to conceal the character of the only flowerpots they may have. In these small buildings are the laundry, dining-room, kitchen, storeroom, halls, cells, and last, but not least, the dungeon. In the yard are stretched the lines for drying clothes and for airing the thin blankets used at night, the garbage cans, and the hopper. What room is left for exercise you can imagine.

"The men prisoners can gaze at the flowers and the water. Not so the women. The bear-pit contains not so much as a rude bench where one might rest for a moment in the sun and air when not at work; and the matron would not allow us to take out a chair—afraid we might hurt the cement, I suppose.

"In the laundry room, and only a few feet from the tubs, is the hopper, an old-fashioned contrivance, about eighteen inches in diameter at the top and narrowing down to about six inches at the base. Into this orifice must go the morning filth from the night buckets, and as it will not hold the contents of more than three at a time the scene is one long to be remembered. There were two large holes in the cement floor at that time, and through them the overflow found its way under dining-room and kitchen, so that these rooms always reeked.

"Every night the 'pit' became the playground of hundreds of the largest rats I have ever seen, which scampered and squealed about, fattening on the refuse of the garbage cans and leaving evidence of their presence everywhere—on stairs, floors, and landings. The smell of the rats, the poisonous gases from the hopper, the odors from the garbage cans, and the buckets and the excretions of a poor diseased dog which had been brought in to kill the rats made up an atmosphere which I do not believe exists anywhere else in the whole world. Small wonder that there were sore throats, rheumatism, fevers, and tuberculosis. The wonder to me was that we managed to survive at all.

"Upstairs, on the east side of the bear-pit, is a row of cells, 7x10 feet, with barred windows. In each of these two and sometimes three women were confined at night. The bedsteads are of wood, years old, and are infested with bedbugs. The men have iron bedsteads, at least some of them do, and are able to wage a more or less successful war against the bedbugs by soaking the framework of their beds in oil and burning it. But we had no way to fight off these parasites, and I was tortured by them during every night of my life in prison.

"Dressers or tables in these cells are made up of grocery boxes. There are generally two chairs in each cell. The straw ticks[10] rest on the boards of the bedstead. The coverings are blankets. No pillow is furnished. The women pick up scraps from the sewing room and make pillows in that way. There is no provision for heating the cells, and in winter we used to go to bed before the sun went down in order to keep warm.

"At the end of the court are three cells slightly larger than the ones I have described, but into which no ray of sun ever penetrates, and they are always damp, cold, and moldy. In the halls are windows opening toward the flowers and

---

[10] A tick is a fabric case stuffed with material to form a mattress. In this instance, the material is straw.

ch. ends p. 333

the garden of the prison proper, but as these windows are painted white and sealed down they serve no purpose save that of furnishing a stingy light.

"Some woman in the past scraped the paint off one of these windows by working a hairpin up from the sill on the outside and making a spot about the size of a dime. I used to watch the women standing with one eye glued to this peep-hole, gazing longingly at the flowers below. I used to gaze there myself when I got the chance. The reason why these windows are painted and sealed is to keep the women from seeing the male prisoners; but it also robs them of sun and air.

"There is a sitting-room, furnished with an old table and a broken-down stove, the broken leg of which was replaced by a discarded flatiron, and the grate supported by an old can. It was a very peculiar stove; it had temperament; I shall never forget it. Instead of warming the room in winter it used to emit puffs of smoke, like a steam engine, hour after hour, all through the gloomy winter days, filling the place with smoke so dense that the only relief was to go outdoors and let the fire die down. Yet this was the only place in the women's department where one could get warm. This same room has windows opening on the courtyard of the main prison, and these windows, like the others, were sealed down and painted on the outside, so that there was no possible chance of ventilation.

"From this room opens another in which there are two ancient sewing machines. These two old soldiers were very cranky and the running of them was a feat requiring infinite patience and endurance; but what of that? We were there to be punished, and the running of these sewing machines was only a small part.

"And then the matron used to act as if she considered herself a special agent of the Almighty, and inflicted upon the women under her charge every indignity she could. Indeed, that seems to be the feeling of all who are placed in charge of prisoners. On these two old sewing machines we were compelled to make all the underwear for the men prisoners, and such other garments as the matron ordered.

"The windows of the sewing room are also painted and sealed, and leading from it is a hall about seventy feet long, into which open the remaining eight cells. At the end of this hall is the bathroom, which is kept locked, so that no one can enter it. There is seldom hot water for bathing purposes, and the women used to heat water on the smoky stove I have described and carry it in pails to their cells. There were no rules regarding the use of the bath, and I knew two prisoners who did not take a bath during the two years I was there. The windows in this hall are also painted and sealed, so that no breath of air ever reaches the toilet or bath.

"At board meeting times we used to be warned to have our cells in good order. All cards were tucked out of sight; all cigarettes and matches were concealed. Various members of the board used to come in, walk down the halls, look into the best cells, and learn nothing. The matron was always close at their heels, and they could make no inquiries of the women that she did not hear. We all knew that a word of exposure or complaint uttered in her presence was far beyond the courage of the boldest woman—it meant humiliation, torture, and the dungeon afterward.

"The dining-room is about 30x20 feet. It adjoins the laundry. There are two tables covered with oilcloth. The dishes are heavy and old. The meat safe, which stands in the northeast corner of the room, is separated from the hopper by only a few inches of ancient wall which is saturated with seepage. Close to the east window are the garbage cans, and only a few feet distant, against the prison wall hang the thirty or forty night buckets.

"At breakfast no one presides, and talking is permitted, but at dinner stern discipline sits enthroned upon a rocker near the door, and all that may be heard is the clatter of knives and forks and the drone of the distant jute mill. At supper time there is a wild scramble for the food, which is

ch. ends p. 333

carried upstairs and eaten in the cells. At 4:30 in the afternoon the key is turned on the unhappy women, and the long, gloomy night is before them.

"The kitchen is a dark, smelly place, with numerous holes in the floor, through which rats find ready entrance. Beyond is the storeroom, and thence a doorway leading into a dark hall about fourteen feet long. It is here that the dungeons are located, two 6x10 cells, called 'holes' by the matron, which are blacker than night, damp, and altogether horrible. A thin straw mattress and a pair of blankets constitute the only furnishing of this awful place. Women are 'thrown' into the dungeon at the pleasure of the matron, without a chance to defend themselves.

"One woman who had not stood upon her feet for years was confined there for eighty-three days because she insisted on having a receipt for valuables that had been taken from her when she came into the prison. During part of that time she was in the jacket. Oh, yes, they use the jacket on women as well as on the men.

"Without light, water, or towels, this poor woman, unable to move save by crawling, survived. She is a living example of what the human body may endure. She was finally brought out into the light, given a pair of crutches, and put to work making buttonholes in the men's garments that are made by the women. Later, for a trifling reply, she was knocked to the floor by the matron, dragged to her cell, and locked in for three months, with no food but bread and water.

"When she was released again she was not permitted to have her crutches. Her mode of locomotion was to sit in a small rocker and hitch along the floor. In order to get anything to eat she had to hitch down eighteen steps, across the yard to the dining-room, and back in the same way. In rainy weather she did not get out at all, but used to depend for food upon the kindness of the other prisoners who ran the risk of being punished by giving it to her.

"And yet a negress who threw three plates at Bertha B——while they were at dinner, cutting a severe gash in the woman's arm, was not even reproved for her act. Indeed, the matron said it served Bertha right, and that she should not have made 'Trixie' mad.[11]

"For a trifling infraction of the rules Etta F——, a half-demented woman, was thrown into the 'hole' for nine days. A little girl, 16 years old, Barbara A——, was put into the dungeon for being 'saucy' and was taken violently ill there during the night. Her cries were heard by the night watch, and one of the men came in and released her, taking her to her cell. The matron's rage when she came on duty in the morning and found the girl had been released I shall never forget.

"On another occasion a seamstress was confined in the 'hole' for two days and nights because she could not make a tailor skirt for the matron. In February 1909, an elderly woman was put in the 'hole' because she was suspected of having found a typewritten letter brought in by the matron from one of the male prisoners and intended for one of the younger women.

"Many other women were placed in the dungeon for the most trivial reasons, and yet certain women who engaged in fights, who blasphemed and blackguarded those who tried to lead a moral existence, were never so much as reprimanded.

"Why were not these things reported to the Warden? Remember, when the doors of the women's department close on a prisoner she is dead to the world, and she is never allowed to see, much less speak, to an officer. If she asks to see the Warden she is insulted.

"'I am the Warden here,' the matron used to say. 'I wouldn't insult the Warden by telling him such a person as you wants to speak to him.'

"One of the very worst things this matron used to do was to repeat the contents of letters. She opens and reads all

---

[11] As evidenced in her mugshot, Bertha's 5 years for "mayhem" may be telling.

ch. ends p. 333

Dis April 4th 1910

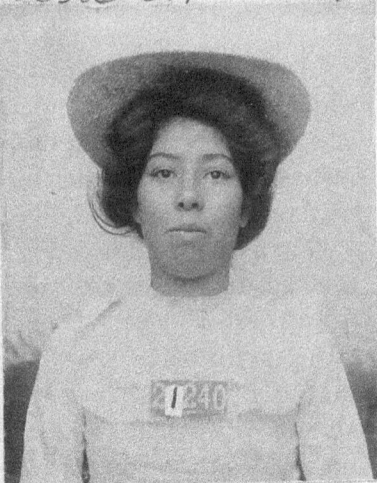

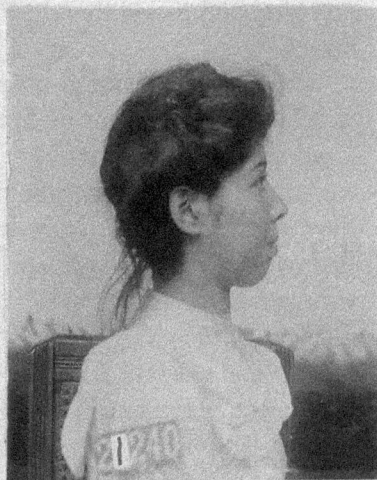

22701

22701 (FEMALE)
BERTHA BORONDA. AGE 31
MAYHEM   5 YRS.
SANTA CLARA. NAT. MINN.
FEB. 29th 08

21240

21240

JULY 14 1905
AGE 16
7 YEARS
CAL.

21240

BARBARA ARADICE
MANSLAUGHTER
EL DORADO.

Name   Bertha Beronda
No.   22701   (female)
County   Santa Clara
Crime   Mayhem
Term   5 years
Received   Dec 29-1908
Discharged   Sep 29-1911
Remarks

letters that come for the women prisoners. Imagine a sensitive woman having the contents of her letters made public to the others, some of whom were of the very lowest order. This was done repeatedly, and I have seen women who were subjected to it weep alone in their cells for hours.

"We were not supposed to see California newspapers, but the matron used to bring in clippings for her favorites. These clippings were always of horrible occurrences. If a paper or book had any case of poisoning, for instance, it would be marked with the name of Cordelia Botkin and handed to that unhappy woman. Cordelia Botkin died in her cell from the effects of softening of the brain, brought on by the mental sufferings she endured. Whether guilty or not, she was human, and I believe God will have mercy. She went through hell before she died.

"The work was not very hard—sewing, scrubbing the floors, cleaning the windows, and general house duties. But each woman had to do her own laundry, and the hot water was scarce. In the matter of clothing we were always in sore need. Each woman was allowed six yards of muslin, six yards of cheap tennis flannel, and two pairs of cheap hose every six months, but woe to the woman who was daring enough to ask for her supply.

"I remember one woman whose supplies were due in April, but she did not get them because her time was up in August. She got along for ten months with two pairs of hose. No underwear, garters, skirts, corsets, or any of the necessary women's garments are furnished. We were supposed to make skirts, night dresses, etc., from the little six yards.

"At the jails women who have been sentenced to the penitentiary are told that all their clothing will be destroyed. This is done to induce them to give away whatever they may have. As a result nearly every woman who arrives brings nothing save what she has on.

"The shoes were heavy cowhide affairs, but even these were hard to get. I have seen women walking about with

ch. ends p. 333

71

Murder. 1st Deg

San. Francisco

Life

Age. 52. Yrs

4 ft 10'1/4

House Wife

Missouri

Rec. May 19/06

Dis ———————

May-19-1906
Age 52.
Life
Mo
21632
Cordelia Botkin
Murder 1 D.
S.F.

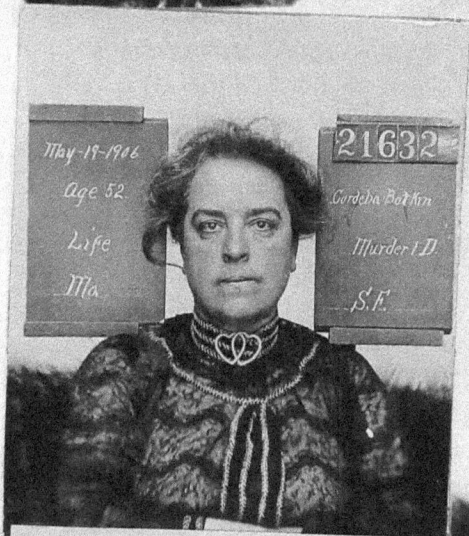

Name Cordelia Botkin
No. 21632
County San Francisco
Crime Murder 1st Degree
Term Life
Received May 19th 1906
Discharged
Remarks

their feet on the floor while waiting the matron's pleasure. If she chanced to be angry with a woman that woman went without shoes until such time as she went to the matron and humiliated herself by apologizing for being alive and begging for shoes.

"The State furnished the women's department with sufficient coarse material for food, but the cooking was so dreadful that all sorts of stomach troubles were prevalent. Those who were not on good terms with the cook, a big negress, serving her third term, and a great favorite with the matron, were subjected to indignities in the matter of food that are simply unprintable. Things were done to dishes, and the portions served, that cannot be told on paper. These acts were known to the matron, who repeated them to the seamstress as good jokes, and she kept this woman in the kitchen knowing what atrocities she practiced. I never partook of the soup at my place without first seeing the other negresses, the friends of the cook, partake of it first.

"When a woman became ill she was to be pitied, for the matron used to act on the theory that anyone who claimed to be ill was faking. A woman with any sensitiveness would suffer long in silence before asking for medical treatment, and the physician was so brutal that most women would drop before asking for him. When he is called into the women's department he is first taken to the office by the matron and told how to treat the particular woman who has asked for him. On one occasion when Mrs. Botkin asked for a lemon—she had rheumatism, and craved acids—he told her to drink vinegar. Another time he was called to treat a little Chinese woman at 8 P.M., and was so incensed at having to leave the saloon—where, according to the matron, he spent most of his time—that he used language so shocking as to disgust even the most hardened women. He was often intoxicated when he came in, and chewed tobacco. He used to expectorate in every direction. An instance of his unfitness was evidenced in his treatment of a little crippled

ch. ends p. 333

Indian woman named Juanita. This poor creature was the scullion in the kitchen, ruled by the negress cook. She carried the heavy pails of coal, made fires, scrubbed the floor, lifted the heavy pots from the stove, emptied ashes, and scoured the dirty pans and tins. In February 1909, she complained of severe pains in her side. The doctor was called and after a brief interview told her she was a faker trying to beat work. Two weeks later she fainted while at work, and she never left her bed until she was carried out in her coffin the following April. When it was seen that she was dying everything possible was done for her, but it was too late. Before she died she told one of the other Indian women that she had been killed by the cook in the kitchen, killed by inches.

"I have been told that the State provides either $50 or $100 for the care of women who suffer childbirth while in prison. In 1907, a young German woman, Lizzie L——, was sent to serve one year for larceny. She had been in jail at San Francisco for some months, and had been so kindly cared for by one of the guards that she arrived at San Quentin in an interesting condition. As the time drew near for her confinement one of the other women, who had been a nurse, went to the matron and informed her that the time was at hand. The matron discredited the information and the child was born inside the prison walls. The matron treated it as a huge joke, and I heard her tell the Warden: 'Oh, well, it doesn't matter. His mother is a thief, and I suppose he'll be one, too.' The Warden smiled and said: 'I suppose you know best.'

"Religious services? Well, the chaplain, your friend, Mr. Drahms, came in five times during the two years I was there. He never spoke to the women save in the presence of the matron. When the Salvation Army women and the California Club members gained an entrance it was the same. And on Sundays no sooner would the door be closed on the departing visitors than the matron would call for a dance. The tables would be pushed back, an old guitar brought out, and some of the women would go through the most degraded

Gr. Larceny
San Francisco
1. Year
Age 23. Yrs
5 ft 4
Servant
Germany
Rec. Apr 5/07
Dis. Feb 5/08

Name Elizabeth Bourika
No. 22100   FEMALE
County San Francisco
Crime Grand Larceny
Term 1 year
Received Apr 5 - 1907
Discharged Feb 5 - 1908
Remarks

contortions, the matron looking on and smiling encouragement. Frequently while religious services were in progress
upstairs those who did not attend would gamble for each other's belongings in the room below. All this on Sunday, mind
you; and each and every person who came there in the hope
of doing good was afterward mimicked by the matron until
it made one's heart sick, and many of the women preferred
spending Sunday in their cells. The only person the matron
seemed to have any respect for was the Catholic priest. That
church cares for its own in its own peculiar way, and in spite
of bolts and bars.

"Several of us formed a class for the study of the Gospel,
but we held only one meeting. We were informed by the
matron that San Quentin was no place for the Bible or religion. The class died a sudden death, and has never been
resurrected. Some of the members of that class are still in
prison. They can testify to the truth of these statements—if
they dare to do so.

"The matron had what she called a 'keen sense of humor.'
I remember an instance when she exercised it at the expense
of an old woman who is serving life. This old woman had
applied for a pardon and her anxiety to hear the result of the
application was pathetic. The matron conceived the idea of
'handing her a lemon.' She arranged with some of the men
who worked in the office, which was directly under the old
woman's room, to talk in loud voices and impart the information that eighteen men and one woman had been pardoned.
The old woman was in the habit of lying with her ear to the
floor so that she might gather such scraps of conversation as
she could from the office below, and the matron knew of it.
So the men, in ignorance of the matron's purpose, and just
to please her, did as she asked. In conversation that night
they made the statement that the Governor had pardoned
eighteen men and one woman. The poor old woman was
so excited when she heard this that she tried to call down
through the floor and learn who the woman was, but they

did not hear her. All that night she walked the floor in an agony of suspense, only to learn in the morning that it was a cruel hoax.

"At one time a young girl had applied for parole, and the parole officer wrote to the matron regarding the applicant. When the matron came in that morning she saw Louise standing on the stairway, and shaking her fist at the girl, exclaimed:

"'Applying for parole, hey? Well, you can bet I'll knock that on the head. I'll tell them you're a tough.'

"This because the girl had incurred the matron's displeasure months before for some petty offense, and had never 'knuckled down' and toadied to the matron after her punishment.

"No woman has ever left San Quentin as good as she went in. There was no chance to become better. The constant terror in which they lived, the awful language they were obliged to hear, the abuse they had to take in silence, the partiality they saw shown daily, the example of a cruel, Godless woman, who broke the Warden's rules with impunity, did not tend to reform anyone, and to a sensitive woman the punishment was beyond description. A Judge who sends a girl like Ruby C—— to such a place should go down on his knees and stay there until the day of his death. He certainly commits a greater wrong than the victim of his judgment.

"Someone will say that women who commit crime should be punished. That may be true, but are they not punished enough by being deprived of home, love, and liberty? Must they be tortured? Can they not have at least the same privileges as the men? Can they not have a little ground instead of asphaltum and boards? Can they not be given enough clothing to keep them warm? Can they not be treated like human beings?

"In addition to the habit of revealing the contents of letters that were sent to the prisoners under her charge, the matron used to eavesdrop at the cell doors to learn what

ch. ends p. 333

Dis Oct 7th 1912.

20447

22933 (FEMALE)
RUBY CASSELMAN. AGE.24
FORGERY.   7 YRS
LOS ANGELES. NAT. CANADA
JUNE.21 '08

20447

22933

Dec-12-1903
Age 26
7 years
Wis

20447

Etta Fitzgibbon
Ass't to Mar.
E.F.

Name	Ruby Casselman	
No.	22933	FEMALE
County	Los Angeles	
Crime	Forgery	
Term	7 years	
Received	June 21, 1908	
Discharged	Mch 21, 1913	
Remarks		

was said of her. She also used to play the women against one another, and each week she had a different spy to report to her. If this spy chanced to be unscrupulous, as was nearly always the case, and was unable to gather any real information, she would manufacture something against other women in order that she might retain the matron's favor for herself. The results of such a pernicious system frequently made women contemplate suicide.

"Sometimes when one of us had incurred the matron's displeasure she would not speak to or notice us for weeks at a time. Meanwhile one would not dare to ask the reason, well knowing that it would bring a tirade of abuse. If one remained silent and did not ask for an explanation the matron would become more and more savage, and then some day, at the slightest pretext, the storm would burst, and the language would be terrible.

"Young girls who had perhaps been wild and wayward, but not vicious, were gradually initiated into smoking, gambling and other vices too awful to mention, by women who were hardened and seemed to take a delight in dragging the young feet into the quagmire from which a woman can never escape. The matron used to take pleasure in telling the prisoners that they were forever branded, and that they could never hope to live a moral life after having been in San Quentin. Those who were weak and despondent naturally became discouraged, and, feeling that they were to be outcasts forever, imbibed as many of the outcast's ways as they possibly could in order to fit themselves to live that kind of life to the best advantage financially.

"I have forgotten one thing, and that was the undergarments made by the women who had no friends or money. Scraps were purloined from the material sent in for the manufacture of the men's underclothing, and when sufficient of these scraps had been accumulated the women used to piece them together and make their own garments in that way. I counted 247 pieces in one garment. Of course, the seams

ch. ends p. 333

in such garments were rather bulky, and one day the matron ordered that no more of that kind of clothing be sent to the laundry, as it 'broke the wringers.'

"On ordinary days we were locked in our cells at 4:30 P.M., but on Sundays and holidays we were shut in at 2:30 P.M. The unlock is at 7 A.M. On Sunday evenings, wearied by the long confinement, the women used to talk to one another across the court, and some of the stories, which everyone could hear, were such as to make the blood curdle. And yet young girls who had been unfortunate enough to be committed to that place were obliged to hear them. Knowing what I do, I would rather kill a girl of mine than have her sent to such an environment for even a week.

"Whenever a woman who was expert with a needle came in she was immediately put to work making garments for the matron. To my certain knowledge, hundreds of yards of crocheted insertion and edging found its way to her cottage on the hill overlooking the prison. Rose P—— was kept busy for two years doing Spanish drawnwork[12] and eyelet embroidery. Mrs. Botkin crocheted shawls and did woven work on lunch cloths and other pieces. Nada L—— had with her when she arrived three beautiful pieces of handwork. In less than a month the matron had them in her possession. The girl gave them to her in order to keep in favor. They were the very last things the prisoner had, but that made no difference. Personally, I donated a yard of silk velvet from the hat which I had on when I entered the prison to make a collar for some man's coat, the matron asking me for it, and saying that she couldn't get any. I got a dose of the dungeon afterward, and it served me right for being so easy. Ruby C—— had several yards of fine linen sent her by friends, and was inveigled into parting with a beautiful shirtwaist which she had embroidered. Grace G—— was kept busy at the very finest kind of silk embroidery, and made not less than

---

[12] Ornamental needlework done by drawing threads to form lace-like patterns.

Dec 28 1905
Age 21
sentence
2½ Years
Cal

21444
Rose D. Porter
Bigamy
Orange.

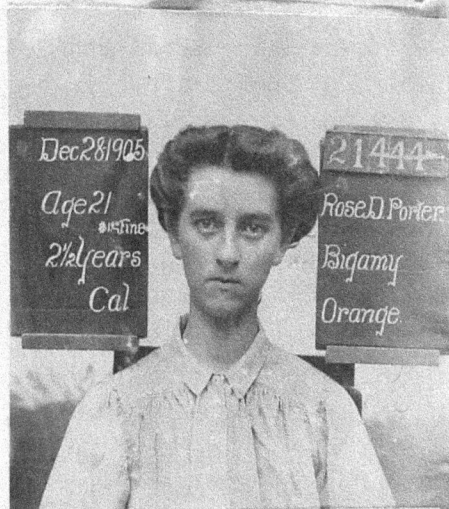

Name Rose D. Porter Female
No. 21444
County Orange
Crime Bigamy
Term 2 r typ & u $100 fine
Received Dec 28 1905
Discharged Dec 28 1907
Remarks

22075
Nada B. Leslie Female
Felony 4 yrs U.S.P.
March 16th Age 29
District S. Calif.
Nat. Canada

Name Nada B. Leslie U.S.P.
No. 22075 FEMALE
County Southern Calif
Crime Felony
Term 1½ years
Received Mch 16 - 1907
Discharged May 28 - 1908
Remarks

a dozen pieces. Some of these women were in turn given extra privileges. In some cases they were made trusties.

"At one time the chaplain arranged that some books should be sent in to us from the men's library. Immediately the matron gave the office of librarian to one of the worst women confined there. She had the selection of the books exclusively, and of course the selections were not elevating.

"One woman, a half-demented negress, was locked in her cell for four years. A month before her ten-year term expired she was taken from this cell and transferred to the insane asylum. Shortly after her arrival there she assaulted one of the attendants with a pair of scissors, and two weeks after she left us she was in her grave. Undoubtedly she was a bad woman, but why was she kept locked in a cell four years before being taken to the asylum?

"The women prisoners are not allowed to receive anything to eat from outside. This always seemed to me to be an unnecessary hardship. Many of the women's friends would have been glad to send them things had they been permitted to do so, and I believe that were prisoners allowed to have such things from those who love them it would tend to keep them from straying so far from the paths of right and virtue.

"Of course, you are wondering why these things have not been told before. One reason is that the women have been afraid to speak, and another is that the majority of them are not of a very high order of intelligence. Someone always has to be the first to let the light in.

"On June 9, 1909, I made all these facts known to the Warden and he promised to investigate them. On October 1st of the same year the matron was removed. I have been told that conditions have greatly improved since that time, but I am sure that they could be much better. As a woman who has suffered, and as one who knows that such a place only breeds vice and hate, I hope the women of California will make an effort to bring about better conditions for women prisoners.

"In telling you this, Mr. Lowrie," she concluded, "I want to assure you that I am not actuated by malice or revenge to anyone. I feel that I paid my debt to the State in full, and I know that I suffered just as much from the effects of seeing others suffer as I did for myself. My hope is that what I have told you will result in benefit to those women who are unfortunate enough to be sent to prison."

26 [1]

---

[1] This chapter or its number was omitted from the original 1912 edition. Research ongoing . . .

27

During the weeks that followed the earthquake[1] the usual regularity of the prison was broken up. It had been a terrible experience to the men in the cells, but their experience was so inconsequential compared with what others suffered that it is not worth telling.

For days afterward the prison ovens were kept hot and bread was baked from morning till night for the refugees in San Francisco. Blankets were also supplied.

Early that summer it was decided to remove the hill back of the prison to make a site for the proposed new buildings. It was an immense undertaking and would require a large force of men.

The population of San Quentin had fallen off after the earthquake and there were not enough prisoners available for the new work—they were all employed in the jute mill and shops. So the State Board of Prison Directors ordered fifty prisoners transferred from Folsom. They arrived on June 30, 1906. They were brought down the Sacramento River on a steamer, handcuffed and chained together, with armed

[1] The 1906 San Francisco earthquake struck the coast at 5:12 A.M. on Wednesday, April 18, with an estimated magnitude of 7.9 and a maximum Mercalli intensity of XI: Extreme. More than 3,000 people died and over 80% of the city of San Francisco was destroyed. It is remembered as one of the worst and deadliest earthquakes in the history of the United States, and the death toll remains the greatest loss of life from a natural disaster in California's history.

guards over them, and in stripes. Of course, under the system, they had to be closely guarded, but had anything happened to the boat they all would have been drowned in their chains.

When the order was issued for the transfer from Folsom to San Quentin the officials at Folsom seized upon the opportunity to get rid of the worst characters confined there. A close canvass[2] of the records was made for this purpose and men of the most vicious tendencies were selected. Quite a number of prisoners who had relatives living in San Francisco made application to be included so that they might be nearer their homes and thus have more frequent visits, but no attention was paid to them. Of course, not all of the fifty who were selected were really vicious, but the officials at Folsom judged them to be so. As a matter of fact, some of them turned out to be excellent men, and several with whom I subsequently became personally acquainted I count among the best men I know.

The fifty prisoners arrived at San Quentin garbed in the hideous Folsom stripes. At San Quentin the stripes are about an inch and a quarter wide and run perpendicularly. The Folsom stripes are about three inches wide and run horizontally. Perpendicular stripes make men look taller than they really are, while horizontal stripes, especially the broad ones, make them appear short.

When these fifty men arrived they looked squat, chunky, and repulsive. All the caricatures of convicts in the magazines and other periodicals favor the horizontal stripes because they make a more offensive showing than do the perpendicular.

These fifty men were not provided with San Quentin clothing, but were assigned to work, and mingled with the other prisoners just as they were. This was a matter of economy. It would have required fifty new outfits had their clothing been changed. It was much cheaper to let them wear the Folsom stripes until they were worn out. Of course, the

[2] Careful examination or thorough discussion; scrutinize.

Folsom clothing could have been shipped back and used where it belonged, and the State would not have lost anything, but no one thought of that.

The "ring-around" stripes made these Folsom men very conspicuous, and after a few days it became evident that they felt the disgrace. Some of them secured sandpaper and "wore out" their clothing in a few hours. But those who were timid dared not adopt this measure and remained conspicuous for months. Still others took extra care of their "ring-arounds" because it had been bruited[3] that the men in the transfer were a "tough lot," and they wanted to enjoy the notoriety of being in that class as long as possible.

Among the fifty were several dangerous lunatics, and the Folsom authorities had sent no word concerning them. One of these, a man serving two years, had a mania for killing, and without apparent cause crushed the skull of the man who was working alongside of him a few weeks after his arrival. The victim died.

His assailant was tried at San Rafael for murder, convicted and sentenced to imprisonment for life at Folsom. Shortly after he arrived there he committed suicide in the dungeon.

Another was Ed C——, a prisoner whom I had seen before. His story illustrates the heartlessness of the system better than any individual case I know.

While I had been in jail before going to San Quentin C—— was brought in, charged with grand larceny. He was about 35 years of age, over 6 feet tall, and weighed 110 pounds. He looked more like an animated beanpole than any human being I have ever seen. We did not discover he was "loco" until he had been in the jail two days. The first intimation we had of his mental chaos was his manner of greeting all questions with grimaces and monosyllables. Then he had several bad nights, when he kept us all awake.

When the time came for his trial he pleaded guilty, but acted so queerly that the judge decided to impanel a jury and

[3] Rumored.

ch. ends p. 349

have them decide as to his sanity. None of the prisoners at the jail were called as witnesses. The District Attorney made an impassioned plea to twelve men, who had been impressed from convenient street corners, asking them not to let this sly faker deceive them, but to return a verdict that would send him to the penitentiary, where he belonged.

The jury promptly found C—— "sane," and he was sentenced to the penitentiary. He came back to the jail grinning. When they handcuffed and shackled him for the journey to Folsom he grinned and jabbered.

After his arrival at Folsom—according to eyewitnesses—he was beaten and kicked from cell to dungeon, from dungeon to rockpile, from rockpile to hospital, and from hospital to dungeon again. At last, to get rid of him, the Folsom authorities shipped him to San Quentin in the transfer.

He was put to work on the "hill" along with the rest of his Folsom brethren. He worked, but, like many insane persons, persisted in taking his time, a sort of go-as-you-please fashion. He was prodded, dungeoned, jacketed, and beaten, and finally found his level in "crazy alley." Day by day he became more pitiable, jabbering incessantly. If offered a sack of tobacco he would refuse it, but if someone threw a Russell-Sage cigarette[4] stump through the palings he would pounce upon it savagely and go off chattering like a monkey. He became thinner and thinner, until it was painful to look at him. Finally he and a man who had softening of the brain were taken from the alley one morning, handcuffed together, and shipped to the insane asylum at Napa.

C—— had no idea where he was going, but showed an inclination to hang back. A few weeks ago, while on a visit to Napa, I passed through the asylum. I kept a sharp lookout for C——, but did not see him.

We did not visit the graveyard.

And while at Napa I could not help comparing the lot of the men I saw there with that of the men in "crazy alley," at

[4] Our research for this brand of cigarette yielded zero results.

San Quentin. At Napa the patients spend nearly the entire day in the grounds. There are trees and shrubs and flowers and lawns, and the space is so ample that they scarcely look like a crowd. Those who are able to work in the gardens and about the buildings. There were many grievous sights, but it was good to see that the unfortunates were given as much freedom as possible and kept close to nature.

But in "crazy alley" at San Quentin it is dark and damp. During the winter months the sun strikes the pavement there for a few minutes in the morning only. During these few moments the dements hug that side; they brighten up in the grateful rays—they sponge in the warmth. Then follows the long, gloomy day, and at night they are herded into their narrow, cheerless cells.

They never get out of the alley, save for a bath, and a shave once each week. Their food is carried there and served to them individually. Owing to the distance and the delay in distribution, it is usually cold when they get it.

The majority of the fifty men who were brought to San Quentin in the transfer were assigned to the "hill." The Legislature had appropriated several hundred thousand dollars for the purpose of erecting new cell buildings at San Quentin, and it had been decided that a good part of it might be spent with profit in removing a large hill to the south of the prison.

A defunct member of the State Board of Prison Directors, who was "out of a job," was appointed "Superintendent of Construction" at a salary of $300 a month.[5] It required very little "superintending," for two hundred convicts to go to work with picks and shovels and wheelbarrows, and all I ever saw him do was sit at the stove in the directors' room at the Warden's office and smoke cigars. His graft[6] lasted several months before he "lost out." A man who really knew something about such work was appointed in his place, and

---

[5] Adjusted for inflation, $300 a month in 1912 would be equivalent to approximately $9,000 a month, or $108,000 a year, in 2023.

[6] The acquisition of money or position by dishonest or corrupt means.

ch. ends p. 349

at less than half the salary. The $300 a month superintendency was one of the rawest cases of graft I have ever known, and I have known many.

Then came a plot for escape. Several of the Folsom men planned to make a "getaway" by water. For this purpose they surreptitiously prepared "patent" rubber suits. They were exposed by a stool-pigeon and the plot was frustrated.

Some time later another one of them tried to sneak off the reservation and was caught. He had on a homemade suit of clothes under his stripes. He had made over a suit of canton flannel underwear, dyed it with inks, and had hoped to escape the vigilance of the guards in the Gatling gun towers.

One of the most remarkable facts in connection with the men who are confined at San Quentin is that a large percentage of them are ex-soldiers. Quite a few are veterans of the Civil War—but their number is decreasing rapidly—so the majority are men who have served in the Philippines.[7] It is a well-known fact that service in the Philippines generally impairs the health and physique of the soldier, and, judging from the number who have been committed to San Quentin and Folsom, it also has a tendency to break down their moral standards.

In a way the Government is responsible for the criminal lapses of its discharged soldiers. At the beginning of the Philippine trouble young men were enlisted in all parts of the United States and shipped to the Orient. After two or three years' service in the enervating climate of the Philippines, with all the demoralizing influences of soldier life and all the unnatural repressions of subordination, these men were brought back to the States, paid off, and discharged from the service at San Francisco. A large percentage of them, bursting with the sense of freedom to do as they chose, proceeded to "have a good time." Generally this "good time"

[7] The Philippine–American War (also referred to as the Filipino–American War, the Philippine War, and previously referred to as the Philippine Insurrection or the Tagalog Insurgency) was an armed conflict between the First Philippine Republic and the United States that lasted from February 4, 1899, to July 2, 1902.

lasted until they were broke, and then came an awakening to the fact that they were stranded in a strange city, thousands of miles from home, and without prospects.

Many of them turned to crime as their only way to keep from starving, and many of them were caught and sentenced to prison. In fact, crimes by ex-soldiers became so common at one time that the magistrates inflicted most severe sentences upon those who were caught and convicted. And yet the Government continued to discharge Philippine soldiers at San Francisco, and does to this day, I believe. It is always a serious matter for a young man to leave the place of his nativity, where he is known, and especially so for young men whom the excitement and adventure of army service lure to the step.

I have talked with dozens of young convicts who have been through this experience, and with almost every man the verdict was: "This would never have happened to me had I been discharged at the place where I enlisted, near home."

The temptation to have one "fling" in a strange and enticing city proved too great for them to withstand. I venture to say that there would be 200 less convicts in the State prisons of California—not to mention the prisons of other nearby States—had the Government transported its soldiers to the places of enlistment before discharging them.

Many of these ex-soldiers draw pensions, especially the veterans of the Civil War. For a number of years after I entered San Quentin, the Rev. August Drahms, himself a veteran, was Notary Public[8] at the prison, and used to charge each man 26 cents for notary service each quarter. He also used to charge a fee of one dollar for witnessing affidavits pertaining to applications for pardon or commutation of

[8] A person legally empowered and authorized to perform certain legal formalities such as witness and authenticate documents, administer oaths, take affidavits and depositions, draw up or certify contracts and deeds, and engage in other activities established by local law.

sentence. His rapacity in this respect finally led to action on the part of the State Board of Prison Directors, who issued an order that no prisoner should ever be compelled to pay notarial charges. Drahms made a fight against this order, but without succeeding in having it rescinded.

Among the veterans of the Civil War whom I knew at San Quentin were several Confederate soldiers. But one of the Union veterans, "Old Shang," was a particularly interesting man. He was a "ten-time loser" the last time I saw him; i.e., he had served nine previous terms either at San Quentin or Folsom. He had practically been "doing life" on the installment plan since the close of the war.

"Shang's" particular weaknesses were "booze" and horse-flesh. During each of his terms of imprisonment, which were always comparatively short, his pension would accumulate, and when his term expired he would go out and get gloriously drunk. Then when his money was gone he would steal the first horse he could get and try to sell it.

The intervals between his various terms were very short. After stealing a horse he would endeavor to sell it to the first person he met, and in this respect he seldom exercised the least cunning or foresight. I remember hearing him tell of one instance of the kind that was very funny, especially to hear him tell it. He had been discharged and had "drunk up" his pension at San Rafael, only three miles from the prison.

"It was the old, old story," said Shang. "Out only a few days, dead broke, and so thirsty I felt like a sponge that had been buried with an Egyptian mummy. That night I decided I'd steal a hoss, but I also decided that I wouldn't get caught, for a change. So I hiked out of San Rafael toward Petaluma, and about midnight I came to a ranch where the barn was some distance from the house.

"It was a dark night and awful foggy, and everything was so still you could hear the hosses in the barn thumpin' half a mile away. It was no trick to crush into the barn, and the first hoss I laid my hands on was a pretty good specimen and I nailed him. I got a saddle and bridle and away I goes. I rode all night in the dark and fog—must 'a' been twenty or thirty miles—and along toward daybreak I came to a ranch.

"'I'll stop here and get breakfast,' thinks I, and I did. They treated me fine, and pretty soon I hinted that I had a fine hoss I'd like to sell. The rancher had an eye to business right away, and we went out to look the hoss over. He seemed kind of surprised at first, and then he offered me $75 for him. I made him raise to $85, and then he told me he didn't have the money on hand, but would hitch up and we could drive into town to the bank and get it. I said all right, and a little while after we started. When we got to town I was kind of surprised to find it was San Rafael, and I couldn't understand how we'd got there so quick. We stopped at the bank and he went inside. He'd been gone about five minutes when I saw the Sheriff coming up the street.

"'Hello, Sheriff,' says I, as he got near. 'Not much doing in your business these days.'

"'No,' he answers; 'not much; but what be you doing with that team?'

"'Oh, this team belongs to Mr. Sheridan, a particular friend of mine, who lives out country a bit. We just drove in on a little pleasure jaunt this morning. He's in the bank getting some dough to entertain me on in town. You known Mr. Sheridan. Sheriff?'

"'Yes, Shang,' says the Sheriff, 'I do know Mr. Sheridan. He just telephoned me to come down and get you for stealin' one of his hosses.'

"'Stealin' one of his hosses?' says I. 'Why, I'm selling him a hoss.'

"'Yes, I know,' says the Sheriff, 'but it just happens it's his own hoss you're trying to sell him. Hop out, Shang, old boy, and come to your old cell in the County Jail.'

"I tried to talk out of it. I couldn't understand the situation

ch. ends p. 349

at all, but he wouldn't listen. And, sure enough, they had me dead right. Do you know what I'd done? I'd yaffled that hoss and then rode around that ranch all night in the fog, and when morning came I tried to sell the hoss to the very man it belonged to. Wouldn't that make your hair curl sideways?

"At first I wouldn't believe it myself, but when the old judge said 'three years' I had to admit that as a crook I was a mutt—and, what's more, I've never changed that opinion. That was twenty years ago, and I've done several bits since then.

"But that ain't all," added Old Shang, a sparkle of mischief coming into his small gray eyes, "that ain't all by a long shot. When I got that three years in do you know what I done? I went right back and stole that same hoss, and you can bet your suspender buckles that I waited for a moonlight night to do it. I got $40 for him in San ——. Oh, never mind where— and I never had more pleasure in my life than I had drinking up that hoss. There was a big crowd in the saloon where I spent the dough, and I guess they must have all thought I was bughouse, for every time I'd call them up to the bar I'd say:

"'Come on boys; let's slop up on his hoofs,' or 'lets guzzle his tail,' or 'let's see how his bloomin' ears taste.' Say, it was great.

"At one stage of the proceedings I was kinder slow between drinks—got to studying on what a fine, artistic specimen of humanity the bartender was, or something like that—I've forgot just what—when up pipes a geezer at one of the tables and says:

"'I don't know who the party is we've been drinking up, but with hoofs and a tail I've got my suspicions—and say, I move that we finish him. Let's see what his bleedin' heart tastes like.'

"So we all lined up once more, and everybody took Dago Red."[9]

Poor old Shang. He spent nearly his entire manhood behind prison bars. The last time I saw him he was tottering eagerly toward the front gate. His tenth "jolt" had been for five years and it had finished him.

*

The fact that clothing is taken from incoming prisoners and given to other prisoners about to be discharged gives rise to an interesting feature of the parole system. The parole law, passed in 1893, empowers the State Board of Prison Directors to make rules and regulations under which any prisoner, other than those committed for life, may be paroled after he shall have served one calendar year of the term for which he has been committed, and life prisoners after they shall have served seven calendar years, at the board's discretion.

The "rules and regulations" established by the State Board of Prison Directors, pursuant to this law, are, briefly, that no application for parole shall be considered until the applicant shall have served one-half of his net sentence and has a perfect prison record for at least six consecutive months immediately preceding the consideration of his case; that he shall have advertised his intention to apply for parole in a newspaper of general circulation in the county where his conviction occurred; that he shall have employment assured him, by affidavit, from some responsible person; that he shall prepare a biographical sketch of his life from boyhood; that he shall furnish his own clothing and transportation, and that

[9] During the late 19th and early 20th centuries, "dago red" referred to a wine made from a blend of assorted dark red wine grapes. The term became synonymous with affordable, basic table wine, especially field blends in California. In the late 1970s and early 80s, there was also a California-based Dago Red brand, but the brand and the term both fell out of favor as "dago" is a disparaging term for a person of Italian, Spanish, or Portuguese descent.

ch. ends p. 349

he shall leave a deposit of $25[10] in the hands of the prison Warden for the purpose of defraying any expense which may be incurred in returning him to prison for infraction of the regulations governing his parole. Also that it shall require the affirmative vote of four members of the board to make a parole legal. The board consists of five members, three of whom constitute a quorum for the transaction of all financial or other business. Three members of the board may revoke a parole and forfeit a prisoner's credits, but it requires four members to grant a parole.

Taking up these rules and regulations in the order of their citation, we have, first, that no prisoner shall be paroled until he shall have served one-half of his net sentence. This rule is arbitrary and works many injustices. One of the purposes of the parole law is to rectify uneven or excessive sentences. It is a well-established fact that many judges impose sentences entirely out of keeping with the nature of the offense and the character of the delinquent. It is a regular occurrence to see a professional crook, a three or four time loser, arrive at the prison under sentence of three or four years, and the same stage deliver a boy, a first offender, with ten, fifteen, even twenty years. The board of directors say that each of these prisoners must serve "half-time" before they can be paroled.

By requiring the applicant to advertise his intention of asking for parole the way is opened for enemies or prejudiced persons to protest against his having it. I have known of instances where legacies or other money matters were involved to such an extent that it was to the interest of persons in the outside world to keep certain men in prison. This advertisement gives them the opportunity to keep posted and to protest against the parole of the individual whom they are interested in keeping out of the way.

By requiring the applicant to have employment assured

---

[10] This rule was abolished by the Board of Directors at the close of the year 1911. Adjusted for inflation, $25 in 1911 would be equivalent to approximately $750 in 2023.

him before his application will be considered it becomes necessary for the man to get employment in advance. This means that a prisoner must secure employment two or three months in advance of the time when he shall, perhaps, be permitted to take it. How many business men are there who can assure a man a position two or three months hence?

And quite frequently, after a prisoner has secured such employment, upon appearing before the board of directors for his "second trial" his application is "postponed" for six months, or a year. It is very seldom that the person who is willing to give him work can arrange to hold the place open, which means that the prisoner must seek and secure other employment before his case will be heard again. I have endeavored to fathom the justice or logic in this rule, but I am unable to do so. It always seemed to me that it would be more logical to parole prisoners on merit, on their good record while in confinement, and with the understanding that they shall not leave the prison until they secure suitable employment.

This system would enable a man to go to such work as he might be able to get without delay. Under the present system it is almost impossible for many of the men to get the necessary employment affidavit, and quite frequently, simply in order to permit the prisoner to get out, persons sign employment agreements charitably—an injustice to the prisoner as well as to the people of the State.

Regarding the "biographical sketch," perhaps it is a sensible rule, but I know of a number of instances where men have remained in prison and served out their full term rather than disclose the names and addresses of their relatives or former employers.

By requiring the prisoner to furnish his own clothing and transportation, and leave a deposit of $25, still greater obstacles are placed in his path. Prisoners who serve out their terms and are discharged are furnished with clothing by the State, but a paroled prisoner must furnish his own. This is

ch. ends next p.

a decided anomaly. If the theory of parole is to get men back to right living it seems to me that the State should be willing to spend a few dollars to accomplish it.

Statistics prove that the paroling of prisoners is a matter of economy, morally as well as politically. Several hundred of the two thousand men now confined at San Quentin, and an equal quota of those confined at Folsom, might just as well be learning to be good citizens, earning their own living, as be costing the State many thousands of dollars a year by being kept in prison.

In many instances men who at the time of their arrival have worn clothing which was of sufficient worth for the State to appropriate and give to discharged prisoners, thus saving the cost of a new suit, are unable to get the funds for parole clothing, and remain in prison as a consequence. If they become embittered and feel that society has wronged them, who shall say that they are not justified?

The $25 which a paroled prisoner is required to leave as a deposit is forfeited to the State as soon as the paroled man is declared a violator. No matter if it only requires a dollar or two to bring him back to the prison from San Francisco, or some other nearby place, the entire $25 is forfeited.

These requirements prevent many worthy men from taking advantage of the opportunity which the law affords for their rehabilitation. The cost of parole ranges from $50 to $75, according to the locality to which the paroled prisoner must go to fulfill his employment pact. A prisoner who has been confined for years, working every day without pay, and who is unable to raise $50, cannot have the same chance as the man who has money, or friends who will supply it for him. And even the men who are fortunate enough to have such friends must start out in debt—an added hardship to an already over-burdened man.

It has been claimed that this expense feature of the parole regulations tends to prevent unworthy and undesirable men from securing the benefits of parole. But this resolves itself into the unwritten and unspoken slogan of our present age of commercialism: to be poor is a crime; a poor man is no good.

Many good persons, learning of these obstacles in the path of the friendless prisoner, have taken a personal interest and have supplied the necessary funds to scores of individual prisoners, and it is gratifying to know that in the majority of cases the beneficiaries have "made good" and have repaid the loan. At the same time there have been ingrates.

Viewed from the standpoint of the prisoner, of the down-and-outer, these rules and regulations are eminently unjust. I feel that way about it. If the law says I may have a chance to prove that I want to redeem myself I do not think it is right that I should have to pay for the opportunity, nor do I think it right that some other person should help me to pay for this privilege by loaning me the money necessary under the rules.

But, to be fair, I am thoroughly convinced that at least three members of the present Board of Prison Directors are not in sympathy with these rules. It is seldom that the five members of the board get together; usually only four attend the meetings, sometimes only three. One of the rules governing parole is that it shall require the affirmative vote of four members to suspend or change the rules, which virtually amounts to a one-man power. The prisoners feel the injustice of this. The present administration of the parole law serves to defeat the purpose of the law.

28

But, although the State Board of Prison Directors have rules governing applications for parole, they "suspend" these rules whenever policy seems to demand it, and it is the poor and friendless prisoners who suffer. Of course, the half-time rule is a usurpation,[1] an assumption of self-righteous wisdom transcending that of the representatives of the people who enacted the parole law and infused it with a spirit of sound common sense by providing that any prisoner, save one serving life, may be paroled at the end of one year if his prison record has been good.

But after having circumvented the intent and spirit of this law, the directors have been inconsistent by releasing favored prisoners on parole before they have served half-time. It must be understood, however, that this half-time rule and other parole regulations do not represent the desires or the judgment of all of the present members of the board. These rules and regulations were framed and adopted by the board as it existed several years ago. The obstacle in the way of change or modification is that one of the members, possibly two, are holdovers from the original board, and oppose new rules.

One member of the board who is not in sympathy with the half-time regulation has consistently objected to its

---

[1] In this context, an encroachment or infringement upon someone's rights.

"suspension" on every occasion that has arisen, not because he believes that prisoners should be kept in confinement until they have served half-time before being granted parole, but because he has hoped to force a change of the rule by making the members of the board who are responsible live up to it. But the half-time rule still stands, and exceptions are still being made to it.

Personally, I know a great many prisoners who should not be compelled to serve half-time; also I know some who should be compelled to serve more than half-time because their daily life and actions in prison clearly indicate that they would not honor the restraints which parole would impose upon them.

Again, even after having served half-time with a perfect prison record, many prisoners are arbitrarily refused a trial on parole. They appear before the board, reply to all questions faithfully—even questions verging on insult, such as would not be tolerated in a courtroom—and are then denied parole without any reason being given for such denial. A man who has obeyed all the prison rules and worked faithfully for years, looking forward to the day when he shall have served half-time as the date when he will get a chance to prove his sincerity and redeem himself, certainly cannot feel very charitable, nor have much respect for a body of men who see him for a few minutes and then arbitrarily tell him that he cannot have a parole.

In my opinion the resident officers of the prison should be the ones to decide when a prisoner is fit for trial on parole, which, of course, connotes that such officers must be men of the highest character and intelligence, and which also necessitates a different internal prison management. The board of directors of an insane asylum or a hospital do not assume to say when the patients shall be discharged. They don't know anything about the patients individually, and even if the patients were brought before them one by one they would not be qualified to assume the responsibility of saying which

ch. ends p. 364

were convalescent and which were incurable. But the officers, the doctors in charge, should know, and do know.

And when a man who has been brought before the State Board of Prison directors and denied parole, after having served half-time, according to their rule, and with a perfect prison record, sees another prisoner who has not served half-time, and whose prison record has not been good, but who has the right kind of extraneous influence, granted that which he has been denied, who can blame him for becoming bitter and holding the law in contempt? What would you feel under similar circumstances? What would any member of the board of directors feel were he a prisoner and doomed to pass through such an experience?

Concrete instances of both kinds could be cited by the score, but one case, that of a man serving twenty-five years who has twice appeared before the board and had his application postponed for two years each time, will illustrate the injustice and inconsistency as well as any other. This man is known as G——, and has been in charge of one of the departments of the prison laundry for five or six years. He first entered San Quentin as a boy, served a short term, and was discharged with the customary $5 and cheap clothing. Of course, a man discharged from prison needs two suits of underwear, and if he has any self-respect he also wants a suit of clothes in place of that furnished him; he feels that the prison brand is upon him so long as he wears the shoddy clothing which the State has furnished him. But he has to eat and sleep, and that costs money. Five dollars doesn't go far when it is all a man has save the clothes on his back.

G—— found it that way, and when in absolute want joined another man in a robbery. G—— was caught and sentenced to twenty-five years at San Quentin. Under the Goodwin act,[2] twenty-five years means fifteen years and three months if the prisoner's behavior is good. So, in G——'s case,

[2] The Goodwin Act of 1864 established a credit system for prisoners that reduced sentence terms for good behavior.

half-time amounted to seven years and eight months. G——
has the capacity for making friends—his very earnestness in
everything he undertakes makes people like him—and at the
approach of his half-time he was urged to apply for parole.

The board heard his case, tried him over again for the robbery, and postponed action on the application for two years.
G—— went back to the laundry and resumed his duty at the
mangle,[3] at which work he is expert. When the two years
rolled around outside friends exerted themselves, and after
considerable effort succeeded in getting G—— a position
in a laundry. One of the directors had become interested in
the case, but was unable to attend the meeting at which it
was heard. So he addressed a communication to the other
members of the board, urging them to give G—— a chance.
It happened, however, that this member of the board was at
loggerheads[4] with one of the other members, and this other
member blocked the parole. It may be a surprise to many
that one member of the board has it in his power to prevent
the parole of a prisoner, but such is the case. It is a one-man
power, pure and simple, as I have seen demonstrated time
and time again.

So G—— went back to his mangle once more, and he is
working at it yet. He has now served ten years—more than
a life termer is required to serve before becoming eligible for
parole; more time than was served by Frank D——, whose
case I cited in a previous chapter.[5] To emphasize the contrast, however, Frank D—— killed his wife in cold blood, was
sentenced to hang, received a commutation to imprisonment
for life, and was paroled at the end of nine years.

Of course, the persons who were willing to give employment cannot hold the position open for him indefinitely,
and, of course, they are justified in thinking that G—— was
denied parole because he is a bad man. Not being conversant

[3] A machine used for smoothing cloth or clothing by roller pressure after washing.
[4] Feuding; in dispute.
[5] Refer back to Chapter 21, pp. 261–262.

ch. ends p. 364

with the system, what else can they think? This means that when G——'s case is again considered he must hustle for another position—hustle from behind prison walls, and in ignorance of the ways of the world, owing to his long confinement.

If this is a logical interpretation of the parole law there must be something wrong with my mind and with the minds of thousands of other men who have suffered these humiliations. If the theory of parole is to redeem men then it is the duty of the State to start the beneficiary under the best possible auspices and to make him feel that his salvation means something to the State.

Eighty-five percent of the men who have been paroled from the prisons in this State have made good. Of the fifteen percent who have violated parole, less than two percent have committed other crimes. Of the men who are discharged at the expiration of sentence, about forty percent are returned to prison in this or some other State, and for new crimes. Many of this forty percent could be redeemed were the parole rules less drastic and were not the last drop of blood exacted from them by making them serve out their terms to the last minute. In fairness to everyone, should not these absurd regulations be abolished?

Quite a number of men have been returned to San Quentin for violating parole in what may be termed a minor way. They have indulged in intoxicating liquor, left their employment, or committed some other minor offense, negative or positive. In every instance, whether serving two years or twenty, all credits have been taken from them. Under the theory that parole is for the purpose of reclamation, why should not some of these men be given a second chance?

Primarily, parole is to test a man, not to prove him, and the very fact that some men fail to "keep" parole is a justification of the parole system. I know a number of men who I am sure will ultimately redeem themselves, and I believe the time will come when a parole violator will not be regarded wholly as a subject for punishment. Rather, he will be looked upon as one who needs help and encouragement. Surely, if the object of prisons is to protect society, the reclamation of the wrongdoer should be the major consideration. Either that or he should be kept in prison for life. And, surely, the harder it is to get a maverick into the herd the greater the satisfaction and merit in its accomplishment.

There is a Chinaman called "Spot" at San Quentin who has the distinction of being the only Chinaman who has broken parole. Still, according to his story, he was merely trying to survive. He left his employment in California, which was very unremunerative, and went to Alaska for the fishing season without permission. When he got back he was arrested and returned to San Quentin.

"I workum hard, I come back, pinchum me heap quick," is the way he tells it.

As a rule, the Chinese are good prisoners and "make good" on parole. Quite recently the Board of Directors paroled two prisoners who had been out on parole before and had been brought back for violation. For violation of parole a prisoner is deprived of all credits, and these two men, serving twenty and twenty-five years, respectively, are now serving their credit periods on parole. Had they not violated parole they would have been discharged some time ago.

It seems to me that this is a splendid application of the parole law. The theory of parole, as I understand it, is to reclaim the lawbreaker and make him a good citizen. This being so, it is logical that the efforts at reclamation should be carried to the last ditch. I believe "Spot" should have a second opportunity. He did not do anything vicious, he did not break the law; he merely went to work outside of his prison (the State of California) without permission.

An incident will illustrate the attitude held by a certain grade of officials in this matter.

One day an officer called Chaplain Drahms into the office to show him the "scrapbook." I was in the next room and could not help hearing all that was said. The "scrapbook" contains the photographs of parole violators from other States, and at that time it contained probably a thousand pictures—an imposing array, well calculated to give the superficial observer an erroneous impression of the parole system. Seeing a thousand photographs of parole violators assembled in one book, page after page of them, is bound to create the impression that the parole system is a failure, especially if this book is considered alone. As a matter of fact, however, it represented parole violators from twenty or more States during the past ten years.

The chaplain became very much excited.

"My, but I'm glad you showed me this," he exclaimed. "Why, they must all break their parole. It's outrageous. It's time to stop this sentimental folly."

"It's only a gang of cranks that stick up for such nonsense," observed the Lieutenant, gloatingly.

"Yes," assented Mr. Drahms, "and we must try to do something to stop it. I'm glad you showed me this. More than a thousand of them! Good gracious!"

At this juncture I began to whistle and then stepped into the room. I had the satisfaction of looking upon two faces that were covered with guilt. I tried to see the matter from their point of view. I could understand the Lieutenant's. He feared that a liberal application of the parole law would reduce the population of the prison and lessen the need for prison officers.

Each prisoner at San Quentin has a number, which is marked on his clothing in indelible ink and which also appears in his photograph. These numbers run consecutively, and the same number is never used more than once. At present the numbers are in the twenty-five thousands, which means that more than 25,000 prisoners have been confined at San Quentin. The numbers at Folsom are in the nine thousands, I believe.

It was not until the year 1888, or thereabouts, that

photographs were taken of prisoners, but since that time there has been quite an accumulation of pictures. All save one or two of the prisoners who have been received since the photograph record was installed have their photographs—front view and profile, hat on and hat off, in citizen's clothing and in stripes, pasted in the albums, each with its respective number underneath.

I have said that this record contains the photographs of "all save one or two" prisoners. If I remember correctly, there are two places in the albums which are blank. At any rate, I am sure there is one place, and the reason is interesting. The prisoner arrived at San Quentin all fight, and his name appears on the register, but he was never photographed. He had a ten-year sentence, and served it in ten minutes. As he stepped inside the prison walls he reached into his pocket and then put his hand to his mouth. Ten minutes later he was dead. The deputy sheriff who had him in charge insisted on getting a receipt, claiming that he had delivered the prisoner alive. So the man's name and crime had to go on the records—and he died as a convict at San Quentin, even though he never wore stripes or suffered having his hair cropped.

In the desire for vengeance so many persons imagine that a prisoner must suffer actual incarceration for years and years in order that he may feel the disgrace and humiliation they hunger to have him feel. Of course, there are many prisoners who do not mind the disgrace of conviction and the loss of social standing—all they care about is the actual confinement of their bodies. But some men suffer more poignantly over the shame than over the physical punishment. The iron sears into the soul of such a man long before he dons stripes and becomes a number living in a cell. I have known scores of such men. Yet the majority of persons think that a man must be reduced to the physical life of a brute before he suffers. The other night I heard Judge Frick of Oakland address a meeting. He declared that he was strongly

ch. ends p. 364

in favor of probation for first offenders wherever the circumstances permit.

"Some persons say that probation is a menace, because it will encourage another person to commit crime," said the Judge, "but let me show you how absurd that is. We'll suppose your next-door neighbor is arrested for embezzlement or forgery, or any other crime. Immediately he is disgraced and dishonored. His home is invaded by the police, his picture and the circumstances appear in the papers, his family is humiliated, many of his friends forsake him, and before he can be placed on probation he must either be convicted or plead guilty. Very well. Now, would you feel encouraged to commit a crime and go through this kind of an ordeal? Of course you would not."

The Judge drew the picture much more graphically than I have, and it impressed his hearers very deeply.

The next morning I sat in the office of a man who is striving with all his might to live up to the doctrine, "Do unto others as you would have others do unto you." For conscientiously and earnestly trying to live and apply this Christ law this man has suffered, and is suffering daily, crucifixion. For years and years he was a hunter—a man hunter—an unmerciful, implacable, blood-lusting Tiger. During the years that he manifested in that way he was popular with the public, he received the plaudits of the crowd, and after a particularly exciting hunt for big game, resulting in the cornering of one exhausted, heartbroken human rabbit, the plaudits resounded more loudly than ever. It made no difference that the larger game had escaped—a rabbit had been caught. Up with the thumbs! Death to the rabbit! It had been a bad rabbit; it had invaded the public garden, emboldened by the larger game. So the rabbit was brought in and held up by the ears, while the hounds jumped and snapped for its life.

And then after it was all over, after the rabbit had been cast into prison, this man, who had bayed and strained with the rest, had a revulsion of feeling. Suddenly it came upon him that the rabbit had died a million deaths while it was being run to earth—it had suffered more in the agony of anticipating its death than it could ever suffer in the death itself. So this hunter began to feel something strange for a hunter—sympathy for the thing he had hunted. And then, when he put himself in the rabbit's place, he saw himself as he really was—his naked soul was covered with muddy-red blotches of hate, revenge, and blood lust. With horrified eyes he looked at himself, endeavoring to see beneath the blotches, hoping, praying that he might catch just one faint glimmer of that light which discloses the soul as divine. At last he saw it. The discovery almost unnerved him. He had found that he was really human and not a self-righteous god. Immediately he was filled with a great desire to let others know what it felt like to be really human. So he forgave the rabbit the wrong it had done, and he determined that he would try to make other "gods" forgive, too.

But when the rest of the hunters learned of it they were aghast! What! Let the rabbit go before it had suffered some more—lots—lots more? Impossible! Had not this rabbit violated the public garden, and were there not other rabbits who were just as much entitled to go free as this rabbit? "Yes," said the ex-hunter; "yes, the other rabbits should go, too, so long as they'll behave, but I didn't help to hunt them. I'm anxious to help my rabbit, the one I helped to exhaust and corner, because I, too, was a rabbit—you are rabbits—and rabbits were not meant to judge rabbits."

But all this went over the rabbit ears, even though the ears were all straight up.

And the other day I sat in this man's office and heard him read some of the letters of execration and insult that self-righteous persons imagine are evidence of their Christianity. He read these letters to a friend who is bitterly opposed to mercy for the rabbit. This friend referred to the rabbit as the most detestable thing on the face of the earth. He kept repeating the most scathing anathemas over and over, while

ch. ends p. 364

the man who has found himself human sat and patiently took it—a sad expression in his eyes and a tired droop in his bearing.

I compared the two men. Both are regarded as successful. One was standing for society as it is today, the other as it will be. How long must the world wait?

✶

When an exceptionally large man is received at San Quentin, none of the stock clothing will fit him, and it becomes necessary to make a special outfit to his measure. Quite a number of exceptionally large men are received, and ordinarily the making of special clothes causes no comment. But one day a prisoner was received whose measurements were so very unusual that a great deal of attention was attracted to him. He arrived at noon, and when the sheriff in charge got off the stage with him no one imagined for a moment that he was a prisoner. He was 14 years old, wore short pants, had a girl's voice, and one of his stockings had a hole in it.

We were standing on the office porch when the man-gate opened and admitted them. The sheriff was a big, strapping man, emphasizing by his very massiveness the diminutiveness of the boy beside him. As they drew near, the Captain of the Yard—Captain Harrison—stepped forward and greeted the officer pleasantly. But when the Sheriff reached into his pocket and handed over a commitment the captain was puzzled. He glanced at the document for a moment and then pushed back his hat.

"This commitment seems to be in order. Sheriff, but where's the prisoner?" he asked.

The Sheriff laughed constrainedly and pointed to the boy at his side.

The Captain regarded the boy incredulously, and then smiled.

"Ha, ha! Pretty good, Sheriff. I came near eating it up. But no joshing, where's the prisoner this calls for?"

He flipped the commitment with his forefinger. The Sheriff became even more embarrassed.

"I hate to say it, Capt'n, but it's no josh. This is the prisoner."

He laid his hand on the boy's tousled head.

Even then the Captain hesitated. Finally it seemed to dawn upon him that the child actually was a prisoner. The Captain was the father of children himself, and he stood regarding the boy—who seemed unconcerned—doubtfully before speaking again. Then he burst out in wrath.

"Great heavens, man, this isn't a kindergarten; it's the State prison. We don't take children here. I'd be ashamed to bring him here if I were you."

This aroused the Sheriff's ire, and he lost patience.

"See here, Capt'n, I've been getting altogether too much of that. It ain't my fault. This kid was sentenced by the court to sixteen years here in San Quentin, and it was up to me to bring him, whether I liked it or not. You don't suppose I enjoyed the job, do you?"

The Captain stuck out his hand. "I beg your pardon, Sheriff," he said, "but it's enough to make any man boil over, sending a child like that to a place of this kind. I don't know what we're going to do with him. I won't receive him, that's all. I'll telephone for the Warden and let him settle it.

"Sit down over there, sonny," he added, addressing the boy, "but I won't tell you to make yourself at home."

The boy seated himself on the "mourners' bench," and the Captain went into his office.

A few minutes later Warden Tompkins came in, and when the situation had been explained to him he was even more wrathful than the Captain had been.

"Why didn't they send him to a reformatory?" he demanded of the Sheriff. "We'll have him transferred at once."

ch. ends p. 364

"You can't," replied the Sheriff, decisively. "He's convicted of murder, and no one can be committed to the reformatory for that. The judge wouldn't have sent him here if he could have helped himself, but he had no choice."

A long conference ensued between the Warden and the Captain. The Warden was for putting the boy in the "female" department, but the Captain opposed it vigorously.

"No, that won't do," he said. "We'll have to make some kind of a special arrangement; it'll never do to send a kid like this to the yard. Ah, I've got it!" he exclaimed. "Let's assign him to the hospital under the doctor's care. He can sleep there nights and stay with the chaplain in the library during the day."

This plan seemed to be a sensible one, and was adopted. But when the boy was taken to the clothing room another problem arose—there was nothing save men's clothes there. Even the smallest sizes were much too large for him. At this discovery the Captain began to see the humorous side of the matter, and turned to the Sheriff, who was standing in the doorway.

"I su'pose you'll send his nursing bottle and the baby carriage by express," he remarked.

The Sheriff grinned, and the boy laughed resentfully.

Another conference took place, and it was decided to send the new arrival to the hospital in the clothes he had on, but before he left his measurements were taken and sent to the tailor shop with an order for a complete outfit.

The next afternoon the clothing was ready and the boy was sent for. He donned his stripes without a whimper, and they made a great change in his appearance, especially the long trousers. They were the first long trousers he had ever had on, and they were—stripes.

Of course, we were all interested to learn the boy's story. According to the prosecution, he had waylaid and killed his employer, a rancher, for the purpose of robbing him, and had been arrested in a town some miles distant while spending the money for candy and ginger snaps.

But according to the boys' story he had been sent to the ranch to work during the summer months, and had been brutally abused by the man whom he killed. He never denied the killing, but claimed he was so incensed at what the man had done, or attempted to do to him, that he couldn't help killing him, and had taken the money as part of his revenge.

I watched this boy grow into a youth. He grew very rapidly, fully a foot or more during the five years he remained in prison before being paroled. He had a good disposition, observed all the rules and regulations religiously, and became very much liked by nearly everyone. A strong effort was made to have him paroled at the end of one year, as provided by law, but it was met by strenuous opposition from the relatives of the man who had been killed and also by some of the officials of the county where the crime occurred.

After hearing the case several times the Board of Prison Directors finally decided that he must serve half-time, according to their rules. A sixteen-year sentence amounts to ten years' actual time; that is, it permits of six years' credits for good behavior. Half-time in this case was five years, and the boy was released on parole exactly five years from the day of his arrival.

In fairness, however, it must be stated that two of the directors, Hon. Warren R. Porter and Tirey L. Ford, were strongly in favor of granting the parole at an earlier time. But it requires the affirmative vote of four of the five members of the board for the granting of a parole.

About a year after Claude—that was his Christian name—came in he was taken from the hospital and assigned to a cell. He was also given employment as messenger for the outside office, which position necessitated his being put on the "second lockup."

One night I saw him standing on the tier in front of his cell, waiting for the key-man to come around and let him in. He stood there gazing out over the wall. The sun was setting behind Tamalpais,[6] and the countryland at the base of the mountain looked cool and restful. The bay was placid in the shimmer of the waning day. The boy looked dismal. There was something tragic in his pose, with one heel resting against his other ankle.

All his boyhood days had been taken from him. He would never romp and play with the boys of his own age. He would never go swimming, or fishing, or hunting until he had become a man, until he had paid the penalty for his childhood crime. A fearful crime it had been—there was no gainsaying[7] that—but—

I don't know what thoughts might have followed had not Claude turned just then and expectorated over the railing.

He was chewing tobacco.

Claude was no longer a boy. He had suddenly become a man—15 years old.

---

[6] Mount Tamalpais is a 2,500 ft. mountain peak in Marin County, California.
[7] Denying.

Paroled Nov. 1st '09

Nov. 1- 1904.
Age. 14.
16 Years.
California.

20863
Claud F. Hankins.
Murd. 2nd Deg.
Yuba.

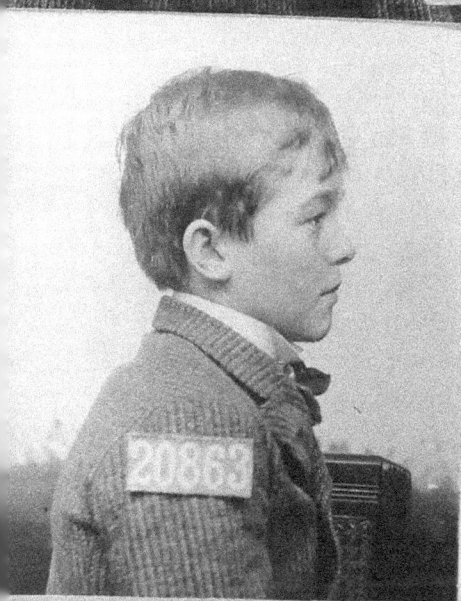

20863

Murder 2nd Deg
Yuba
16 Years
Age. 14 Yrs.
Height 4 ft 11½
Minor
Kansas
Rec. Nov. 1st/04
Dis. Nov. 1st/14

Claude. F. Hankins

San Quentin, California State Prison
at the foot of Mt. Tamalpais

29

Early in July 1907, John C. Edgar, sick in bed and close to death, resigned the Wardenship of San Quentin prison.[1] In the chapters of this narrative dealing with his administration I have told facts very much to his discredit, both as man and as Warden. Those who dislike this criticism, and maintain that I should have had the decency to "respect the dead," must not overlook the fact that I am respecting the dead— the dead that lie in that hideous scar on the landscape which affronts the eye and clutches the heart as one approaches San Quentin.

Certainly I have no desire to say or write anything savoring of unkindness. But facts are facts, and I can no more evade presenting facts about the dead than I can withhold those concerning the living. If I have appeared to judge, it has been through the minds and the hearts of thousands of prisoners and prisoners' relatives, not personally. But we all judge, whether we mean to or not. It is merely one of the indications that the Christian nations have not yet taken up Christianity.

As an individual John C. Edgar had many good qualities. As a prison official of the old school he was a success. But as a Warden of the new school he was a dismal failure.

---

[1] John C. Edgar was warden of San Quentin from 1906 to 1907.

For several weeks before his resignation it had been rumored that John E. Hoyle, at that time the secretary of the State Board of Prison Directors, would be the next Warden. Rumor proved to be correct.[2] As secretary to the Board of Directors he had become known and was popular with the prisoners, and when it was learned that he had been appointed Warden there was a general feeling of relief and satisfaction. Somehow, everyone seemed to feel that he was the right man in the right place.

During the four years that followed I came to know Warden Hoyle very well, and I have a personal regard and admiration for him that is going to make it very difficult for me to write without prejudice in his favor. He has done so many commendable things and his administration has been so much better than any other that it seems carping[3] to point out defects.

But when it is remembered that a Warden cannot change the system and that his duty is to administer affairs to the best of his ability, along the lines laid down by the Prison Directors, it will be readily seen that he cannot be expected to revolutionize conditions in a minute, nor blamed for not doing so. I am certain that if Warden Hoyle had his way San Quentin prison would be much farther removed from barbarism than it is; and yet, in the face of this statement, it must be admitted that he has not done certain things entirely within his power to do, which, were they done, would constitute a long step in the right direction.

A few days after Warden Hoyle took charge two prisoners escaped. They were men who had been transferred to San Quentin from Folsom in the band of fifty that had been brought down to work on the new prison. At the time of the escape these two men were employed in the rock quarry, which is halfway up the hill to the north of the prison. Blasts are set off at the rock quarry at all hours of the day, and these

---

[2] John E. Hoyle was warden of San Quentin from 1907 to 1913.

[3] A petty complaint; critical.

ch. ends p. 379

two men had observed that whenever the gang left the quarry and went up the hillside to get a safe distance from a blast the guards in the Gatling gun towers invariably forgot that they were supposed to be watching the prisoners and "rubbered" to see the blast go off. Taking advantage of this fact, these two men, on going up the hill one afternoon to get out of the way of a blast, could not resist the call of liberty, and kept on going. When the blast went off they were over the crest of the hill, and no one had seen them go.

A few minutes after the quarrymen had returned to work the foot guard discovered that two men were missing. A search of the quarry failed to locate them, and the alarm was sent to Warden Hoyle. After the other prisoners had been counted and locked up the guards, armed with rifles, were sent out to scour the hills.

Word had been telephoned to San Rafael asking the Sheriff of the county to throw the usual cordon of men across the neck of the peninsula, and owing to the very short start which the escapees had secured it was a foregone conclusion that they would be captured.

The various posses had been sent out in conveyances and thrown out in concentric circles of one, two, three, four, and five miles, with instructions to close in toward the prison. Unless the escapees could manage to secrete themselves and elude the searchers until dark there was very little likelihood of their getting away.

I observed the new Warden during all these maneuvers, and while many of his subordinates were madly excited and made all sorts of absurd suggestions, he remained cool and unruffled, maintaining an air of confidence that commanded respect.

About an hour before dark one of the guards who had been sent out discovered the escapees hiding in a tree about four miles from the prison. He fired his rifle to attract other guards, and the two unfortunates were compelled to come down and be captured.

I was standing on the porch of the office, inside the walls, when the two men were brought in. One of them had turned his ankle while running the first half mile, and he came up the walk to the office limping painfully and supported by his convict companion. They were followed closely by a dozen guards, most of whom seemed to be supremely satisfied with themselves. There really wasn't any necessity for these guards to come inside, but they wanted to be in at the finish; they knew the Warden was inside, and they wanted him to know that they had taken part in the chase.

As soon as the escapees arrived at the office, the jute mill whistle was set blowing to notify the guards who were still out on the hills that the escapees had been captured. I had never before noticed how mournful the jute mill whistle was. The long blasts, quivering in the twilight, sounded like the wails of lost souls.

And the faces of the two men who had made the bid for liberty were full of despair. They realized that they were due for punishment, and that by attempting to cut short their imprisonment they had only succeeded in lengthening it. Both were serving long terms, and as an attempt to escape means a loss of credits, these long terms would have to be served to the very end.

As they reached the porch Warden Hoyle dismissed the guards and spoke kindly to the two prisoners. Then he turned to the Captain of the Yard.

"I don't think we'll punish these men. Captain," he said. "Give them some supper and let them go to their cells. They've already been punished enough; and, of course, their credits will be forfeited by the directors."

The Captain looked astonished. He had been regarding the escapees viciously.

"Why, Warden," he replied, "what are you thinking of? Of course they must be punished. If you don't punish them, and punish them good, you'll have escapees every week. You've got to make an example of them."

ch. ends p. 379

The Warden stepped to the end of the porch, and he and the Captain had a long talk. I heard the Captain say something about the "cons always taking advantage of a new Warden" and that it wouldn't do to "show weakness." The Warden looked troubled. Then he yielded to the "judgment" of the Captain and acquiesced in the proposal that the escapees be given a dose of the jacket. Never having seen the jacket applied, he accompanied the party to the dungeon and witnessed the trussing. When he came back he looked very grave and passed out of the front gate with a slow step, and with his head down.

To me this incident was of vital importance. While the Captain had been arguing with the Warden for the punishment of the offenders I had hoped most intensely that the Warden would assert himself and follow the dictates of his own judgment, but when he yielded to the importunities[4] of the Captain—a holdover from a punishment administration—I felt that the future was not so bright with promise as it had seemed.

The two men were kept in the jacket about five days—six hours in, six hours out—on bread and water. One of them suffered with a swollen ankle during that torture. When the Board of Directors met they were deprived of their credits. They are both still in prison. One of them has been an exemplary prisoner in every way, but his face is tense and drawn, and he never smiles. He is serving fifteen years.

What had they done? They had taken advantage of a guard's carelessness, a guard paid to watch them, and had walked off without committing any violence or endangering any lives save their own. The guard responsible for their success in getting away was discharged, a fact which establishes that the two prisoners were, from their viewpoint, justified in going. And yet they could not have been more severely punished had they cut out of their cells at night and fought their way to freedom. At the time of their escape there was

---

[4] Persistent or insistent, especially to the point of annoyance.

no element of a breach of honor involved. They were surrounded by armed guards who could have shot them down
had they been discovered while running up the hill. If these
two men are compelled to serve out their terms—and they
cannot be paroled while their credits are forfeited—it will
be no wonder to me if they return to crime when they are
released with $5. Will it be any wonder to you?

✱

From the very beginning of his administration Warden
Hoyle evidenced an interest in the prisoners as individuals.
This was something new. Other Wardens had maintained
an attitude of exclusiveness, so far as the prisoners were
concerned, and had regarded them collectively as "the cons."
But the new Warden was of different caliber. To him each
individual prisoner was interesting and worthy of notice as
a human being.

During the first three or four months after he took office
Warden Hoyle spent most of his time inside the walls, both
day and night. He spent the days in the various shops—in the
jute mill, in the hospital—and he still makes regular visits to
the hospital, something that no Warden had ever done before.

But he did not confine these daily visits to an inspection
of the places mentioned—he also talked with the men.

A writer in one of the weekly periodicals some months
ago dwelt at great length upon the way in which Warden
Hoyle mingled with the prisoners. The writer thought it
a very remarkable thing to do, and eulogized the Warden for
his fearlessness. Of course, the only inference to be drawn
from such a viewpoint was that the prisoners are a lot of
murderous thugs, waiting to stick a knife into the back of any
freeman who goes amongst them. That article disgusted me.
I believe it disgusted every prisoner who read it. It praised the
Warden because he had the "courage" to trust himself among

ch. ends p. 379

the men under his charge. In other words, it praised him for recognizing the fact that prisoners are human beings. True, other Wardens had never mingled with the men. But to praise a Warden for walking unprotected through the jute mill was puerile;[5] it showed the writer's inability to grasp the real significance of such an act. I give Warden Hoyle absolutely no credit for mingling with his charges, but I do admire the native understanding of human nature that prompts him to do so, because such an understanding is an essential qualification for a Warden to have.

At night the Warden used to come into the office and pore over the photograph album and records. It was surprising how rapidly he learned the names and cases of hundreds of prisoners. And after learning a case he would always ask questions, indicating that he sought motives. Of course, motive is the prime factor to be considered in every crime. Warden Hoyle has the characteristic that recognizes this.

Before long he was conversant with the facts concerning nearly every prisoner under his charge, and it became evident that he was strongly in favor of parole for all deserving prisoners.

Of course, the men learned this and the new Warden became even more popular with them, especially as there had been a marked decrease in punishment and a greater spirit of consideration shown those who violated the rules.

One night while in the office looking over the photograph album the Warden came upon the picture of a "lifer" who had been at San Quentin about fourteen years.

The picture was that of a thin-faced, scared-eyed man with curly hair, and underneath it were the words, "Robbery. Life. San Francisco."

"Who is this man?" asked the Warden, turning and laying his finger on the photograph. "I've never seen him. Where does he work?"

"Big Fitz," the lockup clerk, also serving life, and a man

[5] Immature; juvenile.

with a remarkable ability for remembering names and facts concerning each inmate of the prison, stepped over and glanced at the picture.

"Why, that's L——. He works in sack alley, down in the mill. He's worked there ever since he came here. He's so quiet nobody ever notices him, and he'd never ask for anything. When I worked in the mill I tried to get him to come up and hit the Captain for another job, but he wouldn't do it. He's always been a good prisoner and he ought to get a good job."

"What did he do? What is he here for?" asked the Warden. "This says robbery. What kind of a case was it?"

"Oh, nothing very serious," replied Fitz. "He's just a victim of the black judge that handed a bunch of guys life at the time of the Midwinter Fair. L—— was only a kid then, but he and three other guys, all older than him, coaxed a sucker up into a room to play cards and robbed him. They got his watch and a few dollars, and they were all drunk at the time. The sucker was drunk, too, but he remembered where the room was, and the next day he brought a harness-bull[6] to the place and L—— got pinched along with one other feller. At that time there was quite a lot of holdups going on and the bulls were crazy to pinch somebody. The other guy—you know him, Warden—you remember P——; he was paroled last month—well, he was much older than L——, but he had a drag and got off with twenty years. L—— pleaded guilty and the judge gave him all of it."

"Why, he couldn't have got more if he'd held somebody up on the street with a gun," said the Warden. "I'll have to look into this case."

The next day L—— was sent for, and told his story to the Warden, who instructed him to make an application for parole. L—— prepared the application and a few months later his parole was authorized by the State Board of Prison Directors. But he was friendless and without money. The

---

[6] A uniformed police officer.

ch. ends p. 379

Warden put up the $25 deposit, got clothing, gave L——
sufficient money to start, and through the efforts of Captain
Leale a place was secured for him to work on one of the
harbor boats.

Within six months after his release L—— sent Warden
Hoyle all the money he had advanced. After two years on
parole he was pardoned.

I met L—— on Sutter Street one Sunday night and had
a chat with him. With evidence of considerable pride he took
a bank book from his pocket and showed me an account of
his savings—$1,000.[7]

"Did you have much trouble making good?" I asked.

"Yes and no," he replied. "Of course, the crew on the boat
where I worked at first didn't know I was an ex-con, and
when Christmas came around they had a big feast. Everybody got drunk, and they all wanted me to drink. One guy
threatened to knock my block off if I didn't drink, and for
a few minutes it looked like serious trouble. But I held out
and managed to get ashore. I didn't go back to the boat that
night.

"Then one time an ex-con saw me on the boat and tried to
bleed me, I gave him a piece of money once or twice and then
quit. That made him sore and he went and told everybody
on-board who I was. Of course, the captain knew already, so
it didn't make any difference, as far as my job was concerned,
but some of the crew didn't like it, so I got another job as
soon as I could. It was a lucky thing for me that I was on
parole and that the captain knew."

Whenever a paroled prisoner violates his parole and is
returned to prison the public learns of it. The thoughtless
readers immediately conclude that parole is a foolish procedure. But the public never hears of the men who make good,
many of them in the face of obstacles and discouragements
far worse than those L—— overcame.

[7] Adjusted for inflation, $1,000 in 1912 would be equivalent to approximately
$30,000 in 2023.

It is well always to remember that 85 percent of paroled prisoners redeem themselves and become good citizens. But there is a far more vital fact involved in L——'s case. Under the prison system he was submerged; he was lost; no one knew he was in prison. During fourteen years he worked faithfully, day after day. Wardens came and left, and he worked on. Then, more by chance than by design, a man of insight, and a believer in individualism, was appointed Warden. By looking over the records and making inquiries he learned that L—— was serving life for taking a few dollars.

By presenting the case to the Board of Prison Directors he got L—— paroled. And then by investing fifty or sixty dollars of his own money he got the man started toward self-redemption. Why should there have been such an element of chance? Suppose Warden Hoyle had not interested himself in individuals—where would L——, with his $1,000 bank account, be now?

✱

A few months ago the newspapers all over the United States quoted Warden Hoyle as having said that the duration of a wife's faithfulness to her husband in prison is three years. I am quite sure that Warden Hoyle never made such a statement. He may have said something to the effect that some wives forsake husbands who have been sent to the penitentiary—especially in cases where the husband has been committed for a long term of years—or that sweethearts frequently find solace in some other lover when their first love is taken away and placed behind prison bars, but he couldn't have made the assertion that woman's constancy under such circumstances does not exceed three years, because he takes a personal interest in such cases and knows from experience that the majority of wives remain true to the bitter—or happy—end.

ch. ends p. 379

Some of the finest instances of connubial fealty[8] that it is possible to find may be found at the State prison. The circumstances surrounding such cases are often pathetic. The other night while addressing a public gathering I was reminded of a case of this nature by seeing the husband in the audience. The last time I had seen him he was in stripes, with several years' imprisonment still before him. Had I not seen him in that audience the probabilities are that I should not have thought of his case in connection with this story.

Hundreds of human-interest stories must necessarily be forgotten and never be written because of the impossibility of retaining them in mind. But a face in the crowd, a chance remark, or a moment's conversation often suffices to bring back that which is apparently gone forever.

This young man whom I saw had only been married a short time when the trouble which resulted in his being committed to San Quentin for seventeen years occurred. He was still a boy in years at the time, though he had more than six feet of splendid male physique. She, the girl-wife, was petite and fair.

One night when he came home after his day's work there was one little item short for dinner, and she ran out to the corner grocery to get it. When she returned a few minutes later she had the package, but she was out of breath and crying. He was much concerned, and asked her what had occurred. At first she wouldn't tell him, but finally yielded to his insistence. A man standing on the corner had insulted her as she passed and had then followed her home.

Upon learning this the young husband grabbed his coat and hat and ran from the house. No one but he knows just what occurred, but there was a shot and a man lay dead in the street. The young husband was arrested and charged with murder.

The little wife nearly lost her reason during the weeks that followed while he lay in jail awaiting trial. He insisted that

---

[8] Together, the words connubial fealty mean loyalty to the sanctity of marriage.

she should not be a witness, that he would not have her go on the stand and tell in public what the deceased had said to her.

In this he was supported by his lawyer, who took the view that if the insult to the wife were pleaded in extenuation for the killing the District Attorney would seize upon it to show "motive" and would probably establish that the crime had been premeditated, at least in degree. It would be a risky "defense." The law did not, and a jury would not, justify the husband for killing a man who had spoken insulting words to his wife, especially as he had not been present and some time had elapsed between the insult and the killing.

So the husband decided that he would claim that the man he killed had tried to rob him. He went to trial with that story, was convicted of murder of the second degree and sentenced to imprisonment for seventeen years.

From the day of his arrival, and all through the dreary years that followed, the little wife came regularly to see him. She looked worn and shabby, but always smiled when she met him in the "reception" room. She had secured work in a store and was supporting herself in that way.

During the first year the husband tried to maintain an air of indifference, but the effort was pitifully apparent, and with the passing of time his face became more and more the mirror of his soul, until its expression was one of chronic gloom and despair. His eyes seemed to swim in sorrow. I have looked into many sad human eyes, but none more eloquent of internal death than his.

Each month when the little wife came over to see him she also saw and pleaded with the Warden, and after he had finally convinced her of his helplessness to secure her husband's parole before he had served the Board of Directors' half-time, she resorted to a letter. By chance I saw that letter. The stenographer at the Warden's office, impressed by its pathos, showed it to me. It was written in a schoolgirl hand and was blurred with tears. One sentence stood out above

ch. ends next p.

all the rest. I have never forgotten it. It still recurs to me at odd times. The sentence was:

"Please, Mr. Warden, help him to get out, so that we can have a baby like other married people."

When the young husband had served half-time his application for parole was considered. The little wife exerted and humiliated herself to the utmost in behalf of her husband. She needed him, the store work for so many years had impaired her health, and his prison record had been exemplary. But after having the application before them and subjecting him to the usual grilling the Board of Directors refused him a parole. I forget the exact "action" they took. I think it was a denial of parole, though it may have been a postponement for one year. The applicant tried to ascertain why he had not been granted a parole, but could get no satisfaction. When the board refuses to parole a prisoner they do not give a reason.

This man had complied with every regulation, his conduct in prison had been perfect, he had a tortured, half-sick wife who needed his support, the law of the State, enacted by the people, said he could be paroled, still he was denied, and without reason. It has always seemed to me that the parole law is intended for such cases, if not for every worthy case, but it isn't applied that way. If one member of the Board of Directors conceives an antipathy for an applicant that member can stop the parole.

This reminds me of a juryman in Oakland who voted for a verdict of "murder in the first degree" while the eleven men who were with him voted for acquittal. To all arguments and reason this juryman remained obdurate,[9] and by sticking to his vote managed to "hang the jury."

After the jury had been dismissed and were passing out of the Court House the foreman approached the man who had done the "hanging" and asked him why he had voted that way. The evidence clearly called for acquittal.

[9] Stubborn; not persuaded.

To which the "hang"-man replied in broken English:

"Veil, I didn't like the vay he curled his hair," meaning the defendant.

Unable to restrain himself, the foreman struck the man in the face.

At a subsequent trial the defendant was acquitted.

But to return to the young husband. After he had been refused parole his brother "got busy." This brother lived in a distant State and had brought some influence to bear on the case years before. But meanwhile, on learning that the rules required a service of half-time, he had subsided. Upon learning what had occurred at the expiration of half-time, however, he also acted man-like. He refused to accept such an arbitrary ruling, and by exerting himself to the utmost succeeded in having the case reconsidered and his brother paroled.

The husband and wife are together now, and he is "making good."

Suppose the brother had remained inactive and the denial allowed to stand, who would have been benefited, who would have been "protected"?

30

In December 1907, a prisoner named F. D—— was released from San Quentin. He had only one arm, but had secured an artificial substitute for the missing member while in prison. When he went to the clothing room to dress in his outgoing garments the artificial arm was taken from him, and he was not permitted to take it with him when he left the prison. This was done because it was feared that the arm might be "loaded"—it might contain messages or money. It had been made inside the walls. The presumption is that in allowing him to have this artificial arm made it was hoped that he could work to better advantage for the State while in prison. But by not permitting him to take it out into the world with him, the State, through its subordinate prison officials, denied him the same ability to earn a living when thrown upon his own resources.

I recall another instance of an old man who made a cane for himself while in prison. It was a splendid specimen of inlaid work and was beautifully carved. When his term expired he asked permission to take the cane with him, but was refused.

Of course, under the present system, there must be discipline. Were prisoners allowed to make such things in their cells every outgoing prisoner would want to take something with him.

The present theory is that he is sent to prison to be punished. The majority of persons hold to that view. So long as that is the object and end of imprisonment, the inmates of prisons cannot manifest as human beings—they must be suppressed in every way.

But after this suppression, after this abnormal period, they are expected to go forth into the world of men, where initiative, self-reliance, and responsibility are the first essentials to success in the industrial struggle, and manifest the very characteristics which have been beaten down and obliterated while they have been in prison.

I do not advocate pardon for lawbreakers. I am merely trying to show that the abnormalities of prison life react to the disadvantage of society—that the punishment idea is fundamentally wrong. This is supposed to be a Christian nation. Christ never advocated the punishment of anyone—especially not the punishment of the blind. Men who commit crime should be placed under restraint, but there should be no element of revenge or retaliation and the restraint should last just so long as the delinquent requires it, and no longer.

Under this restraint the wrongdoer should be trained, not browbeaten and humiliated. It is not logical, charitable, nor economical that he should. Twist this as you may, it is irrefutable—if this is really a Christian nation.

I recall two prisoners who were committed from the same county together. Both were ex-prisoners. One had committed burglary of the first degree (night time), and received a sentence of two years for this second offense. The other had committed burglary in the second degree (daytime, and theoretically the less serious offense), and received a sentence of four years on his second conviction.

In both cases the sentencing magistrate was cognizant of the fact of the previous convictions.

Was this a protection of society? I do not mean that they should have received longer sentences. Under the present prison system that would have done no good; it would merely

ch. ends p. 389

have been a greater revenge; but why should these two men have received such unequal sentences, and why should they not be trained to become useful citizens instead of being arbitrarily committed to an abnormal and inhuman existence for a definite time?

So many persons overlook the fact that it is the system, not individuals, that I attack. So long as I earn a living and conform to the laws of the community I want protection myself. I am entitled to it like everyone else. But I do not want to protect myself by wreaking vengeance upon a blind man. I have been blind myself.

The light sentences in the two cases I have cited were imposed because the delinquents had pleaded guilty.

A smallpox patient might just as logically be given a "light jolt" in the pesthouse because he admits having the smallpox. Of course, he may not know that he has the smallpox—he may merely know that there is something wrong with him—but as long as he agrees that it is the smallpox, let him off "light." Don't make any effort to cure him; simply send him to the pesthouse in punishment for having the smallpox, and make it a "light sentence" because he "pleads guilty."

Don't bother about whether a sojourn in the pesthouse, managed by a bunch of politicians, will cure him. Turn him out on society half-cured—it's all right—he has been punished.

Would the man who objected to this be considered a sentimentalist? Would it not have to be admitted that he had the welfare of society, as well as that of the offender, in mind? And if he asked that the pesthouse be placed in charge of capable men and that it be sanitary, would he be branded as having an "awful gall"?

And if he had had the smallpox himself and had been in the pesthouse, wouldn't he know something about it? And would the fact that he had been there with the smallpox disqualify him from telling what he knew, from trying to protect others from such an absurd and dangerous condition?

I remember a boy who came back to the pesthouse for a second "jolt." He was one of four boys who had stolen a tug at Eureka five years before. They had taken the tug out to sea. Not knowing how to handle the boat, they had built a furious fire under the boiler without injecting water, and had set the tug afire. They were rescued just in time to save their lives, and were committed to San Quentin. Subsequently, on account of their ages, they were transferred to the reform school. All this in revenge, in punishment.

One came back to San Quentin after his release from the reform school, and died in the old hospital from the effects of consumption. Another, after his release from the reform school, was committed to the State prison in Nevada under sentence of fourteen years for robbery.

Suppose these boys had been given a trial on probation for the first offense, or suppose they had been committed to the care of the State for training instead of punishment. It would never have become necessary to commit them the second time. Their training, under the proper system, would have effected a cure. They would have remained in the custody of the State until cured. As it is, they are regarded as criminals, and the probabilities are that they will remain in that category.

Were I writing in favor of the present system I might please a great many persons, but I should be true neither to them nor to myself, nor to those who are beginning to see the light on the horizon of civilization.

✱

Each time the Board of Directors meet a mailbox is put up in the yard marked: "Letters for the State Board of Prison Directors." Any prisoner who wishes to communicate with the directors has the privilege of dropping his communication into this box, which is opened at the meeting of the

ch. ends p. 389

board. But it is very seldom that such letters receive any attention, and I have known the box to remain unopened for months.

I distinctly remember one instance when this box was opened at a board meeting. The regular business had been finished and there was an hour before train time. One of the members suggested that the mailbox be opened, and it was done. The first letter which came to the hands of the president was a complaint from one of the prisoners. The president read the letter aloud, and the prisoner was sent for. He came into the room with a questioning look on his face, and the president asked him to state his complaint.

"What complaint?" asked the prisoner. "I haven't any complaint to make."

"Isn't your name G——, and isn't this your number?" asked the president, referring to the letter before him.

"Yes, that's my name and number," replied the man.

"And didn't you write this letter, complaining about so-and-so?"

The prisoner looked puzzled for a moment, and then his face lighted up.

"Oh, sure I wrote it; I remember it now. But I'd forgotten. It was over a year ago I wrote that letter, but I'm all right now, gentlemen."

Reference to the date on the letter established the fact that the prisoner was telling the truth. The board adjourned.

Prisoners are also permitted to write to the Warden. He gets from ten to thirty letters a day from them. Whenever he has the time he sends for some of the writers and interviews them. But, of course, this is not very often, and the result is that men who write to the Warden do not get to see him for months afterward. Many of the letters are of no importance, and it is rather tiresome to send for a man who writes that he has something of vital urgency to impart, only to find it a ruse to get an interview and plead his own case.

On the other hand, it frequently occurs that a man has

been dealt with unjustly. His privileges have been forfeited, or he has been otherwise punished. He writes to the Warden asking for an interview. Two or three months pass before he gets it, and it is then too late to investigate and right the wrong. I know several cases of this kind. It will continue to be so until the officer who deals out punishments is a man of discretion and fairness. Letters to the board, or to the Warden, do not accomplish much.

Talking with a discharged prisoner recently, he told me that he wrote several letters to the Warden complaining that he could not get proper medical treatment, but he never got an interview. This man also told me to be sure and remember to say that prisoners are not supplied with suspenders, towels, or toothbrushes.

"Of course, they get soap, but you know what it is—hard as a rock and full of lye."

When a prisoner is received, even if he has money, he cannot purchase a towel until the end of the month. The suspenders he has on when he arrives are given back to him. But if he is without funds he cannot get another pair during his term of imprisonment. The rules say that trading will be followed by punishment; but, of course, the prisoners trade. What else can a life-timer do if he wants to keep his trousers up?

I well remember the case of a prisoner, a lifer, who came in December 1907. He was given a towel by an acquaintance who had known him "outside." This occurred before the new man had been instructed as to the rule forbidding one prisoner to give anything to another.

The Lieutenant of the Yard saw the new man with the towel and asked him where he got it. The man knew by the Lieutenant's attitude that some rule had been violated, so, in order to protect his friend, said the towel had been given to him by a prisoner whom he did not know; that a strange man had walked up to him and asked him if he had a towel, and on learning that he had not had given him one.

ch. ends p. 389

The Captain listened to this story and then ordered the man to the dungeon—"To show him where he is," said the Captain. So, for not informing against his friend, this man, just beginning a life sentence, was placed in the dungeon.

Of course, there must be certain rules governing such things, but a new man, a man who has just arrived, should not be subjected to punishment. A reprimand would have been more effective.

Sometimes a prisoner arrives intoxicated and is surly or boisterous. Many of the Deputy Sheriffs bringing men to prison feel that it will make them temporarily oblivious of their fate if they have a few drinks. But after a man has been in jail a few drinks make him drunk.

Sometimes Deputy Sheriffs allow prisoners to purchase a quantity of tobacco while on the journey, on the presumption that they will be allowed to have it at San Quentin. But the rule is that the incoming prisoner cannot have anything save his suspenders and a comb. If he has handkerchiefs or a towel with him they are sent to the laundry, and he gets them two or three days later.

On one occasion a one-legged man came in and had some love letters secreted in his artificial leg. There were two letters and a lock of hair, and, of course, they were discovered when the leg was examined. He had been sentenced to fifteen years for arson, and the letters were protestations of undying love from his sweetheart. When he learned that these letters had been discovered and read he was greatly agitated.

"Why did you hide them in the leg?" asked the turnkey. "Didn't you know that we would have given them to you if you'd had them in your pocket?"

"Yes, I knew that. They told me at the jail. But I didn't want anybody else to see them. They're mine, and her name is sacred."

He was given the letters and the lock of brown hair, but not his artificial leg. He went over to the yard on crutches.

Several days later, however, after the leg had been subjected to a thorough examination, it was returned to him.

One morning a guard who had been in San Francisco the day before stopped at the turnkey's office with the information that he had seen "Blackie" B—— working as a streetcar conductor in the city. "Blackie" had been at San Quentin and was a well-known character.

Upon learning that "Blackie" was so employed Mr. Murray, the Lieutenant of the Yard, immediately ex-claimed:

"Gee, the streetcar company ought to know that. What a fine chance for him to pick pockets and swipe jewelry while he's pushin' through the crowd. The next time I go to town I'll cook his goose."

And yet I have heard this same prison officer revile prisoners who returned to prison for a second offense.

"Well, well; back again? You must be stuck on the place. And just in time for Christmas dinner."

That was his usual line of greeting to those who came back after struggling to do right and failing.

On another occasion I heard this same Mr. Murray ask the turnkey if he had observed a certain marriage notice in one of the San Francisco papers.

"That feller, Al G——, is going to get married, and it's dollars to doughnuts she and her folks don't know he's an ex-con. They ought to be told."

In this particular instance Murray may have been right— the girl had a right to know—but he was not right from his point of view, because his motive was to discredit the man more than to protect the girl. G—— had served fifteen years. He had been a quiet, reserved, and manly prisoner.

And this attitude on the part of certain subordinate prison officers toward men who have paid the penalty and have been discharged only went to convince me that the best thing for a discharged prisoner to do is to declare who he is right from the start, and endeavor to work out his salvation in that way.

ch. ends next p.

388 My Life in Prison

Of course, it is a hard thing to do, but I feel sure that it pays in most cases.

Discharged prisoners have no rights that they may feel sure of so long as the possibility of exposure exists. I recall a very interesting case where a paroled prisoner had violated the conditions surrounding him and escaped. The usual order was given for the photographer to make a large number of photographs to be spread broadcast in the hope of apprehending the offender.

While these photographs were being prepared Mr. Murray suddenly remembered that the violator had been very chummy with another prisoner, named G——, while both had been in confinement. G—— had recently been discharged, having served his term, and it occurred to Mr. Murray that the parole violator might have joined his old prison chum, and that they might be together. He suggested this possibility to the Captain of the Yard, and that officer immediately issued an order for the photographer to make photographs of G—— to be disseminated with those of the parole violator, and that the description card should state that in all probability the two men would be found traveling together.

This certainly was a rank injustice to the man G——, who had served his term and been discharged. Because a prison officer imagined that he might be in company with a parole violator his photograph was spread broadcast.

On another occasion I heard the matron (not the present matron) declare that all discharged prisoners should be compelled to work with a pick and shovel, so that they should feel "their degradation." In other words, after paying the penalty exacted by the law, after discharging his debt to society under the present system of dealing with those who violate the law, the offender should be made to feel that he is an outcast and not entitled to an equal chance with other men, no matter how much he may want to redeem himself.

In direct contrast to this attitude toward the discharged

prisoner on the part of some prison officials, I once heard a San Francisco police officer of high rank declare that he always advised discharged prisoners to make a clean start.

"I always tell them to tell the party they go to work for all about it. It pays for them to do that, and I know what I'm talking about."

"And do you really think an ex-con ever amounts to anything?" asked Mr. Murray in moist expectancy. "Do they ever make good altogether?"

"You bet they do," was the emphatic reply. "Of course, some of them don't; but more of them do than most people imagine."

There is a prisoner now confined at San Quentin who was released from Folsom after serving about twenty-five years. He was old and broken in health at the time of his release, and the first work he secured was in a livery stable. But he only held the job one day, and was discharged because he didn't know how to harness a horse. Then he went to work as a laborer, with a pick and shovel. After three days he was discharged again—he was too old and decrepit to "hold his end up."

For several weeks he lived from hand to mouth, until finally, driven to desperation, he committed another crime and was returned to prison. I always felt that the second crime was not a crime at all—at least not his crime.

One of the finest acts I knew Warden Hoyle to do was to aid a prisoner who had been returned to San Quentin for violating his parole. When this man's term finally expired the Warden went out of his way to secure employment for him. Generally, the parole violator gets scanty consideration. Everyone seems to feel that he has had his chance and that there is nothing more coming to him. But in this instance the Warden realized that this particular man was worthy of more encouragement and assistance, that he had a new struggle to face. So he got the man a position. And this man, who had violated his parole, appreciated what the Warden had done, and made good.

31

It is the dead of night, and save for the subdued whir of the lights in the electric tower all is still as the grave. The drab cell-houses, checkered with the apertures of numerous counter-sunk steel doors, resemble four huge tombs. Not even the drone of the waves against the rugged coast a few yards distant penetrates the vast walls that rise on every side and hem in this colony of crime from the world of righteousness, out of which it has been wrested by the strong arm of the law.

"Twelve o'clock, and all-l-l-l's well!"

The blatant voice of the guard in No. 1 post suddenly breaks upon the midnight calm. The cry is caught up and repeated by No. 2, and then, in varying intonations, in voices deep and resonant, in voices harsh and cracked, in squeaky, in shrill, in twanging voices it is tossed and bandied and passed from post to post until every nook and cranny of the great prison reverberates with the multisonous discords.

"Twelve o'clock, and all-l-l-l's well!"

Hundreds of fitful sleepers turn uneasily on their hard, narrow cots in the ill-ventilated cells. Resignedly they recognize the call of the law—their hourly nocturnal nemesis—reminding them that, even in sleep, they are convicts, convicts, convicts—outcasts and pariahs.

And this is midnight of the 31st of December—the call

has ushered them into a new year. To some this means nothing, for time has lost its relation to life—they are "doing it
all." To others—to that row of cells where the lights burn
all night so that a suicide in the dark may not cheat the
gallows—it means the dawn of eternity, their last new year—
a day nearer the "rope." To a few it signalizes the approach
of freedom, the beginning of the year which has been so
patiently awaited, perchance for five, ten, or fifteen years.
To still others it brings hazy recollections of boyhood, of the
gala times spent in celebrating the dawn of the new years
long since dead and gone.

"Twelve o'clock, and all-l-l-l's well!"

The echoes finally die away, and all is again still. Once
more the men and the boys in the bare, cheerless cells fall
into troubled sleep. Not a sound save the shuffling feet of the
second night watch, who come in to relieve the first watch,
and a few gruff "goodnights," as the relieved men turn over
their arms, breaks the stillness.

But hark! What is that noise, faint and far away? At first it
sounds like the moaning of the wind. But presently resolves
itself into the blasts of remote whistles. They are so far away
that individuality is lost, and it sounds like a wail; the element
of rejoicing is absent. A drizzling rain begins to fall as the last
guard passes out of the front gate to his sleep. It has come to
baptize the infant year.

"They're having a great old time in 'Frisco town tonight,"
he remarks, as the gatekeeper softly closes the steel door
behind him. Over on the porch of the office a lone figure is
standing. It is the figure of a tall, broad-shouldered man in
dark clothes and derby hat. It is the Warden of San Quentin
prison. He has been Warden for six months. What is he doing
inside the prison at that hour of the night? Why isn't he at
home and asleep? The guards are all at their posts, and the
prisoners are all securely locked in the black cells across the
quadrangle. The explanation is contained in the remark that

ch. ends p. 403

he makes as he passes the guard at No. 1 post on his way out of the prison a few minutes later:

"Well, it worked. They responded to the call on their honor. Goodnight."

What did the Warden mean by that remark, and who are "they"?

For years and years the prisoners at San Quentin had looked upon New Year's Eve as a time when they might take matters into their own hands. For years and years they had remained awake on the night of December 31, waiting for the midnight call; waiting with wash basins, heavy brogans, stools, and bed slats in their hands. And no sooner did the guard in No. 1 post begin the midnight call than pandemonium broke loose. Iron doors were beaten with stool and cans and shoes. Curses were shrieked from the wickets out into the night. Band instruments were blown in horrible discord. The bass drum in the bandroom was usually beaten into a pulp.

All the repression, all the hate, all the despair of the year was suddenly released and poured forth in a torrent that made fear clutch at the heart. The thing was contagious. Men of quiet dispositions, opposed to the lawless outbreak, would find themselves shrieking and pounding with the others. For three hours the noise would continue. Sometimes it would die down and almost cease when one or two spirits more untamed, more bitter, more lawless than the others, would shriek afresh, and then the outburst would follow with redoubled vigor. Many men took advantage of the occasion to bellow the most horrible curses at the guards or officers whom they disliked. The residents of San Quentin village used to assemble on the little hill just beyond the prison wall to the north and listen to the outburst. The next morning the yard would be strewn with broken stools and demolished buckets.

Many Wardens had tried to stop this New Year's demonstration. Some had placed guards on the tiers with orders to take the numbers of the cells where any noise occurred. Others had posted notices in the yard that any noise at midnight would be followed by a deprivation of all privileges during the new year. Still others had stretched the fire hose with instructions to the guards to play streams of water into the cells and dormitories if an outburst occurred. But all these measures failed of their purpose. They were like waving a red flag before an angry bull.

On one occasion when there was sickness in the Warden's house he had sent a request to the prisoners asking them to keep quiet. Most of them did so, but a few did not. That particular Warden was not liked.

And yet on New Year's Eve of 1907 midnight came and went without a sound save the regulation call. There were no guards posted on the tiers; there were no lines of fire hose stretched from the stand-pipes; there had been no threat of loss of privileges. Old-time prison officials had frequently expressed the opinion that it would never be possible to stop the demonstration on New Year's Eve. Wardens with eight years' experience had been unable to stop it. Surely a young man who had been Warden for only six months could not hope to accomplish it. But the young man did, and by doing so placed a period at the end of decades of misunderstanding between prisoners and their keepers.

What had he done to bring about such an attitude of respect. Had he threatened the men with punishment? Had he doped them with sedatives at the evening meal the night before? No; he had done neither of these things. He had simply had notices distributed in the cells and dormitories asking each prisoner to refrain from making any noise at midnight, and stating that he hoped they would feel that the request was made in good faith, and that he felt confident each one would respond to it.

Why had the men responded? Well, a week before, on Christmas Eve, the Warden had come inside the prison and had been much surprised to see socks hanging from nearly

ch. ends p. 403

every wicket. It had been an amusement for the old-time prison officers to see socks hung out on Christmas Eve, but to Warden Hoyle it was something more than amusing. He promptly sent an officer to San Quentin Point and bought every bit of confection and fruit in the town; and when the officer got back with his load it was distributed in the socks at midnight.

Next morning when the prisoners awoke and found that they had at last been remembered it struck deeply. It was not the first instance of the new Warden's humanitarianism, but it made a deeper impression than anything else he had done. Some may call it sentiment—perhaps it was—but it did not prove so a week later on New Year's Eve. And at each New Year's Eve since that time the whistles and bells at San Francisco, San Rafael, and from the Contra Costa shore have merely served to lull the inmates of San Quentin into deeper sleep.

I have made an incidental reference to Christmas. Perhaps it will interest some readers to know what Christmas means and brings to the prisoners at San Quentin. The fact that it was not mentioned in chronological sequence, and that an incidental reference chanced to bring it to mind, is in itself significant. Christmas means very little to the men in stripes. True, they get a pork dinner, but so far as the Yuletide cheer is concerned the prison walls are impenetrable.

In the first place holiday "time" is observed; that is, the unlock is at 7 a.m. and the lockup at 3 p.m. This is necessary because the guards and officers must have their Christmas freedom; and after eight hours in the yard the prisoners are tired and are glad to return to their cells. At that time of the year it is usually cold and rainy, and, in spite of the wretched ventilation, the cells are preferable to the "bullpen" with its fetid miasma[1] rising from the tobacco stained asphaltum.

Breakfast on Christmas Day consists of sausage, mashed potatoes, bread, butter, and coffee. Dinner, at 2 p.m.,

---

[1] A noxious and highly unpleasant vapor or atmosphere.

consists of roast pork, potatoes, bread, butter, coffee, pie, cake, pudding, and fruit. Butter is never served save on holidays. Owing to the number of meals to be supplied and the limitation of the ovens, the pork is roasted in batches the day before and served cold at the Christmas dinner.

The portion of food served to each man is bounteous, so bounteous that not more than one-third of it can be eaten at the table. On holidays and Sundays the prisoners are permitted to carry food to their cells, and when the men march out of the dining-room after Christmas dinner one is reminded of a line of immigrants landing at Castle Garden.[2] Each man has a large newspaper bundle—and a smile.

Some of the prisoners who do not use tobacco wait at the top of the stairs and bargain for pie and cake. Each prisoner gets half a mince pie, which is worth two rations of tobacco. Cake and pork are each worth one ration.

At the time I worked in the jute mill, "Fatty" was the chief merchant as well as the pawnbroker of the prison. On Christmas and other holidays he used to hire agents, on commission, to wait at the head of the stairs and buy pie and other food. By this procedure he would corner thirty or forty pies. Three or four days after Christmas a half pie was worth four or five sacks of tobacco, and "Fatty" always came out a few hundred rations of "weed" to the good. Moneyed prisoners would buy his supply at the advanced rate, and be glad to get it.

During the week following Christmas the prison physician is kept busy. Many of the men who are able to buy extra rations keep the food too long, and when they eat it the result is disastrous. This is especially true of pork. When a prisoner becomes ill at night he raps on the door of his cell with a tin cup to attract the attention of the night sergeant.

The doctor is not on duty inside the prison at night, but

[2] Castle Clinton or Fort Clinton, previously known as Castle Garden, is a circular sandstone fort located in Battery Park, in Manhattan, New York City. From August 3, 1855, to April 18, 1890, Castle Garden was America's first official immigration center, predating Ellis Island.

ch. ends p. 403

leaves a few remedies with the night sergeant, such as "cramp medicine," salts, toothache drops, and the like. If the man is very sick the sergeant gets two nurses from the hospital with a stretcher, and he is carried into one of the wards where the nurses (prisoners) treat him. If his condition is alarming the doctor is telephoned for.

Some years ago the prisoners at San Quentin were permitted to have food and presents from relatives and friends at Christmas. But when the fight was waged against "dope" this privilege was stopped. It was found that opium and morphine were introduced into the prison in that way. On one occasion a roasted turkey disgorged half a pound of opium "dressing." Confections were utilized for the same purpose. Even towels would be soaked in an opium bath, and on being received by the prisoner would be subjected to a re-soaking. The resultant liquid would be bottled up and imbibed by degrees. Some of the schemes for getting the stuff were really ingenious. So the order was issued that nothing would be permitted in the way of presents at Christmas. That was many years ago, but the rule still holds.

The first year of Warden Hoyle's administration he wanted to permit the prisoners to have the gifts that came for them at Christmas, but was dissuaded by the Captain of the Yard. "Dope" had been effectively stamped out, and save sporadic attempts to introduce it, had been forgotten by most of the prisoners.

The Warden took the stand that it was not right that all the prisoners should be deprived of Christmas cheer because a few of them might take advantage of the occasion to get "dope." But the Captain remained firm. He argued that the prison would be full of "dope" in a month if there was the least relaxation of the rules. So the Warden decided that there should be no Christmas gifts.

I do not know which man was right. I know the condition was awful when "dope" got into the prison, and I know that some men will do almost anything to get it. Even letters are sometimes soaked in opium water, and the turnkey frequently tastes the paper. If it is bitter he sends the letter to the druggist for further examination, and it has often been established that letters contained "dope," which had been soaked into the paper on which they were written. But it seldom occurs now.

In spite of rules many friends persist in sending little remembrances to the prisoners at Christmas time. The men for whom these remembrances are intended are called to the office and permitted to look at them, and then they are either sent back, or put away until the prisoner's term expires. On the day of his release he gets the gift—sometimes several years after it has been received.

When photographs are received in the mail they are not delivered unless the men for whom they are intended give permission to have them dismounted from the cardboard. If they agree to this the photograph is sent to the photographer, who soaks it from the mounting. Books and magazines are not permitted save directly from the publishers. A book or magazine that comes under stamps is confiscated. Even a subscription to a magazine is questioned.

The rule is that anyone desiring to subscribe for a magazine to be sent to a prisoner shall send the money to him so that the order can be placed through the prison office. The same rule applies to books. I know several prisoners who have valuable text books at home, or in the hands of outside friends, but cannot have them sent in. Under Warden Hoyle a Christmas amnesty is proclaimed each year. On that day all lost privileges are restored, and the punishment slate sponged off. This enables every prisoner to start the new year afresh. It is the nearest thing to the Christ spirit that I saw at San Quentin in so far as the body of prisoners are concerned. Of course, I know of individual instances where the Christ spirit has been manifested very beautifully.

But Christ seldom penetrates prison walls. Still, He sometimes comes up from underground.

ch. ends p. 403

In January 1908, a prisoner named R—— was caught making abalone shell ornaments in his cell. The Captain of the Yard inferred that he was engaged in making these ornaments for the guards—that he was trading—and the man was sent to the dungeon and placed in the straitjacket for the purpose of forcing him to divulge with whom he was "doing business." For several days he was kept in the jacket—six hours in, six hours out.

On the afternoon of January 20, 1908, Ed Morrell, whose duty it was to accompany the dungeon officer when he went down there, came into the office and called me into the plate room.

"This R—— case is getting fierce," he groaned. "I can't stand seeing much more of this kind of thing. I feel like throwing everything up and killing some of these torturers. R—— can't stand much more, and yet they intend giving it to him worse than ever. Just now the Captain told Murray to put a coat on him tonight before he goes into the sack, so as to make it tighter. You see, he's shrunk so much since he first went in, that the jacket is getting loose. The coat will make it fit tight—and hotter."

That evening the dungeon-keeper—a prisoner—rushed to the office with the startling information that he thought R—— was dying. The Captain came into the turnkey's office for the keys and went down to investigate. In a few minutes he returned, a look of fiendish satisfaction on his face.

"Has he squealed?" asked Murray, the Lieutenant of the Yard.

"No, the —— —— ——," was the reply, "but he will before I get through with him."

The dungeon-keeper at that time was a Mexican serving forty years. He was not a bad sort of fellow. He had a little shack just outside the dungeon door, and was supposed to prevent anyone from going near the place. He also attended to getting the bread and water for the victims inside.

Men sentenced to the jacket are trussed up at 7 a.m. and

remain that way until 1 p.m. Then they have the freedom of the dark cell until 7 p.m., when they are again trussed up, to remain until 1 a.m., at which hour the sergeant of the second watch takes the jacket off until morning. They are fed a few ounces of bread and water every twenty-four hours. This punishment continues as long as the Captain of the Yard desires.

The R—— case made a lasting impression on me, because it was all I could do to keep Morrell from doing something rash. That night he paced the floor of the office and almost wept.

"Some life will have to be sacrificed again to stop this horror," he declared. "The newspapers won't publish what a discharged prisoner says. Lots of them have tried to tell what happens, but it's no use. So somebody's got to die. And even then I suppose it would be hushed up."

The next morning an extra coat was placed on R—— before he was laced in the jacket. In a few minutes his screams of agony were piercing our brains. I can hear them yet. I shall always hear them. Every man who heard them unconsciously kept as quiet as possible. We moved about with light tread. Without reasoning about it, we wanted those screams to have full sway, to reach everywhere, all through the prison, over the walls, out into the world, into the homes of men and women, into the schools, into the churches. It was not R——, Convict No. 20581, who was screaming; it was not one human soul that was being strangled—it was the composite, the group-soul of all the proscribed. Christianity—civilization—was engaged in the murder of the soul of a convict because he had exercised a talent for making beautiful and delicate things. Art was being crucified by a twentieth century prison system. But the screams did not seem to move those who had it in their power to relieve the victim. Only his fellow convicts suffered with him—

ch. ends p. 403

"And through each brain on hands of pain
Another's terror crept."[3]

The screams had to penetrate two steel doors and wind
through the cellar-like passageway to the outer air. Their
very faintness made them more horrible. It sounded like
a man being tortured in the bowels of the earth. After the
dungeon-keeper had timidly reported at the office twice—he
was always fearful when he came to report screams, because
he was sometimes sent back with a reprimand about being
chicken-hearted—the Captain went down to investigate, but
refused to release the victim. He came back, jangling the keys
at his side and humming "Annie Rooney."[4] After a time the
screams became fainter. Finally they died away.

When the Lieutenant and Morrell went to the dungeon
at the regular hour—the expiration of the six-hour limit,
according to the ruling of the State Board of Prison Directors—they found R—— unconscious.

Morrell came back with his lower lip bleeding. He
slammed the keys down on the table, glanced murderously
at the Captain, and rushed across the yard to his cell. Had
he opened his mouth to speak I do not know what might
have happened.

R—— was carried to the incorrigible ward that evening.
What happened to him up there he will have to tell himself—
if he ever comes out of San Quentin alive.

All the prisoners were in a ferment. Whispers passed from
man to man. It was decided that the demonstration which
had been withheld on New Year's Eve should take place that

[3] The last two lines of the 44th stanza of *The Ballad of Reading Gaol* by Oscar
Wilde. This is Lowrie's second reference to this poem; the first being on p. 97.

[4] Michael Nolan (1869-1910), billed as The Prince of Irish Comedians, wrote
and composed what would become his most famous song "Little Annie Rooney"
in 1889. An instant hit in British Halls, it would go on to become a staple of
North American traditional singing. It's popularity increased more in 1925 after
the success of the film *Little Annie Rooney*, starring a teenage Shirley Temple, and
subsequent newspaper cartoon strip.

April 9 1904
Age 30
20 Years.
California.

20581

A. B. Retaler & T.
Names 2295 4024 49
Paire
Burg 2d Deg 3 Ko

Centra Costa.

night. The men were determined to let the new Warden know that they would meet him halfway, but would not stand for this kind of barbarity. After lockup the demonstration took place. It consisted of pounding on the cell doors, screams in imitation of the sufferer, and the shouting of vile epithets at the Captain of the Yard. It did not last long, but was very intense while it did last. The Warden came down from his residence to ascertain the reason for the disturbance. He asked Morrell what had caused it.

"Why, the men are sore at the deal R—— is getting. They thought that kind of thing was all over, that you wouldn't stand for torture."

The Warden started to speak, but stopped. Then he began asking questions. These questions clearly indicated that he did not realize the extent to which the prisoner had been tortured. He remained about an hour and then went out with his head down and his hands behind him, walking slowly.

I could not help feeling depressed. I knew that the man was big, that he was kindly, that he was honest, that he wanted to be fair and just. When the two prisoners who escaped during the first week of his administration had been subjected to a siege in the straitjacket we all had thought it was because the Warden was new and inexperienced, that he did not fully realize what he was doing.

But here was the same thing over again—a countenancing of torture, and for a comparatively much less serious offense. It looked bad.

Morrell and I discussed the situation at length. He was extremely bitter and aggressive. But somehow, even with R——'s screams still ringing in my ears, I felt a conviction that deep down the Warden was kind and humane and would not tolerate another such barbarity. It seemed inconsistent to feel that way, but I couldn't help it.

"Perhaps he's still feeling his way," I argued. "Perhaps he wants to determine just what the old system really is. Maybe he's playing out the rope to Randolph just to see how far he will go, just to get a line on him, to learn his character."

Morrell snorted and kicked over the coal scuttle. When it stopped sliding he kicked it again.

"Say, you make me tired, absolutely tired," he snarled. "It's that kind of slop that keeps this sort of thing going—that fertilizes it. How would *you* like to be smothered half to death so that the Warden could learn his business and find out you're human? I thought you were different; I thought you could feel a knife when you saw it stuck into another man's heart. But it's the old story—you've got to have the knife stuck into you before you know what a knife really is."

"Don't be too sure of that," I replied. With heat. "I'm not trying to justify torture or anything of that sort, but I know this man is going to be a good man for the prisoners. He's made a mistake, a terrible mistake, but didn't the Legislature investigate the use of the jacket, and didn't they sanction it? And hasn't the Board of Directors made rules for its use, limiting the number of hours it can be applied? The Warden is adjusting himself to conditions as he finds them, but you take it from me, he'll change them. If he came in like a bull in a china shop and tore up things generally I wouldn't have any faith in him—that would show impulsiveness. You'll have to admit that conditions are better than they were, that there has been less punishment, that this Warden is doing many kind things, and has helped a great many men to get started right when they went out. You wait and see."

Morrell cooled down somewhat and replied calmly:

"Yes, what you say is true. He's the best Warden this place has ever had, but I only hope those screams cut into him like they did into me."

32

Recently I spent an evening at the rectory[1] of one of San Francisco's well-known churches. There were six men present—two churchmen, a college student, a neophyte,[2] and two ex-prisoners. The dinner was served by the light of four candles. It will always be a distinct and pleasant recollection.

On entering the rectory with my friend—the student—I was introduced to the ex-prisoner and we shook hands. I knew him and he knew me, but I didn't know whether his status was known to all the others or not, so I said nothing to indicate that I had ever seen him before. When the rector invited me to come and have dinner and spend the evening he told me that another ex-prisoner would be present, but I had no way of knowing that the other guests knew about him, especially when I was introduced to him as if we were strangers.

After we sat down to dinner the conversation drifted to prison conditions. I was talking about a certain aspect of the matter when the other ex-prisoner interrupted. I had been talking about the food served at San Quentin and had inadvertently used the word "wholesome." The rector had asked about the food and I had replied:

[1] The house in which a parish priest or minister lives; parsonage.
[2] A recent convert to a belief or religion.

"Well, of course it isn't what a man would choose to eat, but it's wholesome, and there's plenty of it."

"Wholesome! Wholesome!" exploded the ex-prisoner. "Wholesome! Why, man, how can you sit there and say that? It's rotten, absolutely and unqualifiedly rotten, and you know it. And it's served as if the men were dogs."

In his excitement he had forgotten that some of the persons present were unaware of the fact that he had served time, and there was a noticeable flurry about the table.

"You may call that food wholesome," he continued, "but I'd feel like a butcher if I fed it to hogs. Many a time I've gone into that swill hall after working hard in the mill, and hungry enough to eat nearly anything, and then sat there and just gulped. It would come over me that I was nothing more than a hog. That was on account of the way it was thrown at us, and the dipping into a common dish with the spoons they ate with; but that wasn't all. Don't they soak the beans in soda to make 'em soft? Don't they skim the worms and filth off the dried apples after they've been boiled? Don't they throw the vegetables into the stew all covered with dirt and filth, the same as you'd throw them into a barrel of swill? Wholesome food! I'll tell you what's the matter with you—you're lukewarm; you're getting used to decent living it's coloring you; and you didn't spend a long enough time in the mill and eating in the swill hall to get your craw. You seem to be forgetting that you're talking for 1900 prisoners who can't talk for themselves. I've read everything you've written, and some of it is all right, but hand it out straight, just as it is; there's hundreds ready to back you up."

I stopped eating and looked about the table. Every eye was on the man who was talking, and everybody seemed to be convinced of his sincerity.

"Don't they get enough bread?" I asked, weakly, sparring for time, and trying to defend my position; "and doesn't

ch. ends p. 415

every new prisoner eat with relish when he first comes in? And don't lots of them get fat?"

"Oh, yes, there's enough bread, and fresh fish generally eat pretty well after being starved in the county jail, and they do get fat, but you don't see many men fat after they've eaten that stuff, the same thing over and over and over, day after day, month after month, year after year, do you? I know. I went through it, and I know that I got so I couldn't eat anything: my stomach shook its fist at me every time I tried to eat beans. Why? Because my stomach knew that eating soda day after day, month after month, would put me out of business. And I wasn't the only one. I knew a hundred men who were in the same fix. Did you eat the grub in the main line after you'd been at it a year?"

He turned toward me expectantly.

I was tempted to fabricate, because I had my argument up my sleeve, but he looked at me so searchingly that I told the truth.

"No, I can't say that I did," I replied. "I ate enough to keep alive, but lots of them used to say I was a hophead because I was so thin. It was more a case of being sick of the same old thing, the same old taste, the same old musty, sour smell, than it was the food itself, I think.

"You seem to be forgetting one thing," I added. "There are lots of people in the world who believe that prisoners should be fed that way. Suppose I devoted a lot of space to complaints about the food; suppose I endeavored to show that by feeding human beings that way, and breaking down their health, society was turning prisoners into weak and incapable men and unfitting them to take up the battle of life after their release, and suppose I tried to demonstrate that this treatment was the cause of many second offenses, what would be the result? I'd be branded as a sentimentalist, as a man who wanted to have the prisons turned into pleasure resorts, with first-class hotel meals.

"Even as it is, for trying to show the weakness and waste of the prison system, and for trying to do it frankly, there are many who will maintain that I ought to be squelched. Suppose I saw the matter from your viewpoint alone, and forgot all about the prejudices and blindness of those who don't know and who have never suffered, what would be the result?"

"I don't know," he replied, "but I do know I'm a wreck from eating that grub, or trying to eat it. And I know it's wrecked many another man.

"And there's another thing. How about the deal a guy gets from the croaker when he's sick? Of course, you worked at the office, and I know the doctor is always ready to treat a bon-ton all right. But how about the guys that go into the hospital in the morning, hoping to get some relief, and get kicked out? Let me tell you what happened to me. I had an ulcerated[3] tooth, and I went up to the croaker in the 9 o'clock line.

"'Wasser matter with you?' he shot at me, as if I'd committed some awful crime. My face was all swollen up, and I wasn't feeling any too gay, but I held in.

"'I've got an ulcerated tooth, doctor,' I said, 'and I'd like to get it treated.'

"'Open your mouth,' he ordered, grabbing my chin with one hand and the back of my head with the other. He looked at the tooth and then turned to one of his 'con' assistants.

"'Pull this tooth out,' he ordered, giving me a shove toward the operating chair.

"'Oh, no, you don't,' I objected. 'I don't want it pulled out. It's a good tooth and I haven't got too many left. All I want is to get it treated.'

"'Oh, you want it treated, do you?' he sneered. 'Where do you think you are, anyway? You've certainly got a crust coming in here telling me my business. Now you beat it, and

---

[3] Affected with an ulcer.

ch. ends p. 415

beat it quick. When you get ready to have that tooth pulled out you'll find us doing business here at the same old stand. Git.'

"When I got outside I headed for the office. The Captain was away and the turnkey was on duty in his place. I explained the case to him. He was kind enough, the same as he always was, but he said he couldn't interfere with the doctor.

"'He's running the hospital, you know, and that's his business. But you needn't go back to work. You go over to your cell and lie down.'

"For seventeen days I lay in that cell suffering the tortures of hell itself. Two or three of the guards tried to do something for me, but nothing did any good. If I'd had money at the office I'd gone and seen the dentist on Sunday—you remember he came every Sunday—but I was broke. Finally a feller that knew something about teeth—I s'pose he'd been a dentist outside—slipped into my cell and fixed me up with a little knife that he carried in his hatband.

"I'll never forget those seventeen days as long as I live. It's a wonder to me that I'm working and doing right now. At that time I could 'a' committed any crime on the calendar. But the Father here is my friend; he got me a job, and he's treated me fine, and, anyway, I'd rather do right than cut off my nose to spite my face."

✳

At present there are about 1,900 prisoners confined at San Quentin, with 120 employees to guard them, an average of 16 to 1. Of course, should these 1,900 prisoners ever act concertedly and decide to take charge of things there would be "nothing to it," provided they chose the right leaders. But there is absolutely no danger of such a movement. There are always several hundred men who are either "short-timers" or who have served such large portions of their sentences as to make the forfeiture of their credits too serious a matter to be entertained. Also there are quite a number who honestly feel that they are paying a debt to society—ignoring, for the moment, what society owes them—who would not leave the prison were the walls razed and the bolts, bars, and keys thrown into the bay.

Again, there are some who are always on the watch for a chance to advance themselves by furnishing the officials the least item of information savoring of insubordination or a plot to escape. Practically, when everything is considered, the prisoners are their own jailers. A general uprising is almost impossible. There has not been an escape plot of any note hatched at San Quentin for decades, though a plot of this nature was carried to a more or less successful termination at Folsom in 1903, when thirteen prisoners captured the Warden and some of his officers, used them as a cordon and marched away without being fired upon.

The morning that Folsom "break" took place the news reached San Quentin about 9 o'clock. The man who was turnkey at the time came rushing into the prison from outside with the news.

"Folsom prison has broke loose—all the cons have escaped!" he shouted, breathlessly. "Half a dozen guards killed and about thirty wounded!"

Nothing of this nature had occurred at either prison for many years, and the news was so startling that we instinctively refused to credit it. But as the day wore away the news was confirmed, though in modified form, and not a prisoner in San Quentin but threw out his chest—unconsciously, perhaps—in the knowledge that they could, if they wanted to, do the same thing. A prisoner is so suppressed at all times that he cannot help feeling proud of any assertion of strength or initiative on the part of other prisoners—it is a letting off of steam.

ch. ends p. 415

But though the prisoners at San Quentin have not made a "break," they have enfranchised themselves in another way, and almost as incisively. On two occasions they have gone on strike, closed down the jute mill and disrupted the routine of the prison generally.

The first of these strikes occurred in the late 1890s, and lasted three days. In that strike, however, the prisoners made the mistake of going to their cells at night before they had gained their point. They were promptly locked in, and once under cover were helpless.

A fire hose was dragged from cell to cell, and each man was "wet down" to cool him off. Food was also denied them, and gradually, one by one, they gave up and agreed to return to work. This strike was caused by insufficient food, served without being half-cooked. The prisoners had grumbled at first. Then a few individuals, bolder than the rest, had openly complained, and had been punished, and that brought matters to a crisis. After it was all over there was a marked improvement in the food and in the manner of preparing it.

The strike in 1907, under Warden Edgar, while it did not assume the proportions of the other, was nonetheless serious, and the results secured were just as marked, if not more so.

For months the staple articles of food, such as beans, flour, dried fruits, and vegetables had been wretched, frequently rotten. The contractors supplying these commodities had encroached upon the apathy of the purchasing department until they felt that they could do as they pleased, and supply food that was practically refuse. The flour was weeviled, the potatoes were black and soggy, the evaporated apples were crawling with worms. But the prisoners had to eat these things or starve.

For several months before the strike occurred there was a steady grumble from the table, and many oral and written complaints to the Warden, but without effect. One day when the prisoners returned to the mill after a particularly atrocious meal at noon the word was passed to quit work and assemble in the jute mill yard. A few men were afraid to obey and remained at their tasks. But when the leaders came around and threatened to "knock their blocks off" they saw their folly and joined in.

It was the union man and the scab of the outer world exemplified within prison walls. The principle of a working-man's right to live like a man was at stake. Without realizing it, the prisoners were demonstrating the eternal right of unionism.

At first the guards in the mill tried to prevent the walkout, but soon abandoned the effort, realizing that they were powerless. After everyone was in the yard a council was held and it was decided to send an ultimatum to the Warden. Briefly, this ultimatum was that the Warden should come down to the jute mill yard personally and give them his word that better food would be served, beginning with supper that night. If he did not come down in one hour, or if the six men who were chosen to convey the message were ill treated in any manner, the machinery in the mill would be demolished. If that did not bring results the mill would be burned.

Of course, the fact that a strike was in progress reached the office before the six emissaries—who were passed out of the mill yard by the officer in charge of the double gates—but the report was not taken seriously. After the committee of six had made known the ultimatum, however, the seriousness of the situation was apparent and the Warden decided to go down to the yard parley, as ordered.

I saw Warden Edgar as he and Captain Randolph were on their way to the mill. The Warden's face was a study. During all his years' service as a subordinate prison official, when he was Captain of the Yard, he always despised convicts. Never for an instant had he admitted that a prisoner had any rights that an officer was bound to respect.

Time had patiently waited for him to become Warden

ch. ends p. 415

before searing his soul with the humiliating truth. I am sure
that John C. Edgar began to die at that moment. Had he
followed his natural inclinations he would have ordered extra
guards to the walls of the jute mill yard and had them fire
promiscuously into the crowd.

But that course would not only have meant the destruction of the mill, with possibly a general delivery of the prison,
but also publicity, a publicity which would have blazoned
his lack of ability. After a lifetime of pride such an ending
was unthinkable. It was better, far better, to swallow a small
and bitter dose quietly than to have the public learn of his
incompetency.

Above all, the disturbance must be kept out of the papers,
as other prison affairs had been kept from the papers in the
past—and as they have been kept from the papers since.

So he and Randolph went to the mill. It was a nervy thing
to do, but there was no alternative. The spokesman for the
strikers made known the terms, and the Warden acceded
to them without quibbling. The prisoners took him at his
word—a tribute to the man even in his extremity—and went
back to work.

That afternoon a change was made in the dietary, and
that night a wholesome supper was served. A good deal of
the food on hand was condemned and destroyed, and the
contractors were notified that they would be held strictly to
the terms and specifications of their contracts in the future.
The Warden had promised that none of the leaders of the
strike would be discriminated against in the slightest degree,
and they were not.

But during the years that followed, long after the strike
had been forgotten, some of these men were reported at the
office for infractions of the rules, and then they "got theirs."
The mistake made by the strikers was that they did not
demand a new and more humane Captain of the Yard along
with better "grub." Had they done this, had they reasoned

above their diaphragms, San Quentin prison would now be well advanced toward serving the only purpose for which prisons should be maintained—the protection of society by the humanizing of the prisoners.

But someone has aptly remarked that there are only nine meals between mankind and anarchy.[4]

✳

For many years the average number of prisoners received at San Quentin was less than two a day, but during the past two years this average has been increased to nearly three each day. Of course, there is always a certain degree of interest attached to new arrivals. When a new prisoner steps inside the walls and is brought through the garden to the office the prisoners employed there are prone to speculate on how long he is to stay and what he has done.

As a general rule, the county from which he has been committed is known as soon as he steps inside, because the Deputy Sheriffs from the various counties are familiar figures.

But this interest is not so much in the prisoner himself as it is in the circumstances of his case, and the new arrival is met with no show of feeling. This is the result of familiarity, and not because of heartlessness on the part of those concerned.

Mr. Sullivan, the present turnkey, whose duty it is to receive and interrogate new prisoners, is a man of deep sympathies and excellent judgment. He has been an officer at San Quentin for many years, and though quiet and unobtrusive by nature, has a better insight into the real characters of individual prisoners and knows more about their strengths

---

[4] A quote by Alfred Henry Lewis (1855–1914), an American investigative journalist, lawyer, novelist, editor, and short story writer, which first appeared in the March 1906 issue of *Cosmopolitan Magazine*, in an article entitled "The Day of Discontent: First of the Series of Cosmopolitan Table-Talks in which Vital Problems are Discussed in a Vital Way."

ch. ends next p.

and weaknesses than any man on the reservation. He very seldom makes a mistake in his estimate of a man, and yet he always hesitates before saying anything derogatory to any prisoner. A peculiar aspect of his nature is that he seldom shows any concern for the new arrival by direct speech. Yet men always feel that he is a good man and that he understands them.

In all the years I spent at San Quentin I never heard one prisoner say anything against Mr. Sullivan. This is a remarkable tribute, more remarkable than appears on the surface. No matter how fair and considerate a guard may be, there is always someone ready to "knock" him; not so much as an individual, perhaps, as because he is a part of the law. There are some prisoners who hate the law, and this hate includes everyone who has anything to do with its enforcement.

> "No man e'er felt the halter draw,
> With good opinion of the law."[5]

And yet his kindly manner, his absolute fairness, his ability to reprimand without getting incensed or excited, his sympathy for those who deserve it and his mercy to those who are brought before him for punishment when he is in charge of the inner prison have made Mr. Sullivan beloved by all the prisoners. For years before he became turnkey he had charge of the mess hall during meal hours. When the men filed into the hall and saw Mr. Sullivan—"Old Dan," they call him—standing at his post a feeling of respect instantly came over them.

Only on very rare occasions would disturbances occur. When he was absent the change in the attitude of the men was noticeable, and there was always more or less trouble.

---

[5] Lines 489-90 from Canto III of *McFingal: A Modern Epic Poem*, a mock epic poem written by American poet John Trumbull (1750–1831). The first canto was divided into two and published in 1776, with the third and fourth cantos being published in 1782.

And when he was appointed turnkey and another man was given charge of the mess hall quarrels, fights, and disobedience became common. This was after John E. Edgar became Warden.

It finally got so bad that the Warden went to Mr. Sullivan and asked him to resume his duty in the dining-room at meal times, along with his new duties as turnkey. He did so, and the discipline instantly improved. I know of no greater achievement for a prison officer than this.

The turnkey's duties are arduous and exacting. He is really the busiest man on the prison grounds, though his salary is much less than that of many others who have less to do. He opens and reads all mail—sometimes as many as three or four hundred letters a day—receives all new prisoners, whom he measures according to the Bertillon system, and whose fingerprints are taken in quintuple. He also receives and keeps account of all moneys sent or left for prisoners, turning it in to the Warden each day. He has charge of the historical and individual records, the commitments and the photographs of all prisoners who have ever been received at San Quentin. He is the auxiliary officer for the "female" department. And during the absence of the Captain of the Yard he is in charge of the prison itself, as second officer. Yet I have never seen him lose patience, I have never heard him abuse a prisoner, and I have never known him to act impulsively or unjustly. Add to all this a fine sense of humor and you have a fair picture of "Old Dan." Another thing, and an important fact to remember, is that he seldom says goodbye to an outgoing prisoner without giving him a word of encouragement, an expression of goodwill and the hope that he will "make good."

33

Writing about the man who suffered for seventeen days with an ulcerated tooth emphasized the case of another man whom I saw a few days ago, just after his discharge from San Quentin, where he had served two years. Although his face was not familiar to me, the instant he stepped into the office it was apparent where he had come from. The cheap black hat, the shoddy clothes, the greasy shoes, were unmistakable.

But in addition to these material earmarks he had that furtive, half-frightened expression so characteristic of men who have just been released from prison. It developed that he was without money and had been unable to secure employment. Although there were three or four vacant chairs, he did not sit down, but stood fingering his hat nervously. He did not come all the way into the room, but stood near the door, as if to make a quick egress in case somebody tried to strike him.

"I've been out three days," he said in reply to a question, "and all I want is a chance. I ain't looking for charity ' r nothin' like that, but if I can get work I'm able to do I'll do it, and be glad of the chance."

"What do you work at? Have you a trade?" he was asked.

"No, I ain't got no trade. I used to be a prizefighter before I got drinkin' and got into trouble. See, here's my picture." He reached into his inside coat pocket and produced a frayed photograph of a youth in tights with an American sash about his waist.

"I was some scrapper in them days," he said, proudly. "I was a comer[1] in the lightweight division. This was taken the day before I licked Kid Jackson back in Philly.

"But I guess I'll never be any good again," he went on. "I've got rheumatism in the joints, and sometimes I can hardly walk. They had me in the dungeon over across until the day before I came out. You see, I couldn't get around very fast on account of the rheumatism. I went to the superintendent of the mill and told him the fix I was in. He told me I'd have to see the doctor. I went to the doctor and told him I was sick. I pleaded with him, but I got nothing. He abused me, called me a faker, and I said, 'All right; you take me to the Captain.'

"With that he grabbed me by the neck, and before I knew anything half a dozen bon-tons that worked there in the hospital got hold of me, hit me, beat me up, and threw me out. I went to the Captain, and he put me in the hole for seventeen days—for strikin' the doctor. That was the charge they put against me. I denied the charge and refused to go to the hole, but they had all the best of it.

"The last few weeks I took sick with stomach trouble. I went to the Captain and pleaded with him to excuse me from work so I could get well and strong so I could do an honest day's work when I got out. I was all in. He chased me back to work.

"'If you come near me again I'll put you in the hole for the rest of your time,' he said.

"I was sufferin' with injustice and pain and I wouldn't go. So he put me in the hole until my time was up. I asked to see the doctor after I was down there, but the Captain said 'No; I'm the doctor.'

"So I stayed there without any treatment until 9 o'clock the day before my time was up."

---

[1] A person showing promise of attaining success.

ch. ends p. 424

He was given some money, and arrangements were made for him to be examined by a first class doctor. The doctor's report is now on file. It states that L—— is afflicted with inflammatory arthritis and a heart lesion, indicating some blood irritant in the past.

It may be asked why the man did not apply to some society for assistance.

The last time I visited such an institution the superintendent boasted that the place was empty. "We don't encourage them to stay here," was the way he put it.

I wondered what the place was for and why the people who support it give their money.

Samuel L. Randolph, the present Captain of the Yard, came into prominence a number of years ago when he was still a prison guard. One night, while in a saloon at San Quentin Point, he was shot by a discharged prisoner. There is an old saying to the effect that "where there is smoke there is fire." Of course there was a cause behind this shooting. Even at that early day, long before he had risen to his present position, Randolph was hated by the prisoners. The shooting occurred in the presence of several witnesses, all of whom agreed that it was unprovoked, that the offender had stepped into the saloon "looking for trouble."

The man who did the shooting was known as "Scarry," and he had deliberately returned to San Quentin village, after his discharge from the prison, apparently for the sole purpose of "getting" Randolph. Of course, not having been present, I am obliged to take the word of other persons for what occurred. I have been told that when "Scarry" entered the saloon and threatened Randolph with the revolver Randolph taunted him, walking up to him with the question: "Well, why don't you shoot?" until he got so close that "Scarry" lost his self-possession, dropping his arm and pulling the trigger of the revolver so that the bullet entered the leg of his intended victim. At any rate, there has never been any question as to

Randolph's "nerve." No one has ever been justified in calling him a physical coward at crucial moments.

When I first heard the story of this shooting I didn't understand what had led up to it, and the fact that "Scarry" had been overpowered, jailed, and sent to Folsom for ten years I took as a matter of course. But during the ten years that I saw Randolph nearly every day it became very apparent why he had been shot, and when, on February 22 of this year, another attempt was made to kill him, the viewpoint and feelings of the man who attempted the murder could be readily understood.

Time and time again I had heard prisoners exclaim, "He'll get it some day. Someone is bound to kill him, and when it happens it will be no wonder."

It certainly is not my intention to convey the impression that I am in sympathy with a man who takes, or attempts to take, a human life; but at the same time I understand just how the boy felt when he tried to take Randolph's life.

A week before it happened some of the prisoners knew that it was going to occur, and the matter was discussed between myself and another man. This man had received authentic information that the Captain was to be killed, and told me about it.

"I can't keep it to myself," he declared. "There isn't any doubt but that it's the straight dope, and if I keep still and Randolph is killed, why, I'll be guilty of murder."

There wasn't any question as to the correctness of this view, and Randolph was informed of the plot.

"So I'm to be stabbed if I go through the yard on Sunday?" he mused. "Well, it ain't the first time I've heard that."

On Sunday he strolled through the yard, but nothing happened. Several days before a boy had been brought to the office for some slight infraction of the prison rules, and Randolph had struck him in the face. There is a State law to the effect that an officer or guard shall never strike a prisoner, save in self-defense or to quell a riot. On one

ch. ends p. 424

occasion a half-witted negro had been brought in from the "hill gang." The prisoner was smiling, unappreciative of the solemnity of the moment, when, without warning, he was struck in the face with such violence that he fell. On another occasion a prisoner named W—— still at San Quentin—was given a beating by Randolph in the clothing room.

W—— had endeavored to escape by hiding in the sewer of the new prison and had been "smoked out." A number of guards and prisoners were present in the clothing room while W—— was changing his clothes to go to the "hole," and witnessed the abuse to which Randolph subjected him. A few minutes after it happened an eyewitness described the scene to me, and a few days ago I received a letter from an ex-guard, telling of the same event, stating that he was present and never saw a more cowardly thing in his life, and asking if I was going to "sidestep" telling it. To recount all the instances of Randolph's brutality would make a good-sized volume. Sufficient has here been told to show why prisoners hate and want to kill him.

Although he went through the yard without mishap on the Sunday that had been settled upon as the day when he should be stabbed, the plot was by no means abandoned, and a few days later—Washington's Birthday—as he was passing through the yard a prisoner suddenly rushed from the crowd with a long knife and endeavored to kill him. The knife entered the Captain's back and penetrated deeply, but he grappled with his assailant and managed to hold him until assistance arrived. Then he walked to the hospital.

The man, or boy, accused of the assault was the same person whom Captain Randolph had struck in the face a few days previously. He was escorted to the office and then taken to the incorrigible ward, where he has since been confined.

At the time this attempted murder occurred no mention was made of it in the newspapers—at least not until it "leaked out" days afterward. It has always been the custom when a prisoner committed a murderous assault to take him to the county seat and place him on trial for the offense. But in this case no prosecution was instituted. Naturally, the prisoners wondered why. The reason is apparent. Had this case gone into the courts, Captain Randolph would have been shown to the public in his true character. He had struck a defenseless and helpless prisoner once too often, and even though the prisoner, seething with injustice and hate so that he was ready to commit murder, had struck at the Captain's life, no publicity could be risked—the system was too sacred.

Much that could be written has been left unwritten, and much that has been written has been toned down in order to be entirely fair, or to avoid giving offense to readers. In every instance where individuals have been mentioned in an uncomplimentary way there has been no personality involved, no desire to wound, no motive other than that of showing the injustices and indignities to which prisoners have been and may be subjected under the present system. That the time is at hand when prisons shall cease to be regarded solely as places of punishment and degradation is unquestioned. All over the United States the people, and the people's public servants, are interesting themselves in the conduct of prisons, and clamoring for more logical and humane methods. Already there have been results. The State prisons of California are being conducted today much better than they were conducted four years ago; they are also being conducted much better than they were conducted four months ago. The straitjacket has practically been abandoned at San Quentin; and only a few weeks ago the "tricing up" of prisoners at Folsom was abolished by the State Board of Prison Directors. At a recent meeting of this board the rule requiring paroled prisoners to conjure $25 out of the atmosphere was rescinded. The poor and friendless prisoner now has a chance to redeem himself along with the others. At the next session of the Legislature all forms of corporal torture in the State prisons, as well as legalized murder, should be relegated to the realms of barbarism.

ch. ends p. 424

As has been pointed out in this narrative, Warden Hoyle, at San Quentin, is the most efficient Warden who has ever held that office there. He has fought consistently for better conditions and has gradually reduced all forms of torture and abuse. Give him ten years more, with scope to work out reforms, and he will be the best Warden in America. But in order to attain this honor and distinction—an honor and distinction which any man might well feel proud to attain—he has to act positively. In order that he may act to the best advantage the laws must be changed so that the present system may be done away with. Also all officers and guards—pending the time when they shall be unnecessary—must be compelled to qualify for their positions, and paid accordingly.

Talking with a State Senator at Santa Cruz recently, I was informed that while at Sacramento for the purpose of enacting laws, the members of the Legislature are besieged for their official influence to gain positions in the State institutions for men in need of jobs. It is not a question of fitness that decides who shall have such positions, but purely a question of who can bring the most influence to bear. Under this system many undesirable and incapable men have succeeded in getting positions where they have the lives of fellow-beings in their hands. This is not just, either to the inmates of the institutions or to the taxpayers.

Some day the people will realize the fact that the man at the head of a State prison should be just as capable and efficient as a man at the head of a university, for every aspect of human life and character is contained within the four walls of a penitentiary. And some day it will not even be necessary to have walls of brick and stone at all. Paroled prisoners have no walls, yet 85 percent of them are making good, circumscribed by moral walls which are just as effective as material walls.

State institutions, and especially the State prisons, should be a source of revenue—not an expense—to the State. This may be accomplished coincidently with a course of treatment beneficial to prisoners as individuals. The assertion has been

Randolph is now treating the prisoners with consideration, that he does not send them to "the hole" or "take" their privileges for trivial offenses, especially the first time. Instead he gives them a chance to get straight. This is the probation system carried into the prison community. And the discipline has been maintained.

A few weeks ago I received a signed letter stating that I—a man guilty of two criminal convictions—had an "awful gall" to presume to tell people who have never broken the law how to conduct their affairs. From the standpoint of the old order of things I have had an "awful gall," but from the standpoint of the new order, with the mothers and mothers-to-be holding a voice in affairs, and the general awakening of the genuine Christ spirit in the hearts of men, this "awful gall" is a desirable attribute. I'm glad I have it. I hope I shall continue to have it, as I hope that this book, with its true accounts of some of the saddest phases of human life, will awaken or strengthen in many men and women the sense of comprehension and the urgent desire for helpful action.

Chapter 33

made that it is easy enough to criticize present conditio
easy enough to tear down—but what is to be the new syst

The object of this narrative has not been to tell the rem
but to show the necessity for it. It has not been writte
the nature of an attack, but simply that the taxpayers
the conscientious citizens of the community may know v
they are responsible for. If they are satisfied with the pictu
poorly as it has been produced—no harm has been don
anyone. If they are dissatisfied it is their right and their c
to change conditions.

There are a number of ways in which a change ma
effected—a number of systems whereby prisoners may
benefited and converted into useful citizens while "pay
the penalty" for crime. The New Zealand system is proba
the best, but in the absence of knowledge as to the detai
cannot be stated intelligently. Next to that system, perh
is the indeterminate sentence, with parole, based on indi
ual merit under a remunerative industrial plan whereby
prisoner may support his family while he is confined.

At present new cell buildings, designed to hold 1,(
prisoners, are being constructed at San Quentin. If the p
ent cell-houses and dormitories are allowed to stand the
capacity of San Quentin prison will be 3,500. Add a th
sand for Folsom, and we have provision for 4,500 convi
Surely that doesn't solve the problem! There are close
3,000 convicts in California now. Will an additional 1,5
be desirable?[2] It is not new cells that are required, but a n
system without cells. No human being has ever been be
fited by being confined in a cell. God meant human bein
for fresh air, sunshine, and work.

In concluding this narrative I want to say a few wor
for Captain Randolph and others whom I have criticized
not in a personal way, but as representatives of the syste
A prisoner just released from San Quentin states that Capta

---

[2] As of April 30, 2020, the combined population of both San Quentin and Folsc
was nearing 130% over-capacity at 6,746 convicts.

ch. ends next

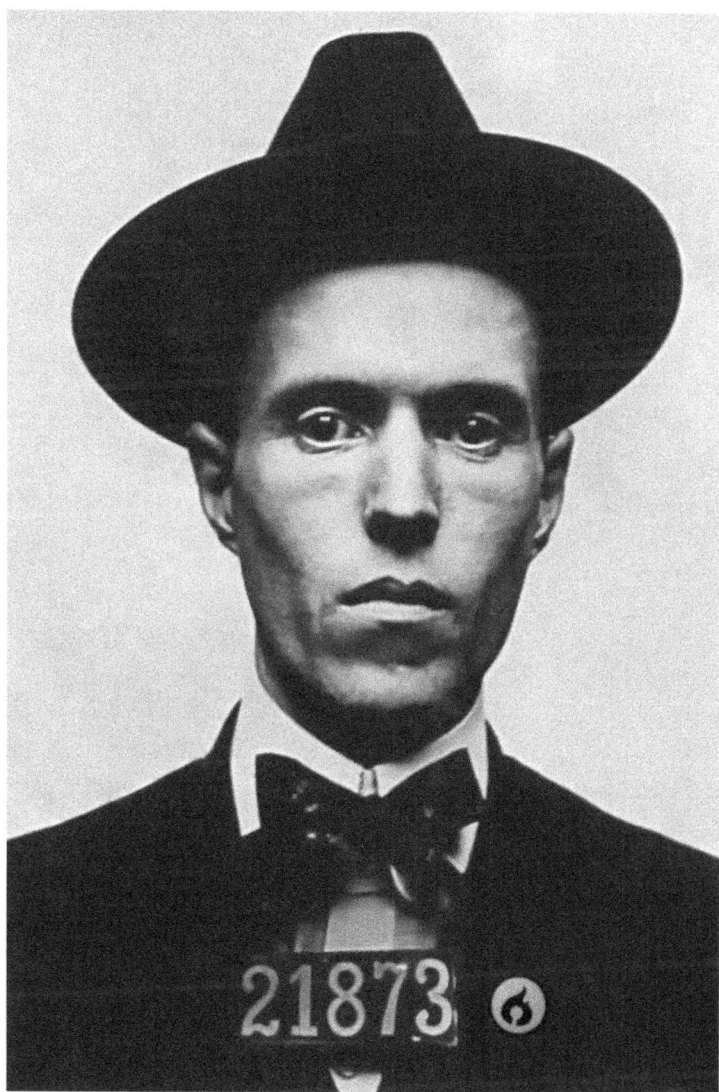

21873 ⑥

Donald Lowrie

HONORARY HEATHEN

21873

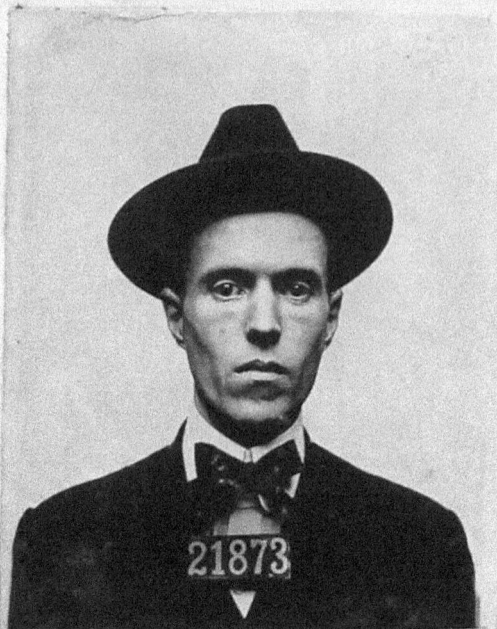

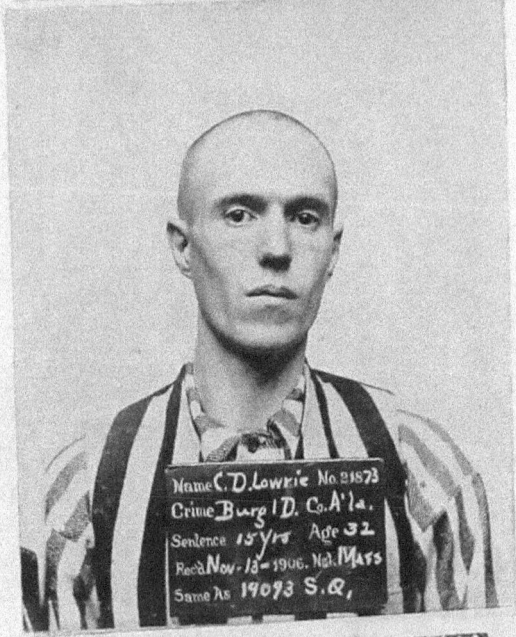

Name C.D. Lowrie No. 21873
Crime Burg 1 D. Co. A'la.
Sentence 15 Y'rs Age 32
Rec'd Nov. 13-1906. Nat. Mass
Same As 19093 S.Q,

Name C. D. Lowrie 2T
No. 21873
County Alameda
Crime Burg 1st Deg. + Pk.
Term 15 years
Received Nov. 13-1906
Discharged Apr. 13-1916.
Remarks Same as 19093.